AF695247

The Dollfuss/Schuschnigg Era in Austria

Contemporary Austrian Studies

Sponsored by the University of New Orleans and Universität Innsbruck

Editors
Günter Bischof, CenterAustria, University of New Orleans
Anton Pelinka, University of Innsbruck

Production Editor
Ellen Palli

Copy Editor
Irène Brameshuber-Ziegler

Editoral Assistant
Tanja Stampfl

Executive Editors
Franz Mathis, UNO Coordinator, University of Innsbruck
Robert L. Dupont, Vice Chancellor, University of New Orleans

Advisory Board

Ingrid Bauer
University of Salzburg
Siegfried Beer
University of Graz
Hans-Georg Betz
Geneva
Evan Bukey
University of Arkansas, Fayetteville
Mario Caciagli
University of Florence
Gary Cohen
Center for Austrian Studies
University of Minnesota
Michael G. Huelshoff
University of New Orleans
Wilhelm Kohler
University of Linz
Jacques Le Rider
University of Paris VIII
Kurt Richard Luther
University of Keele
Andrei S. Markovits
University of Michigan, Ann Arbor
Richard Mitten
Trinity College
Margareta Mommsen
University of Munich
Hanspeter Neuhold
University of Vienna
Max Preglau
University of Innsbruck
Sonja Puntscher Riekmann
Austrian Academy of Sciences
Peter Pulzer
Oxford University
Oliver Rathkolb
University of Vienna
Sieglinde Rosenberger
University of Vienna
Dieter Stiefel
University of Vienna
Franz Szabo
Center for Austrian Studies,
University of Alberta
Ruth Wodak
University of Vienna

Publication of this volume has been made possible through a generous grant from the Austrian Ministry of Foreign Affairs through the Austrian Cultural Forum in New York. The University of Innsbruck and Metropolitan College of the University of New Orleans have also provided financial support. All pictures in this volume are courtesy of the Karl v. Vogelsang-Institut in Vienna.

The Dollfuss/Schuschnigg Era in Austria

A Reassessment

Contemporary Austrian Studies Volume Eleven

Edited by
Günter Bischof
Anton Pelinka
Alexander Lassner

Transaction Publishers
New Brunswick (U.S.A.) and London (U.K.)

Copyright © 2003 by Transaction Publishers, New Brunswick, New Jersey.

All rights reserved under International and Pan-American Copyright Conventions. No part of this book may be reproduced or transmitted in any form or by any means, electronic or mechanical, including photocopy, recording, or any information storage and retrieval system, without prior permission in writing from the publisher. All inquiries should be addressed to Transaction Publishers, Rutgers—The State University, 35 Berrue Circle, Piscataway, New Jersey 08854-8042.

This book is printed on acid-free paper that meets the American National Standard for Permanence of Paper for Printed Library Materials.

Library of Congress Catalog Number: 2002040897
ISBN: 0-7658-0970-2
Printed in the United States of America

Library of Congress Cataloging-in-Publication Data

The Dollfuss/Schuschnigg era in Austria : a reassessment / Günter Bischof, Anton Pelinka, and Alexander Lassner, editors.

p. cm.—(Contemporary Austrian studies ; v. 11)
English and German.
Includes bibliographical references.
ISBN 0-7658-0970-2 (alk. paper)

1. Austria—Politics and government—20th century. 2. Austria—Economic conditions—1918- 3. Dollfuss, Engelbert, 1892-1934. 4. Schuschnigg, Kurt, 1897-1977. 5. Fascism—Austria—History. 6. Austria—Politics and government—20th century—Book reviews. I. Bischof, Günter, 1953- II. Pelinka, Anton, 1941- III. Lassner, Alexander. IV. Series.

DB97 .D656 2003
943.605'1—dc21 2002040897

Table of Contents

INTRODUCTION

TOPICAL ESSAYS

NON-TOPICAL ESSAY

FORUM
Commissioning History: Austria and World War II Restitution and Reconciliation

REVIEW ESSAYS

INTRODUCTION

Alexander Lassner and Günter Bischof

This volume brings renewed investigation to the Dollfuss/Schuschnigg era (1933/34-1938) as part of the ongoing reassessment of the interwar period (1918-1938) within the historical community in America and Europe.[1]

For more than sixty years, scholarly inquiry into the Dollfuss/Schuschnigg era has suffered from divisiveness and politicization perhaps best reflected by the use of the charged terms "*Ständestaat*" (corporate state) versus "Austrofascism." As is well known, the roots of this antagonism reach back to the 1930s, when supporters and critics of the Dollfuss/Schuschnigg governments engaged in a struggle, frequently raucous and sometimes violent. Thus, for example, after the failed socialist revolt of February 1934, men like J. D. Gregory published apologiae for Engelbert Dollfuss's suppression of democracy, while, subsequently, Otto Bauer and Karl Renner lobbied French premier Léon Blum for the removal of Gabriel Puaux as French ambassador to Austria – a man considered by the left as too favorably disposed towards Kurt Schuschnigg.[2] And in the wake of the disastrous Anschluss and the world war, those employing the words "*Ständestaat*" and "Austrofascism" have sought, too often, to defend or to accuse the Dollfuss and Schuschnigg governments, rather than to uncover and consider evidence in as objective a manner as possible. While those on the Right have tended to portray the Dollfuss/Schuschnigg governments strictly as a defensive bastion against Nazi Germany, those on the Left have indicted these governments as decisive contributors to the successful Anschluss through their rejection of parliamentary democracy.

Beyond this contentious issue, and as Thomas Angerer has ably demonstrated, considerable difficulties affected historical research in Austria since World War II. These difficulties included, but were not limited to, the writing of *Koalitionsgeschichtsschreibung* (coalition history) in the late 1940s and 1950s and, until recently, the unwillingness of

Austrian (and non-Austrian) historians to address Austrian collaboration with the Nazis during World War II (the so-called Great Taboo).[3] Other obstacles to historical research on the Dollfuss/Schuschnigg era have remained, and a brief discussion of some of these is necessary.

Among the most serious problems has been the issue of untrustworthy and incomplete evidence. Reliance by historians upon the records of public trials, memoirs and diaries of European statesmen and officials of the interwar period, and such postwar official publications as the *Rot-Weiss-Rot-Buch*, has been regular and extensive. But the degree of willful deceit contained in these works, including blatant lies as well as deliberate, far-reaching, and systematic omissions, can hardly be exaggerated.[4] Exacerbating matters has been the belated release of key documents from American and European archives. Hence, for example, crucial archival evidence from the United States and Italy pertaining to the Dollfuss and Schuschnigg era remained closed until the mid- to late 1980s. Since that time it has lain underutilized or ignored. It is, for instance, the rare scholar indeed who has worked in the archives of the *Ufficio Storico dello Stato Maggiore dell'Esercito*. This is unfortunate since Italian dictator Benito Mussolini conducted his most sensitive diplomacy through his military attachés, all of whom were members of Italian military intelligence. Worse, volumes of published documents—including but not limited to the *Documenti Diplomatici Italiani* (DDI) and the *Diplomáciai Iratok Magyarország Külpolitikájához* (documents on Hungarian foreign policy, all of which contain summaries in German)—have been consistently ignored by scholars writing on the Dollfuss and Schuschnigg era, the late R. John Rath's articles on Dollfuss being a notable exception.[5]

Dovetailing with these issues, many historians have relied too heavily on received wisdom, citing secondary sources far more than primary ones. The result is the propagation of myth based upon limited, flimsy, and/or hearsay evidence. Even when scholars look at primary sources, many do so heavily influenced by what they have read before or have been told, rather than considering the evidence as impartially as possible. A powerful illustration of myth propagation related to the Dollfuss/Schuschnigg era is the so-called fact that the French Popular Front government of Blum and Yvon Delbos refused to undertake a rapprochement with Italian dictator Benito Mussolini—despite the warnings of French diplomats and military officials, who informed Blum that Italian cooperation was vital in order to create security against Nazi Germany and to support Austria militarily in case it was attacked by the Reich.

Here again, the issue of "*Ständestaat*" or "Austrofascism" has exerted its baleful influence. Writers on the Left have tended to defend Blum and Delbos's decision as moral and wise, while chastising the Schuschnigg government as having reaped the bitter fruit of its authoritarian form of government. Meanwhile, authors on the Right have heaped criticism on the French statesmen for being ideologically prejudiced and shortsighted.

But the assertion that Blum and Delbos ignored Mussolini is demonstrably false, and the published documents proving that they made at least one secret effort at rapprochement with the Duce have been obtainable for more than a decade.[6] Nevertheless, work after work maintains that the French statesmen would have nothing to do with Mussolini, whom they regarded, correctly, as responsible for the murder of Italian socialist leader Giacomo Matteotti. This incorrect view of Blum's supposed obduracy includes no less than the recent six-hundred-page French biography of Blum by Ilan Greilsammer.[7] There is simply no way to avoid the reality that the only way to write proper contemporary European history, including that of the Dollfuss/Schuschnigg era, is with the knowledge of the required languages, with extensive research in manifold archives and on published primary sources, and without a political agenda.

Another unfortunate outcome of the fact that so much vital evidence was unavailable for such a long period of time is that scholars relied heavily upon German documents, along with a very limited supply of Austrian documents published in *Der Hochverratsprozess gegen Dr. Guido Schmidt vor dem Wiener Volksgericht*, in order to illuminate events in Austria from 1933 to 1938.[8] The chief problem with having resorted to these sources is that the Nazis and their agents—from Josef Leopold, Franz Papen, and Otto Stein in Vienna to Gerhard Köpke, Konstantin Neurath, Adolf Hitler, Hermann Göring, and Rudolf Hess in Berlin, were pathological liars who, in addition, regularly employed euphemisms of the most insidious kind and were habitually guilty of linguistic perversions. But numerous historians have been blind to the enormous degree of deceit present in the European diplomatic record and, above all, to the perversion of language and of argument in the German documentary record. Similarly, scholars have failed to understand that key members of the Dollfuss and Schuschnigg governments, most especially Schuschnigg, were acutely aware of this situation and, consequently, lied regularly to the Germans.

Given this overall situation, it is unsurprising that a general view has come to dominate the literature on Schuschnigg which portrays him as a naïve academic and/or an incompetent dictator, out of his depth in the battle with Nazism, and not up to the demands of his office. As a lesser statesman, so the argument holds, he believed in a Germanism that precluded any anti-German stance, and, in order to prevent German aggression, he embarked upon a policy of appeasement that included blind, and ultimately ruinous, attempts to obtain Hitler's acquiescence to the central European *status quo*; in the meantime, Schuschnigg and his colleagues mangled the Austrian economy and prepared the ground for the victory of Nazism through their anti-democratic activities.[9]

Within the limits imposed by one volume, this collection of essays seeks to shed new light on the domestic, economic, foreign, and security policy of the Dollfuss and Schuschnigg governments, and to do so *sine ira et studio*. This does not mean that the authors are not critical of Dollfuss and Schuschnigg—such is inevitable in any honest investigation. But where credit is due, it has been given. And where factors beyond the control of Dollfuss and Schuschnigg were at work, attention has been paid.

The article by *Timothy Kirk* takes a needed international approach to the discourse over fascism in Austria. As he notes, views on fascism have, not infrequently, reflected the politics of the author. Kirk highlights some recent methodologies developed to understand fascism, while linking the breakdown of democracy in Austria to a more widespread rejection of parliamentary democracy among members of the mainstream Right in Europe.

Three scholars from the Economics University of Vienna have analyzed macroeconomic aspects of the Dollfuss/Schuschnigg era. *Gerhard Senft* begins by tracing the economic and social preconditions that led to authoritarian rule in Austria. He shows that the Dollfuss and Schuschnigg governments failed to stimulate the domestic economy through vigorous government intervention, which, in turn, helped foreign trade to assume the "pivotal position." While there were some limited successes in the realm of foreign trade, key officials in the Dollfuss and Schuschnigg governments remained mired in 19th century economic thought, with detrimental results for the Austrian economy.

Hansjörg Klausinger investigates the Vienna and Chicago schools of economic theory. After contrasting the two schools' views on policy, he discusses the debate that took place with regard to deflation, "priming the pump," wage cutting, and monetary policy. The author notes that the dearth of activist economic policies in Austria reflected, in some ways, that in other countries. Ultimately, Klausinger writes, the Chicago school had little impact on Austrian policies; and, had Dollfuss or Schuschnigg turned to the Vienna school for direction, they would have been poorly served.

Peter Berger reexamines the economic policies of the League of Nations towards Austria. In contrast to what some scholars have argued—namely that Austria was the victim of League policies—Berger explains that officials in Vienna sometimes forced League representatives to yield to particular Austrian demands. Moreover, those policies set down by the League, far from being universal failures, enjoyed some remarkable successes.

An international approach and a revisionist view characterize the article by *Jens-Wilhelm Wessels* on Austria's economic problems in the 1930s. He accepts the notion that the Dollfuss/Schuschnigg governments pursued restrictive and orthodox economic policies that hampered economic recovery. But he demonstrates that there were other, more important factors which explain the failure of economic recovery in Austria: profound global structural changes (including the expansion of industrialization in the world economic periphery), the contraction of world trade and its slow recovery, and the rise of economic nationalism in Europe and the United States.

Expanding on recent research concerning Dollfuss's personality and *Weltanschauung*, *James William Miller* continues the investigation into why Dollfuss eliminated parliamentary democracy in Austria. The author highlights Dollfuss's conviction that any policy which hurt the interests of the peasantry had to be avoided. Further, Dollfuss operated with an "elitist" and "authoritarian" conception of democracy, in which elections primarily played a legitimizing role. In the end, Dollfuss embraced the notion that authoritarian methods were a more effective way of governing the state.

Helmut Wohnout deals with a long-neglected area of study, namely, the Austrian constitution of May 1934. His focus is on the differences between the corporative constitution as it was written and as it was practiced. In doing so, he also gives us a "map" of how the Austrian government operated. Overall, Wohnout concludes that the corporative elements of the constitution did not develop in any meaningful way, and that, increasingly, power became concentrated in the hands of the chancellor, ultimately leading to a "chancellorial dictatorship."

Alexander Lassner's study derives from a larger work on European international relations from 1932 to 1938 and the origins of World War II. In contrast to historiographical orthodoxy, he shows that the foreign and security policy of the Schuschnigg government was both sound and realistic. Schuschnigg and his colleagues correctly understood that the only way to prevent armed aggression against Austria by the Third Reich was through a politico-military guarantee to be obtained from Britain, France, and Italy. Unfortunately, for reasons that had nothing to do with Austria's form of government, such a guarantee was not forthcoming—with disastrous results.

In the non-topical essay section of this volume, *Megan E. Greene*, a recent graduate of Princeton University, compares the policies of two potent European political movements (far?) right of center—the Austrian Freedom party FPÖ and the Lega Nord of Italy.[10] After a careful definition of the spectrum of right wing politics in Europe, she looks at specific issues such as the two parties' immigration, welfare, and employment planks in their political campaign strategies and their policy impacts in the national governing coalitions. Greene concludes that the Italian Lega Nord adopted more extreme ideologies and policies on the right than the Austrian FPÖ. Nevertheless, the European Union levied sanctions against Austria for FPÖ participation in the governing coalition but not against Italy for Silvio Berlusconi's inclusion of the Lega Nord in his government. It seems to be easier to state an example vis-à-vis EU newcomers and small countries like Austria than vis-à-vis "insiders" like the founding member Italy, one of the larger EU members. This essay, written from a detached American perspective, is published as a contribution to the ongoing and intensifying discussion about center-right coalition building in European politics.

The FORUM *Commissioning History: Austria and World War II Restitution and Reconciliation* deals with the recent upsurge of historical commissions being set up in Austria and all over Europe to confront the World War II past and to deal with the surfeit of war-related memory. Parallel to these commissions the Swiss, German, and Austrian governments have set up reconciliation funds to make late payments to former victims of the massive campaigns of National Socialist property plunder and slave labor exploitation. These major campaigns of restitution settlements and reconciliation efforts need to be seen against a larger post-cold war backdrop of a new "moral economy" or righting the injustices of the past, and a new "guilt of nations" (Elazar Barkan).

A series of Austrian case studies of such commissions and their results are presented in this FORUM. *Brigitte Bailer-Galanda* and *Eva Blimlinger* summarize the establishment and the agenda of the Austrian Historical Commission. *Oliver Rathkolb* introduces his work on various commissions for private industries and banks. *Dieter Stiefel* summarizes his major report on the Austrian record of restitution efforts for forcibly transferred life insurance policies after the Anschluss, commissioned by the Austrian insurance industry. *Margit Reiter* presents her work on the hydroelectric power plant of Kaprun, a study commissioned by the Austrian electricity industry. It shows both the massive utilization of foreign and slave labor by the Nazis during World War II to get Kaprun started and the employment of many former Nazis after the war to get it finished. She also looks at the "myth of Kaprun" in the history of Austrian reconstruction and how the odd labor history was purged from postwar Austrian memory. *Martin Eichtinger* relates the results of the Schaumayer Commission on slave labor and the Reconciliation Fund set up as a result of negotiations with Eastern European and the American governments. This FORUM is part of the ongoing effort of *Contemporary Austrian Studies* to elucidate the complex mix of actions by Austrian victims and perpetrators during World War II and Austrians' postwar memory of their role in the war.

The role of Austrians during World War II is also on the agenda of the three review essays by *Evan Burr Bukey*, *Hermann Freudenberger*, and *Robert Edwin Herzstein*. While Bukey and Freudenberger review important recent works on the vast record of the *Ostmark's* contribution to the political economy of Nazi Germany and the Holocaust, Herzstein revisits the story of one *Wehrmacht* lieutenant, Kurt Waldheim, whose postwar cover-up of his role during the war has become representative and highly symbolic of Austria's long procrastination and failure to vigorously confront its World War II past. A number of book reviews and the annual review of Austrian politics complete this volume.

As always we are very grateful to a number of institutions and people for their unflinching support in helping us complete this volume. We would like to thank the contributors for their timely submission of essays and collegial handling of requests. The UNO-Innsbruck team of Irene Brameshuber-Ziegler, Tanja Stampfl, Gertraud Griessner, and Ellen Palli in Innsbruck did their usual superb job in copy-editing, correcting, proof-reading, type-setting, and shepherding along the two dozen manuscripts of this volume. Helmut Wohnout arrived just in time for helping us obtain portraits of Dollfuss, Hornbostel and Schuschnigg from the ÖVP party archives in Vienna. Dean Robert Dupont of Metropolitan College at UNO and Professor Franz Mathis, the coordinator of the friendship treaty with UNO at the University of Innsbruck, used their financial wizardry to make publication of this volume feasible. Ernst Aichinger of the Austrian Cultural Forum in New York secured support from the Austrian Foreign Ministry in Vienna. At Transaction Publishers, Anne Schneider brought the volume to publication with her characteristic friendly efficiency.

In June 2002, Gordon "Nick" Mueller retires as Director of UNO's Center for Austrian Culture and Commerce and as one of the executive directors of *CAS* to become full-time Director of the National D-Day Museum in New Orleans. It is not using too much hyperbole to note that Nick is the rock on which the unique university partnership between New Orleans and Innsbruck has been built. In 1976, he was the founding father of the highly successful UNO Summer School in Innsbruck, which instigated the UNO – University of Innsbruck partnership in 1983 and the subsequent establishment of a dense network of student and faculty exchanges and many other scholarly ventures. *Contemporary Austrian Studies*, too, is a product of this lasting cooperation. The fact that we go into our second decade of publication attests to Nick's precious vision in trans-Atlantic partnering and the longevity of this university friendship treaty. One of Nick's lasting legacies is that he has stubbornly anchored and institutionalized the partnership in such a way that it can continue without him on the controls. Such shrewd foresight is not always the case in the halls of academe. We will all miss him and his subtle leadership!

Arlington, Virginia/Larose, Louisiana, May 2002

Notes

1. For some recent examples see Gordon Martel, ed., *The Origins of the Second World War Reconsidered* (London: Routledge, 1999); Martin S. A. Alexander, ed., *Knowing your Friends. Intelligence Inside Alliances and Coalitions from 1914 to the Cold War* (London: Frank Cass, 1998); R. M. Salerno, "The Mediterranean Triangle: Britain, France, Italy and the Origins of the Second World War, 1935-1940," Ph.D. diss., Yale University, 1997; Robert Mallett, *The Italian Navy and Fascist Expansionism 1935-1940* (London: Frank Cass, 1998); H. MacGregor Knox, "The Fascist Regime, its Foreign Policy and its Wars: An 'Anti-Fascist' Orthodoxy?," *Contemporary European History* 4 (1995): 347-65; Robert Soucy, *French Fascism: The Second Wave 1933-1939* (New Haven: Yale University Press, 1995); Jacques Nobécourt, *Le Colonel de La Rocque (1885-1946) ou les pièges du nationalisme chrétien* (Paris: Fayard, 1996); Gerhard Stourzh and Birgitta Zaar, eds., *Österreich, Deutschland und die Mächte: Internationale und österreichische Aspekte des "Anschlusses" vom März 1938* (Vienna: Verlag der Österreichischen Akademie der Wissenschaften, 1990).

2. J. D. Gregory, *Dollfuss and his Times* (London, 1935). My thanks to Timothy Kirk for bringing this work to my attention. On the lobbying efforts of Bauer and Renner for the removal of Puaux (and, subsequently, for the accusations leveled against Puaux in the socialist paper *Le Populaire*) see Thomas Angerer, "Die Französische Österreichpolitik vor dem 'Anschluss' 1938," *Vierteljahrshefte für Zeitgeschichte*, 40 (1992): 48, 48 n. 108. For good reasons, Blum and Delbos ignored the efforts of Bauer and Renner and retained Puaux. Indeed, by 1937-38 Blum, Delbos, and Puaux were of much the same mind with respect to the Schuschnigg government. Alexander N. Lassner, "Peace at Hitler's Price: Austria, the Great Powers, and the Anschluß, 1932-1938," Ph.D. diss., Ohio State University, 2001, 564-70, 573-83, 588-91, 607-8, 610, 704-7; see especially ibid., 520 n. 16.

3. Thomas Angerer, "An Incomplete Discipline: Austrian *Zeitgeschichte* and Recent History," in *Contemporary Austrian Studies*, vol. 3, *Austria in the Nineteen-Fifties*, ed. Günter Bischof, Anton Pelinka, and Rolf Steininger (New Brunswick, NJ: Transaction Publishers, 1995), 207–27.

4. For the most recent example of distortions and omissions by a former European cabinet minister of the 1930s, in this case a prior foreign minister in the Schuschnigg cabinet, see Alexander N. Lassner, "Egon and Heinrich Berger von Waldenegg. Biographie im Spiegel: Die Memoiren zweier Generationen," in *Contemporary Austrian Studies*, vol. 9, *Neutrality in Austria*, ed. Günter Bischof, Anton Pelinka, and Ruth Wodak (New Brunswick: Transaction Publishers, 2001), 341-51.

5. Rath made excellent use of the DDI. See R. John Rath, "Deterioration of Democracy in Austria, 1927-1932," *Austrian History Yearbook* XXVII (1996); R. John Rath, "The Dollfuß Ministry: The Democratic Prelude," *Austrian History Yearbook* XXIX (1998); R. John Rath, "The Dollfuß Ministry: The Intensification of Animosities and the Drift toward Authoritarianism," *Austrian History Yearbook* XXX (1999).

6. Lassner, "Peace at Hitler's Price," 247-48, 248 n. 30, 473, 560-61.

7. Ilan Greilsammer, *Blum* (Paris: Flammarion, 1996), 338, 352, 361.

8. *Der Hochverratsprozess gegen Dr. Guido Schmidt vor dem Wiener Volksgericht* (Vienna, 1947), 345-415, 467-578.

9. Prominent examples include the only complete biography of Schuschnigg: Anton Hopfgartner, *Ein Mann gegen Hitler* (Graz: Styria, 1989), 67-68, 128-129. See also Norbert Schausberger, *Der Griff nach Österreich: der Anschluß* (Vienna: Jugend und Volk, 1978), 355; Walter Wiltschegg, *Österreich – der "Zweite Deutsche Staat"? Der nationale Gedanke in der Ersten Republik* (Graz: Stocker, 1992), 100-8: Peter Streitle, *Die Rolle Kurt von Schuschniggs im österreichischen Abwehrkampf gegen den Nationalsozialismus (1934-1936)* (Munich: Tuduv-Verlagsgesellschaft, 1988), passim; Felix Kreissler, *Der Österreicher und seine Nation: ein Lernprozeß mit Hindernissen* (Vienna, H. Böhlau, 1984), 30-35; H. James Burgwyn, "Italy, the Roman Protocols Bloc, and the *Anschluß* Question 1936-1938," *Austrian History Yearbook* XXII (1988): 123, 125, 134, 141, 146. For the most influential and misleading portrayal of Schuschnigg and his foreign/domestic policy in the English language see Jürgen Gehl, *Austria, Germany, and the Anschluß 1931-1938* (London: Oxford University Press, 1963).

10. This paper is an abbreviated and considerably revised and updated version of her senior thesis submitted to the Department of Politics: Megan E. Greene, "Combating Right-Wing Extremism in the European Union: A Case Study of the Austrian Freedom Party and the Italian Lega Nord," Princeton University, 2000.

TOPICAL ESSAYS

Fascism and Austrofascism

Tim Kirk

Fascism determined the political agenda in Europe for a quarter of a century, from its origins in the right-wing political violence that followed the First World War to the defeat of Nazi Germany in 1945. The transformation of Europe from a continent of new parliamentary democracies in 1919 to one of radical right-wing dictatorships in 1939 is unthinkable without fascism, however one defines it, and whatever role indigenous fascist movements came to play in the new authoritarian regimes that sprang up everywhere. Every country in interwar Europe had a fascist movement of one kind or another, however insignificant in terms of numbers or real political clout;[1] and fascism was, more often than not, a common ingredient in the broader political offensive mounted by a dispossessed political class attempting to regain the initiative from a broadly democratic Left.[2] Although only Italy proclaimed itself fascist, the populist rhetoric, authoritarian policies, and above all the monumental symbolism and militaristic rituals of fascism came to define the new political style of continental Europe during the 1930s.

Yet few political movements have been as difficult as fascism for historians and political scientists to pin down. Few of the fascist movements and none of the other right-wing dictatorships of the interwar years adopted the term fascist to describe themselves, and Mussolini's "fascist international" of 1934 failed to take off. Contemporary observers in Italy and abroad were nevertheless in no doubt about the affinities between the Italian Fascist party and its foreign imitators;[3] and admiration for fascism was expressed often and openly.[4] The situation was transformed by the war, the defeat of the Axis, and the revelation of war crimes and atrocities: All forms of generic fascism came to be associated, directly or indirectly, with the Nazis and the Holocaust. Moreover, the postwar order in Europe was explicitly anti-fascist, both in its constitutional arrangements and in its political rhetoric, and the memory of earlier sympathy for fascist movements was repressed. Most postwar European governments claimed some degree of association with anti-fascist forces, and active anti-fascists served in many of them.[5]

The desire to forget the recent past in the interests of present and future political stability was initially compounded by new distractions, above all the immediate and widespread necessity for domestic consensus as a basis for reconstruction and the changing political priorities that came with the cold war. But although there were powerful incentives in postwar Europe to let sleeping dogs lie, fascism has proved to be a "past that will not pass away," and this is because it has always been difficult for Europeans to account for the fascist past satisfactorily without undermining the compromises on which the postwar order was founded. In short, then, the overriding reason for the complexities and ambiguities in the interpretation of fascism is relatively straightforward: After sixty years in which no public figure, political party, or significant organization in the public sphere has been able to espouse fascism openly, it still matters who is accounted a fascist and why.

The particular difficulties encountered by Austrian historians (and historians of Austria) in dealing with the recent past have been well documented elsewhere.[6] Austrians, no less than other Europeans, have been deterred by the political constraints of the present from accounting adequately for painful episodes in the recent past, and historians of "Austrofascism" have found it difficult to break free form the carefully agreed compromises that characterized the "coalition historiography" of the 1950s. The problem is not entirely Austrian: It arises from the lack of an agreed definition of fascism, and this deficiency has been compounded by a failure, for similar reasons, to define the "residual category" of neighboring authoritarian regimes in east central Europe to which the "corporate state" is otherwise ascribed.[7] The following discussion is an attempt to locate, within the broader context of the changing historiographical perspectives of postwar Europe, accounts of Austrofascism from its ideological and political gestation, through its passage to power, to the nature of the regime itself. It will raise the question of whether the origins and development of the dictatorship in Austria did not rest on the same uneasy coalition building between authoritarian conservatives and fascists that brought fascism to power in Italy and Germany.

Postwar Politics and the Historiography of Fascism

Interpretations of fascism have tended to reflect the political orientation of the commentator and changes in the international political climate. This was already the case before the Second World War, when two schools of thought were already emerging. Marxist observers—including, but not only, those directed by the Comintern—categorized both Italian Fascism and Nazism as examples of the same generic fascism that also found expression in the countless other radical right-wing movements across Europe. At the same time, liberals were beginning to equate first Italian Fascism and then Nazism with Soviet Communism, categorizing both the right-wing authoritarian regimes and that of the Left as examples of totalitarianism.[8] It was this second kind of interpretation that gained currency in the west during the early years of the cold war, when it was mobilized as a "device . . . to link the present enemy, communism, with that of the recent past, Nazi-fascism."[9] This is not to say that the term "totalitarian" was no more than a crude propaganda slogan (although it was that too), but it was one that proved, in the first instance at least, to be of limited usefulness. Consequently, the first attempts to describe structural similarities in Stalinism and Nazism proved only superficially convincing to a subsequent generation drawing on more detailed research on each of the two systems.[10] Similarly, rigid interpretations emanating from the Soviet bloc—interpretations which insisted on the indivisibility of a fascism that was essentially the puppet of "capitalism in crisis"—bore the stamp of an official ideology and found little resonance even among western Marxists.

During the later 1960s, however, the conservative orthodoxy was challenged in West Germany, and among western historians generally, by new theories of generic fascism. The revival of interest was led by Ernst Nolte's *Der Faschismus in seiner Epoche* and gathered pace with the general liberalization of the political climate.[11] The challenge was mounted both within the universities and outside, largely by the Left, and often by members of small, marginal (and as it proved, mostly ephemeral) radical groups. In practice, it was often difficult to make clear distinctions between the intellectual posturing of the revolutionaries and the political posturing of many academics, and in these circumstances conservative intellectuals objected to what they interpreted as the undue "politicization" of the universities (while reasserting their own positions from positions of relative strength within the academy). But the new general explanations of fascism, Marxist and non-Marxist alike, came to supplant theories of totalitarianism during the 1970s. They also implicitly challenged other assumptions about fascism, those which limited it to the interwar years and to the two "core" fascist states (Italy and Germany) or reduced it simply to "Hitlerism" or "Mussolini-ism."

Even before the end of the cold war, however, the historiographical landscape was shifting again as the political climate changed. From the late 1970s, a revisionist "new Right" took the initiative on a number of historical questions, and established something of an intellectual hegemony, which forced its opponents to re-examine their own perspectives. Conservative historians in the Federal Republic seized the opportunity to attempt (unsuccessfully) to construct a "usable past" for Germany.[12] A different kind of revisionism was being undertaken in Italy, where Renzo de Felice, the country's foremost scholarly expert on Mussolini, dismissed the foundational anti-fascist mythology of post-war Italy as a development which had undermined Italy's sense of itself and made it "a country irredeemably mistaken."[13] De Felice's assertion in the 1990s that the history of fascism could be read apolitically was welcomed by the resurgent Right, then organizing in a broad coalition which encompassed not only radical right-wing particularists of the Lombard League, but also the euphemistically termed "post-fascist" *Alleanza Nazionale*. The tentative "normalization" of fascism has taken place on two levels, the academic and the political, and new perspectives have been formed—are being formed—in a political context where "post-fascists" increasingly participate in government and decision making at both local and national levels.

The decline in the "fascist paradigm" in the 1980s was not simply the straightforward consequence of the emergence of the "new Right," however. The attempt to construct a satisfactory theory of fascism had been frustrating in other ways, and by the early 1990s it seemed to have run out of steam altogether. It was not just that "totalitarianism" enjoyed a revival in the context of the "new cold war"—although it did (and still does), albeit in modified form.[14] The main problem was that the theoretical approaches that had abounded in the 1970s were never adequately underpinned by sustained empirical work on a comparative basis.[15] The irreducible minimum for a generic theory of fascism was surely a fundamental similarity between Mussolini's Italy and Hitler's Germany, yet in the new perspectives of the 1990s the Third Reich came to be defined in terms that defied meaningful comparison with Italian Fascism. Moreover, historians of the two regimes were increasingly going their own separate ways. Many of those working on Nazism had come to emphasize the singular nature of the Nazis' biological racism and its consequences, a project which extended beyond anti-Semitism and the Holocaust to encompass such subjects as sterilization and family policy as well as the complicity of German medicine, science, and industry in the Nazis' racial projects.[16] The scale of "racial policy" in Italy on the other hand, however broadly defined, was indisputably less than that in Germany. The belatedness of anti-Semitic legislation in Italy, which, in 1938, was foisted on an apparently unwilling Italian public as a consequence of the alliance with Germany, seemed to underline the lesser importance of race in Italy; it is certainly true that the persecution of the Jews was less efficient and enthusiastic in Italy than almost anywhere else in Europe. Finally, the historiographical divergence was compounded by the increasing centrality of "cultural" approaches (in the broadest sense) to new works on Italy, a preoccupation that was seen variously as "secondary" or methodologically problematic for a comparative history of fascism.[17]

These interpretational differences seem less problematic than they once did. Italian historians themselves have challenged earlier, more reassuring assumptions about Italian anti-Semitism under Mussolini. They have argued that Fascist racial legislation was not a "deviation or a falsification of the true Italian spirit," but that the application of the anti-Jewish laws of 1938 throughout Italy constituted a logical premise for the more radical measures (deportation, incarceration, and extermination) implemented in the German-controlled Salò Republic after 1943.[18] Such reinterpretations have located the specific racism of 1938-1945 within a broader reappraisal of Italian attitudes to race since the Risorgimento.[19] In addition, it has become clearer that the eugenic and "biologist" thinking that underpinned Nazi racism was equally well established, if less successful, in Italy (and indeed in much of the industrialized, urbanized world).[20]

In the end it seems that reports of the death of fascism as a comparative analytical tool were premature. Certainly there was something of a retreat from the intense, and intensely polemical attempts to construct general typologies of fascism, at least on the Left, but the 1990s nevertheless saw the publication of several such general accounts of fascism, now from a liberal perspective, and with an emphasis on ideology or doctrine.[21] There has been less progress, on the other hand, towards the satisfactory history of "real existing fascism" that eluded an earlier generation, although collections of essays and conference papers have continued to bring together the research findings of scholars with specialized national research interests.[22] More recently, Robert Paxton has formulated a number of methodological proposals which provide the basis for an understanding of fascism as a developing phenomenon, changing through time and in response to changing contexts and relationships. Paxton argues that historians have concentrated unduly on ideology, since there has rarely been a connection between what dissident right-wing intellectuals set down in the early days of the movement and what fascist parties then set out to do. Moreover, he argues that, since it is in the nature of fascist ideology to draw on the "slogans and symbols of the patriotic repertory of one particular community," varieties of fascism "fit badly into any system of universal intellectual principles. It is in their functions that they resemble each other."[23] If we strive too hard to identify the irreducible essence of fascism to one ideological element or a "checklist" of characteristic features, we can become both reductive and ahistorical. The consequence is all too frequently a series of static snapshots, conveying little sense of depth, broader context, or development in time—what Paxton calls "bestiaries": "a catalog of portraits of one beast after another, each one portrayed against a bit of background scenery and identified by external signs."[24] This characterization applies to the less successful fascisms of smaller states in particular, not least Austria; for although Austria had the misfortune to generate two native fascisms, she has frequently been passed over all too quickly in such general surveys.

Austrian Fascism and Austrofascism

The emergence of two fascisms in Austria between the wars reflected a broader historical division on the political Right between a clerical conservatism united around the Christian Social Party (CSP) and a more fragmented network of secular liberal and national groups, the majority of which came together in the Greater German People's Party (*Großdeutsche Volkspartei*, GDVP) after the First World War. Although it was already a declining force in its Vienna stronghold before 1914, the CSP went on to become the major party of government during the First Republic, and the GDVP was its junior partner in a series of right-wing *Bürgerblock* coalitions during the 1920s, an arrangement which (intentionally) excluded the Social Democratic Workers' Party (*Sozialdemokratische Arbeiterpartei*, SDAP) from political power at the national level. (The Social Democrats remained unassailable as the regional party of government in Vienna, where their successful political and economic programs remained an irritant to their bourgeois opponents.)[25]

Austria's two fascisms reflected in extreme form the ideology and outlook of the more "mainstream" parties in the two broad "bourgeois subcultures." The use of the swastika emblem by regional branches of the GDVP reflected the party's closeness, in the provinces at least, to a more radical *völkisch* tradition, but the Austrian Nazis (organized in the DNSAP) remained outside the newly-formed party; indeed, from 1926, a younger generation of more middle-class and pro-German Austrian Nazis broke away from the party and subordinated themselves directly to Hitler in an Austrian branch of the NSDAP. The DNSAP, now a much less significant political force, withered away. The connections between the CSP and the *Heimwehren*—"home guards" similar to the German *Freikorps*—were more complicated. There was considerable sympathy for Pan-German ideas in south-eastern Austria (above all in Styria and Carinthia), and the Styrian *Heimatschutz* realigned itself with the Nazis in a "national-fascist" camp during the early 1930s.[26] On the whole, however, *Heimwehr* fascists and Nazis represented two distinct varieties of indigenous Austrian fascism. The former was essentially a rural movement of landowners and peasants, largely pro-clerical in its ideology, drawing inspiration from Catholic corporatism for its conception of the state and looking to Italy as a practical model for an independent Austria. The latter was secular, *völkisch* in its outlook, and more urban and petty bourgeois in its social composition. It was increasingly controlled by the German Nazi Party and aspired to Anschluss with the Reich.[27]

There is little disagreement about the fascist nature of either movement. The ideology and policies of the Austrian Nazis were in any case those of the NSDAP. Those of the *Heimwehr* movement were most famously expressed in the Korneuburg Oath of 1930, a rallying call which sought the fundamental renewal of Austria and demanded of all comrades an "undaunted" belief in the fatherland and restless eagerness in a common endeavor. Despite their differences, the two fascisms shared a number of common features. The *Heimwehr*, like the Nazis, "rejected democratic parliamentarism," Marxism, and the "shaping of the economy by liberal capitalism."[28] Both sought the destruction of the labor movement and its political and industrial organizations, and both drew on visions of a society free from class conflict: the Christian *Ständestaat* in the case of the clerical Right and the Nazi racial utopia of the *Volksgemeinschaft*, which also proposed corporate frameworks. The rationale for political change differed in tone. The clerical Right emphasized the restitution of a supposedly traditional authority, and drew on the social ideology of the church; the Nazis dwelt on the need for national rejuvenation.

It is important, however, for an understanding of the breakdown of democracy in Austria, to see the two strands of fascism in the broader context of a more widespread rejection of parliamentarism on the "mainstream" Right, something that was not always emphasized in the era of "*Koalitionsgeschichtsschreibung*." In this respect, of course, the situation in Austria was no different from that in Liberal Italy and Weimar Germany, or indeed in other parts of Europe, where members of the traditional ruling classes and of powerful institutions such as the military, the churches, and the bureaucracy were inclined to see a more authoritarian form of government as the best solution to what they perceived to be unworkable parliamentary systems.[29] Sympathy for anti-democratic thinking in Austria—as elsewhere—was also strong among the established social and economic elites, but was most forcefully articulated by those who dealt in ideas: academics, journalists, and politicians. The most prominent spokesman of the anti-democratic Right was Othmar Spann, whose critique of liberalism and call for an authoritarian corporate state was delivered as lectures to successive cohorts of students at Vienna University and published as a book, *Der wahre Staat*, in 1921. His ideas were taken up by Catholic student groups and were also influential among *Heimwehr* ideologues and on the right of the CSP.[30] Spann was one of a number of so-called "national-Catholic" intellectuals within an academic community that was "an almost ideal environment for irrationalist politics; . . . a veritable 'breeding ground' of fascist and Nazi ideas."[31] Beyond the university, anti-democratic ideas also found a degree of sympathy among the clergy and civil servants.[32]

Politicians were ambiguous in their attitude to parliamentary democracy from the outset. In the Tyrol, where right-wing paramilitary groups had very quickly forged links with their Bavarian counterparts soon after the end of the First World War, political leaders in 1919 began to consider the possibility of a revision of the province's constitution in favor of a system based on estates; and a contemporary pamphlet expressed opposition to "democracy in the vulgar sense as it was created by the French Republic" in favor of a "genuinely Germanic democracy . . . permeated through and through by an aristocratic consciousness of rank."[33] This rejection of representative parliamentary democracy in favor of "true" democracy implementing "objectively correct policies" [*objektiv richtige Politik*] was shared by the leading conservative politician of the 1920s, Ignaz Seipel. As a young theologian before the First World War, Seipel had argued that a Christian people owed allegiance to its leader "not on account of a party resolution or electoral manipulation, but for the simple reason that he is the leader."[34] Only such a leader could articulate the will of the whole people rather than the sectional interests of a nation inexplicably divided against itself. During the mid 1920s, Seipel developed a concept of "true democracy," a term which became one of the dominant slogans of the Christian Social Party towards the end of the decade. It was a conception that was dismissive of public opinion and the "masses," and one which made a disturbing distinction between Parliament itself, and the pluralistic political culture on which it rested: "True democracy" was opposed to the dependence of Parliament on parties especially after the loss of the monarchy, which had been a "corrective" to the evil of party rule.[35]

This critique of parliamentary democracy became shriller towards the end of the 1920s. Anti-democratic impulses gathered pace as the *Heimwehr* emerged as an independent force to be reckoned with, and as the beleaguered Left of the Christian Social Party lost ground to the centralizing tendencies of the right-wing leadership and its Pan-German Allies: Symbolically, for the elections of 1927, the party leadership preferred to forge a "unity list" with its anti-clerical coalition partners than to respect the feelings of the party's own Christian democrat wing in the provinces. The Unity List nevertheless lost seats in elections to the *Nationalrat*, and the situation was further inflamed by the events of July 1927. Criticism of republican institutions intensified in the political uncertainty that followed Seipel's resignation in 1929, and increased pressure for a revision of the constitution came from various quarters on the right, above all from the *Heimwehr*. Like Seipel's calls for "true democracy," the campaign was couched in a familiar anti-parliamentary rhetoric.[36] The stakes were raised by *Heimwehr* leaders, who threatened that if Parliament permitted "a few

Jews [*Judenbuben*] with red carnations" to prevent reform, it would go ahead without them; they submitted their plans for a corporate state in September 1930 against a background of provocative *Heimwehr* demonstrations.[37]

In any event, the constitutional reforms were far more limited in scope than the extreme Right had demanded and represented a reversal for the *Heimwehr*. In fact, the revised constitution was a triumph of democratic co-operation between the parties that "testified to the political acumen of the leadership of the three political camps" (and ought to have revealed the hollowness of rightist anti-parliamentary rhetoric).[38] The national elections of 1930 confirmed, however, that the "mainstream" Right, in conditions not dissimilar to those outlined by Robert Paxton as necessary for the success of fascism, was no longer able to wield power alone, but was reluctant to accept the legitimacy of a Social Democratic Party that was increasingly popular with the electorate. In these conditions, argues Paxton, "some fascist leaders . . . are willing to reposition their movements in alliance with . . . frightened conservatives," and in 1932 the Christian Social Party was compelled to rely on the support of the *Heimwehr* to form a new government with a majority of one.[39]

The immediate catalysts for political change were reminiscent of conditions in Italy and Germany at similar junctures. The center-right had been able to live with parliamentary democracy for as long as it had been able to maintain its own dominant position at national level, but now saw its electoral support leach away to the extreme right, while support for the center-left remained relatively stable. As in Italy and Germany, the arithmetic of parliamentary majorities was to prove a decisive factor in the breakdown of democracy. In 1930, the CSP won its smallest share of the vote since the establishment of the republic (35.7%) while some 9%of the vote went to the two fascist movements. (The *Heimwehr* campaigned independently in 1930.) Between 1931 and 1933, virtually every constituency in the country voted again in regional and local elections which established a pattern of Nazi electoral gains that seemed to echo developments in Germany itself. In provincial parliaments and local councils up and down the country the non-clerical Right (Pan-Germans and Agrarian League) was virtually eliminated and replaced by Nazis. Finally, the Nazis won 41% of the vote in municipal elections in Innsbruck—not a traditional German nationalist stronghold. The significance of these shifts in electoral allegiance was clear: If another general election were held soon, it might well make the Nazis by far the biggest right-wing party in the *Nationalrat*.[40]

The difficulty for the bourgeois parties of retaining control of Parliament and other institutions was compounded by the political violence on the streets. The country was in the grip of a protracted political and economic crisis which seemed insoluble. The only way to resolve it within the frame-work of parliamentary democracy would have been a "grand coalition" bringing together the Social Democrats and the Christian Social Party. Quite apart from the purely political antagonisms that stood in the way of such a solution, this would have meant the Social Democrats sharing responsibility for the imposition of ever more draconian austerity measures on its own supporters. In addition, the failure of just such a coalition had marked the end of parliamentary government in Germany in 1930.

The tension was raised by the *Heimwehr*'s abortive "march on Vienna" in 1931 and by the formation of a new administration by Dollfuss in 1932, a government which brought the *Heimwehr* into power and ended the possibility of Social Democratic toleration of the government. Co-operation with the SDAP was now unthinkable. Leading industrialists, more eager than ever during the depression to reduce the cost of wages and social policy, had met Chancellor Buresch in 1932 and urged against any attempt to achieve a consensus with the Social Democrats, arguing instead in favor of greater powers for the executive.[41] Dollfuss made his own views clear in 1933, when he spoke of doing "everything step by step to force the Marxists to their knees," and Schuschnigg later recalled that the coalition with the Social Democrats had been rejected as impractical since 1931.[42] In fact, Dollfuss followed the example of Heinrich Brüning, who had used presidential decrees to circumvent the German *Reichstag* and revived the War Economy Enabling Act of 1917 in order to govern not only without being accountable to the *Nationalrat*, but without the Austrian president's own "strictly circumscribed" power to issue decrees. The law was first used on 1 October 1932 to pass an order making members of the *Creditanstalt* liable for the bank's losses, and was applied with retroactive force. The Social Democrats demanded that the order be withdrawn but members of the *Nationalrat* were advised by the chancellor's adviser, Robert Hecht, that its use was perfectly legitimate even in peacetime.[43] The Social Democrats' concerns were noted in cabinet, but Hecht assured the ministers that the law was now a part of the new constitution and could be seen as a "general economic enabling law."[44] As in Germany, government by decree marked the end of parliamentary democracy: The War Economy Enabling Law was used to suspend local elections in 1933, for example. It was most useful, however, in the suspension of Parliament itself.

The Establishment of the Corporate State

The breakdown of democracy and the establishment of the dictatorship has attracted as much—if not more—attention from historians than the Austrofascist regime itself, and the focus has been on two events in particular: the suspension of Parliament in 1933 and the brief "civil war."

There is some disagreement about the interpretation of these events between those historians who do not see dictatorship as the intended or even inevitable outcome of the crisis, and those who find the evidence for a concerted drive towards dictatorship overwhelming. In the former perspective, the suspension of Parliament was the consequence of an unfortunate sequence of events involving obduracy and lack of judgment on both sides. In March 1933, the Social Democrats and Pan-Germans joined forces to prevent the government from punishing striking railway workers with disproportionate severity, and Karl Renner, the chairman of the *Nationalrat*, declared their motion carried. When his decision was challenged by the government, Renner resigned, and his own resignation was followed by that of his two deputies. The president could, in these circumstances, have dissolved Parliament and called a general election but did not do so. Instead Christian Social Party leaders met the following day and resolved to govern by means of the Enabling Law until the opposition parties could be persuaded to agree to a revision of the constitution. Certain provisions in the constitution were suspended immediately and all political meetings were banned.

The interpretation of these events has always been contested. The next day Dollfuss declared himself "in favor of a healthy representation of the people" and a supporter of parliamentary government, but added that Parliament had made itself impossible.[45] By September he had warmed to his theme: Parliament had abolished itself [*sich selbst ausgeschaltet*] and must never be allowed back. Instead, there should be a "social Christian German state of Austria, on a corporative basis, and under strong authoritarian leadership."[46] The notion that the Austrian Parliament had abolished itself was greeted with skepticism at the time—a British foreign office memorandum noted that Dollfuss had in effect "carried through a *coup d'état*," and *The Times* noted that the Austrian government seemed "in no hurry to return to parliamentary forms."[47] The British journalist G. E. R. Gedye "found the Ringstrasse blocked with barbed wire entanglements and rifle-rests. The grounds of the Hofburg were crowded with mounted police with slung carbines, storm companies with rifles, hand grenades and steel helmets," and reported that deputies were being prevented from entering the chamber by the police.[48] But the suggestion that the Austrian Parliament brought about its own ruin has been remarkably persistent. Analyzing the transition from democracy to dictatorship half a century after the event, Ulrich Kluge emphasized the role of "undemocratic impulses that determined the 'self-destruction of Parliament'" rather than conspiracy, an approach which provoked a sharp critical response from Rudolf G. Ardelt.[49] Both agreed, however, that this episode is central to an understanding of the way in which the corporate state was constituted. Helmut Wohnout has judged the events surrounding the parliamentary session less important for future developments than the government's decision to exploit the situation in order to introduce further constitutional reforms and rule without Parliament.[50] More recently R. John Rath, in one of a series of essays on the life of Dollfuss, summarized the situation succinctly: "The resignation of all three presidents of the *Nationalrat* made it possible for its enemies to abolish it by asserting, with at least a modicum of truth, that it had dissolved itself."[51] Kluge emphasizes the very close relationship between the sudden end of Parliament and the finalization of careful plans for authoritarian government which enjoyed broad support both in the Christian Social Party and among economic interest groups, and which rested on the precarious coalition between political Catholicism, Pan-German agrarians, and the extremist *Heimwehr*":[52] An alliance of conservatives, radical fascists, and rural economic interests not entirely dissimilar to the government coalition that appeared to be forming in Germany at the same time. All that remained was to place the authority of the new regime on a permanent footing.

The crisis in Parliament provided the opportunity to suspend the constitution; the political space to finish the job was provided by the abortive uprising of Social Democratic industrial workers in response to provocation from the government and the *Heimwehr*. Government policy was deliberately confrontational, and it is difficult to draw a clear line between the actions of the police and those of the *Heimwehr*, effectively the paramilitary wing of the governing coalition. The SDAP leadership was under pressure from its rank and file to take decisive action but was afraid that any response to government intimidation of workers might unleash a civil war which the Left would inevitably lose. Its tactical error was to name specific government measures which the party would counter with general strike, which meant that the government could avoid a crisis while proceeding with the dismantling of the democratic state, and proposals for constitutional reform on a corporate basis were presented to the cabinet in December 1933.[53] This process gathered pace with renewed pressure on Dollfuss from Mussolini, who wanted to see the establishment of a fascist state in Austria. In February, leaders of the Social Democratic paramilitary organization, the *RepublikanischerSchutzbund*, were arrested, provocative house searches for *Schutzbund* weapons were instituted by the public security minister, *Heimwehr* leader Emil Fey, and at the same time the provincial leaders of the *Heimwehr* attempted to mount a rolling *coup d'état*.[54] National labor leaders counseled caution, but local *Schutzbund* leaders in Linz resolved to undertake resistance, and a conflict broke out which quickly spread to Vienna, where a series of armed clashes took place. Although resistance was probably stronger than the government had expected, order was restored in a few days. 131 civilians were killed in the fighting, 25 of them women and children, and over 350 were wounded, while on the government side there were 55 dead and over 250 wounded. The SDAP was dissolved on 12 February, and within two weeks over two thousand of its members were arrested. Summary courts were set up, and nine death sentences were carried out in the capital almost immediately. Thousands more Social Democrats were then prosecuted in the ordinary courts in trials that continued into 1935.[55] The Vienna city council and senate were dissolved immediately, and a commissioner was instead appointed by the government. Finally, a new—arguably fascist—constitution was promulgated on 1 May.

The role of Dollfuss was crucial to these events. If in 1932 "no one dreamed that he would become a fascist dictator,"[56] his impatience with democracy and preference for an authoritarian corporate order were well known and well documented at the time, not least by his admirers. J. D. Gregory, a contemporary apologist for the then recently established *Ständestaat*, tells us that "Dollfuss had already postulated a 'German corporate state' in 1915."[57] Nevertheless, recent studies of the chancellor's career have been relatively sympathetic. Much has been made, for example, of the undoubted sincerity of his political beliefs, an approach that is only possible if one is prepared to take the chancellor on his own terms. Laura Gellot, for example, has argued that "Dollfuss's political philosophy . . . cannot be understood if confined or analyzed according to liberal definitions of democracy and dictatorship,"[58] his philosophy was a product of the rural values of the peasant milieu, in which he was raised, and this is borne out by James Miller's study of the chancellor's agrarian policy.[59] As Rath has shown, however, the chancellor's political priorities involved support for agriculture, particularly the more affluent farmers, at the expense of industry, urban workers, and the rural poor.[60] Moreover, they were responsible for provoking opposition from the Social Democrats and the industrial lobby alike, and thereby contributed to the difficult political position in which Dollfuss found himself in the early 1930s.

The Nature of the Corporate State

Chancellor Dollfuss's commitment to Catholicism and to the social teaching articulated in *Rerum Novarum*, was also central to his political ideas: The new regime was officially designated "Christian." Otto Bauer went further and described the regime as an alliance between clerical fascism and *Heimwehr* fascism, thereby raising what has been one of the central questions in the debate. Ernst Hanisch, among others, has vigorously contested this kind of interpretation. He argues that the corporate state was never fully fascist but remained "semi-fascist," and not least because the church constituted "something of a barrier against full fascism." The regime, "supported and legitimized by the Catholic church," had totalitarian tendencies but never managed to overcome the extensive "free spaces" that remained.[61] This was also true, of course, of both the "core" fascist states, with the qualification that the church was less inclined to legitimize the regime. In both Italy and Germany, a measure of agreement was reached between the regime and the church—bringing about a greater degree of co-operation in the former than had existed for several decades, and both Mussolini and Hitler encountered opposition from the church. The difference in Austria was not only that the Church was much closer to the dictatorship but that Catholicism was a defining ingredient in an "Austria ideology" that drew on the memory of the Holy Roman Empire, and cast the Austrians as "supranational" and the truncated territory of the republic as a passing phase. If there were dreams of a new Reich among the right-wing Catholic intellectuals of Vienna, it was of a restored "universal" Holy Empire that would trump the "*Kleindeutschland*" to the north and encompass non-Germans as well.[62] The reality was more prosaic: Christian motifs were used to symbolize the corporate state, and the Catholic identity was an important part of the Austrian identity propagated by the regime, not least as Austria asserted its independence under pressure from Germany; but the universality of the Austrian identity is less convincing if measured by attitudes to non-German minorities.

Exactly how the corporate state would have developed under Dollfuss is, of course, impossible to know. In any event, he was assassinated during a botched Nazi coup in July 1934, and the development of the corporate state took place under his successor Kurt von Schuschnigg. The new constitution abolished elected institutions and established an impotent Parliament and four advisory "councils;" the real power was concentrated in the executive. The corporative system that was to underpin the new regime, based on seven estates representing different sectors of the economy, never fully materialized. The reality of the Austrian corporate state was even more of a sham than that in Italy. In the absence of a genuine fascist mass movement in Austria, the symbolic unity of the regime was expressed by the Fatherland Front (*Vaterländische Front*, VF), which had been set up by Dollfuss shortly after the suspension of Parliament in 1933. It was now the only permitted political organization, adopted all the external paraphernalia of a fascist movement, and articulated the regime's ideology. It, too, was a fraud. Whereas the roles of the Partito Nazionale Fascista (PNF) and the NSDAP became also relatively directionless once their respective leaders had won power, the VF had no period of political struggle from which to retire. Its initial membership was built up by absorbing organizations rather than enlisting individuals, and it never really mobilized authentic popular support for the regime.[63]

Kluge distinguishes between a theoretical dualism based on authoritarian government on the one hand and a "democracy" of occupational estates on the other, but concludes that real political power was exercised in accordance with a "modernized neoabsolutism," ostensibly provisional and with the notional objective of overcoming the country's immediate crisis. In practice, he concludes, the system suffered from the same absence of a reciprocal constitutional relationship between state and society that had eluded the parliamentary system but is essential to the politics of a modern state.[64] In the absence of evidence for any real popular resonance on the part of the corporate state, there have been those who have found in it 'a foundation for the future of a workable Austrian identity."[65] There are grounds for skepticism about this new-found identity in the light of the Anschluss euphoria of 1938 and of postwar opinion polls suggesting that a substantial number of Austrians still thought of themselves as Germans. "To this day," writes Fred Parkinson, "the term *nation* and *national* refer automatically and implicitly, without any need for explicit affirmation, to the German nation."[66] Dollfuss and Schuschnigg, he goes on, so abused the term "patriotism" that people were alienated rather than convinced. Similarly, Evan Bukey, one of the most knowledgeable historians of Austrian public opinion in this period, has been scathing about the regime's attempts to mobilize popular support for an Austrian identity when, at the same time, it sought to silence those who said otherwise.[67] The confusion seems to lie in the methodological approaches of the two schools of thought. Those who dismiss the idea of an emergent Austrian national consciousness between 1934 and 1938 have attempted to assess popular feeling, while those who find it have tended to refer to the regime's intentions, and to the ways in which a separate Austrian identity was promoted and discussed among those sympathetic or close to the regime. Much of this identity rested on a political and cultural nostalgia for the imperial past and a sentimentality associated with traditional values, expressed not least in public sculpture and monuments, and in a Biedermeier revival among the chattering classes: an Austrofascist chic, which, although predominantly reactionary, could not dispense with elements of modernism.[68] (The attempt to reconcile the two is captured in Fritz Seibel's fashion sketches of men wearing smart country clothes.)[69] What comes across most clearly from the visual and material culture, however, is that much of what is new reflects not a national identity but a recognizably international modern style. The direct impact of Austrofascist aesthetics seems to have been limited to a new vogue in religious painting and a spurt of church building. The situation for literature and the performing arts was perhaps rather more directly influenced by the regime's intolerance. A contemporary theatre critic, Jura Soyfer, wrote that a future theater historian would have to "dismiss this epoch with a few sad words; John Warren adds that "although the Austrian government was able to use the theater for its own ends, the confused state of Austrian loyalties continues to emerge from many of the key productions."[70]

If a cohesive national identity failed to emerge in Schuschnigg's Austria, it was perhaps not least because the government had alienated the majority of the population that had so overwhelmingly rejected it in the last free elections. In 1932, some three-quarters of the Austrian electorate had voted in elections of one kind or another, and the Christian Social Party had won just over of a quarter of their votes.[71] The party also lost control of the Lower Austrian *Landtag* and with it of the *Bundesrat*. In 1933, local elections were put back to 31 October to avoid disruption to the tourist industry, but were then postponed indefinitely. The *coup d'état* of 1933-34 imposed a regime that ruled against the will of most of the people; whether it was a fascist regime remains an open question, despite the attention it has received. Few of the many interpretations of the corporate state have been willing either to discount elements of fascism entirely or to argue strongly that the Dollfuss-Schuschnigg regime was unambiguously fascist. Something approaching a consensus has emerged over the last forty years, however. It is agreed by most that the *Heimwehr* movement was the vehicle for a native Austrian fascism, one that was strongly influenced by Italian Fascism, but was nevertheless, by 1931, self-consciously fascist in its own right.[72] Ernst Hanisch, a historian more skeptical of the extent and influence of fascism, has written recently that the "Austrian dictatorship was based on an alliance of authoritarian Christian Socials with a *Heimwehr* that was fascist in important respects [*in wesentlichen Teilen*], and was entrusted with the important security ministry."[73] Gerhard Botz has suggested a developmental approach to the analysis of the regime, which takes account of the fluctuating influence of fascism. He suggests a phase of authoritarian semi-dictatorship between March 1933 and January 1934, during which time the regime was becoming more fascist, followed by a phase of semi-fascist dictatorship between February 1934 and October 1935, or the middle of 1936. This period, he argues, was characterized by a balance of power between authoritarianism and fascism, while Christian corporatism was evident only in the regime's ideology and made no impact on social reality at all. Finally, the last two years of the regime were marked by a decline in the influence of the *Heimwehr*, which was determined as much by the changing relationship between Italy and Germany as by any internal developments. The reactionary officers and aristocratic landowners among the *Heimwehr* leadership had lost their protector, and now they also lost position and influence. The *Heimwehr* itself was dissolved, along with other organizations not conforming to the regime's requirements, a development observed with some nervousness by the church, but one which, Botz argues, was part of an effective *Defaschisierung*. On balance, he concludes, the regime was comparable with the authoritarian dictatorships in Portugal, Greece, and Spain.[74] Emmerich Tálos and Walter Manoschek, while retaining the term "Austrofascism" to characterize the regime, emphasize the failure of the Fatherland Front to mobilize support and develop into anything other than a "functionally limited instrument of government." Similarly, the organization of society into the new structures prescribed by the regime's ideology never took place, making nonsense of the term "corporate state." The political structure of the regime, they argue, was characterized by the principle of authoritarian rule and the central importance of the executive.[75] More recently, Tálos has argued that the term "Austrofascism" remains a valid one for the Austrian system of rule between 1934 and 1938 so long as there is no definitive definition of the term "authoritarian regime" in the sense in which it is applied to the other, in many ways similar dictatorships that were established in central and eastern Europe in the 1930s and 1940s.[76] And this, in a sense, is at the heart of the matter: As long as definitions are vague or inconsistent, "checklists" vary, and no clear line is drawn somewhere on the continuum between "authoritarian" and "fascist," the issue cannot be resolved.

Tálos qualifies his use of the term "Austrofascism" by distinguishing between his own use, which is based on scholarly research, and the manner in which it has frequently been used to make party political points. It may be that the term "fascism" itself is ultimately not so much inaccurate as unhelpful in advancing our understanding of the Austrian dictatorship, because it deflects attention away from the political realities of the system and its social and economic consequences. As Robert Paxton has argued, it is difficult to generalize about fascism because its different manifestations are invariably colored by the political culture and history of the different national contexts. This is true even of the manifesto and movement stage of development, and although fascist ideology exerted a considerable influence on European politics generally between the wars, few fascist movements ever achieved any measure of real political power, even as junior partners. Where fascists did join governments, they did so initially in coalitions based on compromises with conservatives or more mainstream nationalist movements, with whom they shared at least some beliefs and objectives, and only in Italy and Germany did fascism gain the upper hand. Much of the recent writing considered here suggests that Austrofascism, an alliance of avowedly fascist *Heimwehr* leaders and *fascisant* authoritarian conservatives, was in many ways more successful than many similar movements, but was in the unique position of being one of two native fascisms, and was squeezed by the popular success of its rival, the Nazi party. Moreover, in so far as there was an attempt to institute a specifically fascist dimension to the regime—the Fatherland Front—it was a failure. Finally, the dominant element in the coalition was that rooted in the authoritarian conservative tradition and not the fascist *Heimwehr*, and it appeared to be moving towards a more uniform bureaucratic authoritarianism as soon as the circumstances permitted. In any event, this development too was cut short by the German annexation of Austria in 1938.

Notes

1. See Stein Larsen, J. P. Mykleburst, and B. Hatvet, *Who Were the Fascists?* (Bergen: Universitetsforlaget, 1979).

2. The different ways in which this was achieved are described in Charles Maier, *Recasting Bourgeois Europe. Stabilization in France, Germany, and Italy in the Decade after World War I* (Princeton: Princeton University Press, 1975).

3. Renzo de Felice cites a report drawn up by the Italian foreign ministry in 1934: *Movimento fascisti esteri*, cited in *Mussolini il duce. 1. Gli anni del consenso 1929-1936* (Rome: Einaudi, 1974), 588.

4. Richard Griffiths, *Fellow Travellers of the Right: British Enthusiasts for Nazi Germany, 1933-39* (Oxford: Oxford University Press, 1983). See also N. J. Crowson, ed., *Fleet Street, Press Barons and Politics. The Journals of Collin Brooks, 1932-1940* (Cambridge: Cambridge University Press, 1998). Sir Percival Phillips, *The 'Red' Dragon and the Blackshirts. How Italy Found her Soul. The True Story of the Fascisti Movement* (London: Associated Newspapers, 1922) is a very early example of the genre of pro-fascist apologetics which was to be popular for the best part of twenty years.

5. Tim Kirk and Anthony McElligott, *Opposing Fascism: Community, Authority and Resistance in Europe* (Cambridge: Cambridge University Press, 1999), 3.

6. See, for example, Thomas Angerer, "An Incomplete Discipline: Austrian *Zeitgeschichte* and Recent History," in *Contemporary Austrian Studies*, vol. 3, *Austria in the Nineteen-Fifties*, ed. Günter Bischof, Anton Pelinka, and Rolf Steiniger. (New Brunswick: Transaction Publishers, 1995), 207-51.

7. Emmerich Tálos, "Zum Herrschaftssystem des Austrofaschismus: Österreich 1934-1938," in *Autoritäre Regime in Ostmittel- und Südosteuropa*, ed. Erwin Oberländer (Paderborn: F. Schöningh, 2001), 143-62, here 161.

8. Ian Kershaw, *The Nazi Dictatorship: Problems and Perspectives of Interpretation*, 4th ed. (London: Arnold, 2000), 20-27.

9. R. J. B. Bosworth, *The Italian Dictatorship. Problems and Perspectives in the Interpretation of Mussolini and Fascism* (London: Arnold, 1998), 54.

10. Ian Kershaw and Moshe Lewin, *Stalinism and Nazism. Dictatorships in Comparison* (Cambridge: Cambridge University Press, 1997); Ian Kershaw, "The Nazi State: an Exceptional State?," *New Left Review* 176 (1989): 47-67, here 49-51.

11. Ernst Nolte, *Der Faschismus in seiner Epoche* (Munich: Piper, 1963).

12. See Richard Evans, *In Hitler's Shadow: West German Historians and the Attempt to Escape from a Nazi Past* (London: I. B. Tauris, 1989).

13. Bosworth, *The Italian Dictatorship*, 19.

14. See, for example, Emilio Gentile, *Il mito dello Stato nuovo: Dal radicalismo nazionale al fascismo*, 2nd ed. (Rome: Editori Laterza, 1999), xiv-xviii.

15. See Tim Mason, "Whatever Happened to 'Fascism'?," in *Reevaluating the Third Reich*, ed. Thomas Childers and Jane Caplan (New York: Holmes and Meier, 1993), 254-62. Mason himself was one of the few historians to undertake original research on both Nazi Germany and Fascist Italy.

16. Renate Bridenthal, Atina Grossmann, and Marion Kaplam, eds., *When Biology became Destiny: Women in Nazi and Weimar Germany* (New York: Monthly Review Press, 1984); Gisela Bock, *Zwangssterilisation im Nationalsozialismus. Studien zur Rassenpolitik und Frauenpolitik* (Opladen: Westdeutscher Verlag, 1986); Michael Burleigh and Wolfgang Wippermann, *The Racial State: Germany 1933-1945* (Cambridge: Cambridge University Press, 1991); Lisa Pine, *Nazi Family Policy 1933-1945* (Oxford: Berg, 1997); Detlev Peukert, "The Genesis of the 'Final Solution' from the Spirit of Science," in Childers and Caplan, *Reevaluating*, 234-52.

17. Mason wrote of "secondary issues, such as Fascist aesthetics and 'faschistische Öffentlichkeit'" (Mason, "Whatever Happened to Fascism?," 256) and Bosworth has found the work of some "culturalist" historians of Fascism problematic and limited: "[I]n a curious and not always well-considered way, among Italianists Rankeanism mingles with postmodernism" and "in their determination to be apolitical and to treat Fascism in its own terms, the culturalist historians often credulously report what Fascism said rather than critically exploring what it meant" (Bosworth, *Italian Dictatorship*, 26-27). See also the *Journal of Contemporary History* 31 (1996), a special edition devoted to Fascist culture. Bosworth makes an exception of the work of Ruth Ben-Ghiat, and with good reason. See Ruth Ben-Ghiat, *Fascist Modernities: Italy 1922-1945* (Berkeley: University of California Press, 2001).

18. See Paola Di Cori, "Le Leggi Razziali," in *I luoghi della memoria. Simboli e miti dell'Italia unita*, ed. Mario Insenghi (Rome: Editori Laterza, 1998), 463-76, here 464-65. The quotation is from David Bidussa, *Il mito del bravo italiano* (Milan: Il Saggiatore, 1994).

19. See, for example, Alberto Burgio, ed., *Nel nome della razza. Il razzismo nella storia d'Italia 1870-1945* (Bologna: Il Mulino, 1999).

20. For a comparison of pro-natal policy in Italy, Germany, and France see Maria Sophia Quine, *Population Politics in Twentieth-Century Europe* (London: Routledge, 1995).

21. For example, Roger Griffin, *The Nature of Fascism* (London: Routledge, 1991); idem, *Fascism* (Oxford: Oxford University Press, 1995); Stanley Payne, *A History of Fascism 1914-45* (Madison: University of Wisconsin Press, 1995); and Roger Eatwell *Fascism. A History* (London: Vintage, 1996).

22. See especially Larsen, Mykleburst, and Hatvet, eds., *Who Were the Fascists?*; Detlef Mühlberger, ed., *The Social Basis of European Fascist Movements* (London: Croom Helm, 1987); Martin Blinkhorn, ed., *Fascists and Conservatives: The Raical Right and the Establishment in Twentieth-Century Europe* (London: Routledge, 1990); Richard Bessel, ed., *Fascist Italy and Nazi Germany: Comparisons and Contrasts* (Cambridge: Cambridge University Press, 1996).

23. Robert O. Paxton, "The Five Stages of Fascism," *Journal of Modern History* 70 (March 1998): 1-23, here 5.

24. *Ibid.*, 10.

25. See Jill Lewis, "Red Vienna: Socialism in One City 1918-27," *European Studies Review* 13 (1983): 335-55.

26. On the political situation in Styria see Jill Lewis, *Fascism and the Working Class in Austria 1918-1934* (New York: Berg, 1991).

27. See Gerhard Botz, "Soziale 'Basis' und Typologie der österreichischen Faschismen im innerösterreichischen und Europäischen Vergleich," in *Faschismus in Österreich und international. Jahrbuch für Zeitgeschichte 1980/81*, ed. Bernhard Perz, Hans Safrian, and Karl Schulpfarrer, 15-77; idem, "Varieties of Fascism in Austria," in Larsen, Mykleburst, and Hatvet, *Who Were the Fascists*, 192-99; F. L. Carsten, *Fascist Movements in Austria: From Schönerer to Hitler* (London: Sage, 1977). In a review of the historiography of the movement Franziska Schneeberger, "Heimwehr und Bauern – Ein Mythos," *Zeitgeschichte* 16.4 (1989): 135-45, challenges the "myth" that the *Heimwehr* was a peasant movement.

28. Carsten, *Fascist Movements*, 167-87.

29. See, for example, Fritz K. Ringer, *The Decline of the German Mandarins. The German Academic Community 1890-1933* (Cambridge, Mass.: Harvard University Press, 1969); Michael Burleigh, *Germany Turns Eastwards. A Study of Ostforschung in the Third Reich* (Cambridge: Cambridge University Press, 1988).

30. Anton Staudinger, "'Austria' – The Ideology of Austrofascism," in *Austria in the Thirties: Culture and Politics*, ed. Kenneth Segar and John Warren (Riverside: Ariadne Press, 1991), 1-24; Helmut Wohnout, *Regierungsdiktatur oder Ständeparlament? Gesetzgebung im autoritären Österreich* (Vienna: Böhlau, 1993), 22-24.

31. John Haag, "Marginal Men and the Dream of the Reich: Eight Austrian National-Catholic Intellectuals," in Larsen, Mykleburst, and Hatvet, *Who Were the Fascists?*, 239-48, here 244.

32. Gerhard Oberkofler, "Einige Dokumente über die Funktion der Beamtenschaft beim Aufbau des 'Austrofaschismus'," *Zeitgeschichte* 2, 9.10 (1975): 216-26.

33. Carsten, *Fascist Movements*, 169.

34. Robert Stöger, "Der christliche Führer und die 'wahre Demokratie'. Zu den Demokratiekonzeptionen von Ignaz Seipel," *Archiv* 2 (1988): 54-67, here 61.

35. Ibid., 64.

36. As a proto-authoritarian shot across the bows, the anti-parliamentary language was not dissimilar to Sidney Sonnino's call of 1897 for a return to the *Statuto* and other attacks on the Italian Parliament by authoritarian conservatives in pre-Fascist Italy.

37. *Alpenländische Heimatwehr*, Folge 3, September 1929, cited in Rainer Hubert, *Schober: "Arbeitermörder" und "Hort der Republik"* (Vienna: Böhlau, 1990), 269.

38. Walter B. Simon, "Democracy in the Shadow of Imposed Sovereignty: The First Republic of Austria" in *The Breakdown of Democratic Regimes*, ed. Juan J. Linz and Walter Stepan (Baltimore: Johns Hopkins University Press, 1978), 80-121, here 101.

39. Paxton, "Five Stages of Fascism," 13.

40. Tim Kirk, *Nazism and the Working Class in Austria* (Cambridge: Cambridge University Press, 1996), 33-39.

41. Ernst Hanisch, *Der lange Schatten des Staates: Österreichische Gesellschaftsgeschichte im 20. Jahrhundert* (Vienna: Ueberreuter, 1994), 302.

42. Jill Lewis, "Conservatives and Fascists in Austria 1918-1934," in *Fascists and Conservatives*, 98-117, here 111.

43. Adam Wandruszka, "Historische Einführung," in *Protokolle des Ministerrates der Ersten Republik* VIII, vol. 1 (Vienna, Verlag der österreichischen Staatsdruckerei, 1980), xvi.

44. Ministerratsprotokoll Nr. 828, 5 October 1933, ibid., 596.

45. R. John Rath, "The Dollfuss Ministry: The Demise of the Nationalrat," *Austrian History Yearbook* XXXII (2001): 125-47, here 131.

46. Emmerich Tálos and Walter Manoschek, "Zum Konstituierungsprozeß des Austrofaschismus," in *"Austrofaschismus": Beiträge über Politik, Ökonomie und Kultur 1934-1938*, ed. E. Tálos and W. Neugebauer (Vienna: Verlag für Gesellschaftskritik, 1984), 31-52, here 43-44.

47. See Stein Larsen, J. P. Mykleburst, and B. Hatvet, *Who Were the Fascists?* (Bergen: Universitetsforlaget, 1979).

48. G.E.R. Gedye, *Fallen Bastions* (London: Gollancz, 1939), 84.

49. Rudolf G. Ardelt, "Der Ständestaat – ein postparlamentarisches System?," *Zeitgeschichte* 13.3 (December 1985): 109-19; Ulrich Kluge, *Der österreichische Ständestaat 1934-1938. Entstehung und Scheitern* (Vienna: Verlag für Geschichte und Politik, 1984).

50. Helmut Wohnout, *Regierungsdiktatur oder Ständeparlament?*, 57.

51. R. John Rath, "The Dollfuss Ministry: The Intensification of Animosities and the Drift toward Authoritarianism," *Austrian History Yearbook* XXX (1999): 65-101.

52. Kluge, *Ständestaat*, 56-57.

53. Ministerratsprotokoll Nr. 911, 15 December 1933, Beilage H, *Protokolle des Ministerrates der Ersten Republik* VIII, vol. I.

54. Gerhard Botz, "Der Aufstandsversuch österreichischer Sozialdemokraten am 12. Februar 1934. Ursachen für seinen Ausbruch und Mißerfolg," in *Krisenzonen einer Demokratie. Gewalt, Streik und Konfliktunterdrückung in Österreich seit 1918* (Frankfurt am Main: Campus, 1987), 181-99, here 191, 95-150.

55. Everhard Holtmann, *Zwischen Unterdrückung und Befriedung. Sozialistische Arbeiterbewegung und autoritäres Regime in Österreich 1933-1938* (Munich: Oldenbourg, 1978).

56. Rath, "The Intensification of Animosities," 65.

57. J. D. Gregory, *Dollfuss and His Times* (London: Hutchinson, 1935), 321.

58. Laura Gellot, "Recent Writings on the Ständestaat, 1834-1938," *Austrian History Yearbook* XXVI (1995): 207-37, here 211.

59. James William Miller, *Engelbert Dollfuss als Agrarfachmann. Eine Analyse bäuerlicher Führungsbegriffe und österreichischer Agrarpolitik 1918-1834* (Vienna: Böhlau, 1988). See also James Miller, "Agrarian Politics in Interwar Austria" (Center for Austrian Studies, Working Paper in Austrian Studies 1992-93, Minnesota, 1992). See also James Miller's essay in this volume.

60. Rath, "The Intensification of Animosities," 67-75.

61. Ernst Hanisch, "Der politische Katholizismus als ideologischer Träger des 'Austrofaschismus'," in *Austrofaschismus*, 53-73, here 54.

62. Staudinger "Austria," 15-16.

63. Emmerich Tálos and Walter Manoschek, "Politische Struktur des Austrofaschismus (1834-1938)," in *"Austrofaschimsus,"* 75-119.

64. Kluge, *Ständestaat*, 87-90.

65. Gellot, "Recent Writings," 213.

66. Fred Parkinson, *Conquering the Past. Austrian Nazism Yesterday and Today* (Detroit: Wayne State University Press, 1989), 314-15.

67. Evan Burr Bukey, *Hitler's Hometown. Linz, Austria, 1908-1945* (Bloomington: Indiana University Press, 1986).

68. See, for example, Margerethe Lasinger, "Wie modern war doch die Biedermeierzeit: 'Die Pause' und andere Kulturzeitschriften im Ständestaat," in *Kunst und Diktatur. Architektur, Bildhauerei und Malerei in Österreich, Deutschland, Italien und der Sowjetunion 1922-1956. Eine Aussstellung des österreichischen Bundesministeriums für Wissenschaft und Forschung*, ed. Jan Tabor (Baden: Verlag Grasl, 1994), 260-76; Barbara Feller, "Sichtbarmachung der Vergangengheit. Kunst-am-Bau und neue Monumente in Österreich 1930-1938," in ibid., 282-93.

69. Georg Rigele, "Ein Kontrapunkt zum Fremdenverkehr. Ernst Krenek und die österreichische Kulturpolitik 1928-1938," in ibid., 242-51, here 247.

70. John Warren, "Austrian Theatre and the Corporate State," in *Austria in the Thirties*, 267-91, here 267.

71. Jürgen W. Falter and Dirk Hänisch, "Wahlerfolge und Wählerschaft der NSDAP in Österreich von 1927 bis 1932: Soziale Basis und parteipolitische Herkunft," *Zeitgeschichte* 15 (1988): 223-44.

72. Carsten, *Fascist Movements in Austria*; Botz, "Varieties of Fascism in Austria."

73. Hanisch, *Der lange Schatten des Staates*, 313.

74. Gerhard Botz, "Faschismus und 'Ständestaat' vor und nach dem 12. Februar," in *Krisenzonen*, 211-236. Laura Gellot points out that the church perceived this shift as "increasing fascistization"; see Gellot, "Recent Writings," 214. See also Laura Gellot, *The Catholic Church and the Authoritarian Regime in Austria 1933-38* (New York: Garland Pub., 1987).

75. Tálos and Manoschek, "Politische Struktur."

76. Emmerich Tálos, "Zum Herrschaftssystem des Austrofaschismus," 161-62.

Economic Development and Economic Policies in the *Ständestaat* Era

Gerhard Senft

The *Ständestaat*—as the authoritarian regime governing Austria from 1934 to 1938 named itself—is still very much *terra incognita* for historians. For a short period, research in the field flourished, but in recent years interest in the field has been muted at best.[1] Accordingly, the scholarly community has not even agreed on some fundamental issues: Is it permissible and acceptable to use the term "Austro-Fascism" to designate the political system applied by the governments of Engelbert Dollfuss and Kurt Schuschnigg?[2] Was the Austrian *Ständestaat* primarily a dictatorship enforcing an essentially business-friendly political course or was the emphasis rather on premodern anticapitalist concepts?[3] In order to obtain a clear categorization, it would be best to look at the social implications of the *Ständestaat*. After all, the problem becomes even more complex when the critical observer looks at its "corporate" economic policies, which, at first glance, appear largely contradictory. Interestingly enough, ultra-protectionist measures stand side by side with anti-interventionist concepts comparable to those by liberal economists such as Ludwig Mises or Fritz Machlup. The ideas developed by corporate thinkers such as Othmar Spann or Walter Heinrich certainly shaped the structure of the corporate state, yet altogether the *Ständestaat* shows so many facets that it is extremely difficult to describe its character. This essay is an attempt to illuminate the key features of the economic policy situation of 1934–38 and includes a more long-term perspective on issues of economic development.

The Route to the *Ständestaat*

Any attempt to describe the interwar period in Austria as an "age of uncertainty" needs to take into account the shaping moments and events of the previous period. Not only did the traditions of the imperial authoritarian government still have massive aftereffects, but the long-term consequences of the economic backwardness of the Habsburg empire, which had become increasingly pronounced in the first half of the 19th century, began to pose particularly grave problems. Although measures that aimed to give impetus to industrial development were still taken during the monarchy, the lack of continuity and momentum slowed down economic growth. The changes that arrived in the last years of the 19th century were nevertheless sufficiently great for important elements of society to perceive a certain progress interspersed by painful ruptures. As a consequence, people in Austria failed to mentally cope with the industrial upheavals and tended to escape into premodern attitudes and ideas.

This negative trend was further exacerbated by the breakup of the Habsburg monarchy. The greatly skewed economic structure, the partial shortage of raw materials, and the enormous changes that followed for the export sector constituted serious difficulties, but the new Republic of Austria continued to be the economically favored part of the former monarchy. Doubts about its viability were thus chiefly of a socio-psychological nature and did not derive from any reasonable review of economic facts.[4] Nevertheless, these doubts complicated the efforts to find a specifically Austrian identity: Torn between a longing to continue the fairy-tale operetta of the monarchy and the desire to assume the role of a "second German state," Austrians were unable to find a separate and distinct national identity. Similarly, the conflict between modernity and anti-modernity flared up again in the transition phase after the First World War. The old alliance of traditional and bourgeois elites had lost much of its importance. At the academic level cultural pessimists deplored the process of social erosion and warned against the terrors of the "ungovernable masses." The working class, enjoying more participatory rights and social policy successes, sent clear signals of its growing assertiveness. In the interwar period, the newly practiced ideas of fairness and social security were repeatedly used by opponents of these ideas to ignite the discussion of social distribution.

In the 1920s, Austria tried to adapt to new conditions and circumstances. Its development was impeded by the postwar inflation, which reached its climax in 1922, the stability crisis in 1923, and a series of bank collapses, which started in 1924. In the second half of the 1920s, the economy in Austria achieved some consolidation, but still suffered from structural weaknesses, a chronic trade deficit, and a high unemployment rate. Between 1923 and 1929, the Austrian GDP rose from ATS 8,562 million to 11,358 million, the production index went up from 72 to 100 (in real terms, at prices of 1937), and the general business index from 62 to 100.[5] The global economic crisis had a disastrous effect on the economy of the small country. The depression caused sales to plummet, which in turn caused increasing numbers of companies to collapse and the unemployment rate to explode. Between 1929 and 1933, unemployment jumped from

8.8% to 26%.[6] The general business index and production index dropped below the level of 1923, and the GDP even below the level of 1913.

All ingredients for disaster were in place when social and political conflicts came to a head in the wake of the economic decline. The discussion raged over the need to cut "excessive social burdens," and the grave situation was further exploited to settle old accounts with the "modernists."[7] The "modernists" included all those who looked for new social approaches away from traditional communalities, who trusted in democracy and progress to achieve an ascending future development of society, in short those who had never stopped propagating the "ideas of 1789." Instead, ideas were increasingly shaped by a belief in a prestabilized harmony, in line with an idealized image of the Middle Ages. *Berufsständische Bindung* (ties based on corporations of employers and employees) was the magic word that was to repair the systemic failure. The corporate idea of a "social equalization of interests" aimed to desubstantialize the democratic rule of law and to rescind earlier compromises achieved between the classes. Forcing workers and employers into corporations ("onward to old goals," as Josef Tzöbl called it)[8] should take the sting out of all class struggles. Its advocates expected the *Ständestaat* not just to alleviate the social crisis but also to achieve a complete rearrangement of the economy. In Austria, it required the abolition of parliamentarism and a dramatic civil war to clear the path for a corporate state system. The resulting decline in social accomplishments was brazenly obvious. With the absence of free unions of laborers, workers were de facto left at their employers' mercy. The effects of the crisis were, without interference, distributed "from the top down," with the concrete results of wage cuts, cutbacks in the labor law, and serious changes in the social security and pension systems.[9]

Key Economic Players

The "refeudalization" of Austria[10] affected mainly the institutional framework of its society, but the theoretical ideas of the corporate thinkers certainly had an impact on the daily practice of business as well. For its main support, the regime looked towards farmers because the ideal of a "sound peasantry" was to counteract all social manifestations of decadence.[11] Accordingly, protecting the farm sector from the negative influence of a "liberal-capitalist global economy" was a first priority. In the 1930s, protectionism was the norm and Austrian farming was screened for foreign influences. The price level of farm products was kept stable by applying a rigid quota system for dairy products and livestock farming. Subsidies were designed to give priority to farm products over commercial and, in particular, industrial products. Shifts in beverage sales clearly illustrate this point: In 1937, the sale of wine was up by 28% compared to 1929, whereas beer sales had declined by 57%.[12] Similarly, commercial policies were clearly anti-modernist. The Whitsuntide Conference of Catholic Sociologists in 1933, which was supported by Chancellor Dollfuss and which was also attended by a number of senior civil servants, recommended more consideration of small and medium sized enterprises (SMEs) since "the growth of large-scale industries had repeatedly caused misery and distress."[13] The access restrictions that were adopted when the trade and commerce sector was restructured eliminated the last remains of a liberal industrial code; and when in the mid-1930s the guilds were reintroduced, it became obvious that the return to the Middle Ages was progressing at full speed.

Industry benefited from the *Ständestaat*'s authoritarian approach to conflict resolution, which appeased the workers, lowered wage costs, and reduced the "social burdens." Nevertheless, upon closer consideration, the disadvantages suffered by the industry were greater than the advantages gained: Not only did the government fail miserably in the area of cartel formation, but its rigid financial policies precluded all potential opportunities for expansion. The actual improvement of infrastructure between 1933 and 1938 was entirely disproportionate to the propaganda efforts expended on, for example, road construction; no serious thought was given to developing the Danube as a modern waterway; the electrification of the railways, while continued in 1933 after having come to a standstill in the late 1920s, still lagged behind. Energy generation was similarly neglected. Contrary to recommendations by experts of the Austrian Board of Economic Efficiency and in spite of the evident shortage of coal, construction of hydropower plants virtually ceased in the 1930s.[14] Oil was found by chance rather than systematic exploration, and it was with great hesitation that the refining capacities were adapted to the growth of production. That the industries in the 1930s were at all able to increase their supply was mainly due to foreign trade and, specifically, the new boom in the armament industry. It appears obvious that no genuine economic success story could have been achieved from such a course of restriction.

Nevertheless, anti-modern resentment did not prevail in all aspects of the *Ständestaat*. When the new Austrian leaders adopted the new constitution in the spring of 1934, they found out that rolling back certain standards would not be all that easy: Banks, to take but one example, refused to follow the path stipulated by the theorists of the *Ständestaat*. Rather than being dissected into small units, which would have been in line with the corporate concept, banks went through a process of monopolization that was unique in the history of Austria. Walter Eucken's comment that the corporate practice went hand in hand with centralization and singularization of power was fully confirmed by the Austrian corporate regime.[15] Its not inconsiderable deviations from the ideological ideal, though, show that the Austrian *Ständestaat* was indeed a contradictory and incomplete project. Practical imperatives, deliberate contrivance, and even chance shaped the appearance of the corporate system. At times, it even included modernist spots on its hide. For example, the dramatic contraction of tourism revenues in the 1930s made it imperative to modernize the tourism industry; occasionally, the corporate government also made an effort to show a modern face towards its western trade partners.[16] An action extremely untypical of the authoritarian regime was its abolition of the application fee charged for new telephone lines, which made for a growth of almost 25% in the density of telephone coverage between 1929 and 1936.[17]

The fact that the *Ständestaat* identified the stability of its currency ("Alpine Dollar") and a balanced budget as its main economic goals demonstrates that it had failed to draw proper conclusions from the global economic crisis.[18] Attempts to stimulate the national economy, as were made by a number of other countries in 1932/33, remained much too weak in Austria since they lacked genuine conviction on the part the government. The economy of the small country thus remained exposed to the whims, the ups and downs of the global economy, and only export considerations could occasionally break through the prevailing stagnation. The nadir of the depression was reached when all blast furnaces were shut down in Austria, but in 1934 the first tender shoots of recovery were emerging. Heavy industry in particular profited from an increase in exports, and a faint mood of optimism spread in the chemical, electrical, and automotive industries. Other sectors, such as the textile industry, still remained in the doldrums, overall employment continued to be low, and liquidity in general had not improved. The armament drive launched in 1935 benefited the heavy, automotive, and textile industries. But Austrian industries still suffered from their overcapacities. In terms of their domestic sales, plants operated by the paper mills were twice as large as needed, and bottle glass producers were working at 30% of their capacity.[19] The order books of iron and steel producers were only half as full as in 1929.[20] The shutdown of the *Marchegger Maschinenfabrik* in 1935 was deeply symbolic for the situation in the machinery industry.

In 1936, the global economy continued on its path to recovery. The upswing made itself felt in Austria as well, especially in the pig iron and crude steel production, and gave another boost to the textile industry. The production index per cotton spindle rose from 141 in 1935 to 160 in 1936 (1929 = 100).[21] The extremely low level at which restructuring actually took place can be exemplified by the mechanical engineering industry: Its capacity utilization rate only rose from 36% in 1935 to 40% in 1936.[22] In other manufacturing sectors, the situation was virtually hopeless, in spite of the momentum from the international upswing. Thus, window glass production, for instance, was at a standstill for about seven months in

1936.[23] Industries producing goods for the military sector enjoyed another growth year in 1937. Japan alone purchased 1,145 freight cars of hot-rolled bars in the first ten months of the year, at a value of ATS 15.32 million—a spectacular rise over the previous year.[24] In 1937, the crude steel sector was at last able to surpass its 1929 production volume. But the upswing came to an abrupt stop in the autumn of the year. Growing demand for raw materials had pushed up prices: Between October 1936 and October 1937, world market prices rose by 35.5% for hard coal, by 73% for pig iron, by 21.8% for zinc, by 23.4% for lead and by 16.2% for copper.[25] In the context of a still unstable global economy, this upsurge in prices and the resulting damper on demand were certainly the main causes for the setback in 1937. It had been the highly sensitive capital goods sector which had chiefly fuelled the upswing in the mid-1930s, and it immediately felt the slowdown in the second half of 1937. The effect was a renewed downturn of business and curtailment of output. Particularly affected were the textile and paper industries; some operations even had to return to short-time working.

The short upturn of the Austrian industries had not sufficed to eliminate their structural imbalances. They were unable to operate at full capacity, and even crude steel capacities remained partly unutilized during the upswing in 1937. In this context, it is interesting to note that Austrian industries shifted to the raw and base material sector. The industrial development throughout the 1930s is reflected in the price index for key industrial stocks: After reaching a low of 43.5 points in 1933, the index recovered and rose to 94.3 points by 1937. (See Table 1: Price index development of the 34 main industrial stocks in Austria.) In March 1937, it reached its high point, only to decline again in the second half of the year. As the monthly reports of the Austrian Institute of Business Cycle Research noted, "... with this, the prospects to raise capital by issuing shares have, for the time being, diminished."[26]

In the 1930s, investment activities in Austria, which were rather weak throughout the interwar period, even failed to meet the rates of the previous decade. Mirroring the fluctuations of the business cycle, the ratio of gross investment to GNP at market prices was 6% in 1924. It grew to 10% during the consolidation phase up to 1929. During the depression it dipped to 5%, and reached just 7% in the following upturn until 1937. Fluctuations were greater when it came to the investment volume. Between 1924 and 1929, real gross capital expenditure (total investments) grew by 81%, only to fall off by 60% until 1933, and to rise by just 57% between 1933 and 1937. It should also be noted that most investments compensated for the retirement of old, no longer usable assets so that the volume of real fixed assets was, at most, maintained, but not added to.[27] Neither investments nor changes in consumption could provide a crucial impetus for the production section. Industrial output in 1937/38 was below that of 1929.[28]

Table 1: Price index development of the 34 main industrial stocks in Austria

Year	Index	Year	Index
		1932	52.3
1927	113.9	1933	43.5
1928	110.5	1934	48.5
1929	100	1935	64.4
1930	81.5	1936	81.9
1931	61.6	1937	94.3

(1929 = 100)
Source: *Monatsberichte des österreichischen Instituts für Konjunkturforschung*, vol. 12, no. 2, 26 February 1938, 63.

Agricultural production was characterized by some special circumstances. Farm and raw material prices had flagged even before the onset of the global crisis. Due to the farmer-friendly course steered by the Austrian government, protectionism flourished. In 1930, an increase in customs duties on agricultural products launched the first phase of an all-out agricultural interventionism. But it quickly became clear that with higher customs duties farm prices could no longer be protected. Thus, the second stage of protectionist government intervention followed, which included direct subsidies, support buying, and import bans on, for example, rye, barley, and livestock. Dumped exports, particularly frequent for dairy products, were a critical component of the policy. The desired effect was achieved when the price level for most farm products in Austria was stabilized, while it continued to decline on the world market. However, the various price supports were found to be extremely expensive. The last attempt to help the farm sector in its crisis was to directly restrict production. With the emergence of a planned economy in the agricultural sector, the degree of self-sufficiency went up, but negative effects also became obvious. Prices for farm products rose to a level that was hurting consumption. In addition, agricultural intervention, which had first triggered a wave of investment in livestock and dairy production, now seemed to be misdirected as the production cuts took effect.[29]

Yet, even the agricultural sector gradually began to feel the financial policy restrictions put in place by the authoritarian state (for example in terms of its debt rate and subsidies). Nevertheless the planned-economy structures and domestic protectionism were, if possible, enhanced even further. Pricing for farm products continued to be divorced from the effects of the world market. When in 1934 the sugar beet harvest for the first time exceeded domestic demand, the acreage was to be reduced by one eighth in the following year,[30] in accordance with the motto of limiting production rather than cutting prices for consumption. A reduction in the quantity of production raised harvest values. Hence, the computed contribution of farming to the GDP rose noticeably in the 1930s, as compared to 1929. The index of farm purchasing power in January 1938 was substantially higher than the index average of 1930.[31] (See Table 2: Volume of Austrian farm production.)

Table 2: Volume of Austrian farm production

Year	Production	Year	Production
		1933	2.9
1929	6.5	1934	2.4
1930	4	1935	2.4
1931	4	1936	2.3
1932	3.3	1937	2.4

(In 1000 metric tons)
Source: *Monatsberichte des Österreichischen Instituts für Konjunkturforschung*, vol. 12, no. 2, 26 February 1938, 66.

In view of the fact that there was virtually no policy impetus to improve the economic situation in Austria, foreign trade was placed in a pivotal position. Considering the threat of a global crisis, it was not unusual that Austria, like other countries, installed an external trade regime of massively regulatory proportions. In 1931, high protective tariffs were introduced, followed by import and export bans, exchange controls, and quotas. Barter clearing replaced monetary clearing; special agreements led to a system of preferential tariffs. In 1933, international trade in Austria experienced its lowest point, with the volume of foreign trade being about a third of the level of 1929.[32] Subsequently, restrictions were tentatively relaxed (for example by easing the foreign currency regime). By 1934, external trade had slightly improved, which was partly due to the conclusion of the Roman Protocols (by Austria, Italy, and Hungary). Exports rose by 7.7%, imports by 1.5%.[33] That year, Austria's main trading partners were Germany, Czechoslovakia, Hungary, Italy, Yugoslavia, and Poland. The positive trend continued in 1935. At that time, a noticeable shift in trading partners occurred when Italy became a primary importer of Austrian products. By 1937, one quarter of Austria's total exports went to the Roman Pact states. The trade deficit shrank again because Austria was able to reduce imports from its main trading partners. The international upswing of 1936 improved foreign trade conditions for Austria as well. With industrial capacities available, order books filled. The sanctions imposed by the League of Nations on Italy for its war in Abyssinia made Austria more valuable as its supplier. The devaluation of the gold currency bloc and the rising world market prices could not dampen the optimism of 1936. Nevertheless, it turned out that the growth of global trade could not keep pace with the expansion of production, since most countries were still betting on stimulating their domestic economies. The change from finished products to raw materials and semi-finished goods that characterized Austrian exports needs to be seen in this light.[34] It was in 1936 that Austria began to direct its focus westward and thus greatly improved its export rates. Compared to the previous year, Austrian exports to the United States rose by 40%, to France by 33%, and to Great Britain by 35%.[35] From the foreign trade perspective, 1937 was a similarly successful year for Austria. The trade deficit reached its lowest value during the interwar period. Without food imports, Austria had already achieved a trade surplus. Yet, it needs to be noted that the foreign trade volume in 1937 was still markedly below that of 1929, and that Austria's share of the world trade had declined significantly. When we compare foreign trade in terms of international and Austrian trade using the quantum index (index of foreign trade excluding price fluctuations), we find that the decline of foreign trade in Austria between 1929 and 1933 was much more precipitate than elsewhere and that, in spite of the recovery, Austria still could not catch up with the global situation. (See Table 3: Quantum index and foreign trade.)

Table 3: Quantum index and foreign trade

Year	Global	Austria
1929	100	100
1932	74.5	53.1
1933	75.5	50.9
1934	78	53.8
1935	82	56.6
1936	85.5	57.3
1937	--	67.9

Source: *Monatsberichte des österreichischen Instituts für Konjunkturforschung*, vol. 12, no. 2, 26 February 1938, 52.

In Austria of the 1930s, banks and insurance companies were the greatest trouble makers. A series of bank collapses, accompanied by an unfortunate merger strategy, climaxed in May 1931 with the crash of the *Credit-Anstalt*, the last remaining major bank. When the bank's balance sheet deficit became known (ATS 140 million), loan funds were quickly withdrawn and gigantic amounts of capital left the country. The bank crisis led to a currency crisis when the reserves of the National Bank melted to less than one-twelfth of their original stock and the minimum cover ratio was reached. The rescue package put an enormous drain on the public budget. By assuming the debts, the state became the bank's majority shareholder.[36] Because the *Credit-Anstalt* had merged with the *Wiener Bankverein* and continued the business activities of the *Niederösterreichische Eskomptegesellschaft* (of which the *Österreichische Industriekredit-AG* was left as a kind of holding company), only one major bank remained when the reconstruction was completed in 1934. The *Merkurbank* was mostly in German hands, and the *Zentraleuropäische Länderbank* operated as a French bank. In the Austrian business setting, the *CA-Bankverein* was left with a quasi-monopoly.[37]

The terror of the *CA* collapse was still vivid when a new disaster hit—the so-called "*Phönix* Scandal" in March 1936. *Phönix*, a life insurer operating in more than twenty countries, reaching as far as Africa and the Middle East, was by far the largest insurance company in Austria during the interwar period. Founded in the 1880s, it had expanded enormously during and after the First World War, and it regularly advertised its business benchmarks. Thus, the scandal, described as "one of the worst insurance affairs of all times," came as a surprise.[38]

What had happened? After the sudden and unexpected death of Wilhelm Berliner, the company's managing director, it became known that ATS 250 million were missing from the balance sheet of the Austrian affiliate. The ensuing hectic investigation brought to light some unpleasant details. The scandal was perfect when it was found out that the deficit was not the result of insufficient coverage of the premium reserve but of dubious money transfers to political parties, public personalities, and journalists.[39] The greatest public excitement was generated by bribes and similar payments, which actually constituted only a fracture (some 3%) of the total loss. Several causes triggered the collapse of *Phönix*: The management's expansive strategy lacked a solid and proper foundation. Next to unsound premium rates and excessive advertising, non-insurance activities (i.e. savings deposits) caused major problems for the company. Finally, hardly any of the affiliates in the many countries where *Phönix* had been active was able to furnish a positive balance sheet.

Those responsible for economic policy were aware that a repetition of the *Credit-Anstalt* solution was not feasible since it would have put an enormous burden on the population and might even have caused a currency devaluation. Ludwig Draxler,[40] federal minister of finances, developed a plan for the entire insurance sector, including its employees, to share the rescue costs[41] with the *Phönix* clients.[42] In April 1936, a rescue company was formed under the patronage of two banks and two major insurance companies. It was named *Österreichische Versicherungs AG* (*ÖVAG*) and took over the insurance stock after *Phönix* was liquidated. Canceling the contracts was prohibited by law; liability vis-à-vis those insured by foreign branches of *Phönix* was limited to a deficiency guarantee.[43] Of the 1,300 *Phönix* employees, only 200 found work at *ÖVAG*. Even though the state had committed a gross breach of its duty of supervision, its claims were ranked before those of the *Phönix* employees in the bankruptcy proceedings, which had major repercussions on severance payments. When all insurance employees in Austria had their salaries cut, a wave of protests ensued. Josef Dobretsberger, the social minister of the time, was unwilling to accept responsibility for these hardships and resigned from the Schuschnigg cabinet. In its financial reports, the League of Nations commented: "The bankruptcy of the Phönix Life Insurance Company was supported by the country without great disturbance."[44] This was a mendacious assessment since the problems of the *Phönix* pensioners and of the employees who had lost their jobs in the liquidation remained unsolved.[45] The *Phönix* affair remained a key component of the defamation campaign pursued by the National Socialists.

Economic Policy and Policy Alternatives

In order to assess the whole spectrum of economic policies in the 1930s, it will be necessary to include several key economic benchmarks and links. Of considerable value appears to be the GDP development during the First Republic. Following the foundation phase of the Republic, Austria profited from the international upswing which had started in the mid-1920s. During that period, Austria's GDP no longer showed the growth rates of the earlier phase, but still recorded a steady upwards movement and, in 1928, the level of 1913 was at last surpassed. After plummeting during the global economic crisis, the GDP stagnated and showed very few, faint signs of recovery. While growing again in the 1930s, it still remained far from the heights achieved in the late 1920s.[46]

The situation in the 1920s and 1930s is clearly reflected in the general business index, which sagged from 100 to 59 points between 1929 and 1933, and took considerable time to pick up again (72 points by 1937).[47] The gradual improvement of the economic situation in Austria as of 1934 did not extend to consumer goods sales. In that year, food production, the ready-to-wear industry, and shoe manufacturers still suffered from a decline in demand.[48] In 1935, for the first time since 1929, consumer goods reported an increase in sales, but there were still sectors, such as the food industry, which had no reason to be optimistic.[49] The common rule of thumb that rising sales of production goods will entail stronger consumption did not apply to the economic situation of Austria in the 1930s. By 1936, consumer goods sales were once again falling off substantially, which greatly affected the food industry and fuel consumption.[50] The decline continued into 1937. While food sales recovered slightly, durable consumer goods showed no indication of any alleviation of the situation.[51] It became obvious that most households postponed their major consumption decisions. (See Table 4: Indices of production and consumer good sales, 1929 to 1937.)

Table 4: Indices of production and consumer good sales, 1929 to 1937

	Producer goods	Consumer goods
1929	100	100
1930	81	98
1931	64	94
1932	58	79
1933	57	69
1934	63	67
1935	70	70
1936	74	66
1937	94	65

Source: *Monatsberichte des Österreichischen Instituts für Konjunkturforschung*, vol. 12, no. 2, 26 February 1938, 67.

Up to 1937, consumption shrank alarmingly at all levels. Between 1933 and 1937, the food supply to the markets of Vienna plunged from 7,932,964 metric tons to 5,701,400 metric tons. Between 1931 and 1937, meat consumption in Vienna fell from 143,061.4 metric tons to 105,661.6 metric tons.[52] Similar dents were recorded in the clothing and shoe sectors, as well as the luxury food sector. The decline in consumption was due to the deteriorating income situation and a widespread feeling of insecurity. In 1935, bakers' wages were down by 5%, compared to 1931, wages in the metal industry were down by 5%–10%, and in the construction industry by almost 30%.[53] Thus, a skilled worker in the metal industry in Vienna had his hourly wages cut from ATS 1.39 in 1929 to ATS 1.33 in 1933, and to ATS 1.28 in 1937,[54] while the cost of living remained essentially constant.[55] Endemic unemployment and the decline in mass income, which in the course of the 1930s even dropped below the level of 1913, were bound to have a disastrous effect on the general purchasing power.

Representatives of the authoritarian regime pointed to their success in keeping the currency stable and reducing external debt.[56] They missed their goal of achieving a balanced budget, but the financial restrictions associated with that goal were sufficiently massive to cause great damage to the Austrian economy. Not only the monetary sector but also federal expenditure showed signs of deflation. The lack of any anti-cyclic impetus meant that the Austrian economy contracted or shifted to a lower level. By 1938, unemployment had surpassed the 20% threshold, and the number of bankruptcies in the 1930s presented a similarly gloomy picture.[57] Examples of idle capacities were particularly drastic in mining: In 1935, seven graphite mines were operating and twenty-nine were shut down; two lead and zinc mines were active while fifty-seven had ceased their operations; two copper mines were working and twenty-seven had closed. Mining of aluminum, antimony, sulfur, and some other ores was discontinued entirely.[58] The onset of the international revival in 1935 failed to improve Austria's economic situation in general. In foreign trade, the restrictive regime had a counterproductive effect. Abroad, a devaluation of the currency was constantly expected so that imports from Austria kept being delayed.[59]

The effects of the restrictions in economic policies were particularly ominous when looking at employment, wages, and social progress. The conservative policy of restricting money supply was partly the consequence of Austria's foreign debt,[60] but to a greater degree the policy was determined by the "home-made" fear of inflation. That such fears were unfounded was clearly demonstrated by Switzerland. It was due to a different approach to the economy that Austria's neighbor, in spite of its lesser endowment with resources, ranked far before Austria in terms of economic growth between 1913 and 1938.[61] Switzerland was just as affected by the global crisis, but it managed quickly to shake off the deflationary pressure by devaluating its currency on 26 September 1936. Whereas Austria refrained from increasing its money supply (notes in circulation plus current accounts debts) between 1930 and 1937—and, indeed, money circulation was markedly below the rate of the 1920s[62]—Switzerland more than doubled its money stock.[63] Constantly diminishing unemployment and the fact that domestic inflation could be kept under control confirmed that the Swiss had chosen the right path.[64] Increasing the money supply, which offered the prospect of boosting the total investment volume and purchasing power in a situation of idle capacities, was apparently less risky than many Austrians thought. Activities to stimulate business in Austria were limited to floating bonds (but the proceeds from bonds were only partly used for public investments) and a few tentative make-work programs.[65] In 1935, the launch of the "Battle for Work" started the most comprehensive employment program developed by the *Ständestaat*. But the impetus derived from it was so weak that its effects vanished immediately upon termination of the initiative—1936 was once again a year of "budget reform." The volume of public investments in 1934–1938 was utterly insufficient to compensate for the crisis-induced shortage of demand by the private sector.[66]

Caution—the *leitmotif* of Austrian economic policy—was driven by the desire to maintain the economic theories of the 19th century. "The widespread notion of 'pump-priming' the economy is a great misunderstanding,"[67] said Ernst Streeruwitz in 1936, aligning himself with the many warners against new tools to combat the crisis. In accordance with the orthodox view, Austria was to master the crisis-prone situation of the 1930s by adapting: i.e., remove "rigid wages," cut unemployment benefits, consolidate and balance the state household, and prune disproportions in the production structure. Credit expansion and devaluation were seen as tools of an inflationary policy. Among the great innovators of economic theories widely attacked in Austria, John Maynard Keynes stands out. The economic policies developed on the basis of his *Treatise on Money* (1930) referred to cyclic dynamism determined by the savings-investment ratio. Keynes felt that an expansive fiscal policy could be effectively used to encourage an economic upswing, on condition that interest rates were low and (as a prerequisite for the latter) that monetary policy would be autonomous (independent of the constraints of the gold standard).[68] Advocates of the Austrian guild-based economy dismissed "Keynes and his disciples"[69] as "inflationists,"[70] as "prophets of cheap money."[71] Even after 1936, the year in which Keynes published his main œuvre, which comprehensively and systematically outlined the foundations of his practical proposals,[72] no positive response came from Austrian economists. Yet, due to the insistence on the pursuit of orthodox models, the economic policy in Austria was put in a straightjacket that it could no longer shake off.

Nevertheless, even before the New Deal was launched in the United States, which signaled a political turnaround for the economy, a few "pre-Keynesian" approaches had begun to emerge in Austria, isolated from the mainstream economists.[73] Of the many make-work programs, the plan proposed by Otto Deutsch and Alexander Vértes stimulated the most animated discussion at the academic level. Deutsch and Vértes advocated a large-scale public investment program to eliminate rampant unemployment in the medium term. The program was to be financed by a major money-raising scheme (domestic bonds, capital to be raised by newly formed corporations, and "delivery credits"). Compared to earlier make-work schemes, their plan included a number of new features that represented a dynamic macro-economic approach with a clear affinity to Keynes' ideas. The concept included the basic concept of an overall economic equilibrium (i.e., a proper ratio between "saving" and "investing") and applied a multiplier theory (which focuses on the effect of an investment on expenditures).

At the core of the Deutsch-Vértes scheme was the insight that the propensity to invest needs to be encouraged in order to overcome an economic crisis. The fact that investment in Austria remained below the required level was, however, not so much due to the central bank policy but rather to the monopoly situation in the monetary and banking sector, which had a dampening effect on business. Even though the discount rate was substantially lowered by the central bank in the years before the mid-1930s,[74] effective interest rates remained so high that loans were beyond the reach of many companies. Still, after 1934 the situation for the banks improved. Savings deposits rose from ATS 2,087 million in 1934 to ATS 2,249 million in 1935, and again to ATS 2,327 in 1936 and ATS 2,348 million in 1937.[75] With the exception of the *Phönix* collapse, which was accompanied by a short-time withdrawal of money, liquidity of the banks was steadily on the increase. In 1937, the *CA* again distributed a dividend to its shareholders, for the first since 1929. Still reeling from the shock of the global economic disaster, banks proceeded with extreme caution, terrified of bad loans. "Liquidity existed only to the extent to which money is in the bank. It was necessary to regulate the gap between the rates of interest for deposits and for loans; this gap was much too high," was the message of a cabinet meeting in March 1935.[76] But this insight remained without noticeable consequences for the businesses in need of loans.

The numerous local initiatives to overcome the credit shortage also had a pre-Keynesian touch. The greatest fame in this respect was achieved by the "free money" experiment in Wörgl in Tyrol.[77] In mid-1932, the mayor and council of the small town at the Inn river in Tyrol decided to run a regionally limited "money creation scheme." Supported by the local *Raiffeisenkassebank*, so-called "*Arbeitswertscheine*" (work coupons) were issued to finance projects of the community, which was suffering from a massive financial bottleneck. The coupons were covered by amounts in the schilling currency and in bills of exchange. The envisaged 1% depreciation per month was intended to accelerate circulation of the money. With this scheme, Wörgl obtained financial coverage for a number of make-work programs. The coupons opened up a second money stream, demand jumped, and, because of accelerated circulation, the funds quickly returned to the community budget by way of tax revenues. The scheme had its greatest success in reducing unemployment. While the number of jobless in Austria grew from 468,000 in 1932 to 557,000 in 1933 (i.e., by about 20%), the employment situation improved substantially in and around Wörgl.[78] An Austrian newspaper wrote about a "flourishing town in crisis-ridden Austria," and the monetary experiment was also closely watched at the international level.[79] The idea of the depreciation money spread to many other communities in Austria. Wörgl's neighbor Kirchbichl joined the system in January 1933; large majorities of the population of Brixlegg, Hopfgarten, Schwaz, and Lilienfeld were in favor of attempting a similar scheme, and even the council of Linz discussed the experiment.[80] The government eyed the progress of the scheme at Wörgl with great suspicion. Citing Article 122 of the National Bank Act, it requested in early 1933 that the experiment be stopped. A negotiation marathon followed which led right up to the supreme administrative court. On 18 September 1933, the currency of Wörgl was given its death sentence.[81]

When we look at the sectors involved, we find that SMEs were the greatest beneficiaries of small-scale self-help schemes. They had experienced the great crisis at a slight delay but with equal severity. Even though the state put considerable efforts into protecting the commercial sector, the resulting monopolization did not improve the sector's economic situation. In contrast to the industries, which were able to profit from the international upswing in the mid-1930s, prospects remained bleak at the SME level. Consumer purchasing power remained weak domestically, so that SMEs inevitably fell victim to the restrictive policies. In addition, SMEs were unable to modernize since the credit policy pursued by commercial banks made it virtually impossible to obtain a reasonably priced loan. The various self-help projects, aimed at initiating a local upswing, exercised their greatest benefit on local small-scale businesses. From this angle, these schemes were even more important since SMEs were a clear majority in the Austrian business structure.

The industrial sector was underwhelmed by the ideas of depreciation money and similar schemes.[82] Most of the Austrian industrialists had little to gain from regional small-scale self-help programs. They perceived their main opportunities to be in the expansion of export markets, and so they looked to Western Europe, the United States—or Germany. Their group included quite a few advocates of the Anschluss to Germany. Already before 1938, the Federation of Austrian Industrialists initiated an official approach to Nazi Germany. Otto Friedländer, a representative of the chamber of trade, describes the pro-Anschluss mood in his literary document *Maturajahrgang 1907*: In June 1937, in the Lower Austrian abbey of Karbach, a group of ex-pupils meets to celebrate the 30th anniversary of their *Matura*, the university-qualifying examination. Among them is an industrial tycoon who clearly voices his opinion in the increasingly heated political debate. "Business is always about surviving the next day," he says. "After you've survived a crisis, nobody asks you how you did it. I am known as a rather successful industrialist. As such I say and can only say: what they are doing out there with the economy [in Nazi Germany, G.S.] is quite simply impressive. And that is what I told Schuschnigg and [National Bank President, G.S.] Kienböck to their face."[83]

Internationally, there were essentially three financial and currency models which were implemented in the 1930s. The Anglo-Saxon and some of the Nordic countries stressed currency policy as an element of actively influencing the business cycle. The anti-deflationary measures first taken in Great Britain in 1931 and in the U.S. in 1933 had a strong impact on economy and employment. A second group of countries, which included Austria, viewed the crisis of the 1930s mainly as a consequence of the collapse of trust in the international credit system and proceeded to re-establish that trust by way of conservative financial and currency policies. The third approach to coping with the crisis produced Nazi Germany as its most extreme example. The National Socialist regime sought to neutralize the economic imbalance primarily by massive state intervention. The armament program played a dominant role in this scheme, especially in the context of aggressive territorial expansion. With financing handled mainly by printing new banknotes, the Nazi regime had to take flanking measures such as systematic exchange controls and authoritarian price and wage controls. The regime showed key features of "conservative modernisation" (Barrington Moore); i.e., it aimed at renewing and increasing the efficiency of the technological-economic system while at the same time curtailing social achievements.[84]

At the turn of 1937 to 1938, Nazi Germany had important reasons to concentrate on annexing Austria. The rapid expansion of its military sector had put enormous burdens on the German economy, which then entailed a shortage of foreign currency, a decline in raw material stocks, labor bottlenecks, and an increasing shortage of industrial capacities.[85] It was not just the idle production potential and the large pool of skilled labor which made Austria the first target of German expansionism. Austria's hoard of gold and foreign currency was significantly larger than that of the German Reich. Austria was rich in raw materials, such as timber, iron ore, and magnesite. Its production ratio of normal to special steel (which was preferred by the armament industry) was of particular interest to Germany. Austria boasted companies which enjoyed an excellent reputation far beyond the borders of the small country (e.g. in the chemical industry sector). In addition, its hydropower capacities promised vast resources of sustainable energy. A final bonus was the suitability of Austria as a marshalling area for further expansion to southeastern Europe. By winning new territory and people, the resultant Greater Germany was bound to become Europe's top country.

In the war games of German imperialists, shaped by the requirements of a war economy, Austria was assigned not much more than colonial status. But it was not just the numerous attempts to intimidate and humiliate

Austria which eventually made the small Alpine republic "ripe for annexation." Some key prerequisites were found in "German-Austria" itself, such as the unhesitating imitation of fascist models by the *Ständestaat*. In terms of ideology, political Catholicism similarly prepared the ground. It developed, for example, population policy goals such as getting women back to the home and hearth in order to reverse the falling birthrate, "which in its rapidity and scope surpasses everything we know in this field..." and which "occurred almost exclusively within the Germanic peoples."[86] When the libertarian philosopher Moritz Schlick was killed by an assassin from the political right,[87] the *Ständestaat* press added insult to injury: "The weekly *Die Schönere Zukunft* delivered the following obituary: 'The Jew is a born a-metaphysician [*Ametaphysiker*], he loves logocism [*Logozismus*] in philosophy, mathematicism [*Mathematizismus*], formalism and positivism, all characteristics that Schlick united within himself to the greatest extent.' And an anonymous 'Professor Austriacus' foresaw that the murder would serve a 'truly satisfactory solution of the Jewish question.' All this while the Nazi party was still illegal! The *Linzer Volksblatt* sounded the authentic clerico-authoritarian voice: Schlick had spoiled 'precious national porcelain, children of the home soil, of noble build, from the spiritual power reservoir of our agricultural estate.' Declared a 'must-Jew,' [*Muâ-Jude*] his truly liberal attitude attributed to 'Austro-Marxism,' he was stamped a guilty victim whose murderer was in truth innocent."[88] The fact that resistance against German National Socialism was so weak in Austria had primarily economic causes. The dire straights caused by the *Ständestaat* regime—"Austria is suffering from a heavy budgetary pressure . . ." observed the League of Nations[89]—left no route open to escape economic misery, and offered no means to establish trust in the viability of the country.

Notes

1. A wider interest in the subject was limited to a short period in the 1980s. A selection of publications on the Ständestaat includes Winfried R. Garscha, "Katholisch und deutsch. Anmerkungen zur Ideologie des Austrofaschismus," *Aufrisse. Zeitschrift für politische Bildung* 5, no. 1 (1984): 25-26; Ulrich Kluge, *Der österreichische Ständestaat 1934–1938. Entstehung und Scheitern* (Vienna: Verlag für Geschichte und Politik, 1984); Dieter Stiefel, "Utopie und Realität: Die Wirtschaftspolitik des Ständestaates," in *Tirol und der Anschluß. Voraussetzungen, Entwicklungen, Rahmenbedingungen 1918–1938*, ed. Thomas Albrich, Klaus Eisterer, and Rolf Steininger (Innsbruck: Haymon Verlag, 1988), 403-35; and Emmerich Talos and Wolfgang Neugebauer, eds., *"Austrofaschismus" – Beiträge über Politik, Ökonomie und Kultur 1934–1938* (Vienna: Verlag für Gesellschaftskritik, 1984). Noticeable among more recent publications are Gertrude Enderle-Burcel, *Christlich-Ständisch-Autoritär. Mandatare im Ständestaat 1934–1938* (Vienna: Dokumentationsarchiv des österreichischen Widerstandes, Österreichische Gesellschaft für historische Quellenstudien, 1991); and Emmerich Talos, "Zum Herrschaftssystem des Austrofaschismus: Österreich 1934–1938," in *Autoritäre Regime in Ostmittel- und Südeuropa 1919–1944*, ed. Erwin Oberländer (Paderborn: Ferdinand Schöningh Verlag, 2001), 143-63.

2. For an analytical categorization of the *Ständestaat* regime within the range of government systems see Ernst Hanisch, "Der Politische Katholizismus als ideologischer Träger des 'Austrofaschismus'," in Talos, Neugebauer, "*Austrofaschismus*," 54; Klaus-Jörg Siegfried, *Klerikalfaschismus. Zur Entstehung und sozialen Funktion des Dollfuß-Regimes in Österreich. Ein Beitrag zur Faschismusdiskussion* (Frankfurt/M.: Verlag Peter Lang, 1979); Willibald I. Holzer, "Neues vom 'Ständestaat'. Aktuelle Literatur zu Wesen und Gestaltwandel des österreichischen Diktaturregimes 1933/34–1938," *Zeitgeschichte* 12, issue 3 (December 1984): 96; idem, "'Faschisierung' von oben? Das Beispiel des sogenannten 'Autoritären Ständestaats'," in *Bericht über den sechzehnten österreichischen Historikertag in Krems/Donau, 3–7 September 1984*, ed. Verband Österreichischer Geschichtsvereine (Vienna: Veröffentlichungen des Verbandes Österreichischer Geschichtsvereine, 1985), 145; (Gerhard Botz in his comments on Holzer's paper: p. 155); Hans Jürgen Krüger, "Faschismus oder Ständestaat. Österreich 1934–1938," PhD. diss., University of Kiel, 1970; Hans Mommsen, "Theorie und Praxis des österreichischen Ständestaats 1934–1938," in *Das geistige Leben Wiens in der Zwischenkriegszeit*, ed. Peter Heintel, et al. (Vienna: Österreichischer Bundesverlag, 1981), 174-93, esp. 186; Andreas Rasp, "Der Austrofaschismus – Ein abhängiger Faschismus," *Aufrisse. Zeitschrift für politische Bildung* 5, no. 1 (1984): 27-29; and John R. Rath, "The First Austrian Republic – Totalitarian, Fascist, Authoritarian or what?," in *Beiträge zur Zeitgeschichte. Festschrift Ludwig Jedlicka*, ed. Rudolf Neck and Adam Wandruszka (St. Pölten: Verlag Niederösterreichisches Pressehaus, 1976), 163-81.

3. While Siegfried Mattl describes the economic policy pursued by the *Ständestaat* as "financial dictatorship," Roman Sandgruber perceives a strongly anticapitalist trend in its politics. Siegfried Mattl, "Die Finanzdiktatur. Wirtschaftspolitik in Österreich 1933–1938," in Talos, Neugebauer, "*Austrofaschismus*", 133-61. Roman Sandgruber, *Ökonomie und Politik. Österreichische Wirtschaftsgeschichte vom Mittelalter bis zur Gegenwart*, Österreichische Geschichte, ed. Herwig Wolfram (Vienna: Ueberreuter Verlag, 1995), 398.

4. Friedrich Hertz, *Ist Österreich wirtschaftlich lebensfähig?* (Vienna: Verband österreichischer Banken und Bankiers, 1921), 25. See also Gustav Stolper, *Deutsch-Österreich als Sozial- und Wirtschaftsproblem* (Munich: Drei-Masken-Verlag, 1925); Österreichisch-deutsche Arbeitsgemeinschaft, ed., *Das österreichische Wirtschaftsproblem*, Denkschrift der österreichisch-deutschen Arbeitsgemeinschaft (Vienna: Verlag Hölder-Pichler-Tempsky, 1925).

5. Österreichisches Institut für Wirtschaftsforschung, ed., *Österreichs Volkseinkommen 1913 bis 1963* (Vienna: Selbstverlag des Österreichischen Instituts für Wirtschaftsforschung, 1965), 38. *Monatsberichte des Österreichischen Instituts für Konjunkturforschung*, vol. 12, no. 1, 25 January 1938, 66 and 67.

6. Dieter Stiefel, *Arbeitslosigkeit. Soziale, politische und wirtschaftliche Auswirkungen am Beispiel Österreichs 1918 bis 1938* (Berlin: Duncker und Humblot, 1979), 29.

7. Anton Orel, *Revision der modernen Wirtschaftsauffassung. Eine gemeinverständliche Philosophie und Geistesgeschichte der Wirtschaft und ihrer Beziehungen zu Religion, Kultur, Recht und Gesellschaft, insbesondere zu den sozialen Fragen*, 5 vols. (Mainz: Matthias-Grünewald-Verlag, 1930).

8. Josef Tzöbl, "Auf neuen Wegen - zu alten Zielen," *Arbeitsfriede. Österreichische Volksschriften* 4 (1934): 44-47.

9. Between 1933 and 1937, the wage share of the national income declined from 58.8% to 54.8%. Anton Kausel, *Österreichs Wirtschaft 1918–1968* (Vienna: Verlag für Geschichte und Politik, 1968), 20. For the sociopolitical changes see, in particular, Emmerich Talos, *Staatliche Sozialpolitik in Österreich. Rekonstruktion und Analyse* (Vienna: Verlag für Gesellschaftskritik, 1981); Gerhard Melinz, "'Christlicher Ständestaat' und autoritäre Sozialpolitik'," *Historicum. Zeitschrift für Geschichte* (Spring 1999): 15-20.

10. Thomas Meyer, *Stand und Klasse. Kontinuitätsgeschichte korporativer Staatskonzeptionen im deutschen Konservativismus* (Opladen: Westdeutscher Verlag, 1997), 198.

11. The 1936 propaganda movie *Ernte* (Harvest) idealized peasantry and criticized the "pleasure-seeking life of the big city."

12. "Rückblick auf das Jahr 1937," in *Monatsberichte des Österreichischen Instituts für Konjunkturforschung*, vol. 12, no. 2, 26 February 1938, 41.

13. Alois Schrattenholzer, "Die Gemeinschaftsgerechtigkeit als Grundlage der sozialen Ordnung," in *Neuer Staat – neue Wirtschaft im Lichte der katholischen Sozialidee*, ed. Studienrunde katholischer Soziologen (Vienna: Verlag der Studienrunde katholischer Soziologen, 1933), 37.

14. Richard Hofbauer, *Österreichs zukünftige Energiewirtschaft* (Vienna: Springer Verlag, 1930), 24.

15. Walter Eucken, *Grundsätze der Wirtschaftspolitik* (Tübingen: Rowohlt Verlag, 1963), 105.

16. "Ständestaat Österreich im neuen Wirtschafts-Europa," (Baden/Vienna: Wirtschaftsverlags- und Zeitungsgesellschaft, 1935).

17. Stephan Koren, "Die Industrialisierung Österreichs – Vom Protektionismus zur Integration. Entwicklung und Stand von Industrie, Gewerbe, Handel und Verkehr," in *Österreichs Wirtschaftsstruktur gestern – heute – morgen*, vol. 1, ed. Wilhelm Weber (Berlin: Duncker und Humblot, 1961), 542.

18. Oskar Morgenstern, "Bemerkungen zur wirtschaftspolitischen Lage Österreichs im Hinblick auf die internationalen Abwertungen" (Unpublished manuscript, Vienna, 23 November 1936), 1.

19. "Gesamtbild der wirtschaftlichen Entwicklung Österreichs in den Jahren 1935/36," *Wirtschaftsstatistisches Jahrbuch 1936*, vol. 11, ed. Kammer für Arbeiter und Angestellte für Wien, 98.

20. "Rückblick auf das Jahr 1937," *Monatsberichte des Österreichischen Instituts für Konjunkturforschung*, vol. 12, no. 2, 26 February 1938, 31.

21. The textile industry was one of the few areas where some progress was made in streamlining production. Between 1926 and 1935, annual production of spun cotton grew by more than 80%. The fact that the textile industry streamlined its production without consulting any of the workers' interest groups generated a not inconsiderable amount of social conflict. "Allgemeine Übersicht," *Monatsberichte des Österreichischen Instituts für Konjunkturforschung*, vol. 10, no. 9, 26 September 1936, 200.

22. "Handel und Verkehr," *Österreichisches Jahrbuch 1936*, no. 17 (Vienna 1937): 143.

23. "Chemische Industrie. Glasindustrie. Papierindustrie," *Wirtschaftsstatistisches Jahrbuch 1937*, vol. 12, ed. Kammer für Arbeiter und Angestellte für Wien, Vienna, 134.

24. "Österreichs Wirtschaft im Jahre 1937," *Das Gewerbe. Hauptblatt des Gewerbebundes*, vol. 3, no. 1/2, January 1938, 2.

25. "Die internationale Wirtschaftslage," *Monatsberichte des Österreichischen Instituts für Konjunkturforschung*, vol. 11, no. 12, 23 December 1937, 271.

26. "Rückblick auf das Jahr 1937," *Monatsberichte des Österreichischen Instituts für Konjunkturforschung*, vol. 12, no. 2, 26 February 1938, 27.

27. Even in 1929, when the best values were recorded, both the ratio of gross investment and the investment volume remained under the 1913 level. Österreichisches Institut für Wirtschaftsforschung, *Österreichs Volkseinkommen*, 17.

28. Koren, *Industrialisierung Österreichs*, 307.

29. "Rückblick auf das Jahr 1936," *Monatsberichte des Österreichischen Instituts für Konjunkturforschung*, vol. 9, no. 2, 26 February 1935, 37.

30. "Rückblick auf das Jahr 1934," *Monatsberichte des Österreichischen Instituts für Konjunkturforschung*, vol. 9, no. 2, 26 February 1935, 37. "Rückblick auf das Jahr 1935," *Monatsberichte des Österreichischen Instituts für Konjunkturforschung*, vol. 10, no. 2, 29 February 1936, 36.

31. *Monatsberichte des Österreichischen Instituts für Konjunkturforschung*, vol. 12, no. 1, 25 January 1938, 19. "Rückblick auf das Jahr 1937." *Monatsberichte des Österreichischen Instituts für Konjunkturforschung*, vol. 12, no. 2, 26 February 1938, 66.

32. Österreichisches Statistisches Zentralamt, ed., *Der Außenhandel Österreichs in der Zeit zwischen den beiden Weltkriegen* (Vienna: Verlagsbuchhandlung Carl Ueberreuter, 1946), 19.

33. "Rückblick auf das Jahr 1934," *Monatsberichte des Österreichischen Instituts für Konjunkturforschung*, vol. 9, no. 2, 26 February 1934, 41.

34. The change in the structure of Austrian exports made the country more susceptible to price and sales fluctuations on international markets.

35. "Rückblick auf das Jahr 1936," *Monatsberichte des Österreichischen Instituts für Konjunkturforschung*, vol. 11, no. 2, 26 February 1937, 42-43.

36. For an in-depth discussion of the *Credit-Anstalt* crisis see Aurel Schubert, "The Credit-Anstalt Crisis of 1931. A Financial Crisis Revisited," PhD. diss., University of South Carolina, 1985. Dieter Stiefel, *Finanzdiplomatie und Wirtschaftskrise. Die Krise der Credit-Anstalt für Handel und Gewerbe 1931* (Frankfurt/M.: Knapp Verlag, 1989).

37. Peter Eigner, "Die Verflechtungen zwischen den Wiener Großbanken und der Industrie 1895 bis 1938," in *Historische Betriebsanalyse und Unternehmer, Festschrift Alois Mosser*, ed. Herbert Matis (Vienna: Veröffentlichungen der Österreichischen Gesellschaft für Unternehmensgeschichte 19, 1997), 197.

38. "Sanierung des Phönix," *Der österreichische Volkswirt*, vol. 28, no. 27, 4 April 1936, 518.

39. Isabella Ackerl, "Der Phönix-Skandal," in *Das Juliabkommen von 1936. Vorgeschichte, Hintergründe und Folgen* (Minutes of the Symposium in Vienna on 10 and 11 June 1976), ed. Ludwig Jedlicka, Rudolf Neck (Vienna: Verlag für Geschichte und Politik, 1977), 241. See also Peter Ulrich Lehner, "Am Rande berührt – Auswirkungen großraumwirtschaftlicher und weltpolitischer Vorgänge auf das österreichische Versicherungswesen," in *Assekuranzmosaik des ausgehenden 20. Jahrhunderts, Versicherungsgeschichte Österreichs*, vol. 5, ed. Wolfgang Rohrbach (Vienna: Verlag Holzhausen, 1997), 93-245.

40. Ludwig Draxler, Federal Minister of Finances, at the 40th Meeting of the Federal Economic Council, 24 March 1936. Österreichisches Staatsarchiv, Archiv der Republik, Protokolle des Bundeswirtschaftsrates 1934 bis 1938, vol. 3, 929.

41. Between late 1935 and late 1936, the assets of Austrian insurance companies shrank by almost ATS 431 million. Österreichisches Statistisches Landesamt, ed., *Statistisches Jahrbuch für Österreich 1938* (Vienna: Verlag Ueberreuter, 1938), 167.

42. For the reconstruction of *Phönix* see "Die Regelung der 'Phönix'-Frage," *Die Industrie. Offizielles Organ des Bundes der österreichischen Industriellen*, Beilage, *Privat-Versicherungsfragen*, vol. 5, no. 2, 10 April 1936. "Allgemeine Versicherungsgesellschaft Phönix," *Der Österreichische Volkswirt*, Beilage, *Die Bilanzen*, vol. 28, no. 50, 12 September 1936, 386-87.

43. "Liquidation des Phönix," *Österreichischer Volkswirt*, vol. 28, no. 28, 11 April 1936, 538.

44. League of Nations, *Financial Position of Austria in the First Quarter of 1936*, 18th Quarterly Report, by M. Rost van Tonningen, Geneva, 24 April 1936, 2.

45. On the issue of the insurance employees see Ackerl, *Phönix-Skandal*, 242, 248, and 278.

46. Österreichisches Institut für Wirtschaftsforschung, *Österreichs Volkseinkommen*, 38.

47. "Rückblick auf das Jahr 1937," *Monatsberichte des Österreichischen Instituts für Konjunkturforschung*, vol. 12, no. 2, 26 February 1938, 67.

48. "Rückblick auf das Jahr 1934," *Monatsberichte des Österreichischen Instituts für Konjunkturforschung*, vol. 9, no. 2, 26 February 1935, 21 and 30.

49. "Rückblick auf das Jahr 1936," *Monatsberichte des Österreichischen Instituts für Konjunkturforschung*, vol. 10, no. 2, 29 February 1936, 31.

50. "Rückblick auf das Jahr 1937," *Monatsberichte des Österreichischen Instituts für Konjunkturforschung*, vol. 11, no. 2, 26 February 1937, 29.

51. "Rückblick auf das Jahr 1937," *Monatsberichte des Österreichischen Instituts für Konjunkturforschung*, vol. 12, no. 2, 26 February 1938, 39.

52. Österreichisches Statistisches Landesamt, *Jahrbuch 1938*, 73 and 75.

53. "Rückblick auf das Jahr 1935," *Monatsberichte des Österreichischen Instituts für Konjunkturforschung*, vol. 10, no. 2, 29 February 1936, 29.

54. Österreichisches Statistisches Landesamt, *Jahrbuch 1938*, 178.

55. Österreichisches Statistisches Landesamt, *Jahrbuch 1938*, 239.

56. Large-scale devaluation at a global scale had a highly positive effect on Austria's debt problem. The external debt share of the Austrian federal debt could be substantially reduced up to 1938. Österreichisches Statistisches Landesamt, *Jahrbuch 1938*, 276.

57. Österreichisches Statistisches Landesamt, *Jahrbuch 1938*, 243.

58. Hans Bayer, *Ein Blick in die österreichische Volkswirtschaft* (Vienna: Verlag der Kammer für Arbeiter und Angestellte in Wien, 1936), 18. Österreichisches Statistisches Landesamt, *Jahrbuch 1938*, 178.

59. Morgenstern, *Wirtschaftspolitische Lage Österreichs*, 14.

60. The economic policies of Austria were observed by the League of Nations until autumn of 1936; this circumstance forced the restrictions. For the role of the League of Nations in Austria see Peter Berger, *Im Schatten der Diktatur. Die Finanzdiplomatie des Vertreters des Völkerbundes in Österreich, Meinoud Marinus Rost van Tonningen, 1931 – 1936* (Vienna: Böhlau Verlag, 2000).

61. Norbert Schausberger, *Der Griff nach Österreich. Der Anschluß* (Vienna: Verlag Jugend & Volk, 1978), 472.

62. The velocity of money circulation can be determined from changes in the current account turnover. To that end, the current account turnover rates of the Austrian National Bank, the Postal Savings Bank, the *Wiener Giro- und Kassenverein*, and the *Saldierungsverein* will have to be used to calculate the velocity of money circulation in interwar Austria.

63. "Internationale Wirtschaftszahlen," *Monatsberichte des Österreichischen Instituts für Konjunkturforschung*, vol. 12, no. 3, 11 April 1938, 94. Clearly, this enormous increase in the money supply was also related to the flow of foreign currency into Switzerland. Nevertheless, there was no big difference between the two countries, since both the Swiss Franc and the Austrian Schilling were considered "escape currencies" in the 1930s. The League of Nations noted in its financial report of 1933: "The instability of many foreign currencies contributed also to achievement by inducing holders of assets in foreign currency to transform them into Schillings." See League of Nations, *Financial Position of Austria in the First Quarter of 1933*, 9th Quarterly Report, by M. Rost van Tonningen, Geneva, 15 February 1934, 9.

64. "Internationale Wirtschaftszahlen," *Monatsberichte des Österreichischen Instituts für Wirtschaftsforschung*, vol. 12, no. 3, 11 April 1938, 95.

65. Only about a third of the proceeds of the issues raised between 1933 and 1937 was used for employment policy purposes. For an in-depth study see Dieter Stiefel, *Die große Krise in einem kleinen Land* (Vienna: Böhlau Verlag, 1988), 199.

66. A major factor to explain the restraint certainly was the rescue of the banks completed in 1934, which cost the state a fortune. A small part of these costs would have sufficed to achieve considerable progress in electrifying the Austrian railways, for example.

67. Ernst Streeruwitz, *Österreichs Wirtschaftsstruktur* (Brixlegg: Heimat-Verlag, 1936), 64.

68. Hansjörg Klausinger, "Die Alternativen zur Deflationspolitik Brünings im Lichte zeitgenössischer Kritik. Zugleich ein neuer Blick auf die Borchardt-These," *Wirtschaft und Gesellschaft*, vol. 24, issue 2, 1998, 186.

69. "Öffentliche Investitionen als Krisenheilmittel," *Der österreichische Volkswirt*, vol. 29, no. 26, 27 March 1937, 503.

70. "Keynes über den Ankurbelungsfaktor," *Der österreichische Volkswirt*, vol. 25, no. 25, 18 March 1933, 578.

71. "Keynes für weitere Zinsverbilligung," *Der österreichische Volkswirt*, Beilage, *Die Bilanzen*, vol. 28, no. 22, 29 February 1936, 165.

72. John Maynard Keynes, *The General Theory of Employment, Interest and Money* (London: Macmillan, 1936).

73. Felix Butschek, "Präkeynesianismus in Österreich," *Wirtschaft und Gesellschaft*, vol. 19, issue 2, 1993, 171-82.

74. The discount rate in 1931 was 10%; in 1935 it was 3.5%. See Hans Kernbauer, *Währungspolitik in der Zwischenkriegszeit. Geschichte der Österreichischen Nationalbank von 1923 bis 1938* (Vienna: Österreichische Nationalbank, 1991), 329 and 395.

75. "Rückblick auf das Jahr 1937," *Monatsberichte des Österreichischen Instituts für Konjunkturforschung*, vol. 12, no. 2, 26 February 1936, 64.

76. Odo Neustädter-Stürmer in the cabinet meeting of 28 March 1935. While Minister Reither plainly spoke of "usury" by the banks, Minister Stockinger felt "that the banks had been saved and that they were now again ruining the economy." Österreichische Gesellschaft für historische Quellenstudien; Österreichisches Staatsarchiv, ed., *Protokolle des Ministerrates der Ersten Republik*, Kabinett Dr. Kurt Schuschnigg, Abteilung IX, vol. 2, 989/2 (Vienna: Verlag der Österreichischen Staatsdruckerei, 1993), 385.

77. See Erich Hans Wolf, *Katastrophenwirtschaft. Geburt und Ende Österreichs 1918 bis 1938* (Zurich: Europa Verlag, 1939), 89, 94, 96, and 113; Mattl in Talos, Neugebauer, "*Austrofaschismus*," 152-54; "Ausgabe von Freigeld durch die Gemeinde Wörgl," *Der Wiener Tag*, 22 July 1932; "Umlaufzwang des Geldes," *Neues Wiener Tagblatt*, 28 March 1933; "Die Wörgler Währung," *Volkszeitung*, 12 June 1933; "Wörgl – ein Wendepunkt," *Tagblatt*, 16 August 1933; Hans Hollitscher, "Schwundgeld," *Neue Freie Presse*, no. 24.765, 23 August 1933.

78. Between mid-1932 and mid-1933, the number of unemployed in and around Wörgl fell by 25%. See Fritz Schwarz, *Das Experiment von Wörgl* (Bern: Genossenschaftlicher Verlag freiwirtschaftlicher Schriften, 1951), 52; Stiefel, *Arbeitslosigkeit*, 29.

79. "Blühende Stadt im Krisen-Österreich," *Der Morgen*, 8 Mai 1933.

80. Stadtarchiv Linz, minutes of the town council of 15 December 1933; René Perin, "Schwundgeld," *Neue Freie Presse*, no. 24.752, 10 August 1933.

81. See "Das Schwundgeld von Wörgl vor dem Verwaltungsgericht," *Die Stunde*, 30 April 1933; "Schwundgeld verboten," *Tagblatt*, 22 August 1933; "Ausgabe von Schwundgeld ist strafbar!," *Reichspost*, 19 November 1933.

82. "Kardinalfehler der Schwundgeldlehre," *Die Industrie. Offizielles Organ des Bundes der österreichischen Industriellen*, vol. 40, no. 45, 8 November 1935, 6.

83. Otto Friedländer, *Maturajahrgang 1907* (Graz: Styria Verlag, 1963), 25 and 26.

84. Gerhard Senft, "Tyrannei und Modernisierung. Der techno-ökonomische Wandel im Dritten Reich," in *Auf in die Moderne. Österreich vom Faschismus bis zum EU-Beitritt*, ed. Österreichische Gesellschaft für kritische Geographie (Vienna: Promedia Verlag, 1996), 16-77.

85. Schausberger, *Griff nach Österreich*, 433.

86. Wilhelm Schmidt speaking at the Whitsun meeting on social reform organized by the *Studienrunde katholischer Soziologen* in Vienna in 1933. Wilhelm Schmidt, "Die gesellschaftliche, wirtschaftliche und biologische Neuordnung der Familie," in *Neuer Staat – neue Wirtschaft*, 104.

87. Michael Siegert, "Der Mord an Professor Moritz Schlick," in *Attentate, die Österreich erschütterten*, ed. Leopold Spira (Vienna: Löcker Verlag, 1981), 123-33.

88. Hilde Spiel, *Die hellen und die finsteren Zeiten. Erinnerungen 1911 bis 1946* (Reinbek/Hamburg: Rowohlt Verlag, 1991), 135.

89. League of Nations, *Financial Position of Austria in the Third Quarter of 1934*, 12th Quarterly Report, by M. Rost van Tonningen, Geneva, 12 November 1934, 2.

How Far Was Vienna From Chicago in the 1930s? The Economists and the Depression[1]

Hansjörg Klausinger

1. Introduction

Today, highlighted by the Nobel Prize winners Friedrich August Hayek and Milton Friedman, Vienna and Chicago are regarded as the founding centers of two distinct schools of (classical) liberalism.[2] As the Great Depression of the 1930s was undoubtedly the greatest challenge to the liberal-capitalistic system, it appears to be worthwhile to compare the diagnoses and therapies coming forward from Vienna and Chicago at this time. Whereas Hayek was directly involved in the debates about crisis policy, Friedman—almost a generation apart from Hayek—was not, so that we have to contemplate the views of his precursors in Chicago, to which he has linked himself by emphasizing the existence of an unbroken "oral tradition."[3]

After a short overview of the theoretical foundations, the main emphasis of this essay lies on the relevant policy advice. To begin with, I will contrast the general views on policy, before turning specifically to the Great Depression and the debate on four major points: the perception (or misperception) about deflation, the need for pump priming, the role of wage cutting, and the norms for monetary policy. Finally, I will speculate about the relevance of the economists' policy advice for actual policy making.

At first, however, some stocktaking is necessary. In the 1930s, Austrian economics was on the move. In its fourth generation, with such eminent young scholars as Friedrich August Hayek, Gottfried Haberler, and Fritz Machlup (and the older but most influential Ludwig von Mises),[4] the Austrian School showed signs of theoretical progress in the fields of money and business cycles and embarked on new controversies about capital theory and economic calculation in socialism. Yet, when the decade was over, the Austrian School had largely dissolved. First, it appeared to have suffered defeat in all three crucial controversies,[5] and its members—with the exception of the U.S.-based neo-Austrian school of Mises—either turned away from economics proper or integrated into the mainstream of neoclassics. And second, this process of dissolution and integration was much furthered by the emigration of the most prominent Austrians to the English-speaking world. So, in these debates on how to deal with the Great Depression, we also witness Austrian economics in its last flowering (that is, before its revival some decades later).

When talking about the old Chicago School, I refer to the liberal core of economists within a rather heterogeneous department, that is Frank Knight and Jacob Viner, as well as the younger members Henry Simons and Lloyd Mints.[6] Of these Viner and Simons were most pronounced in their published views on depression policy in the 1930s. Simons declared himself for the liberal cause—very much a minority view in these times—in his "Positive Program for Laissez Faire." Compared to the fate of the Austrian School, that of Chicago was just the opposite: thanks to Friedman's agitating power it survived in the minds of economists not only as a distinct school, but as a triumphant one.

2. Business Cycle Theories and Policies

The point of departure common to both approaches is the quantity theory of money, which, in a nutshell, rests on the equation: $MV = PY$.[7] M denotes the stock of money, V its velocity (i. e., how often on average a unit of money is put to use within a period), P the price level, and Y the real national product (or output). The left-hand side of this equation can be interpreted as the nominal aggregate demand, i.e. the demand for commodities as a whole, measured in money units. (Austrians and Chicagoans alike prefer the term "effective circulation of money.") Assuming that M is independent from the other variables and that there are no significant (reverse) reactions of V, we can conclude that the aggregate demand is determined by the money supply. Now if, as usually is the case in the short run, the price level is rigid to some extent, then changes in M, and therefore in MV, will be transmitted to Y, with P less than proportionally affected. Thus, we observe real (short-term) effects of monetary expansions and contractions. (Conversely, if in the long run the output is fixed, independently from the left-hand side of the equation, then monetary factors will determine the price level.)

Here two important notes on definitions are in order. First, according to contemporary usage, the terms *inflation* and *deflation* typically refer to changes in the quantity of money (M) or, at most, to changes in "effective circulation" (MV), but not to changes in the price level.[8] And second, there is also widespread agreement that the proper definition of the quantity of money, although always to some extent arbitrary, should include currency (as the main part of central bank money) as well as the checking deposits at the commercial banks.[9] As the non-bank public is free to choose the proportion in which it uses currency and deposits for transactions and, similarly, the banks have some leeway in deciding how much reserves (the other part of central bank money) they hold against those deposits, it is (or should have been) evident that the quantity of money (*M*) is determined interdependently by the central bank, the banking system, and the non-bank public.[10]

After these preliminaries, we have now reached the point where the interpretations of the two schools depart. Let us first look at the explanation of the business cycle by the Chicago School, as it is a typical variation on the quantity-theory theme.[11] The specific aspect of this school's explanation is that money and velocity exhibit an endogenous cyclical pattern, so that in the upswing both will increase (without any intervention of monetary policy) and, conversely, in the downswing both will decrease. As regards velocity, this pattern is due to the positive effect of prosperity and confidence on velocity ("dishoarding" in the upswing, "hoarding" in the downswing). Yet, the crucial factor is the elasticity of the money supply as a consequence of fractional-reserve banking (i.e., the practice that banks are only required to back a fraction of their deposits by reserves). As indicated above, the banking system can bring about an increase in the quantity of money if it is ready to create money, i.e. deposits, by extending the volume of credit and thereby accepting a lowering of the ratio of reserves to deposits. So, typically in the upswing, when business earnings are high and optimism is unshattered, banks will easily respond to the increased demand for credit by investors. Conversely, in the downswing (and more so during a depression), banks become eager to build up reserves and call back loans—thereby reducing the volume of their deposits. Thus, with a do-nothing policy of the central bank, the effective circulation of money is prone to grave cyclical fluctuations. When such fluctuations meet with imperfectly flexible prices (and in particular costs, mostly consisting of wages), the typical business cycle (as exhibited in the pattern of output) will result. As regards the depression, it is noteworthy that the Chicagoans claim the liquidation of credit and the ensuing deflation can easily give rise to a cumulative downward process, a "vicious spiral"[12]: "The bottom of an uncontrolled deflation, for all practical purposes, is nonexistent . . . ."[13]

For the Austrian theory of the business cycle, often characterized as an "over-investment theory," monetary factors are the ultimate cause of the business cycle, whereas the explanation of the (upper) turning point relies on real or structural maladjustments—alien to the traditional quantity theory. The monetary factor that starts the upswing is inflation, whatever its cause. (Note that inflation means just an increase in effective circulation.) As money is typically injected into the economy in the form of an additional supply of funds in the capital market, inflation is mirrored by the fact that the prevailing money rate of interest is below the equilibrium or "natural" rate. It is the divergence of these two rates that sets in motion a process of disequilibrium.[14] In short, the excessively low money rate of interest leads to over-investment, i.e., a shift of resources from producing consumption goods to producing investment goods. This is where the theory of the business cycle gets linked to the rather idiosyncratic Austrian capital theory. The increased ratio of investment to consumption goods, implying also an increase in the capital-labor-ratio (or "more roundabout methods of production"), could only be sustained—so the theory goes—if the necessary supply of funds to the capital market were forthcoming from voluntary saving instead of from injections of money ("forced savings"). As this will typically not be the case, the investment boom must eventually falter. At the beginning of the downswing, the state of the economy is characterized by an excess capacity of capital goods that cannot be utilized, though, because of a lack of savings (somewhat confusingly described as "capital shortage"). Thus, it is a lack of utilizable capacity (combined with the immobility of resources) that causes output to decline in the depression (and not a lack of aggregate demand). So, the depression is the inevitable consequence of the boom. The only way out of depression is to facilitate the re-establishing of the original equilibrium: by liquidating excessive capacity, by promoting savings, by redistributing income away from labor, and by reversing the distortions in the price structure. Obviously, in this view rigid wages are seen as an obstacle to recovery.

One particular feature of this theory must be noted: Inflation as *the* cause of the boom (and then of depression) need not be accompanied by a rising price level. For in a growing economy where the effective circulation is fixed, the price level should indeed fall; thus, as in this case, even a stable price level might signal inflation. In hindsight, the Austrians identified as the cause of the depression in the United States the fact that during the long boom of the 1920s the price level had been kept stable instead of having been allowed to fall. Accordingly, the ultimate outcome of this inflationary boom was a deep depression.[15]

Turning from theory to policy advice, two questions have to be distinguished: First, how to generally avoid business cycles by applying structural remedies, and, second, what to do once the depression has set in. For the Chicago economists, and in particular for Simons, the elimination of the causes of business fluctuations points to two areas for reform: One is the restoration of the flexibility of prices, costs, and especially wages by fostering competition and combating monopolies and cartels (trade associations as well as trade unions). Evidently, the more flexible prices and costs are, the less fluctuations in aggregate demand will affect output. The mitigation of such fluctuations, and of the "instability of credit"[16] in general, constitutes the other area, that of financial reform. The aim of this reform is to retransfer the responsibility for the working of the monetary system from the banking system to the state. This should be accomplished by abandoning the fractional reserve system, replacing it with the requirement that banks hold a 100% reserve against deposits (i.e., those banking liabilities that could function as a means of exchange). Thereby, the monetary authority would be able to directly control the quantity of money. However, it is not supposed that this control should be left to discretion; on the contrary, monetary policy is to be subjected to simple and publicly known rules. For the long term, the goal of Simons' financial reform was yet more ambitious, namely to "approach an economy where all private property consisted in pure assets, pure money, and nothing else. This . . . is the financial good society."[17]

It is immediately obvious that none of the proposed measures of long-term reform would have contributed to recovery from depression. Amidst a depression characterized by falling prices and a squeeze in profit margins other short-term expedients were called for. In this regard, the Chicago economists discuss two options.[18] The first option—balanced deflation—is to cut wages by a cooperative action (engineered by government leadership) and to simultaneously support the price level so that a more acceptable profit margin can be reestablished. The second option is inflation (or reflation), meaning here a rise in the price level brought about by a stimulation of the aggregate demand with wages held constant.

Compared with the advice coming from Chicago, that from Austria is simpler and almost entirely prophylactic. As the depression is the inevitable consequence of the boom (and, in fact, the longer the boom, the more severe the depression will be), the only way to avoid depressions is simply to prevent booms by abstaining from inflation. Like the Chicagoans, the Austrians believe in the prevalence of cumulative expansions and contractions of credit, so that to realize this aim the central bank would "have to act persistently against the trend of the movement of credit in the country . . . ."[19] However, apart from that, Hayek just points to "the old truth that we may perhaps prevent a crisis by checking expansion in time, but that we can do nothing to get out of it before its natural end, once it has come."[20] Such a policy of doing nothing must therefore refrain from any attempts at expansionist monetary policy, in particular from reflation or pump priming, and must accept the limits prescribed by the rules of sound finance and the gold standard. However, inasmuch as the depression is not only a reaction to the preceding inflation, but also to policies causing or favoring "capital consumption"—excessive taxes, social duties and/or wages—it necessitates a policy of retrenchment and the breaking of rigidities.[21]

A better understanding of the opposing views may be achieved by making the conceptual distinction between primary and secondary depression. This distinction is based on the task that the depression is supposed to fulfill—if there is one. For the Austrians such a task or, as one might call it, a "cleansing function" of the depression clearly exists, as the boom has brought about an unsustainable structure of production that must be liquidated. As long as this process of liquidation goes on, the depression is primary (or in its primary phase). Therefore, when referring to a primary depression, it makes good sense conceptually to speak of its "natural end" (as Hayek did). In contrast, the (phase of) secondary depression is characterized by the dominance of cumulative processes without any economic purpose. The Chicago School puts depressions mostly into this category, flatly denying the very existence of a natural end to depressions. It is evident that the differing policy prescriptions follow neatly from these different conceptual views of what a depression is all about.[22]

3. Addressing the Great Depression

Now we shall look at how Austrian and Chicago economists reacted to crucial questions arising from the experience of the Great Depression, namely the perception of deflationary policy, the evaluation of pump priming, the role of wage cuts, and the long-term norm of monetary policy.

The perception of and the reaction to deflation

As the Great Depression was characterized by a simultaneous fall in prices and output, this implied deflation defined as a decrease in effective circulation (*MV*). The crucial question therefore was whether this deflation was brought about by monetary policy—i.e., the result of *deflationary policy*—and whether it should have been counteracted by expansionary measures.

For Chicago economists the answer is clear: the depression is the consequence of deflation—mainly brought about by the shrinking volume of bank money: "There has been . . . a fairly continuous and unprecedentedly great contraction of credit [i.e. deposits] during the entire period."[23] Furthermore, the policy of the Fed (i.e., the Federal Reserve System) resembles "a program of drift, punctuated at intervals by homeopathic doses of belated inflation or deflation and rationalized by declarations of impotence . . . ."[24]

This is not so for Austrian economists. Although deflation, signifying a departure from equilibrium (or neutral money), represents an evil to be avoided (by saving without investing),[25] the Austrians unanimously reject expansionist policy as an appropriate answer when confronted with massive signals of deflation, as during the Great Depression. This Austrian position can be justified in two regards: first, by outright denial of the existence of deflationary policy and, second, by considering this kind of deflation (as it happened) an indispensable part of the liquidation process which warranted no interference. To some extent both interpretations supplement each other: Just as the boom is the result of inflation, deflation is necessary to reestablish the equilibrium of the economy—and therefore need not be regarded as harmful.

A few illustrations of this Austrian view may suffice. In 1932 Hayek characterizes the policy of the Fed as "the first attempt at a large scale to revive the economy . . . by a systematic policy of lowering the interest rate . . . for preventing the normal process of liquidation, and that as a result the depression has assumed more devastating forms and lasted longer than ever before."[26] After constructing monetary indicators for the United States, Lionel Robbins (of the London School of Economics) denies a monetary contraction. His calculations "should be sufficient refutation of the charge that the [Federal Reserve has] deliberately brought about deflation."[27] Machlup, after consistently claiming that deposits "must be considered money" and defining deflation as "the destruction of money," flatly states that in this sense "no country has pursued a deflationary policy."[28] Finally, in its report on the events of 1932, the Austrian Institute for Business Cycle Research compares the development of output with that of currency plus deposits at the central bank and finds money in circulation as possibly excessive.[29]

A look at the figures clarifies the fallacy of the Austrian view. The definition of money accepted by Austrians and Chicagoans alike corresponds closely to *M1* of modern statistics. For the United States, *M1* declined from August 1929 to March 1933 by 28% against an increase of central bank money of 17.5%.[30] In Austria the cumulative decrease in *M1* over the four years from 1929 to 1933 was 40%,[31] whereas central bank money stayed roughly constant (in spite of a sharp increase in 1931).[32]

The explanation for the apparent ignorance of the Austrian economists might be found in the fact that despite their (valid) definitions of inflation and deflation they never ventured to look at the relevant figures.[33] Rather they satisfied themselves with examining the level of (nominal!) interest rates[34] and indicators of central bank money (such as currency in circulation or bank reserves). Unfortunately these indicators rendered the wrong answers, which, however, had the advantage of fitting their theoretical preconceptions.

The case for pump priming

Next, I inquire into the policy options that are feasible in a state of deep depression, such as that of the U.S. economy in mid-1932. At that time, the Fed reacted with a campaign of expansionist policy by massive open-market purchases—only to stop it after a few months.

The most pertinent exposition of the Austrian view with regard to "pump priming" (*Ankurbelung*) as a remedy against deflation is presented in a short paper by Fritz Machlup.[35] According to Machlup, unaided monetary policy cannot be successful as even at a zero rate of interest no profitable investment projects will be forthcoming due to the rigged cost structure.[36] This view, which reflects the prevailing concept of a "credit deadlock,"[37] is also shared by the Chicago economists. Under these special circumstances the only effect of injecting central bank money "would be to increase the cash reserves of the banks or decrease the indebtedness of the member banks to the Federal Reserve system."[38]

Therefore, as the only way out, the state would have to step in and substitute government expenditure for the lack of private investment (and thus credit demand). This would actually increase aggregate demand and, in terms of the quantity theory, relocate the money from the excess reserves of the banks into the cash holdings of private firms and households (which could be expected to spend the cash rather than leave it idle). In addition, this would solve the problem of credit deadlock, resulting from either a lack of credit *demand*, or a reluctance of the banks to *supply* credit to private customers due to risk aversion—for the government (at least the U.S. government) ought to be considered a safe debtor.[39]

Indeed, both Austrians and Chicagoans share the belief that monetary policy could be made effective by combining it with fiscal policy, by, for example, having the banks (or the central bank) finance a budget deficit. While both schools regard this as a *feasible* policy, they disagree on whether it is desirable in the long run. Machlup, for instance, considers this an example of sheer inflationism, the return to that kind of policy that caused the boom and would in turn cause an even deeper depression.[40] For the Chicagoans, what is feasible is also desirable, in this context; thus, they make this method the primary mechanism in their program of how to execute a policy of price level stabilization. There is ample evidence for their advocacy of countercyclical fiscal policy combined with monetary policy: surpluses in the boom and deficits in the recession, directly connected (by central bank financing) to decreases and increases in the money supply as the future recipe for stabilization.[41] Simons goes as far as to urge the integration of the central bank with the treasury and to put the responsibility for stabilization on the latter one.[42] Yet, from an analytical point of view, this policy is considered monetary, working its way through the mechanisms of the quantity theory.

The role of wage cuts

There is a consensus among both schools that wage rigidity (or an excessive level of wages) is a vital source of the depression. From the

Chicago point of view this is simply due to the effects of wages on prices and profit margins as resulting from the mechanics of the quantity theory.[43] The Austrians add another complication to this picture: In their view, inflation leads to a rise in wages during the upturn, as labor is bid away from lower to higher stages of production, and thereby to a redistribution of demand towards consumer goods; both these maladjustments must be eliminated during the depression in order to restore equilibrium. Obviously, this task is made more difficult by downward rigid wages.

So—even if for slightly different reasons—both schools agree that a necessary step towards the restoration of equilibrium is to lower wages relative to the price level (or, as the Austrians would put it, relative to the whole structure of prices). The first best (and, to the Austrians, the only) way to achieve this would be to cut nominal wages and to reestablish the price-cost margins required for an increase in supply. This corresponds to Viner's proposal of "balanced deflation," which, as he points out, must be supplemented by a policy preventing the price level from falling. How this wage cut should be achieved, though, is not totally clear: In the long run, the restoration of competition in the labor market is the obvious aim; however, in the short run, Viner looks for some kind of social compact to achieve lower wages,[44] whereas the Austrians put their faith in the breaking of rigidities by means of (ever more) deflation.[45]

Viner and Simons further believe that a policy of balanced deflation would only be effective if carried out immediately, which is improbable under the prevailing circumstances. As Viner puts it: "I still believe that even if nothing is done costs will eventually probably fall sufficiently to restore a profit margin. But I am becoming more and more convinced that there is a serious risk that they won't do so quickly enough to forestall wholesale economic collapse . . . ."[46] Therefore, the Chicagoans are sufficiently pragmatic to opt for the second-best alternative: inflation. This consists simply in raising prices (with wages still constant) by means of stimulating demand up to the point where an acceptable profit margin is again achieved, followed by a policy of price level stabilization. Before April 1933 such a policy of inflation was considered with some skepticism because of the difficulty of implementing it within the limits of the gold standard; yet after America's departure from gold, it became an unambiguous policy advice.[47]

The Austrians also discuss such a policy—identifying Keynes as one of its originators—and predictably dismiss it as inflationism. Again, they invoke their ever present argument that it would introduce into the system just those maladjustments which the depression is supposed to purge from it.[48]

Lessons for monetary policy

Although not directly relevant as a remedy for depression, the debate of the 1930s also dealt with the appropriate norms for monetary policy to be followed in the future. As noted above, the Austrian prescription is to approximate a state of neutral money as close as possible by avoiding inflation or deflation. In practice this means a stable (i.e., constant) quantity of money. From the Chicago point of view, represented most consistently by Simons, the primary aim is to replace a discretionary policy with a policy governed by rules. In this regard the "prescription . . . of a simple, explicit rule"[49] is more important than its specific content. Relevant proposals range from the stabilization of the quantity of money to that of its effective circulation and eventually that of the price level (i.e., of M, MV, and P, respectively)[50] In his later pronouncements, Simons endorses, though reluctantly, the rule of price level stabilization for "the significant future" because the preferred rule of a stable quantity of money is predicated on a complete financial reform and the elimination of all near monies.[51]

Simons' eventual endorsement of price level stabilization runs counter to both the Austrians' quest for a stable quantity of money as well as to Friedman's propagation of a rule of constant money growth (some decades later).[52] However, there are two distinct sets of arguments. The *first* refers to the stability of the velocity of money. Simons starts from the assumption that velocity fluctuates throughout the business cycle and that these fluctuations have to be compensated by the countercyclical use of fiscal and monetary policy as outlined above. Therefore, by stabilizing the price level he ends up with a variable money growth rule. (The drawback clearly envisaged by Simons is that stabilizing the price level is more discretionary than stabilizing money.)[53] The *second* set of arguments pertains to the question of the optimal rate of inflation (inflation, in its usual meaning, being the rate of change of the price level). Whereas Simons opts for a constant price level, the Austrians—in order to avoid inflation, as they defined it—are ready to accept a falling price level in the presence of technical progress and growth. Thus, after sorting this out, we can conclude that the opposition of the Austrians is solely based on the second set of arguments, whereas Friedman's opposition is predominantly based on the first one.

Finally the contrast between Vienna and Chicago also becomes obvious in the evaluation of the gold standard. To the Austrians it is, despite its imperfections, a truly international currency and thereby a safeguard against monetary nationalism and inflation.[54] Yet, in the Chicago view it is to be subordinated to the management of the (national) currency: "The utter inadequacy of the old gold standard . . . seems beyond dispute."[55]

4. The Interaction of Economic Theory and Economic Policy. Some Speculative Remarks

Evidently, in these turbulent times, both schools developed their ideas with an eye to applying it to the failing economy. Yet, how much did they actually influence economic policy during the Great Depression? The following section sketches some speculative answers to this question.

Two preliminary distinctions have to be emphasized. The first refers to the different political audiences: The Chicago School more or less exclusively addressed its policy advice to the U.S. government (of Hoover and Roosevelt) whereas the situation was more complicated for the Austrians. At first, the Austrian School naturally responded to the Austrian economic situation; however, due to emigration (and the establishment of a stronghold at the LSE) their advice and criticism soon turned to British, American, and even international economic policy. The second distinction refers to two alternative channels of influence: a direct influence on policy makers on the one hand and an indirect influence on public opinion on the other hand.

At first glance, there is a presumption that in such times of unprecedented events the advice of economists (especially those of less extreme opinions) is typically not well-received. Viner's description might be considered quite realistic: "The economist . . . has little prestige with the American public, . . . and the public prefers to take its economics from newspaper editors, politicians, bankers, and men who in happier days were able to accumulate or inherit a million dollars or more."[56] As far as I can see, this is also borne out by the general lack of evidence about the first channel of influence.[57] The Chicago School—despite its participation in many conferences that gave rise to memoranda, appeals, telegrams to the president—had little impact on actual policy. Neither the timid policy of Hoover nor the more resolute, but incoherent policy of Roosevelt took their advice seriously into account.[58]

The same appears to be true for the influence of Austrian economics on economic policy in their home country. During the 1930s, the ties between Austria and the Austrian school of economics began to loosen, with the most well-known members of the school emigrating one after another[59]. In 1930, Ludwig von Mises was still able to exert some influence by his co-authoring the report of the *Wirtschaftskonferenz*, which argued predictably for a strategy of cost cutting.[60]

However, already in the *Credit-Anstalt* crisis, almost all the measures of economic policy—the bail-out of the bank, the pegging of the exchange rate and the ensuing loss of exchange reserves, and eventually the introduction of exchange controls—ran counter to the advice of the Austrian economists.[61] It is perhaps not merely a coincidence that Machlup—who had written a weekly column in the *Neues Wiener Tagblatt* for three years, preaching the insights of the Austrian school—gave up this activity in 1934 when an increasing number of his manuscripts were left unpublished under the pressure of (self-)censorship.[62] The only remaining economist of repute who indeed played some role as an advisor to the Ministry of Commerce and the Austrian National Bank was Oskar Morgenstern. Yet, as noted above, he was somewhat of an outsider, being not so tightly committed to the world view of classical liberalism typical of the Austrian school (at least under the guidance of Mises).[63] So, in the end, there is in my opinion no convincing evidence for a direct link between the policy advice of the Austrian school and the actual economic policy of the Dollfuss-Schuschnigg era.

However, the relevance of the second channel effective through public opinion should not be underestimated. There is scarcely any country where adherents to a more activist policy did not point out the severe obstacles posed by the belief that any deviation from old-honored rules, such as a balanced budget or the gold standard, might lead to catastrophe—if under the heading of "uncertainty," "shake of confidence," or "inflationary expectations."[64] In his memoirs Herbert Hoover blames the force of such convictions for his lack of success: "The 'leave-it-alone liquidationists' headed by Secretary of the Treasury Mellon felt that government must keep its hands off and let the slump liquidate itself. Mr. Mellon had only one formula: 'Liquidate labor, liquidate stocks, liquidate the farmers, liquidate real estate.' He held that even a panic was not altogether a bad thing. He said: 'It will purge the rottenness out of the system.'"[65]

As much as abiding to those rules was emphasized by the Austrian view, it appears that, with regard to public opinion, the Austrians were more successful than their more reform-oriented colleagues from Chicago (and elsewhere). In the end, either the economic policy remained bound by those rules—"fettered by gold"[66]—or, where those rules were discarded early, the room for maneuver was only timidly used. As it were, although other countries abandoned the gold standard mentality in the 1930s—Great Britain in 1931, the United States and Germany in 1933, and even France in 1936—Austria clung to it until the bitter end. However, the persuasive powers of the Austrians were hardly grounded in the government sharing their liberal beliefs, but in the coincidence of their proposals with a conservative aversion to experiments, the yielding to foreign pressure, or the welcome opportunity for using them as a pretext for a rollback on social policy. For in other fields—most visibly in the restriction of international trade, capital flows and migration, and in the interventionist stance with regard to farming and industrial policy—liberal prescriptions simply failed to impress Austrian policy makers.

5. Conclusion

This comparison of the varieties of liberalism as advocated in Vienna with Old- (and by implication New-)Chicago revealed that within traditional economic theory based on a pro-market ideology there existed a broad spectrum of opinion, in particular with regard to monetary management. It ranged from the Austrians' rather extreme policy advice of doing nothing to the proposals of the Old Chicago School that combined proto-Keynesian remedies with a price level anchor for monetary stability (with New-Chicago monetarism somewhere in between).[67] Indeed, in the eyes of Simons and his colleagues there was no need for a Keynesian revolution as a prerequisite for activist policy, but rather the need for a thoughtful application of traditional theory.[68]

Finally, against the background of current (macro-)economic opinion on the Great Depression, the Chicago view appears to provide one of the more reasonable recipes for fighting the depression. This cannot be said of Austrian economics, in spite of its possible indirect influence on actual economic policy in the 1930s.[69] Therefore, as it seems, not only was Vienna indeed far away from Chicago, but it was also further away from the truth.

Notes

1. The paper benefitted from helpful comments by Günter Bischof, Eric Frey, and J. Ronnie Davis, without however implicating them with any responsibility for the final product. This work was done during my Schumpeter fellowship at Harvard University; the hospitality of the Weatherhead Center for International Affairs and the financial support from the Schumpeter Society and the Austrian Ministry of Education are gratefully acknowledged.

2. The contribution by Karl-Heinz Paqué, "How Far is Vienna from Chicago? An Essay on the Methodology of Two Schools of Dogmatic Liberalism," *Kyklos* 38 (1985): 412-34, concentrated on methodological aspects; for a recent view of the Austrian critique of Friedman's positivism see Bruce Caldwell, "Hayek: Right for the Wrong Reasons?," *Journal of the History of Economic Thought* 23 (2001): 141-51.

3. In fact, Friedman asserted on the one hand that the Chicago School of the 1930s anticipated those policy conclusions commonly associated with Keynes and the Keynesian revolution, and on the other hand that his own brand of monetarism was firmly based on the Chicago "oral tradition"—which, as it seems, is one assertion too much to be consistent. See Milton Friedman, "The Monetary Theory and Policy of Henry Simons," *Journal of Law and Economics* 10 (1967): 1-13, especially 7-9; and idem, "Comment on the Critics," in *Milton Friedman's Monetary Framework. A Debate with His Critics*, ed. Robert J. Gordon (Chicago: University of Chicago Press, 1974), 132-77; for a critique see Don Patinkin, *Essays On and In the Chicago Tradition* (Durham: Duke University Press, 1981), especially chapters 10-12.

4. These authors also provide the main sources for the following discussion. See Ludwig Mises, *Theorie des Geldes und der Umlaufsmittel* (Munich: Duncker und Humblot, 1912); and idem, *Die Ursachen der Wirtschaftskrise* (Tübingen: Mohr, 1931). Friedrich August Hayek, *Geldtheorie und Konjunkturtheorie* (Vienna: Hölder-Pichler-Tempsky, 1929; reprint, Salzburg: W. Neugebauer, 1976); idem, *Prices and Production* (London: Routledge, 1931); and idem, *Profits, Interest, and Investment* (London: Routledge & Kegan Paul, 1939). Gottfried Haberler, "Money and the Business Cycle," in *Gold and Monetary Stabilization. Lectures on the Harris Foundation 1932*, ed. Quincy Wright (Chicago:

University of Chicago Press, 1932), 43-74. Fritz Machlup, *Führer durch die Krisenpolitik* (Vienna: Springer, 1934; reprint, Vienna: Manz, 1998). Among contemporary economists Joseph Schumpeter and Oskar Morgenstern are not included because, despite their Austrian origin, they were not truly members of the Austrian school. I will also draw on Hansjörg Klausinger, "Schumpeter and Hayek: Two Views of the Great Depression Re-Examined," *History of Economic Ideas* 3 (1995): 93–127; and idem, "'Austrian Economics in Two Minutes.' Fritz Machlup as a Journalist" (Paper delivered at the History of Economics Society Meeting, Winston Salem, 2001).

5. See Mark Blaug, "Hayek Revisited," in idem, *Not Only an Economist* (Cheltenham: Edward Elgar, 1997), 87-94. The winners in these controversies were of course Keynes, Knight, and Lange, respectively, the latter two themselves Chicagoans at a time.

6. With regard to the Chicago School the main primary sources are: Henry C. Simons et al., "Banking and Currency Reform" (University of Chicago, Department of Economics, Unsigned Mimeograph, 1933), reprinted in *Research in the History of Economic Thought and Methodology. Archival Supplement* 4 (1994): 31-49; Henry C. Simons, *A Positive Program for Laissez Faire. Some Proposals for a Liberal Economic Policy* (Chicago: University of Chicago Press, 1934); idem, "Rules versus Authorities in Monetary Policy," *Journal of Political Economy* 44 (1936): 1-30; idem, "Hansen on Fiscal Policy," *Journal of Political Economy* 50 (1942): 161-96; and idem, "Debt Policy and Banking Policy," *Review of Economic Statistics* 28 (1946): 85-89. All contributions by Simons but the first one are reprinted in Henry C. Simons, *Economic Policy for a Free Society* (Chicago: University of Chicago Press, 1948), the relevant quotations are to this edition. Jacob Viner, "International Aspects of the Gold Standard," in Wright, ed. *Gold*, 1-39; idem, *Balanced Deflation, Inflation, or More Depression* (Minneapolis: University of Minnesota Press, 1933); and idem, "Inflation as a Possible Remedy for the Depression," in *Proceedings of the Institute of Public Affairs, Seventh Annual Session* (Athens: The University of Georgia, 1933), 120-35. Frank H. Knight, "The Business Cycle, Interest, and Money: A Methodological Approach," *Review of Economic Statistics* 23 (1941): 53-67; as reprinted in idem, *On the History and Method of Economics* (Chicago: University of Chicago Press, 1956), 202-26. For the development of the Chicago School see Melvin W. Reder, "Chicago Economics: Permanence and Change," *Journal of Economic Literature* 20 (1982): 1-38.

7. For the quantity theory see Mark Blaug, "Why Is the Quantity Theory of Money the Oldest Surviving Theory in Economics?," in Blaug, *Not Only an Economist*, 114-35.

8. See the definition in Machlup, *Krisenpolitik*, 40-41, where the zero point between inflation and deflation corresponds to the so-called state of "neutral money"; see also Viner, *Balanced Deflation*, 20, and his "use [of] the term inflation to mean an increase in the total amount of spendable funds, whether consisting of coin, paper money, or bank deposits subject to check."

9. For the Chicago School definition see above. On the Austrian side the interpretation is less clear-cut; however, the definition given in the text is confirmed, among others, by Machlup, *Krisenpolitik*, 40-41 and 61.

10. For an algebraic formulation see Milton Friedman and Anna J. Schwartz, *A Monetary History of the United States, 1867-1960* (Princeton: Princeton University Press, 1963), 51n. We must not, however, impute a precise understanding of this mechanism to all the participants in the 1930s' debate.

11. The Chicago view was shared and, to some extent, preceded by Ralph Hawtrey (at His Majesty's Treasury), Irving Fisher (at Yale), Lauchlin Currie (at Harvard), and others; see David Laidler, *Fabricating the Keynesian Revolution* (Cambridge: Cambridge University Press, 1999), 183-88, 228-39.

12. Viner, *Balanced Deflation*, 7.

13. Simons, "Hansen," 188. See Knight, "Business Cycle," 224: "Indeed . . ., just what sets a boundary to a movement of general prices in either direction, and especially the downward movement, becomes something of a mystery."

14. Such a divergence may be due to exogenous movements in either the natural rate or in the money rate. The former case, with commercial banks being slow in adapting their lending rate, corresponds closely to the view of the Chicago school; the latter, typically thought of as the effect of inflationary policy by the central bank, represents the Austrian School. Note, however, that the first case figures prominently in Hayek's *Geldtheorie* of 1929 (80-81) but not in his later expositions; see Harald Hagemann and Michael Landesmann, "Lowe and Structural Theories of the Business Cycle," in *Political Economics in Retrospect. Essays in Memory of Adolph Lowe*, ed. Harald Hagemann and Heinz D. Kurz (Cheltenham: Edward Elgar, 1998), 117-18.

15. I could not find any evidence for the opinion that the Austrians had *predicted* this outcome. To the contrary, Hayek asserts: "The secret of the duration of the boom in the United States is thus to be sought precisely in the fall in prices. . . ." See Friedrich August Hayek, "Das intertemporale Gleichgewichtssystem der Preise und die Bewegungen des 'Geldwertes'," *Weltwirtschaftliches Archiv* (1928); translated in *The Collected Works of F. A. Hayek*, vol. 6, *Good Money*, Part II, ed. Stephen Kresge (London: Routledge, 1999), 218.

16. Laidler, *Fabricating*, 113, shows that in this literature the term "credit" is synonymous to "deposits," not to "loans."

17. Simons, "Debt Policy," 236.

18. These two options are examined in Viner, *Balanced Deflation*.

19. Friedrich August Hayek, *Monetary Nationalism and International Stability* (Geneva: Longmans Green, 1937); as reprinted in Hayek, *Good Money*, 97.

20. Hayek, *Prices*, 87.

21. This last point is vigorously stressed in Mises, *Ursachen*, 15-21.

22. For the distinction between primary and secondary deflation in the 1930s and the policy conclusions derived from it see Hansjörg Klausinger, "German Anticipations of the Keynesian Revolution? The Case of Lautenbach, Neisser and Röpke," *European Journal of the History of Economic Thought* 6 (1999): 378-403, especially 382-85.

23. Viner, *Balanced Deflation*, 22. Simons, *Positive Program*, 74, also refers to a "contraction" of money.

24. Viner, "International Aspects," 28.

25. Machlup, *Krisenpolitik*, 174.

26. Friedrich August Hayek, "Das Schicksal der Goldwährung," *Der deutsche Volkswirt* 6 (1932); as translated in Hayek, *Good Money*, 164.

27. Lionel Robbins, *The Great Depression* (London: Macmillan, 1934), 17; see also Frank Steindl, *Monetary Interpretations of the Great Depression* (Ann Arbor: University of Michigan Press, 1995), 54-57.

28. Fritz Machlup, "Dollarinflation?," *Neues Wiener Tagblatt*, 12 March 1933; and idem, "Was ist eigentlich Deflation?," *Neues Wiener Tagblatt*, 25 March 1934; my translations.

29. "Rückblick auf das Jahr 1932," *Monatsberichte des Österreichischen Institutes für Konjunkturforschung* 7 (1933): 15.

30. See Friedman and Schwartz, *Monetary History*, 333 and Table A-1. The decrease in Friedman and Schwartz's preferred *M2*-series was even sharper, namely 35%.

31. See Aurel Schubert, *The Credit-Anstalt Crisis of 1931* (Cambridge: Cambridge University Press, 1991), Table 6.1, 104.

32. Calculated from "Notenumlauf und Giroverbindlichkeiten" in *Monatsberichte des Österreichischen Institutes für Konjunkturforschung* 9 (1934): 49.

33. These aggregates were not readily available from official statistics then; however, it would have been possible to construct them with sufficient accuracy, as for example Lauchlin Currie did for the United States. See Steindl, *Monetary Interpretations*, 61-62.

34. Note that with near-zero nominal rates the real rates correspond roughly to the rate of deflation which in the United States of 1931 and 1932 approximated 10%.

35. Fritz Machlup, "Zur Frage der Ankurbelung durch Kreditpolitik," *Zeitschrift für Nationalökonomie* 4 (1932): 398-404.

36. Ibid., 399.

37. The term "credit deadlock" was coined by Ralph Hawtrey; see Steindl, *Monetary Interpretations*, 117.

38. Viner, *Balanced Deflation*, 22; Simons, "Hansen," 186, extends this view even to the period of recovery in the late 1930s. Of course, this is in contradiction to Friedman and Schwartz's counterfactual argument that the Fed, by persevering in expansionist open-market policy, would have ultimately succeeded.

39. The new view of credit deadlock as a deficiency of credit supply was put forward by Ben Bernanke, "Nonmonetary Effects of the Financial Crisis in the Propagation of the Great Depression," *American Economic Review* 73 (1983): 257-76. In a close reading of Viner, "Inflation," both demand and supply factors can be found.

40. See Machlup, "Ankurbelung," 402.

41. Simons, "Rules," 175: "The powers of the government to inject purchasing power through expenditure and to withdraw it through taxation – the powers of expanding and contracting issues of actual currency and other obligations more or less serviceable as money – are surely adequate to price-level control." For an overview of similar proposals in the United States during the 1930s see J. Ronnie Davis, *The New Economics and the Old Economists* (Ames: Iowa State University Press, 1971).

42. See Simons, "Rules," 174; in idem, "Debt Policy," 239, he also speaks of the "fiscal [sic!] stabilization of the value of money."

43. In this respect, the Chicago view is severely critical of the economics of the New Deal; see Viner, *Balanced Deflation*, 12, for criticism of "the high-wage fallacy."

44. The deflation should be induced by "governmental action"; see Viner, *Balanced Deflation*, 13.

45. See Fritz Machlup, "Die Geldtheorie von J. M. Keynes," *Der Österreichische Volkswirt* 24 (1932): 967–70, here 969; and Friedrich August Hayek, "Der Stand und die nächste Zukunft der Konjunkturforschung," in *Festschrift für Arthur Spiethoff* (Munich: Duncker und Humblot, 1933); as translated in Hayek, *Profits*, 171-82, here 176.

46. Viner, *Balanced Deflation*, 10.

47. For this change of mind see Viner, *Balanced Deflation* and Viner, "Inflation," with the former text written before, the latter after the United States' departure from gold.

48. See for example Machlup, "Geldtheorie," 969.

49. Simons et al., "Banking Reform," 33.

50. Ibid., 43-45.

51. See Simons, "Rules," 171-74.

52. Indeed, Robbins, *Great Depression*, 20, attributes the Austrian view to "the majority of economists of repute." For Friedman's criticism see Friedman, "Monetary Theory," 10-13.

53. Simons, "Rules," 169.

54. See Hayek, *Monetary Nationalism*, 49-61.

55. Simons, "Rules," 169. However, before 1933 at least Viner's position was more guarded: "The gold standard is a wretched standard, but it may conceivably be the best available to us;" Viner, "International Aspects," 37.

56. Viner, *Balanced Deflation*, 5. For a similar diagnosis for Austria see Peter Berger, "Ökonomische Macht und Politik," in *Handbuch des politischen Systems Österreichs. Erste Republik 1918–1933*, ed. Emmerich Talos et al. (Vienna: Manz, 1995), 406.

57. Eric Hobsbawm perceptively comments on the relation between "the supply of good economists" and "the fortunes of national economies": "Pre-1938 Austria, where such theorists were plentiful, distinguished and *consulted by governments*, was not an advertisement for economic success until after 1945 when, as it happens, it had lost all its distinguished older theorists without acquiring comparable replacements" (emphasis mine); yet, this might exaggerate the (direct) power of Austrian ideas. See Eric Hobsbawm, "Historians and Economists: I," in idem, *On History* (New York: The New Press, 1997), 100.

58. On the economists and the economic policy of Hoover and Roosevelt see William J. Barber, *From New Era to New Deal* (Cambridge: Cambridge University Press, 1985); and idem, *Designs within Disorder* (Cambridge: Cambridge University Press, 1996).

59. For example, Hayek left Vienna for a professorship at the London School of Economics in 1931; Haberler vistited Harvard in 1931/32 and worked at the League of Nations from 1934 to 1936, when he became professor at Harvard University; Machlup spent three years in the United States and in Britain before he became professor at Buffalo in 1936; and, finally, Mises left Austria for a fellowship in Geneva. See Harald Hagemann and Claus-Dieter Krohn, eds., *Biographisches Handbuch der deutschsprachigen wirtschaftswissenschaftlichen Emigration nach 1933* (Munich: K. G. Saur, 1999).

60. For a devastating critique see Fritz Machlup, " Die Währungs- und Kreditkrise," *Schmollers Jahrbuch* 62 (1932): 373-88.

61. See Machlup to Dr. Hugo Glaser (6 April 1934), in Fritz Machlup Papers, box 55, folder 18. There are also ten typescripts of columns that the *Tagblatt* apparently refused to print (Fritz Machlup Papers, box 86, folders 3 and 4).

62. For Morgenstern and the Austrian school see Urs Rellstab, *Ökonomie und Spiele. Die Entstehungsgeschichte der Spieltheorie aus dem Blickwinkel des Ökonomen Oskar Morgenstern* (Chur: Ruegger, 1991), chapter 3.

63. With regard to countercyclical fiscal policy Viner complains: ". . . it was only [the] alleged fears as to the ill effects of these deficits, and the panic which the big business world professed to foresee if these deficits should recur, which have made this method of depression finance seriously risky." See Viner, *Balanced Deflation*, 18-19.

64. Herbert Hoover, *The Memoirs of Herbert Hoover*, vol. 3, *The Great Depression, 1929-1941* (New York: Macmillan, 1952), 30.

65. On the power of the gold standard mentality see Barry Eichengreen and Peter Temin, "The Gold Standard and the Great Depression," *Contemporary European History* 9 (2000): 183-207.

66. Note that by the beginning of the 1980s the new Chicagoans considered Simons' program as "highly interventionist" and a deviation from liberal creed; see Ronald Coase's remark in Edmund W. Kitch, ed., "The Fire of Truth. A Remembrance of Law and Economics at Chicago, 1932-1970," *Journal of Law and Economics* 26 (1983): 178.

67. See Henry C. Simons, "Keynes' Comments on Money," *The Christian Century* 53 (1936); as reprinted in *John Maynard Keynes. Critical Responses*, vol. 3, ed. Charles R. McCann (London: Routledge, 1998), 91-93.

68. For a critique from the standpoint of modern macroeconomics, see Bradford DeLong, "'Liquidation' Cycles: Old-Fashioned Real Business Cycle Theory and the Great Depression," *NBER Working Paper* 3546 (1990).

The League of Nations and Interwar Austria: Critical Assessment of a Partnership in Economic Reconstruction

Peter Berger

Introduction

During the twenty years of its precarious existence, the interwar Austrian Republic constantly depended on foreign credit. In 1923, the first of two large, internationally guaranteed reconstruction loans was floated under the auspices of the League of Nations. Its purpose was to liquidate the detrimental consequences of hyperinflation and enable the government to carry out urgent budgetary reforms. The outlines of a reform strategy were laid down earlier in a contract between Austria and four guarantor nations (Geneva Protocols of 1922), and then specified in a reconstruction law passed by the Austrian Parliament. Experts nominated by the League Secretariat set up a monitoring office in Vienna, which was entrusted with the task of supervising financial and economic reorganization work until 1926.

After a break of five years, League supervisors returned to Austria in August 1931, when the preparations for issuing a second international loan started. Once again, the granting of the loan was linked with far-reaching monetary and fiscal reforms (Lausanne Protocol of 1931). Having to act under the watchful eyes of foreign financial commissioners thus became the rule rather than the exception for Austria's political leaders, between the early 1920s and the late 1930s.

For the League of Nations, successful co-operation with Austria in financial and economic matters (the term "financial control" was carefully avoided in Geneva) turned out to be immensely valuable. It publicly underscored the League's technical expertise, and, when Austrian budget recovery first became visible around 1924, it gave the secretariat and financial committee staffs a boost of confidence. Yet, outside League circles, and above all in Austria, the relationship between Geneva and Vienna triggered a range of more ambiguous reactions.

Austrian public opinion, influenced by press campaigns from both left and right papers against what was dubbed "western financial colonialism," could not be expected to warmly welcome League of Nations interference. Yet, during the 1920s, the country's two major political parties, Catholics and Socialists, while not always in agreement with specific aspects of financial reform, did support the League's work in general. In the case of the Catholic *Christlichsoziale Partei*, this attitude resulted from the fact that League functionaries were seen as strong allies against "marxist" political ambitions in Austria. On the opposite side of the political spectrum, the Social Democratic Party realized the danger emanating from a coalition of international financiers and local conservatives eager to dismantle existing (and costly) social legislation. But it refrained from undermining League action in Austria, probably because some top figures in its ranks, such as Otto Bauer, speaker of the Socialist deputies' club, saw no genuine alternative to the 19th century-style liberal economic wisdom preached by Geneva. A third political grouping with considerable weight in Austria's Parliament, the Pangermans (*Grossdeutschen*), deeply resented the obvious anti-German bias of League financial reconstruction work. For them, salvation lay in close economic cooperation and, ultimately, political unification of Austria with the neighboring German Reich. However, in 1922-23 the party backed the Catholic chancellor's plea for western financial support, fearing to lose its cabinet posts in the government led by clergyman Ignaz Seipel.

After 1931, the impact of the Great Depression placed the issue of League interference in the center of the struggle between Austria's four contending political forces, i.e., the Catholic *Christlichsozialen*, the Italian-sponsored Fascist *Heimwehr*, the Social Democrats, and the Nazis (who had completely absorbed the former Pangerman camp). The adherents of the swastika saw in the League's presence in Austria a despisable instrument of "international capitalist Jewry," designed to block the country's economic progress, which, according to them, would be attained through association with Germany and Adolf Hitler. Ironically enough, the acting representative of the League of Nations in Vienna between 1931 and 1936, the Dutchman Rost van Tonningen, showed increasing sympathy for the National Socialist cause, which forced the secretariat to prematurely withdraw him from his post.[1]

Austria's Social Democrats—fighting a losing battle against both the swelling Nazi tide and the ruling alliance of Catholics and *Heimwehren* determined to outperform Hitler's followers in anti-Marxism—half-heartedly opposed Geneva's fiscal and monetary strategies but, after 1933, learned to appreciate the League's interest in Austria as a bulwark against German expansionist appetites. Closer relations between the Socialist Party and Geneva had no chance to develop, however, due to the abortive uprising of Austrian workers in February 1934 and the subsequent repressive measures taken against the defeated Left by the dictatorial governments of Chancellors Dollfuss and Schuschnigg. To conclude this short summary of Austrian attitudes towards the League in the thirties, we must look at how the *Heimwehren* and *Christlichsozialen* dealt with Geneva during their joint period in power. The Fascist *Heimwehren* seem to have been too inhomogenous to formulate a common view on either political or economic implications of foreign financial intervention. Some leading *Heimwehr* figures like *Prinz* Rüdiger von Starhemberg repeatedly showed interest in increased foreign loans (or donations, for that matter) to finance the government's soaring military and police expenditure. Others wanted all western loans repaid and the League out of Austria as quickly as possible. Such views sometimes originated from resentment against the Anglo-French dominance in the League's Financial Committee and the wish to improve Austro-German relations. But equally present was the motive to get rid of an organization like the League which stood in the way of more active strategies of social policy in times of economic hardship. Not only the "left wing" of the *Heimwehren* but also a large faction within the Catholic camp were in favor of moderate inflationist policies benefiting the jobless and poor. However, the power wielded by the "capitalist" wing of the Catholic establishment, whose head was the president of Austria's central bank Victor Kienböck, left little room for heterodox experiments. Kienböck served as secretary of finance in Chancellor Seipel's cabinet, which brought the League to Vienna in the early 1920s. In the mid-1930s, he still advocated co-operation with Geneva, more or less along the lines of the past. This implied policies which defended a strong currency and strict limits on state expenditure. For Kienböck, as for most Christian Social politicians of his caliber, the value of the League's presence in Austria depended on its willingness to support government, banking, and industry in their fight for Austria's economic competitiveness, to be achieved through low wages and an equally moderate level of corporate taxation.

The Question of Foreign "Finance Dictatorship" in Retrospect

Before entering into a discussion of how the League of Nations achieved or did not achieve its goals in Austria economically and otherwise, I will briefly dwell upon some post-1945 commentators' judgments concerning the financial reconstruction programs of the 1920s and 1930s. Both League-sponsored Austrian reconstruction schemes were in fact "tasks as political as it is possible to be," to quote the words of a high-ranking Geneva official.[2] This is why few retrospective comments can be considered as being merely "technical." Instead, they tend to reflect their authors' politico-economic *Weltanschauung*, sometimes consistent with, but (as we will see) in most cases contradicting, the professed creed of the architects of interwar financial reforms.

It is not really surprising that League activities in interwar Austria have earned little appreciation from scholars writing after the Second World War. As two authors, historian Karl Bachinger and economist Leonhard Bauer, have most recently pointed out, the decades following victory over Nazism were devoted to the building of European welfare states.[3] So complete was the abandonment of pre-1939 economic orthodoxy, and so overwhelming the triumph of the new "Fordist" paradigm (i.e. the conviction that high capital returns were dependent upon increased purchasing-power of the masses) that few people bothered to defend interwar policies of budgetary retrenchment. In an economic world shaped by Keynesian ideas, Montagu Norman—the Bank of England's interwar governor and chief instigator of League financial policies—lost whatever guiding function he may have possessed.

Among the publications denouncing the deflationist tendencies of the League's financial schemes in Austria, Siegfried Mattl's article of 1984 occupies a prominent place.[4] Mattl, echoing earlier criticisms by Charles Gulick, Erich Hans Wolf, Karl Ausch, and others, mainly questions the economic wisdom of not having devalued the Austrian currency in the mid-1930s, and of still having aimed for a budget equilibrium when half a million Austrians or more were without jobs. He puts the blame equally on the League of Nations' financial recommendations to Austrian ministers, and on the Austrian central bank's governor Kienböck. Kienböck, with his political roots in the most bourgeois circles of the *Christlichsoziale Partei*, is accused to have turned a blind eye on the unemployment problem while rushing to help ailing commercial banks and bank-owned industries whenever such help was needed. Hence, the term Mattl employs to characterize the League's and Kienböck's regiment during the great depression is "*Finanzdiktatur*" (finance dictatorship).

Other Austrian historians, too, have embraced the concept of *Finanzdiktatur* in Austria, and they did not always limit its use to the analysis of the 1930s. In a book first published in 1974 on the history of the Austrian schilling (and re-edited on the occasion of the schilling's replacement by the EURO),[5] authors Karl Bachinger and Herbert Matis acknowledge that thoughts about state-generated economic growth and full employment cannot fairly be expected to have entered the minds of interwar decision makers, foreign or Austrian. Nevertheless they blame foreign, i.e. League of Nations and Bank of England, influence for having limited Austria's freedom to deviate from the path of rigid financial orthodoxy. The League's first commissioner-general in Austria, Alfred R. Zimmerman, is depicted by Bachinger and Matis as "the most powerful figure of his host-country,"[6] issuing orders to local dignitaries like a white officer in colonial Africa. Before being appointed to Vienna, Zimmerman for many years filled the post of burgomaster of the Dutch port city of Rotterdam. There already—his biographer Jacques Bosmans tells us[7]—he earned the reputation of an unwavering partisan of financial austerity. One need not share the views of Zimmerman's overtowering influence on Austrian policies to assume that the impression left by League actions on contemporaries and historians alike would have been much less dictatorial and "deflationist" with another commissioner-general in charge.

Summing up post-1945 opinions on the League's financial experiments with interwar Austria, it is safe to say that a significant group of historians has seen the Austrian republic as a victim rather than a beneficiary of foreign interference. More often than not, historians argued that fiscal and monetary strategies imported from abroad were applied without giving much thought to the special requirements of a small Central European community suffering from the consequences of war, political disintegration, and hyperinflation. Two important qualifications were made, though, by some commentators who acknowledged (a) that leading economic decision makers in Austria, notably Victor Kienböck, embraced the ultra-orthodox financial principles of their times without reservations, and (b) that conservative Austrian politicians welcomed the League's role as executioner of these principles, mainly because responsibility for an anti-labor bias of economic reforms could be heaped on someone else's shoulders.

A third aspect, however, seems to have been generally overlooked in the debate among historians. Repeatedly during the interwar period, but mainly in the 1930s, Austrians urged League functionaries to consent to policies which were irreconcilable with any kind of consistent economic reasoning, whether orthodox or not. In some cases, Geneva yielded to such pressure and thus became a tool for purely political ends of the Austrian government. While discussing the progress of League work between 1922 and 1936, I shall try to highlight these instances of breach of principles.

The First Austrian League Reconstruction Scheme (1922-26): A Case of Applied Neo-Classical Economics?

What became known in Austrian economic history as *die Genfer Sanierung* was in fact a conservative national government's strategy to redress state finances by use of foreign loans, and to stabilize a strongly depreciated currency by pegging it to the gold-based U.S. dollar.

The four-year period preceding the signing of the 1922 Protocols of Geneva—which entitled Austria to foreign financial aid—had been a time of missed fiscal opportunities. Various efforts to balance Austria's state budget without, or with just a little, support from abroad failed. Among these efforts was State Secretary Joseph A. Schumpeter's *Finanzplan* of 1919, proposing, along with other measures, high taxes on domestic private property. More actively than Schumpeter, the Social Democratic Party pressed for taxing Austria's big fortunes. Yet, such plans were doomed to fail after elections in 1920 gave Catholics and Pangermans a comfortable majority in Parliament. In the summer of 1922, the rise to chancellorship of Ignaz Seipel, the most influential figure of the *Christlichsoziale Partei*, marked a new stage in the ascendancy of Austria's political Right. By skillfully exploiting the Entente powers' mutual suspicions about their respective allies' striving for politico-economic preponderance in the Danube basin, Seipel managed to unite France, Britain, Italy, and Czechoslovakia in an effort to guarantee Austria's political independence, and to strengthen her economically with an international loan. Seipel's success had two immediate political consequences. First, the League of Nations, represented by a commissioner-general residing in Vienna, was awarded the function of prime coordinating agency for Austrian financial reforms and supreme arbitrator in conflicts between Austria and her creditors. Second, plans for a political union between Austria and Germany (not actively pursued since 1919, but still widely popular in Austrian Socialist and Pangerman circles) had to be renounced officially for a period of at least twenty years.[8]

The Seipel government's swift abandonment of the Anschluss concept—owed to the chancellor's strategic choices as much as to foreign (mainly French) pressure—was something that Seipel's opponents never forgave him. Many Austrians would grudgingly accept financial dependence on their ex-enemies of World War I and even the presence of a League "controller"in Vienna, but they felt deeply humiliated by the Geneva Protocol's first paragraph vetoing Austro-German unification. Given the potentially destabilizing force of frustrated Austrian Pangermanism, the decision to link financial reconstruction to a ban against the Anschluss can be questioned—as was done by historian Grete Klingenstein, among others.[9] In hindsight, the *Anschlussverbot* of 1922 was of no practical value anyway. It failed to prevent Hitler from occupying Austria in 1938 and a majority of Austrians from welcoming their country's incorporation into the *Reich*.

But our main concern here cannot be the foreign policy aspect of the first League reconstruction scheme. Rather, we will focus on its economic and social impact. Conventional historical wisdom in Austria associates the League's activity between 1923 and 1926 mainly with exaggerated efforts to fight a general rise in prices. League experts influenced by the Bank of England are thought to have been overcautious in their attitude towards public investment, which had detrimental consequences for national employment. Further criticism is directed, in retrospect, against moves to lay off public servants, make state and provincial administrations more effective and "lean," and keep their borrowing under tight control. To sum it up, the League of Nations is held responsible, together with its friends in the Austrian government, for having created massive deflationary pressure on the economy. How just are these allegations?

In search of an answer it is convenient to divide the timespan between 1922/23 and 1928 into four distinct phases. The initial phase began with League commissioner Zimmerman's arrival in Austria (December 1922) and expired shortly before the Viennese stock exchange suffered drastic losses in March 1924. During our first period under review, financial reconstruction efforts were mainly directed at lowering state expenditure via the dismissal of personnel employed by the confederation, provinces, and the federal railroads. All in all, about 60,000 public servants lost their jobs. Doubtlessly, this put a heavy strain not only on the individuals and families afflicted, but on society as a whole. The influence of the League commissioner-general was highly visible in all matters of budgetary retrenchment. Austria's minister of finance was compelled to furnish him with preliminary budgets at the beginning of each month of the fiscal year. Four weeks later the commissioner compared factual budget figures with the estimates he held in hands. Only when the deficit was within the limits foreseen did he consent to covering it with foreign loan funds. Whatever League credit money flowed into Austria was kept on accounts administered by the League commissioner's office. Thus, an effective brake was put on Austrian public spending behavior.

On the monetary front, the greatest achievement of 1923/1924 undoubtedly was the stabilization of the Austrian crown after years of inflationary turmoil. Operating as of 2 January 1923, the new Austrian National Bank aimed for an exchange rate of 71.060 crowns to one U.S. dollar, thereby launching a "lighter" Austrian money than some experts had expected. This was hardly a deflationist move, but it met with understanding and support from the League of Nations' Financial Committee and commissioner-general Zimmerman. A member of Zimmerman's Viennese staff, Rost van Tonningen—later appointed League commissioner himself—wrote about the advantage of restricting the gold value of Austria's currency: "As a matter of fact the leaders of the [Austrian National] Bank had the good fortune to choose a level of stabilisation which was so low that wages could subsequently be increased to a very considerable extent without upsetting the equilibrium of the country."[10]

The bank of issue's cautious choice of not aiming at prewar gold parity had problematic effects, too. An undervalued Austrian currency contributed to the growth of a speculative bubble at the Viennese stock exchange, where international investors sought to profit from bargains in Central European companies' shares. The bubble burst after little more than a year, and speculators were forced to sell equity as a result of losses incurred from an unexpected rally of the French franc. These events marked the beginning of a new stage of Austrian financial reconstruction stretching from spring 1924 well into the summer of the next year. It was a crucially important stage inasmuch as it earned the League Financial Committee and its endorsers at the Bank of England the definite reputation of unflagging deflationists. Actually, Montagu Norman and his partisans in Geneva were deeply worried about what they considered an "inflationary" practice of Austria's bank of issue, i.e., the rediscount of bills without any guarantee that the cheap money thus created was not used for speculative purposes. Richard Reisch, Austrian central bank governor at the time, maintained that in times of crisis his institution was obliged to keep industrial and commercial credit afloat, even at the cost of an occasional abuse of lent money for bourse speculation. In an attempt to neutralize Reisch's strategy, League commissioner Zimmerman, acting more or less upon Norman's orders, tightened his grip on both Austrian credit policies and the budget. Government plans to beef up public investment after the 1922-1924 period of enforced retrenchment were undermined by new, restrictive League rules on state spending. Pressure was put on the Austrian bank of issue to accept co-responsibility for keeping consumer price rises within internationally accepted limits. And once again, an effort to curb the cost of public administration and diminish the number of state employees was requested from Austria's political leaders.

In hindsight, one can hardly deny the restraining effect upon Austria's economic growth caused by the League's budgetary and credit guidelines operative during 1924 and the first half of 1925. League commissioner Zimmerman's vetoes against major public lending projects worked into the same direction. Without his interference, the Austrian railways, for instance, would have had the chance to borrow considerable sums from investors abroad. Putting these moneys to productive use would have helped keeping Austrian unemployment in check. The railway loan failed to materialize, and the Austrian government, under League pressure to prevent budget deficits at all costs, had to confront a steep rise in the number of jobless during the winter of 1924/25. Nevertheless, if we look at the whole period between March 1924 and August 1925, it seems unwarranted to speak of the presence of deflation in a technical sense. Austrian banknote circulation, instead of contracting, remained stable. And the cost of living measured by the consumer price index even increased, from 126 to 143 (January 1923=100).[11]

Whatever fears of continuing inflation the League's financial experts may have had in the middle of 1925, they were compelled by political events to prepare their retreat from the shores of the Danube. This happened during the third stage of Austrian financial reconstruction, which lasted for about a year and ended with the closing of the League commisioner's Viennese office in June 1926. One of Zimmerman's ex-aides stayed in Vienna, though, and exercised a mild control of the Austrian state debt on behalf of the League of Nations' Financial Committee until mid-1928. What were the political factors causing the League to pull out of Austria head over heels? Mainly, Geneva was alarmed by a remarkable growth in strength of the Austrian Anschluss movement during the first half of 1925. Partisans of Austro-German unification claimed that the economic hardship suffered by hundreds of thousands of Austrians could have been avoided if German economic assistance had been installed in the place of Anglo-French loans. The stock exchange crisis of March 1924, and the procyclical monetary and fiscal strategies applied to fight the consequences of the crash, doubtlessly fuelled the resurgent Anschluss propaganda. In order to take the wind out of Pangerman sails, the League sent two experts to Vienna and entrusted them with the task of inquiring into Austria's general economic situation. The report presented in September 1925 to the League Secretariat by French banker Charles Rist and the editor-in-chief of the Royal Economic Society's "Economic Journal," Charles Layton, painted a rosy picture of healthy Austrian state finances and a stable currency. According to Rist and Layton, Austria's future economic prosperity depended on increased exports to other countries in eastern and central Europe (and not so much to Germany!), for which the political cooperation of the governments involved would be crucial. As it was obviously not a financial experts' job to lay foundations of friendship between the states of the Danube basin, Rist and Layton paved the way for the League commissioner's departure from Vienna.[12]

But before Zimmerman could leave, the problem of how to use the remainder of the 1923 League of Nations Austrian loan had to be solved. Some 40% of the original loan sum of 650 million gold crowns still rested on various bank accounts instead of being spent for balancing state budgets. The reason for this somewhat surprising fact were extraordinarily high tax receipts of the Austrian confederation after December 1922. While the minister of finance easily balanced his consecutive budgets by means of tax surplusses, the entire cabinet expected the League's signal to "liberate" unused loan money, thus making it available for public investment purposes. Indeed, the League Financial Committee—after initial hesitation—consented to earmark some 300 million gold crowns for the electrification of Austrian rail tracks and for laying long-distance underground telegraphic cables. In doing so, it added a somewhat pre-Keynesian flavor to what had been, until then, a mere exercise in conventional fiscal and monetary stabilization practice. The complete success of that exercise had to be obvious to anyone watching the developments of 1928-1930. In 1930, Austria confidently floated a new investment loan on all major western financial markets. The clouds of the Great Depression did not yet darken the economic horizon of eastern and central Europe. But within months, the picture would change dramatically.

The League Returns to Austria: Initial Rescue Strategies (1931-1932)

The second League interference with Austrian economic and financial developments came in 1931, after the announcement of imminent bankruptcy by the country's largest commercial bank, the *Credit-Anstalt für Handel und Gewerbe*. Austria's banking system had been in dire straits since the early 1920s. But as most of the ailing banks were discretely taken over by stronger competitors and only a few (for example the *Centralbank der Deutschen Sparkassen*) actually crashed,[13] the public remained largely unaware of the deep structural crisis resulting from a cumulation of misfortunes. These included the loss of the Habsburg Empire's large industrial clientele, the extinction of assets during a period of prolonged inflation, and the proliferation of unsound business practices linked with the stock exchange boom of 1922/23. The League of Nations experts associated with the commissioner's office at Vienna were of course informed about the precarious state of Austrian banking. But in 1922 a clear choice had been made to limit League action to restoring budgetary equilibrium and monetary stability. Hence, Geneva lacked practical experience when, in 1931, Austria's government called on the League as well as the Bank of International Settlements (BIS) to help reshape the banking sector (together with the national budget and the currency, endangered by foreseeable consequences of the *Credit-Anstalt*'s fall).

In fact, the task the League faced in Austria in 1931 basically consisted in fighting the impact of what was to become the Great Depression, spilling over from the United States to large parts of Europe. Being a small, open economy dependent on foreign credit, Austria suffered simultaneously from shrinking exports and from growing difficulties to service her existing foreign loans. Measures which seemed promising if one wished to revive export trade (like devaluation of the national currency) ran counter to the equally desirable goal of holding the cost of the foreign debt in check; and thus they were eschewed. Meanwhile, tax returns diminished due to restricted business activity, and soaring public outlays for the social system (mainly unemployment doles) pushed the national budget's deficit to record heights. Federal Chancellor Karl Buresch, whose request for League assistance came after the promulgation of a series of laws giving extended state guarantees to all *Credit-Anstalt* creditors, presided over a coalition cabinet in which the *Christlichsozialen* held the majority of posts. But parliamentary support for Buresch's cabinet was too weak to launch an all-out attack against, in the eyes of conservatives, the prime obstacle to economic recovery: far-reaching social legislation and excessive non-wage labor costs. With the League Financial Committee's weight thrown into the scale, Buresch hoped to tip the political balance to his favor. A new League loan would enable him to solve the budget problem. And pressure from Geneva would assist to overcome the Social Democratic Party's resistance against lowering social welfare expenditure and wages. In Austrian banking, as in most industrial branches, unjustifiably high wages and wage related costs were considered to block the road to profitability.[14]

If we read the statements issued by foreign experts after a first round of fact-finding missions in Austria in August and September 1931, the cure they had in mind for the ailing Austrian economy appears clearly orthodox and deflationist. In some cases, policy recommendations were wrapped in harsh criticism of the way Austrians had dealt with their financial and economic plight so far. Among those who did not conceal their dissatisfaction was Gijsbert Bruins, a Dutch monetary specialist who, on behalf of the BIS, investigated the Austrian bank of issue's most recent crisis management. Bruins left no doubt that in his view "the governing idea behind [Austrian reconstruction policies] must be the cheapening of production and the reduction of present consumption which is not justified by the situation, in order to improve the trade balance and the balance of payments, so far as that lies within Austria's own power." He then went on to attack Austrian economic policy makers in all but diplomatic words: "In other countries which have been confronted with similar difficulties in recent months the difficulties have served to stimulate the effort required. . . . In Austria, the necessary effort was not made at the psychological moment, i.e. at the time of the acute crisis of the currency, nor was it made later to any considerable extent."[15]

Similar denouncements of Austrian sluggishness came from another prominent financial diplomat dispatched to Vienna in August 1931, Meinoud M. Rost van Tonningen. Rost was later to become the League's acting representative in Austria, and it was largely due to his personal influence that in 1933 and 1934 the Geneva Financial Committee tolerated some credit expansion to ease political pressure on the Dollfuss government. But in 1931, with Dollfuss's predecessor Buresch still in power, Rost held radically deflationist views on what had to be done in Austria. He advocated drastic reduction of public spending, tightening of the bank of issue's discount credit to commercial banks, management of the *Credit-Anstalt* by non-Austrian directors ("to provide backbone"), defense of the schilling currency by means of capital controls, and—most emphatically—an enforced downward adjustment of all wages and wage-related costs. A particularly noteworthy aspect of Rost's economic scheme in the early 1930s was his penchant for methods irreconcilable with representative democracy. Repeatedly he stressed the advantage of salvaging the economy by emergency decrees (*Notverordnungen*), thus echoing voices from within the Austrian governing coalition that demanded plenary powers to circumvent "Marxist obstruction" in Parliament. League officials in Geneva, though, were careful not to openly associate themselves with such ideas, and they certainly refused to make "financial dictatorship" a precondition for rescue loans to Austria.

The League's strong commitment to orthodox financial practice, and the Austrian government's wish to create a situation in which organized labor would not find the time to oppose economic reforms along conservative lines, combined to produce remarkably quick results for Austrian fiscal years 1931 and 1932. In fulfillment of specific promises made by Chancellor Buresch at a meeting with the League Financial Committee on 17 September 1931, Austria completely wiped out her budget deficit over the next fifteen months by means of drastic cuts in public expenditure and simultaneous tax increases. Unexpectedly, even the Social Democratic deputies voted in favor of a budgetary reconstruction law, which was passed on 3 October 1931 *(Budgetsanierungsgesetz)*, though it was clearly foreseeable that Austrian workers would pay a dear price for balancing the budget. Indeed, 1932 witnessed a steep rise in the number of the unemployed (21.7% of the workforce as compared to 15.4% in 1931[16]) while nominal wages of jobholders fell by more than 5%.[17] The share of the three lowest brackets of wage-earners in the overall yield of Austria's income tax increased, while that of four higher brackets diminished.[18] Popular consumer goods like beer were subjected to heavy taxation. But despite the surge of nominal tax rates, real tax revenue diminished in line with contracting mass purchasing power. The resulting dilemma reinforced the government's tendency to cut back capital investment. While in 1931 4.2% of all public expenditure had been devoted to investment purposes, this ratio fell to 0.6% in 1932.[19]

Whatever views one may hold on fiscal retrenchment in times of economic crisis, the measurable results of Austrian budget stabilization were doubtlessly impressive. In the field of currency management, the Austrian National Bank and the ministry of finance performed less convincingly. Since the near-collapse of the *Credit-Anstalt* in May 1931, Austrian holders of bank accounts had displayed growing concern about the stability of the schilling. Withdrawals from commercial banks and conversion of domestic currency into foreign exchange gained momentum after the Austrian state had assumed full liability for the *Credit Anstalt*'s outstanding debts (26 June 1931). In October 1931, Austria introduced exchange controls to impede capital flight—a measure prompted by fears that the devaluation of the British pound might encourage international speculators to launch an attack on the schilling.

Capital controls produced the predictable result of an emerging black market for non-transferable claims in Austrian currency. In this market, schillings were traded 20-30% below the official exchange rates. That, in turn, caused Austrian partisans of currency devaluation—mainly exporting industrialists, but also spokespersons of organized labor—to question the wisdom of adhering to an obviously untenable schilling-gold ratio. Similar arguments were voiced by monetary experts associated with the League of Nations, most of them British. As an illustration, I quote from a statement of Sir Frederick Leith-Ross, member of the "Mixed Committee" charged with preparations for the Austrian rescue loan: "The maintenance of gold parity will necessitate, having regard to the level of world prices, a very heavy strain, not merely on the industrial and financial system of [Austria], but on the political and social organization. . . . It will certainly be less difficult to restore equilibrium by devaluation of the currency which will enable costs to be adjusted to prices with much less friction."[20]

Failure to reduce deflatory pressure on the Austrian economy by means of currency devaluation can be attributed almost solely to the governor of Austria's central bank, Victor Kienböck. Appointed to his post in February 1932, Kienböck, a trained lawyer and staunch defender of the gold standard "rules of the game," first refused to acknowledge the reality of an illicit market for the schilling. Later he grudgingly allowed Austrian exporters to circumvent capital controls and sell foreign currency directly to importers at rates approximately 25% above the central bank's quotations (*Privatclearing*). But official recognition of the schilling's depreciated state did not come before spring 1934, when Austria's National Bank brought the book value of its gold reserves to parity with "private-clearing" rates. Compared with the extent of currency depreciation in other European countries, the schilling's delayed downward adjustment was insignificant and certainly failed to enhance competitiveness of Austrian export trades. However, two points can be raised in defense of Kienböck's policies. First, given the enormous size of Austria's foreign debt, yielding to the demands of "devaluationists" would have meant a notable increase of the country's debt service bill. And, second, the logic of conservative reform demanded a lowering of production costs in all sectors of the Austrian economy. At repeated occasions Kienböck stressed the pivotal role of his bank of issue in forcing the national wage level down (for example by denying credit to firms with excessive payroll costs).[21] Currency depreciation as an easy way to gain comparative export advantage would have thwarted such efforts from the beginning and, hence, had to be avoided—if one accepted the rationale of mainstream trade theory.

Politics as the Decisive Factor in Austria's "Financial Reconstruction" after 1932 and Resulting Attitudes of the League

It is important to note that Austrian budgetary and monetary reconstruction unfolded in 1931 and early 1932, prior to the flotation of an international rescue loan, and even before size and scope of such a loan were defined in the document later known as the Lausanne Protocol. Also, many important steps to consolidate Austria's banking sector preceded the arrival of League financial assistance. The *Credit-Anstalt*'s huge domestic debt with the bank of issue (approximately 700 million schillings) was transformed into a debt of the Austrian confederation and divided into two parts. The larger section was to be repayed out of the proceeds of a planned domestic loan. Redemption of the other part was postponed until after 1946. In January 1933, all foreign creditors of the *Credit-Anstalt* agreed to a settlement by which their existing claims against the bank (422 million schillings) were exchanged for new preferential shares (70 million schillings), bonds of a holding company created to sell off industrial assets formerly in the *Credit-Anstalt*'s portfolio (140 million schillings), and "live claims" to be honored over a period of 7-16.5 years (212 million schillings).[22]

Just a couple of weeks after the conclusion of the *Credit-Anstalt* settlement, two other large Viennese banks turned to the state for help. Both the *Wiener Bankverein* and the *Niederösterreichische Escomptegesellschaft* had accumulated enormous debts and could only be kept afloat by means of a rescue operation that would cost the taxpayer 100 million schillings, and the National Bank another 40 million schillings. The decision to intervene on behalf of the banks was made public after a three-day emergency meeting of the cabinet council (18-20 March 1933). It was openly backed by the League of Nations' representative in Austria, Rost van Tonningen.[23]

The banking decrees of March 1933 (like other economic measures discussed below), which seriously infringed the principle of liberal economics to avoid public subsidizing of private business, should be seen in context with the troubled situation of Austria's government then in power. The cabinet of Engelbert Dollfuss, a Christian Social agricultural expert who replaced Karl Buresch as chancellor in May 1932, initially commanded a majority of one single vote in the Austrian Parliament. Under permanent threat of defection by renegade MPs of the Christian Socials' smaller coalition partners (the Pangermanic *Landbund* and the Fascist *Heimwehren*), Dollfuss managed to secure parliamentary approval for the Lausanne Protocol of 15 July 1932, thus clearing the way for the long-awaited League of Nations loan.[24] But the extended and bitter fight in both chambers of Austria's legislative body over ratification of "Lausanne"—opposed on economic grounds by the Social Democrats, and on political grounds by the Pangermans—fatally weakened the chancellor's commitment to democracy. Other factors contributed to this development. While being exposed to increasing pressure from ultra-right *Heimwehr* leaders, who wished to transform Austria into an authoritarian state, Dollfuss also had reasons to fear National Socialist successes at the polls. Prior to the formation of his cabinet, the Nazis had won landslide victories over both the Catholic and Pangerman parties at communal elections in Vienna and Innsbruck. As a result of this, the Social Democrats demanded nationwide elections in the fall of 1932. They expected the National Socialists to gain enough bourgeois votes to either force the demoralized *Christlichsozialen* into a left-center coalition, or to join a government themselves, in which Socialists would play the leading role. The spectre of an "unholy" alliance of Austro-Marxists and followers of Hitler led many Christian Social politicians, otherwise sceptical of methods of "government by decree," to believe in the merits of at least temporary suspension of parliamentarism.

The course of events, from the crucial appointment of Emil Fey (head of the Viennese *Heimwehr*) to the post of state secretary of public security in October 1932, to the forced dissolution of the Austrian Parliament on 15 March 1933, need not be described here. Suffice it to say that the League of Nations representative in Vienna, as we learn from a diary he kept during the year 1934, claimed a decisive share in the destruction of Austrian democracy. Rost van Tonningen left no doubt about why he preferred a semi-Fascist dictatorship exercised by Dollfuss to parliamentary rule. Like Italy's Benito Mussolini—the most outspoken supporter of the Dollfuss-regime among foreign statesmen—Rost believed that a crushing defeat of Austria's Social Democratic Party through elimination of its stronghold in the national assembly (*Nationalrat*) and subsequent government by emergency decrees would greatly facilitate containment of the Nazi peril. The developments after March 1933 proved this theory wrong as Hitler's Austrian followers, encouraged and financed by the new Nazi rulers of Germany, committed a series of terrorist bombings to chase Dollfuss out of office. In reaction to the National Socialist violence, Rost van Tonningen, in his capacity as self-proclaimed "best friend of Austria," recommended that the Dollfuss government (1) invigorate its assault on Marxism and end Social Democratic dominance of the federal capital Vienna by use of military force, (2) expropriate the financial assets of Vienna's "red" municipality and use them to cover military and police expenses, and (3) ask the League of Nations' permission to depart from orthodox methods of credit restriction stipulated by the Lausanne Protocol. The point here was to gain some elbow-room for state-financed job creation programs, designed to reduce the appeal of Nazism and Socialism to frustrated unemployed workers.

Let us now resume our discussion of the main characteristics of Austrian League reconstruction work in the wake of Dollfuss's authoritarian coup. To an extent which is often downplayed by economic historians, Geneva-based financial experts departed from their earlier deflationist views and allowed themselves to be guided primarily by their desire to warrant the stability of the Dollfuss regime. Just a week after armed police had denied Austrian members of Parliament access to the *Nationalrat* building in Vienna (15 March 1933),[25] the League assented to state subsidies on behalf of the *Bankverein* and *Escomptegesellschaft*. As noted above, this was clearly in contradiction to liberal economic principles. But League experts could justify their step by pointing to the expected beneficial effects to Austrian economy of an emergency decree on wage-cuts in the banking sector (*Bankenentlastungsverordnung*), issued by the government as part and parcel of the two-bank rescue package.

No justification other than fear of political turmoil in Austria existed for the League's surprising preparedness to deviate from the stipulations of the Lausanne Protocol concerning employment of the proceeds of the international and the domestic loan floated in summer and fall 1933, respectively. The original agreement required that the 300 million schilling yield of the foreign loan be utilized for repayment of earlier Bank of England and BIS loans in favor of the *Credit-Anstalt*, and for repayment of state debts to the bank of issue. The purpose of the domestic loan, as originally intended, was to provide the state with means for purchasing *Credit-Anstalt* bills from the National Bank. However, haunted by the prospect of Dollfuss losing his two-front battle against Socialist and Nazi opponents, League Financial Committee members—urged by Rost van Tonningen—gave authorization to spend loan proceeds totalling 265 million schilling*s* for job-creating public investment schemes. Somewhat earlier, the committee agreed to a proposal made by Austria's finance minister to split the government budget into two parts. "Irregular" expenses (i.e. outlays for stimulation of the economy) would find their place in the so-called *Extraordinarium*, while recurrent regular expenditure covered out of tax receipts remained to be shown in the *Ordinarium*. The extraordinary budget soon proved its value as a device for cheating, i.e., concealing common state deficits. Only a fraction of it did actually serve to finance productive investment programs, while the lion's share was diverted to cover the cost of an army and police buildup against "red" and "brown" threats, partly imaginary, partly real. During 1934, most of the Dollfuss government's expenses incurred in the civil war of February and in the crushing of the Nazi putsch of July got transferred into the *Extraordinarium*. Despite warnings from a French member of the League Financial Committee, Gabriel Dayras, that Austrian budget figures did not mirror the true state of things, the League remained silent. Dayras also pointed at the largely illusory character of Dollfuss's effort to check unemployment: The 1933 domestic loan, he wrote, was wasted for nothing but a bogus scheme of public investment, "*un prétendu programme d'outillage national.*"[26]

As a last instance of League leniency towards Austrian violations against rules of sound finance, I will, very briefly, discuss Dollfuss's agrarian policy. With his political strength firmly rooted in (eastern) Austrian peasantry, the chancellor could not afford to fully expose the farming sector to the imponderables of the Great Depression. As a result of this, agrarian protectionism became a dominant feature of Austrian management of economic crisis after 1932. More than that: Whenever state assistance to suffering sections of industry or trade was considered, agricultural lobbies claimed their share in the rescue programs, irrespective of an existing causal connection. A case in point were the banking reconstruction acts of March 1933. They were linked with a generous government donation of forty million schillings to peasant mortgage debtors. Similarly, when in the spring of 1934 the *Wiener Bankverein* and *Niederösterreichische Escomptegesellschaft* were merged into the recapitalized *Credit-Anstalt*, agriculture managed to extract from the Dollfuss government a sum of ten million schillings to reduce farmers' debts. While League of Nations experts were utterly critical of such practice, they refrained from serious protesting for the sake of domestic stability in Austria.[27]

League Presence during the Schuschnigg Era: Resurging Deflationism, and the Ultimate Triumph of Politics

Engelbert Dollfuss was murdered on 25 July 1934 by an SS-squad storming the Vienna federal chancellery in a futile attempt at bringing Austria's National Socialists to power. Dollfuss's popularity in Western Europe, after reaching its peak at the time of the London economic conference of June 1933,[28] had considerably suffered since the brutal display of government military force against Socialist workers in the civil war of February 1934. But to his last day he was considered a valuable partner in western containment strategies against Hitler's Germany. Few expected his place to be easily filled by another Austrian politician. Succession to his office by a pro-German Catholic lawyer, Kurt Schuschnigg, consequently did not fail to alter the relationship between Austria and the League of Nations. This was largely due to the fact that the League's representative in Austria, Rost van Tonningen, had been Dollfuss's close friend and confidant in political matters. Rost felt no such loyalty towards Schuschnigg. Instead, he began to talk with admiration of Hitler and developed a strange taste for the National Socialist economic policies employed in Germany, especially for Hjalmar Schacht's methods of dealing with the

Reich's foreign creditors and for public works like the German *Autobahn* project.

The psychological causes for Rost's attraction to National Socialism are not our topic here. But we must take into account the impact of his growing Nazi and German sympathies on his work as a League functionary. This impact was already discernible in late summer 1934, when Rost, together with the Bank of England's Ernst Niemeyer, succeeded in convincing Austria's foreign creditors at the League's September session in Geneva to agree to a conversion of the outstanding portion of the 1923 international loan. For Austria, this rescheduling operation brought the double advantage of lowered interest rates and a three year suspension of debt service. Western creditors and the League could pride themselves to have prevented Austria from following Schacht's example of a one-sided moratorium at the price of an average 2% reduction of their return on investment.[29] There are good reasons to believe that Rost would have recommended to Schuschnigg a deferral of debt repayment in the case of a failure of the Geneva negotiations.

In spite of the positive effects of loan conversion on the Austrian budget of 1935, the remaining 160 million schilling deficit forbade state funding for substantial job-creating schemes. This is why the Schuschnigg government, fearing the impact of Hitler's successful employment policies on Austrian public opinion, proposed a new domestic labor loan (*Arbeitsanleihe*). League representative Rost van Tonningen lobbied the financial committee to get the Austrian plans approved and even submitted detailed proposals for the utilization of the forthcoming loan proceeds. Austria should follow Hitler's example and build superhighways and aerodromes. In fact, the size of public works put into effect in 1935 remained negligible, as huge portions of the fresh loan were employed to cover ordinary state expenses. Knowing that a major effort at balancing the budget would be required, Schuschnigg appointed a new minister of finance from the ranks of the *Heimwehr*, Ludwig Draxler, in October 1935. Within one year, Draxler managed to reduce Austria's budget deficit to approximately 34 million schillings, less than 0.5% of the gross domestic product.[30] This astonishing result was achieved while the Austrian economy suffered from a drastically overvalued schilling. Due to the National Bank's refusal to participate in a round of European currency devaluations, Austria's competitors in world markets enjoyed a comparative exchange rate advantage of between 5% and 32%.[31]

Surprisingly little attention was payed not only by Austrian economic decision makers, but also by the League of Nations to the foreseeable political effects of Draxler's fiscal restraint program. As Erich Hans Wolf, an economic publicist who emigrated to Switzerland in 1938, correctly pointed out, uncompromising Austrian deflationism (applauded by the

League) would damage mass morale and result in overwhelming support of a Nazi takeover by the man in the street.[32] Wolf was wrong in supposing, though, that both Kienböck's refusal to devaluate the schilling and Draxler's decision to balance the budget in 1936 were elements of a pro-German conspiracy. The Anschluss was neither in the interest of Austria's central bank governor nor desired by the finance minister. The same cannot be said of Rost van Tonningen, representative of the League in Austria, who became fatally involved with National Socialism. Eager to see his host country freed from the "fetters" of Anglo-French credit, and convinced that joining the German Reich would serve the Austrian economy better than staying in the orbit of the League's "Shylock-system," Rost abruptly tendered his resignation on 3 August 1936. His move came shortly after Chancellor Schuschnigg's conclusion of a "peace-treaty" with Hitler, in July 1936. Together, these events sealed the fate of a partnership between Austria and the League of Nations, which, in spite of occasional tensions, successfully defended Austrian independent statehood for more than fifteen years.

Notes

1. Peter Berger, "Meinoud Marinus Rost van Tonningen. Vertreter des Völkerbundes in Österreich. Ein Forschungsbericht," *Zeitgeschichte* 11/12 (1990/1991): 351-78.

2. Pelt Papers P.103:12, Control of Austria (1922), Archives of the League of Nations, Geneva.

3. Karl Bachinger and Leonhard Bauer, "Daktylogramme des Gesellschaftlichen," in *Auf Heller und Cent. Beiträge zur Finanz- und Währungsgeschichte*, ed. Karl Bachinger and Dieter Stiefel (Frankfurt: Ueberreuter, 2001), 539-72.

4. Siegfried Mattl, "Die Finanzdiktatur. Wirtschaftspolitik in Österreich 1933-1938," in *Austrofaschismus. Beiträge über Politik, Ökonomie und Kultur 1934-1938*, ed. Emmerich Tálos and Wolfgang Neugebauer (Vienna: Verlag Jugend und Volk, 1984), 133-59.

5. Karl Bachinger and Herbert Matis, *Der österreichische Schilling. Geschichte einer Währung* (Graz: Styria, 1974); Karl Bachinger, Felix Buschek, Herbert Matis, and Dieter Stiefel, *Abschied vom Schilling. Eine österreichische Wirtschaftsgeschichte* (Graz: Styria, 2001).

6. Ibid., 65.

7. Jacques Bosmans, *De Nederlander Mr. A.R.Zimmerman als Commissaris-Generaal van de Volkenbond in Oostenrijk 1922-1926* (Nijmegen: Gebr.Janssen, 1973).

8. Nicole Pietri, *La reconstruction financière de l'Autriche, 1921-1926* (Genève: Centre europèen de la Donation Carnegie, 1970).

9. Grete Klingenstein, *Die Anleihe von Lausanne. Ein Beitrag zur Geschichte der Ersten Republik in den Jahren 1931-1934* (Vienna: Böhlau, 1965).

10. RvT 54, "The Book," 24, Netherlands' Institute for War Documentation, Amsterdam.

11. Peter-Robert Berger, *Der Donauraum im wirtschaftlichen Umbruch nach dem Ersten Weltkrieg* (Vienna: VWGÖ, 1982), 477.

12. Pietri, *La reconstruction financière*, 145ff.

13. Fritz Weber, "Vor dem großen Krach. Die Krise des österreichischen Bankwesens in den zwanziger Jahren," Habilitation, Salzburg University, 1991.

14. Dieter Stiefel, *Die große Krise in einem kleinen Land. Österreichische Finanz- und Wirtschaftspolitik 1929-1938* (Vienna: Böhlau, 1988).

15. Peter Berger, *Im Schatten der Diktatur. Die Finanzdiplomatie des Vertreters des Völkerbundes in Österreich Meinoud Marinus Rost van Tonningen, 1931-1936* (Vienna: Böhlau, 2000), 170f.

16. Dieter Stiefel, *Arbeitslosigkeit. Soziale, politische und wirtschaftliche Auswirkungen – am Beispiel Österreichs 1918-1938* (Berlin: Duncker & Humblot, 1979), 29.

17. Bachinger, et al., *Abschied vom Schilling*, 41.

18. Stiefel, *Die große Krise*, 101.

19. Ibid., 50.

20. Memorandum on Monetary Situation in the Danubian Countries, 25 April 1932, Bank of England Archive, London.

21. Berger, *Im Schatten der Diktatur*, 229.

22. Ibid., 262f.

23. Ibid., 272ff.

24. R. John Rath, "The Dollfuß Ministry: The Democratic Prelude," *Austrian History Yearbook* XXIX (1998, Part 1): 161-94.

25. Gordon Brook-Shepherd, *Österreich* (Vienna: Paul Zsolnay Verlag, 1995), 374.

26. Berger, *Im Schatten der Diktatur*, 323.

27. Ibid., 346.

28. Ibid., 372.

29. Ibid., 365f.

30. Bachinger, *Abschied vom Schilling*, 23.

31. Berger, *Im Schatten der Diktatur*, 445.

32. Erich Hans Wolf, *Katastrophenwirtschaft. Geburt und Ende Österreichs 1918-1938* (Zurich: Europa Verlag, 1939).

Economic Performance and Micro-Economic Development in Austria, 1929-1938

Jens-Wilhelm Wessels

I. Introduction

The Austrian economy of the interwar period was crisis-ridden. It suffered from inflation, underwent stabilization crises and erratic growth in the 1920s, and hardly attained the prewar national income level before the Great Depression hit. Then the impact of the slump was enormous. While Austria already had a low level of economic growth, the decline of its national income and industrial production until 1932 was comparable to that of Germany and the United States. Between 1929 and 1933, the value of exports in this trade-dependent country dropped to nearly half its original value and finally reached its absolute low point of the interwar period.[1] Whereas other countries had surpassed or attained pre-crisis levels of national income by the late 1930s, Austria had only reached 86.5% of the 1929 Gross National Product (GNP) by 1937.[2] The actual pre-World War I per capita income level was not surpassed until 1950.[3]

Austria has been known for its unusually restrictive and orthodox economic policy. Only for a short period in the late 1920s, due to moderate prosperity, its economic policy became a bit more progressive. During the worst years of the depression and thereafter, however, this trend was once again reversed. In spite of only sluggish recovery, Austria's policy strictly adhered to orthodox financial principles, while counter-cyclical interventionist policies were increasingly applied elsewhere.[4]

Considering the concurrence of poor economic performance with the restrictive policy of the First Republic and the proto-fascist *Ständestaat*, it is no surprise that Austria's policy-making of that period has not only been harshly criticized by contemporary journalists[5] and many modern scholars,[6] but has also been regarded as a major factor in the economic disaster of the interwar period.[7] Furthermore, historiographers have shown a direct connection between this policy, economic misery in the 1930s, and the apparent ease of the takeover of Austria by National Socialist Germany in March 1938.[8]

However, while it is certainly true that deflationary policy impeded economic recovery, the micro-economic development shows that these policy implications have been overestimated; long-term structural preconditions, circumstances, and transformations were the primary determinants of economic growth. The main precondition was the fact that Austria was a small, advanced, industrialized, and trade-dependent country, constrained by an international economic environment of nationalism, retrenchment, protectionism, and stagnant world trade. The combination of this precondition and this economic environment resulted in massive disadvantages for Austria: It diminished the potential effects that economic policies could have had in a small national economy and restricted Austria's competitive position in international markets.

II. Structural Determinants of Performance

1. Worldwide transformations

In addition to the depression, two global structural shifts were taking place during the interwar period that were, under the circumstances, more difficult to face for small advanced countries than for the largest industrialized nations. The first major shift manifested itself in the modern industrialized countries, which underwent a transformation process from traditional industries (such as iron and steel, coal, and textiles) to modern industries (such as chemical, electric, and motor industries). The latter were based on the large-scale application of innovations of the late 19th century. The transformation was also accompanied by an increasing employment of new technology by old industries. Moreover, this change went hand in hand with the emergence and dissemination of mass consumption markets that combined high purchasing power with a favorable distribution of wealth. This "second industrial revolution" within modern economies was distorted in interwar Europe and caused the move towards the classical advanced 20th century economy to be increasingly focused on the concentration of growth and development on advanced large national economies.[9]

The theoretical framework for this structural approach is based on Schumpeter's endogenous growth theory.[10] It describes economic growth and development as the constant repetition of revolutions within industrial structures at the core of the evolutionary process of capitalism, and as largely unrestrained by political or intentional events.[11] These transformations were visible in long-term business cycles.[12] The "process of creative destruction"[13] based on a permanent change of industrial structures to the large-scale application of new technology, production, and consumption processes determined to a great extent long-term economic growth and development. However, in interwar Europe, this process was distorted and slowed down, causing the differences of international competitiveness and productivity of national producers in various countries to increase. In an effort to shield their markets from foreign competition, these differences, in turn, resulted in intensifying protectionism and retrenchment of producers to their national economies. The most influential national producers in various countries pushed for trade protectionism in an attempt to equaliże the lower "productivity of labour, land, and capital of [their] national economy with the superior productivity of other countries . . . ."[14]

The second long-term structural transformation was an intensifying and accelerating expansion of industrialization in the world economic periphery and in the advanced countries outside of Europe, such as the United States and Canada. The most prominent areas of intensifying industrialization in the periphery were in particular Japan and Russia, South-Eastern Europe, some of the British colonies, and, to some extent, India and China. The war in Europe actually facilitated this process of peripheral industrialization as the traditional European domination of international markets was temporarily checked. Peripheral industrialization primarily relied on the emergence, growth, and development of the classical traditional industries of the 19th century. Thus, many of those industrial sectors that stagnated in the old industrialized countries began to expand rapidly in the periphery during the interwar period and contributed to the emergence of productive over-capacities, to the slow growth of world trade, and to the increase in competitive pressures on many traditional industries in Europe.[15]

Naturally, these processes and changes were detrimental to the economic growth and development in countries such as Austria, which had relatively large export industries with small domestic markets and little economic leverage on international markets.

2. Export dependence and economic policy

In this environment of global structural changes, small advanced countries largely depended on international trade for their economic growth. This dependence, together with the constraints it placed on these countries' national policies, was a main factor determining their economic performance. This can be illustrated by a simple comparison of relative export rates with growth rates of national income. (See Table 1: Relation of Exports to National Product and Growth in 1936 and 1928.)

Between 1928 and 1936, the average export rates of the smaller countries declined faster than those of the large industrialized countries. At the same time, world trade contracted to a greater extent and recovered much more slowly than industrial production.[16] The trade in value and volume never recovered from this blow until the war.[17] After 1933, world production increased again due to an upswing of industrial domestic markets, but world trade never came close to the growth rate of industrial production.[18] The fact that advanced small countries relied heavily on foreign trade for economic growth can be seen in the lower growth rates of these countries, at a time when foreign trade was stagnating. Although the average export rate (20%) was substantially higher, the average increase of Austrian, Belgian, Czechoslovak, and Danish national income over six years, starting from the incredibly low level of 1932, was just 10.3%. It is also interesting to note that the two most industrialized successor states of the Austro-Hungarian Empire had a much lower export rate than the advanced small countries of Western Europe. This reveals their still lower level of integration into the modern international economic system of trade. Larger countries like Germany, France, the United Kingdom, and Italy enjoyed an average growth rate of 24.4%, even though their average value of exports was only 6.4% of the national income. In the 1920s, their average export rate had been twice as high. In 1936, they could regain fairly high growth rates with a lower export rate because most of these countries were able to focus their economic expansion on the resources and demand of their large domestic markets. Trade was of only secondary importance to them. It was far easier for the large countries to incite sufficient domestic demand for higher growth and structural change than for the small national economies with their relatively large national producers and small domestic markets. Moreover, a reduction of trade also hit a small country more severely because export industries generally suffer much more from contracting trade than industries producing for home markets.[19] As Austria had a relatively large export industry, the country's vulnerability to the decline of international trade was far greater than that of almost all other industrialized countries.

Thus, for the Austrian economy, already constrained by enormous financial problems, it was practically impossible, albeit feasible in theory,[20] to compensate a loss of foreign trade demand that amounted to around 20% of the national income; this was the average annual value of exports in the 1920s, or about half of the Austrian industrial production, the usual portion of industrial output sold abroad.[21] As the export demand dropped dramatically already in 1930 and hardly recovered after 1933, Austria was heavily hit by the massive decline of world trade. Recovery was barely possible since the volume of world trade itself only slowly recovered. The value of Austrian exports in 1936 only reached 60.4% of its pre-depression level, but this was still higher than the value of exports of most European industrialized countries, which, on average, only reached about 46.5% of their 1929 export value level.[22] The vital difference, though, is that many of these countries were not as dependent on foreign trade. When Austrian export figures finally increased considerably in 1937, it was mainly due to the higher foreign demand for armament, particularly in the most important neighboring countries of Germany, Italy, and Czechoslovakia.

Table 1: Relation of Exports to National Product and Growth in 1936 and 1928

	Austria	Belgium	CSR	Denmark
GDP Growth Rate 1932-1937:	7.8%	9.7%	9.7%	14%
Export Share of GNP in 1936:	14.8%	33%	12.4%	20%
Export Share of GNP in 1928:	24.5%	55.4%	29.7%	29%

	Germany	France	UK	Italy
GDP Growth Rate 1932-1937:	50.4%	7.8%	23%	16.4%
Export Share of GNP in 1936:	8.3%	4.2%	8.6%	4.4%
Export Share of GNP in 1928	13.6%	12.5%	14.7%	8.7%

(In million national currency at current prices)
Source: Compiled from various data.[23]

Therefore, Austria's major source of income, export sales, was harshly curtailed by the precipitous reduction of imports from its most important trading partners. The massive loss of export demand could not be compensated. In the period of most dramatic export contraction (1929 to 1933), the theoretical average annual deficit of export demand, compared to its 1929 level, amounted to more than 707 million Schillings. That was about 6% of the 1929 GNP. Thereafter, it amounted to 850.5 million Schillings until 1937. Under the financial and political circumstances, it would have been impossible for the national economic policy to even attempt to substitute this loss, neither before nor after 1933. The Austrian government would have had to compensate for a loss of aggregate demand in the amount of more than 6.2 billion Schillings between 1930 and 1937![24] Only the annexation of Austria, the ensuing incorporation into the German economy, and aggressive Nazi economic policy brought a compensation for the massive deficit of demand. Compared to the 1929 export level, the theoretical annual deficit of demand amounted to 549 Schillings in 1937.[25] The following year, after the Anschluss, the Austrian economy benefited from 750 million Schillings worth of German state orders and investments, or nearly 8% of the 1937 GNP.[26] In 1939, unemployment in Austria was virtually wiped out.

III. Micro-economic Development

The limitations of Austria's economic policy and of its structural preconditions, circumstances, long-term transformations, and their negative effects were directly reflected in the business of the largest Austrian industrial joint-stock companies. Only the development of some of the most important companies will be examined here.[27]

In Austria, as in most countries, the depression and incomplete recovery during the 1930s had catastrophic consequences for all industrial sectors. Not only did they undergo an unprecedented slump, but almost all enterprises were unable to recover from this blow before 1938. Pre-depression investment, demand, and production levels could not be reached again. The production capacity remained under-employed and unchanged. It is safe to say that the process of secular transformation, the increasing growth of new industries, and the application of new technologies drastically slowed down, or even stopped altogether in the 1930s. The retreat of Austria's most important trading partners to economic nationalism and domestic growth, in addition to the protectionist economic policies that went along with this process, directly harmed Austria's export-oriented enterprises. Furthermore, the export demand structure reflected the effort of rearmament in its immediate neighbors. Surprisingly though, most enterprises survived the depression and were able to cope with and adjust to the stagnating growth and development.

The performance of the various industrial sectors was quite different. Between 1933 and 1937, the growth rates of most industrial sectors were considerable. However, this only appears so at first sight because production levels of nearly all branches had fallen so low before 1933. Compared to the incredibly low production levels after the precipitous decline, vehicle production, for example, was now nearly five times as much as before. Iron production increased by 166%, iron and steel processing by 98%; the output of the paper industry rose by 22%, and the textile and leather production by 49%.

However, when comparing production levels of 1929 and 1937, the picture is very different. Almost all industrial sectors had not yet regained their pre-depression production levels by the end of this period. The iron and steel processing industries, as well as the wood, chemical, and vehicle manufacturing industries were still around 30% below their 1929 production levels. Only mining, oil, magnesite, and the iron producing industries nearly recovered their pre-crisis output levels. Among other traditional industries, only paper (7.8%) and textiles (17%) surpassed their pre-depression levels. Of the modern industries, only the electricity supply industry considerably expanded its output (17.6%).[28]

Since capacity was under-utilized and business activity and prospects were low, the incentive for investment and depreciation was depressed.

Until 1937, aggregate investment only reached a bit over half of the already low 1929 investment level. The annual investment rate was merely between 5.1% and 7.4%, whereas it had been 9.9% in 1929.[29] While the productive capital asset had only been moderately increased in the late 1920s, with investment rates of between 5% and 10%, there was an actual reduction of capital asset during the depression. Thereafter, low profit prospects induced companies to lower depreciation and investment. The investment rate was below 5%, resulting in a general stagnation and deterioration of productive assets.[30]

1. Traditional industries

1.1. The mining industry: Veitscher Magnesitwerke AG

The *Veitscher Magnesitwerke AG* is a typical example of the decline of European industry during the interwar period.[31] It is also a good example of how little companies and whole branches of industry, in this case the magnesite industry, were influenced by politics and economic policy. The *Veitscher* company clearly shows that disintegration, inflation, deflation, a well as economic and currency policy shifts had little effect on the development of industry at the time. Instead, the management was much more concerned about the partial loss of formerly very important markets, the creation of worldwide over-capacities, peripheral industrialization, cartel agreements, and the international business cycles of the various national iron and steel industries because these factors essentially determined the performance.

In the mining industry, in fact among all other branches of industry in Austria, the development of the Austrian magnesite industry was quite unique. It held a special position of strength within the modern world economy, as it played a key role supplying a vital natural resource for the worldwide production of iron and steel. Magnesite, in its various forms, was a very important material for the production of iron and steel because it formed the basis of the heat resistant material for blast furnaces. As this material had to be renewed regularly with continuing iron and steel production, constant demand was ensured. Therefore, magnesite production completely depended on the business cycle development of the international iron and steel industry.

The Austrian magnesite industry was the oldest and largest of its kind and had a world monopoly before the war.[32] At that time, magnesite was processed almost exclusively in Austria, in large amounts with high quality. The boom of this industry culminated in the year 1913. Its major customers were the North American and West European iron and steel industries. Of course, World War I temporarily overthrew this market domination because the Austrian monopoly was suddenly cut off from world trade, and because iron and steel industries abroad began to explore and exploit other sources of magnesite supply. Before the end of the war, the American iron and steel industry had started to mine magnesite of lower quality in Washington state.[33] The Western European countries had also built-up their own magnesite mining industries. However, these were inefficient and the mines were of low quality so that they could only exist in war economies. Moreover, the mines of North America and Western Europe could not satisfy market demands. Therefore, after 1918, Austrian firms partially recovered the magnesite market.

Still, the Austrian magnesite mining industry had lost large shares of the world market as more production capacities had not only been developed in America and Europe, but also in Asia. Russia, for example, had the largest magnesite deposits in the world and became the largest producer in the 1930s. Also in Manchuria large deposits were found and exploited. The results were over-capacities in the worldwide magnesite production of the interwar period. Asian markets, especially the important Japanese market, were lost for the Austrians, and the vital markets of the United States and Western Europe had to be shared with other local producers.[34]

However, *Veitscher*, by far the biggest magnesite company in Austria, continued to be one of the largest suppliers of this natural resource in the world and dominated the European magnesite cartel, founded in the mid-1920s.[35] Thus, it was in a fairly safe position, even though it could not regain its prewar market position and production volume. Essentially, the company was financially prosperous, while its real economic development stagnated. Although production was modernized and rationalized, its output was far lower than before the war.

The world economic depression had catastrophic effects on the production and sales performance of this highly export-dependent industrial sector, since its main customer, the world iron and steel industry, went through a dramatic decline in the early 1930s.[36] Total Austrian magnesite exports declined from almost 120,000 tons to 33,000 tons in 1932. The largest customer of *Veitscher*, the North American iron and steel industry, reduced its demand by 94% between 1929 and 1932.[37] The dissatisfying import agreements of 1929 with Harbison and General, the main importer of the United States, had to be discarded in the face of crisis.[38] In this period, *Veitscher's production shrunk by 79%, and the total Austrian production by 68%.*[39] *After 1931, Austria was overtaken by Soviet Russia as the largest producer of magnesite in the world.*

Financial standing

Financially, the blow was by far not as heavy. *Veitscher's* financial standing remained excellent and could easily resist crisis shocks, even of this magnitude, although its gross profits declined from almost 4.2 million Schillings to one million Schillings by 1932. Because the firm was unable to lower expenses accordingly, a minor deficit of 40,000 Schillings ensued in 1932. The company's management was also forced to lower the high dividend of 18% to 6% in 1931. The entailing increase of creditor value was easily covered by substantial financial reserves. Already by 1933, *Veitscher* had made a profit of 613,000 Schillings, and in 1936 the company reached its pre-crisis profitability level again. Furthermore, it had large bank deposits, and the value of liabilities remained well below debtor value. The management could once again afford to assume the payment of very high rates of dividends. While only 110 of the 297 large Austrian enterprises[40] could pay any dividend at all, and most of them only disbursed between 3% and 8%,[41] *Veitscher* was able to grant a 20% dividend in 1937.[42] With this financial background it was easily possible to maintain depreciation and investments on sufficiently high levels, enabling the management to modernize and increase the value of capital assets, even though the firm's capacity was under-utilized most of the time. The value of productive capital increased from 13.5 million Schillings to 17.5 million Schillings between 1924 and 1937, including a total depreciation of 12.5 million Schillings.[43]

Business activity

By mid-1930, a decline in demand was noticed as a result of the diminishing iron and steel production abroad. Yet, this was still a minor blow compared to the following two years when the capacity utilization of the world iron and steel industry dropped to 25%. In 1932, magnesite export sales, declining another 46%, reached rock bottom.

The *Veitscher* company experienced another upswing in 1933. Austrian exports nearly doubled and the American iron and steel works were again the main customers. Also, British iron and steel producers substantially increased their demand. However, due to falling prices, the rise of profits was not proportionate to the increase of production and sales. The low prices were, to some degree, the result of the dollar depreciation. Although production and sales were rising and financial development was positive, recovery progressed very slowly. In 1934, still only 26% of the capacity was employed. This slow upswing was commensurate to the slow recovery of the world iron and steel industry.

Similar to the development of the main Austrian iron and steel producer, the *Österreichisch-Alpine Montangesellschaft*,[44] *Veitscher* production also benefited from the rearmament boom starting in the mid-1930s. From 1935 onwards, production and export sales finally started to pick up, and markets began to change, reflecting the shift of demand in Europe.

Whereas American demand stagnated after 1933, demand from iron and steel producers in the authoritarian states was sharply increased. Between 1933 and 1937, German producers bought between 31% and 44% of Austrian magnesite exports.[45] Total exports more than doubled. In the same time span, total Austrian magnesite production increased by more than 60%, reaching nearly 400,000 tons in 1937, about 91% of the 1929 output.[46] Only Soviet Russian production was higher. The majority of total Austrian magnesite exports went to the rearming states in Europe. Furthermore, magnesite brick—about one-third of the total value of sales—was delivered to Germany, France, Britain, the Scandinavian countries, India, and South Africa. Total Austrian brick export doubled after 1933.[47] Although the capacity utilization was still only 40%, in 1935 and 1936 *Veitscher* production and export sales experienced a massive expansion. The importance of the American market for Austrian magnesite producers declined, as only a fraction of sales went to the United States. This market was well protected by tariffs and was now completely in the hands of the national importers and Canadian producers.

2. *Modern industries*

2.1. Electrical engineering industry

2.1.1. International development

The electrical engineering industry proved to be the most stable, crisis-resistant, and successful sector of the interwar period. Considering all the domestic electricity supply companies and the four large electrical engineering companies in Austria, the *Österreichische Siemens Schuckert Werke*,[48] the *Allgemeine Elektrizitäts-Gesellschaft Union Austria* (AEG),[49] the *Österreichische Brown-Boveri Werke AG*,[50] and the *Elin Aktiengesellschaft für Elektrische Industrie*, this sector was of considerable size for a small country.

Until the late 1920s, domestic demand for electrical engineering was increasing, but the companies' proportion of total sales declined slightly. The Austrian market could not offer sufficient employment. Thus, the four companies increased their export sales in the second half of the 1920s in order to utilize their capacity of production sufficiently. They benefited from a steady demand from the international markets. The above-average growth of the electrical engineering industry in industrialized Europe and America was generally due to the change from steam-powered electricity generating engines to new combustion engines and hydropowered engines. Demand for electricity generators of all types, based on hydro- and conventional combustion engine power, increased enormously.[51]

By far the largest producers and exporters of electrical power generating machinery were Germany, the United States, Britain, and Switzerland.

The next largest group of producers included Sweden and France, followed by Italy, the Netherlands, and Austria. The latter three had about the same export capacity, between 1.7% and 3.3% of the world trade in electrical goods. Between 1925 and 1929, export growth was the strongest in Germany, with an increase of 43.6%. The American electrical engineering industry was much less oriented to foreign markets and its export sales increased only by 15%. Austrian export expansion amounted to 30%, well within the European average.[52]

Thus, at the time, export conditions were favorable, as demand for high-end technology of electromechanical machinery was rising abroad, even though tariffs were fairly high[53] The major Austrian export markets were Germany, the area of the successor states, and the Balkans. Some products went to Russia and also to areas outside of Europe. The main competitors on the Austrian market were German firms and on the markets in Eastern Europe, German and American companies, such as General Electric, the German *AEG* and *Siemens*.

The *Österreichische Siemens* and the Austrian *AEG*, as the only and largest representatives of their German mother firms, had certain market shares in Eastern Europe delegated by their parent firms. The *Siemens* plant in Austria was the largest investment of the German *Siemens* in Central and Eastern Europe.[54] Because the Austrian market was much too small for them, these firms were forced to export to the areas of South-Central and Eastern Europe. The Austrian *Siemens* had factories in each of the main successor states. Both originally German firms, *AEG* and *Siemens* were the main competitors of the only electrical engineering company that was purely Austrian, the *Elin AG*. This firm will be discussed later. *Brown-Boveri* was a Swiss subsidiary company.

The depression changed the relatively favorable trade conditions for the Austrian companies, since national producers increasingly retrenched to their domestic markets, focusing business on a considerable expansion of electricity supply in all advanced and developing countries and on recovering the market demand in the 1930s. The rate of expansion varied, according to the volume, rate of expansion, development before 1929, and the size of the economy. In Austria, however, the rate of expansion, compared to the Netherlands, Switzerland, and Belgium, was among the lowest. British and German rates of expansion were well above those in the small countries.[55]

Unlike the development of the 1920s, the increase in production of electrical machinery and goods in the 1930s was primarily based on domestic growth and demand, while the importance of foreign trade for national producers worldwide declined. During the depression and thereafter, world trade in electrical goods of all sorts suffered heavily from the decline and slow recovery of the overall world trade and the fall of prices.

Of course, this had a particularly strong impact on the export-dependent Austrian electrical engineering industry. (See Table 2: Indices of the Value and Volume of Exports of Electrical Products of Austria, Germany, and the World.)

Table 2: Indices of the Value and Volume of Exports of Electrical Products of Austria, Germany, and the World

Years	Value of Austrian Exports	Value of German Exports	Value of World Exports	Index of Value of Austrian Exports	Index of Volume of Austrian Exports	Index of Value of German Exports	Index of Value of World Exports	Index of Volume of World Exports
1929	51.5	639	2,294.8	100	100	100	100	100
1930	50.7	-	2,181.4	98.5	107.5	-	95.1	96.9
1931	39.4	-	1,648.7	76.5	69.4	-	71.8	78.6
1932	21.2	354	1,012.2	41.2	38.9	55.4	44.1	53.0
1933	18.9	249	834.9	36.7	35.5	39.0	34.6	52.6
1934	19.9	226	866.3	38.6	42.5	35.4	37.8	62.8
1935	15.9	233	904.0	30.9	36.6	36.5	39.4	70.0
1936	17.3	266	1,000.8	33.6	45.3	41.6	43.6	80.8
1937	22.4	328	1,236.0	43.5	84.0	51.3	53.9	95.8

(In million Reichsmark (1929=100))
Source: Compiled from various data.[56]

Whereas the Austrian value of exports in this industrial sector expanded by 122% in the 1920s, it soon started to drop and hardly recovered after 1933.[57] The drop of prices was revealed in the difference of decline of value and volume of export between 1929 and 1937. Value declined by more than 56%, while volume only fell by 16%. The volume of world exports of electrical products, though, nearly recovered by 1937.

The trade conditions were almost equally poor for other countries but, again, national producers in large countries were able to take advantage of their home markets. This was especially true for Germany, where rearmament supported this process. German export value, for example, also dropped by nearly half, still a bit stronger than the value of world exports. However, the value of German production only shrank by 22% before 1937 and its workforce slightly expanded.[58] Compared to 1928, total sales had increased by 19% by January 1938. Domestic sales of German electrical engineering companies increased by 36.8%, whereas export sales dropped by more than 40%. Apparently it was possible for the German electrical engineering industry to evade the declining foreign trade and divert sales to the domestic market. In addition, this industrial branch benefited from the massive rearmament demand. Between 50% to 80% of the employment of some companies was generated by rearmament orders.[59] However, just like the representatives of the German heavy industry, *Siemens*, for example, did not trust the state investment-led boom and feared over-expansion.[60]

Even though it was an important national producer,[61] the Austrian electrical engineering export industry played a minor role in world markets and faced fierce competition. This situation proved to be a major disadvantage in the international economic environment of the 1930s. The German industry still remained the most important exporter of electrical products, with a more than 26% share of world exports. It was followed by the United States (25.5%), Britain (19.5%), and the Netherlands (8%). The Austrian export industry ranked number ten in the world with only a 1.9% share of world exports in 1937. Thus, it was still behind the industries of Japan, Sweden, Belgium, Luxembourg, Switzerland, and France.[62] Therefore, not only did this industrial sector suffer from slow expansion of electricity supply at home, but it was also strongly affected by the decline of trade while its economic leverage on world markets was negligible.

Generally, for all Austrian companies, the 1930s were difficult years.[63] Since the home market remained stagnant and public orders came to a halt, the companies had to increase their export rates, even though foreign trade was not nearly as buoyant and smooth as in the late 1920s. Moreover, currency fluctuations and competition from counterparts in the large countries constituted huge problems. International markets had contracted, national markets were in the grip of national producers and protectionist policies, and foreign trade competition was fiercer than ever, which explained the contradiction of development between volume and value of exports. Thus, this situation constituted a dilemma for relatively large companies with a small market. In order to withstand unfavorable trade conditions, increasing specialization of export items with low demand elasticity was necessary. By and large, this industry was damaged by the decline of trade, national retrenchment and structural distortions, but the nature of its advanced products and its export orientation allowed it to stay afloat relatively well. The most trade-oriented of the four major Austrian companies, the *Elin*, enjoyed the most favorable economic performance. Until 1934, *AEG*, *Siemens,* and *Brown-Boveri* made deficits, while the independent *Elin*, focusing on its foreign business, made small profits.

Only by the late 1930s, a very moderate recovery occurred due to slow increases in public and semi-public investment and Austria's indirect participation in the international rearmament boom. It should be noted, though, that even the large German electrical engineering companies, which benefited from the four-year plan, were only able to recover their volume of production after the mid-1930s; they did not uncover their value of turnover until the last few years of the decade.[64] The German *AEG*, for instance, surpassed its 1928 value of turnover only in 1939.[65]

2.1.2. Elin *Aktiengesellschaft für elektrische Industrie*

Financial standing

The *Elin*,[66] the second largest electrical engineering company during the late 1920s,[67] tumbled into the depression with stable finances and consolidated export business. Debts and bank credits were small, especially because a sterling loan was used. The balance sheet reveals the abrupt halt of rapid expansion of business in 1929 and 1930. The balance sheet value declined by 26% by 1934. Its financial standing, however, remained very stable. Unlike almost all other Austrian companies of the traditional and modern industries, the *Elin* was able to balance its profit and loss account and to make minor profits during the depression and throughout the 1930s, without having to undergo a profound financial reconstruction. In 1930, its gross profits only declined by 1.4% and net profits only by 26%. After 1931, minute net profits and small investments were made. *Elin* managed to avoid deficits not only because of its excellent financial standing and stable business in 1929, but also because of its drastic expense cuts of 9% in 1931 and even 20% in 1932. Furthermore, after 1933, the company still benefited from a reduction of debt service because of sterling depreciation. It also took advantage of profits from the depreciation of the sterling bond. However, in spite of the increasing turnover after 1933, it was not possible to make higher net profits as prices continued to be depressed.

Business activity

Notwithstanding the business decline on the Austrian market already in late 1929, *Elin's* management was able to increase the company's turnover by enforcing an increase in export sales, especially in highly developed finished products. As the recession worsened in 1930, and the demand from private and public domestic orders lessened (in particular from the hydropower plants), it became expedient to press export business forward even more. The permanent search for employment on foreign markets had highest priority. In 1930, 60% of the turnover was sold abroad. Transmission lines and power plants, including a transformer station, were built and delivered to Poland, Bulgaria, and Greece. In 1931, when business continued to worsen, the *Elin* management continued to make the right policy choices, and remained focused on foreign markets, whereas the other electrical engineering firms were contractually bound by their parent companies to limit diffusion of their exports. Orders from Yugoslavia, Egypt, and South Africa increased. Soviet Russia, augmenting its total value of imports of electrical engineering products to 116 million Reichsmark in 1931, still remained an especially important customer.[68]

1932 and 1933 were the most difficult years. Again, domestic demand declined much more than foreign demand. Particularly, special and highly developed products, such as specific welding equipment and various types of rectifiers, were able to stand their ground on international markets. The manufacture of such products, and also of incandescent lamps, remained stable. With this expansive and aggressive export business, it was possible to contain the drop of total value of turnover (-35%) within the year 1932. Very new types of welding sets, allowing the construction of large-sized steel supporters, were sold in the Netherlands. A large diesel power plant was delivered to the Assuan dam. The city power system of Guirga, Egypt, was extended. From Bulgaria, the *Elin* accepted orders for a 20 kilometer transmission line and a transformer station. In Poland and Yugoslavia, rectifier plants and high voltage rectifiers were constructed.

The low mark of domestic sales in early 1933 was well compensated by reviving exports in the second half of the year. Once again, most successful were the sales of highly developed special products of electrical engineering, such as welding equipment. To be able to maintain and increase export business and to remain competitive after 1933, *Elin* enlarged its range of production of other highly developed electrical items. Research and development (R&D) of high quality technology was advanced. The machinery department developed more than one hundred new products, among them new types of electrolytic rectifiers, stage-selector switch controls, protective switches for electric motors, special oil drilling engines, high powered squirrel-cage motors, direct-current machinery, and new electric stoves. The management remarked that currency and trade restrictions were less harmful to their business than the year before, even though the dollar was devalued.[69] Foreign sales continued to increase until 1938, as exports went to fifty-four different countries. Business improved with up to 80% of the total value of turnover being exported. While the sales to Russia declined after 1932, deliveries to and construction in the Near and Far East, South America, and South Africa could be extended.

In 1934, *Elin* could still not make any substantial profits, even though it utilized 70% of its capacity and still expanded its export business. Continuously falling international prices remained the main problem. In 1934 and 1935, the average prices of electrical machinery dropped by around 16% and those of other electrical products by 10%. Even the huge German electrical engineering industry required supreme efforts to keep up profitability of foreign trade.[70] Yet, *Elin* could expand foreign trade, and export business was successful. Moreover, by the mid-1930s, orders from public investment slowly began to increase again. *Elin* did the switchgear installations for the railway plant in Mallnitz and made a few deliveries to Viennese power plants.

While there was hardly any stimulation from the Austrian home market, in 1935 and 1936 foreign sales continuously rose so that the rectifier and neon light factories had to be enlarged. In both years turnover increased by 15%. The export rate was augmented to 80% of the turnover value. However, the competition on world markets had become increasingly fierce, with the currency depreciation of the gold bloc countries and government export bounties directly supporting foreign competitors. Profit margins could not be raised. Research and development was enforced, while the management continued to expand foreign trade to new overseas markets. In 1936, the extension of the export business stopped. The export rate went slightly below 80%. In the following year, public investment finally offered increasing employment, but until the war the business remained focused on markets abroad.

2.2. Motor industry

2.2.1. International development

The most significant characteristic of the Austrian automobile industry was its strong export orientation,[71] which was in sharp contrast to the strictly home-market-oriented and protectionist car manufacture industries of the five large states that dominated world production: the United States, Britain, France, Germany, and Italy. Ironically, this export concentration, coupled with a lack of comparable international productivity, was essentially one of the main problems of this Austrian industrial sector. It was a perfect example of a modern industrial branch in a small country that did not enjoy the advantages of the equal or more capital and technology intensive mass-producing counterparts in the large industrialized countries. In Europe and the United States, car manufacture and sales were strictly tied to the various large domestic markets of the big modern countries because the sales of these mass-produced durable goods depended on the limited mass consumption power of the various national economies. In 1938, foreign sales among these five large powers only amounted to 5% of their total exports of motor vehicles, since each group of national producers controlled its own market. Thus, the world motor vehicle trade mainly consisted of outbound trade from these large countries to small and less developed countries.[72] This tendency was enhanced by protectionist trade policies that supported the interest of national car manufacturers.

The Austrian automobile industry did not fit into this general pattern and directly suffered from the split and controlled structure of foreign national markets. Considering the advantageous production and trade conditions of the larger foreign producers, it is surprising that the Austrian manufacturers held their ground as well as they did. There was always a large Austrian export surplus of automobiles. Still, export performance was erratic, revealing its dependence on international business cycles in the countries of its most vital markets.[73] During the depression, export sales dropped enormously. The Austrian industry suffered especially from the decline of prices enhanced by increasing production of mass-produced smaller and cheaper vehicles. Prices dropped by more than half in the late 1920s, which forced companies to increase their productivity permanently.[74] The fact that exported Austrian vehicles were on the average much more expensive than imported vehicles,[75] reveals the lower productivity of Austrian manufacturers.

Besides the most important German market, the main markets were those of the Western industrialized countries. Some vehicles were also sold on the markets of the successor states. Trade conditions were generally hostile already in the second half of the 1920s, as European car manufacturers had been able to exclude their national markets from international competition and imports. The countries with the highest purchasing power, naturally the countries that had automobile industries themselves, imposed the highest import tariffs.[76] Not only the export sales situation was difficult for Austrian vehicle manufacturers, though. The domestic market was not only far too small for national production facilities, but also had a relatively low consumption level.[77]

However, before 1929, the growth of the Austrian vehicle industry could bear international comparison. (See Table 3: Production of Automobiles and Utility Vehicles, 1926-1929.) The table clearly demonstrates to what extent the motor vehicle industry in the United States dominated world vehicle production, with a share of more than 85%.

Table 3: Production of Automobiles and Utility Vehicles, 1926-1929

Years	Germany	GB	France	Italy	Belgium	CSR	Austria	US	World
1926	45.5	198.0	192.0	64.8	6.0	7.0	5.3	4300.9	5035.2
1927	114.9	211.8	191.3	54.6	6.5	10.2	8.7	3401.3	4159.0
1928	137.9	211.9	223.6	59.8	8.2	13.2	9.4	4358.7	5203.1
1929	127.9	238.8	245.6	54.1	7.0	14.7	9.1	5358.4	6277.5

(In thousand)
Source: *Statistisches Jahrbuch für das Deutsche Reich* (1933), 69 (international survey).

The depression abruptly ended the upward movement of production. Although in all countries, the average growth rates of vehicle production were higher than the total industrial production,[78] the world vehicle industry, which tripled its output after the depression, did not recover pre-crisis levels until 1937. (See Table 4: Production of Automobiles and Utility Vehicles, 1929-1937.)

The production performance of national producers in authoritarian states was, by far, the best, partially because their production and consumption started from comparably low levels, and partially because public policy supported these increases. Between 1932 and 1937, Germany increased its output more than six times, Italy two and a half times, and Russia even more than eight and a half times. As the only country with a liberal economic system, British performance (+113%) was truly remarkable. Most other European producers, and not even the United States, did not recover their 1929 output levels. As expected, the producers in small advanced countries tended to experience the slowest recovery. In 1937, Czechoslovak production was nearly 5%, Austrian 33%, and Belgian production even 79% (in 1936) below the 1929 level.

Table 4: Production of Automobiles and Utility Vehicles, 1929-1937

Years	Germany	GB	France	Italy	Soviet Russia	Belgium	CSR	Austria	US	World
1929	127.9	238.8	245.6	54.1	1.7	7.0	14.7	9.1	5358.4	6277.5
1930	96.0	236.6	230.7	42.7	8.5	4.7	16.8	3.2	3355.9	4126.5
1931	77.6	226.3	209.2	29.3	20.6	3.2	17.0	4.4	2389.7	3048.6
1932	51.6	232.7	180.7	29.1	25.4	2.2	13.6	2.4	1370.7	1977.0
1933	105.5	286.3	198.2	42.0	49.7	1.4	10.0	1.2	1920.0	2675.7
1934	174.7	342.5	198.2	44.8	72.5	0.7	9.9	2.1	2753.1	3735.8
1935	247.1	403.7	178.6	49.2	97.1	0.8	10.0	3.1	3946.9	5126.7
1936	301.9	461.4	209.3	51.1	137.0	1.5	12.0	6.4	4454.1	5815.8
1937	326.5	507.7	206.7	75.1	220.0	-	14.0	6.1	4809.0	6350.3

(In thousand)
Source: *Statistisches Jahrbuch* (1937), 81 and (1938) 83 (international survey).[79]

Even to a greater extent than in the 1920s, most of the production growth was based on national demand, while foreign trade stagnated. Vehicle manufacturers in large countries retrenched to their domestic markets and were protected by high import duties. For example, of its total vehicle production in 1935, Germany only exported 9.5%.[80] By far the most trade-oriented manufacturers among the larger countries were British producers, exporting about 19.4% of their output, which amounted to 14% of the value of the world market.[81] However, the majority of this export went to the Commonwealth countries, where it benefited from preferential tariffs. Furthermore, the British market was highly protected by the McKenna duties, imposing a tariff of 33.3% on imported cars,[82] which hardly gave a chance to small national producers with lower productivity. The export rate of the French car industry was around 10% in 1936.[83]

Of course, for big national producers in large modern countries, declining foreign trade was by far not as harmful as it was to export-dependent producers in small advanced countries. In large countries that underwent an economic boom and where the number of persons per car was still high, producers still enjoyed private and public demand in their home markets. This was the case for Germany, Italy, and Russia. In large countries in which economies underwent stagnation or only moderate recovery and where the number of people per car was very low, producers naturally faced low demand, saturated markets, and a slow increase of output. This especially occurred in the United States, but also in France.[84] Very large national producers in the authoritarian states and in Britain not only benefited from large markets, but also enjoyed the combined advantage of massively reduced unit prices and a reduction in the cost of car ownership. In the U.S. market, this process had already been fully exploited in the 1920s. In the case of a general upswing, these price reductions entailed a sudden spurt in demand. While the number of units produced after 1933 increased in nearly all countries, prices continuously declined because mass production became more efficient and widespread. In Germany, for example, average car prices in 1935 were 25% below those in 1929.[85] In 1937, they were 56% below prewar prices.[86]The British industry was able to reduce car prices even more. In 1935, motor vehicles were about one-third cheaper than in 1929.[87] Whereas some countries quickly surpassed the volume of production in 1929, the value of production never recovered prior to the war.[88]

Consequently, foreign sales of the Austrian motor industry were heavily hit by the combined effect of declining prices due to constantly increasing international productivity and collapsing, stagnating trade, resulting from the national retrenchment of producers in large advanced countries. One of the main problems was that small national producers with small home markets were unable to lower prices as much as the large national producers in Germany or Britain, not to speak of manufacturers in the United States. Moreover, there was a huge disparity between home and export market prices so that for most producers prices at home were far more profitable. For instance, for most German companies export sales actually resulted in deficits, which could only be compensated by increased and higher priced domestic sales. Therefore, if national producers wanted to export at all, their home markets had to be large enough to expand the volume of domestic sales to an extent that allowed a dramatic reduction of production costs through rigorous extension of mass production, rationalization, and modernization. Essentially, overpriced home market sales were bearing the costs for the losses in export sales.[89] While it was very difficult even for the German vehicle manufacturing industry to benefit from this process,[90] it proved to be impossible for the Austrian industry to raise its production capacities to international standards in order to run a profitable export business. In 1937, the average price of one exported Austrian car was still 39% higher than that of an average imported foreign vehicle.[91] This way, Austrian firms were unable to make profits from foreign trade and had no choice but to retrench to their home market as well.

Thus, the export of Austrian vehicles and engines underwent a major crisis in the 1930s.[92] The only option for Austrian producers was to regain control over the domestic market, and to revive international trade. Yet, the Austrian domestic market did not offer adequate compensation because the home market demand had declined during the depression and recovered only slowly until 1937.[93] In Austria, therefore, as in all other small advanced countries, the production levels of the late 1930s were far below pre-crisis output levels. This process is reflected in the development of the *Steyr-Daimler-Puch AG*, the country's largest vehicle manufacturer.

2.2.2. Steyr-Daimler-Puch AG
Financial standing

Since the highly indebted *Steyr Werke*,[94] the largest Austrian producer, had conducted a risky business policy in the late 1920s, it underwent a massive financial breakdown already in 1929, resulting in a deficit of more than 24 million Schillings. Only after state reconstruction slowly enabled the *Credit-Anstalt* (*CA*) to financially stabilize Austria's largest automobile producer, it was possible to balance the profit and loss account in 1932. A massive remittance of debts, capital stock reduction, and revaluation had been necessary. The balance sheet revealed a 31% reduction of liabilities, the majority of which included bank credit. By 1933, it was almost possible to balance the value of creditors and debtors.

The *Austro-Daimler Puchwerke AG*,[95] which merged with *Steyr* in 1934, had also been running massive debts, which had to be lowered by debt remittance of the *CA*, capital stock reduction, and subsequent revaluation. After the merger, capital stock was raised to 13.2 million Schillings, and the reduced debts of *Daimler-Puch*, still close to 13 million Schillings in 1933, had to be assumed. However, thanks to improving business after 1935, it was possible to considerably reduce the bank debts. In spite of the financial breakdown in the depression and difficult trade conditions thereafter, the renamed *Steyr-Daimler-Puch AG* made surprisingly high profits in 1935 and 1936. Profitability was with 12% in 1936 and 20% in 1937 well above the level of the late 1920s.

Business activity

Before the crisis, the *Steyr Werke* must have produced well over 6,000 automobiles annually, of which a fluctuating share of roughly 50% to 80% was exported. Then, during the depression, conditions rapidly changed. The workforce was reduced from 6,200 to less than 1,500. Although the company continued to provide nearly all of Austria's car output, its home market share declined and remained low. Moreover, its export rate dropped to 50% or less. In 1932, *Steyr* sold 1,800 cars (some of which had been in stock),[96] of which less than 500 were outbound sales.[97] The main export areas were still Germany, Hungary, Poland, and Switzerland. Total domestic sales amounted to 2,268 cars, of which *Steyr* sold only 1,368. Thus, its home market share was slightly more than 60%.

In 1933, the turnover value increased by 20%, but net profits and total exports still declined. The export rate of car sales increased to 50%. Two thirds of all ball bearing sales were exported. The home market share continued to decline while the proportion of imported products increased. Of the 1,433 brand-new automobiles licensed in Austria,[98] *Steyr* only had a share of 45%.

After the merger in 1934, the *Steyr-Daimler-Puch AG* basically constituted the only automobile manufacturer as well as the only motorcycle producer in Austria. Besides the *Alpine-Montangesellschaft* and the rubber goods producer *Semperit*, it was the largest company in the country. It took over the production of the large, more luxurious *Daimler* cars, as well as of the *Puch* motorcycles. The *Daimler* factory in Wiener Neustadt was closed and all production capacities were concentrated in Steyr. In spite of this concentration, competitiveness did not improve and business only slowly began to pick up. Foreign trade stagnated and did not surpass its 1931 level until 1937. In 1934, total sales only increased by 20%, of which half was generated by the car production, 30% by bicycle and motorbike output, and the rest by ball bearing and car battery production. The company's domestic market share slightly augmented. Nevertheless, of the more than 1,700 licensed new automobiles, its share was still just 54%.

In the following two years, production could be raised by more than 150%, finally allowing for higher capacity employment and acceptable profitability. This still slow upswing was mostly based on the rising demand of the home market, due to moderate general recovery, a reduction of car running costs, and a massive decrease of Austrian automobile prices. With its low cost, mass-produced compact car, the so-called "Steyr-50," *Steyr-Daimler-Puch* gained an increasing share of home market sales, rising from approximately 59% in 1935 to 82% in 1936. At the same time, the export volume stagnated until 1936. The export rate was only around 10%. In 1935, the total turnover value increased by 30% and 75% of its capacity was utilized. The following year, the company used 70% of its car manufacturing capacity and 100% of its motorcycle production capacity. The total turnover increased by 43%.

Thus, only after the mid-1930s was the volume of home demand large enough to introduce profitable mass production of cheap cars. This process, in turn, enabled the company to regain control of its home market, which had been flooded by cheaper imported cars. In addition, home sales of mass-produced compact cars proved to be far more profitable than export sales of larger obsolete cars in the late 1920s. Earning power had considerably improved, and in 1936 the net profit was 24% above its highest pre-crisis value of 1927. However, Austrian car manufacturing was still far from full capacity utilization as the volume of output was still considerably below its 1929 level. Furthermore, because of its disadvantages as a national producer with a small domestic market, *Steyr-Daimler-Puch* was unable to compete on international markets and could not revive its once lively, but unprofitable, export business. Therefore, even though the productive capacity had been considerably modernized and improved in the 1930s, there was still a great potential for expansion and productivity increase.

IV. Conclusions

The effects of restrictive economic policy on enterprises, such as the sudden termination of public demand, were obvious only in very rare cases. The economic performance of the majority of Austrian industrial joint-stock companies was not primarily determined by economic policy. The analysis shows that a multitude of factors influenced financial and real economic performance. Main determinants of growth and development were relative productivity, international competitiveness, demand elasticity, as well as the level and rate of the successful application of new technology to keep up with international demand and market changes. However, the development and improvement of these determinants were restrained by the two structural long-term transformations after the war. Equally important was that the Austrian companies' adjustment to these changes was complicated by their international market position. As minor national producers with a small and impotent home market, they faced the competition of large industrial sectors of the big advanced countries. This naturally entailed a serious disadvantage of competitiveness, especially in a hostile environment that limited trade.

The traditional sectors tended to experience the negative implications of the structural changes and the disadvantageous market position of small national producers much more than the modern industries. Most traditional companies were directly affected by the competition from modern sectors, by peripheral industrialization, worldwide over-capacities, and the deterioration of their formerly vital markets. Therefore, most of these firms were not only severely hit by the depression, but they were also much more affected by economic policy measures, such as stabilization policies, protectionism, currency devaluation, tight money policies, and restrictive public investment.

While many of these traditional enterprises were large national producers in Austria, their economic leverage on international markets was small. The *Veitscher*, the *Alpine*, the engine factories, and most other large traditional machine building enterprises suffered from over-capacities in their sectors, experienced stagnation already in the 1920s as other much larger national producers dominated the world markets, and were heavily hit by the slump. The *Alpine* began to recover pre-crisis levels of production, turnover, and investment only after the manufacturing capacities of all neighbor states were already fully employed. The engine factories would never be able to return to the international markets and domestic demand remained insufficient. *Veitscher* was also a classical victim of the global changes that occurred after World War I. Its financial standing remained stable, yet it would never regain its prewar position in world markets due to the global rise of competing industries. Other very important examples of Austrian industrial sectors whose market positions were directly affected by global structural changes of increasing industrialization and economic shifts in the modern states, were the textile and the paper industries.[99]

Even the modern Austrian industrial sectors suffered from this phenomenon. In the 1920s, the disadvantages of a small home market for a car manufacturing became soon apparent, since already then this sector was hardly able to adopt the low international market prices and made only minor profits. *Steyr-Daimler-Puch* attempted to keep up with unprofitable export trade before the crisis, and had to almost completely terminate outbound sales in the 1930s. At least this enterprise was able to control its home market after introducing cheaper mass-produced cars in the mid-1930s.

Even the most competitive and advanced companies were able to expand export business only by supreme effort. Essentially, this was merely possible for *Semperit* and *Elin*, whose business policies were exemplary.[100] Flexible and forced exports of advanced high-quality products, the introduction of new and better products with the help of research and development, the introduction of a diversified production range, and a constant effort to increase productivity and competitiveness were the secret to moderate business performance in the 1930s.

In general, companies of the modern sectors, or companies with a strong commitment to foreign trade and a flexible business policy, tended to perform better than those that retrenched to the stagnant home market or only produced traditional goods. The *Elin AG* chiefly based its slow and partial recovery on outbound trade. Retrenchment was always the wrong choice. Generally, though, in the 1930s, there was no chance for anyone to expand capacities and make substantial profits.

In the end, only a few companies were able to break out of this position of constraint. The constant revolution of industrial structures, as well as the process of transformation and reorientation towards new types of production, production methods, and consumption, was enormously restrained in the 1930s, due to the distortion of structural transformations, the intensifying economic retrenchment, and economic nationalism. Production and business of nearly all enterprises stagnated until the mid-1930s. They only *began* to recover in 1936/37.

Notes

1. See *Monatsberichte des Österreichischen Instituts für Wirtschaftsforschung, Österreichs Volkseinkommen 1913 bis 1963*, special issue (Vienna, 1965): 42.

2. Ibid.

3. Angus Maddison, "Economic Policy and Performance in Europe 1913-1970," in *The Fontana Economic History of Europe,* vol. 5, *The Twentieth Century-2*, ed. Carlo M. Cipolla (London: Fontana Books, 1977), 449.

4. See Dieter Stiefel, *Konjunkturelle Entwicklung und struktureller Wandel der österreichischen Wirtschaft in der Zwischenkriegszeit, Forschungsbericht Nr. 135* (Vienna: Fachverlag für Wirtschaft und Technik, 1978), 80: "Die Weltwirtschaftskrise wurde allgemein als Wendepunkt in Wirtschaftstheorie und Wirtschaftsauffassung betrachtet. Zwischen 1930 und 1935 liegen in der Wirtschaftspolitik Welten. Nicht aber so in Österreich. Die österreichische Wirtschaftspolitik hatte aus der Weltwirtschaftskrise keine Schlüsse gezogen."

5. The major contemporary economic journal persistently criticizes deflationary economic policy. *Der Österreichische Volkswirt. Zeitschrift für Industrie und Finanzen* (Vienna: Volkswirtschaftliche Verlagsgesellschaft, 1923-1938).

6. See Alexander Fibich, "Die Entwicklung der österreichischen Bundesausgaben in der Ersten Republik (1918-1938)," PhD. Diss., University of Vienna, 1977, 19: "Eine wesentliche Ursache dieser wirtschaftlichen, gesellschaftlichen und politischen Misere war sicher nicht zuletzt eine falsche Wirtschafts- und damit auch Budgetpolitik." See also Fritz Weber, "Staatliche Wirtschaftspolitik in der Zwischenkriegszeit. Zum Investitionsverhalten der öffentlichen Hand 1918-1938," in *Handbuch des politischen Systems Österreichs. Erste Republik 1918-1933*, ed. Emmerich Tálos et al. (Vienna: Manz, 1995), 547; and Peter Berger, "The Austrian Economy, 1918-1938," in *The Economic Development of Austria since 1870*, ed. Herbert Matis (Aldershot: Elgar, 1994), 273 and 274. Berger talks about an irresponsible deflationist policy.

7. See Hans Kernbauer, "Zur österreichischen Wirtschaftspolitik in der Ersten Republik: Ein Überblick," in *Banken, Währungen und Politik in Mitteleuropa zwischen den Weltkriegen*, ed. Alice Teichova (Vienna: Böhlau, 1997), 45: "Den wirtschaftspolitischen Maßnahmen der Bundesregierung und der Österreichischen Nationalbank, die freilich sehr stark von ausländischen Einflüssen von Seiten des Finanzkomitées des Völkerbundes und der Bank von England abhängig waren, ist eine große Verantwortung für die unbefriedigende Wirtschaftsentwicklung zuzuschreiben." Stiefel has a similar view: "Eine der Ursachen dieser zögernden wirtschaftlichen Erholung [zwischen 1925 und 1929] war die in Österreich betriebene Wirtschaftspolitik, die mehr als in anderen Ländern am Wechselkurs orientiert war und auch nach Aufhebung der Völkerbundkontrolle den 'Blick auf die Finanzprobleme

und auf die internationale Kreditfähigkeit Österreichs' konzentrierte." Stiefel, *Konjunkturelle Entwicklung*, 38.

8. Weber, "Staatliche Wirtschaftspolitik in der Zwischenkriegszeit," 550 and 548.

9. This was especially obvious in Germany, France, and Great Britain. See Ingvar Svennilson, *Stagnation and Growth in the European Economy* (Geneva: United Nations, Economic Commission for Europe, 1954), especially the chapter on "Transformation and Growth of Early-Industrialised Countries," 44ff.

10. One of the latest works based on Schumpeter is Philippe Aghion and Peter Howitt, *Endogenous Growth Theory* (Cambridge, MA: MIT Press, 1998).

11. See Gerhard Mensch, *Das technologische Patt. Innovationen überwinden die Depression* (Frankfurt a. M.: Umschau Verlag, 1975), 18; and Joseph Alois Schumpeter, *Kapitalismus, Sozialismus und Demokratie*, 4th ed. (Munich: Francke, 1950), 136-37.

12. Joseph Alois Schumpeter, *Konjunkturzyklen. Eine theretische, historische und statistische Analyse des kapitalistischen Prozesses*, vol. 2 (Göttingen: Vandenhoeck & Ruprecht, 1961), chapter XV. Until World War II, three Kondratieff cycles have been discerned. The last to be observed lasted from 1897 until the downswing of 1939. Between 1787 and 1932, economists have counted eleven Juglar cycles. See Walter Assenmacher, *Konjunkturtheorie*, 8th ed. (Munich: Oldenbourg, 1998), 17-18. The long-term cycle theory is rejected by many economists today. See Jürgen Heubes, "Juglar-, Kondratieff- und Kitchin-Zyklen," *Wirtschaftswissenschaftliches Studium* 9 (1980): 383-85.

13. Schumpeter, *Kapitalismus*, 134-42.

14. Heinrich Liepmann, *Tariff Levels and the Economic Unity of Europe. An Examination of Tariff Policy, Export Movements and the Economic Integration of Europe, 1913-1931* (London, 1938; reprint Philadelphia: Porcupine Press 1980), 360.

15. In a similar fashion, this has already been suggested by studies of the League of Nations: See League of Nations, Economic, Financial and Transit Department, *Industrialization and Foreign Trade* (New York: United Nations, 1948), 81. Already in the 1930s, scholars noted these developments. See, for example, Rolf Wagenführ, "Die Industriewirtschaft. Entwicklungstendenzen der deutschen und internationalen Industrieproduktion 1860 bis 1932," *Vierteljahreshefte zur Konkjunkturforschung*, ed. Institut für Konjunkturforschung, special issue 31 (1933).

16. The value of trade shrunk by more than 50%, the volume by almost 30%, whereas world exports decreased by about 60% between 1928 and 1932. See Deutsches Institut für Konjunkturforschung, *Wochenbericht des Instituts für Konjunkturforschung*, vol. 6, no. 32 (1933): 138. See also "Die Lage des Welthandels," *Wochenbericht*, vol. 10, no. 26 (1937): 143-44.

17. In 1936, it only reached 86%, and the value of world trade only reached 59% of its 1929 level. See *Wochenbericht*, vol. 10, no. 26 (1937): 146.

18. "Weltproduktion und Welthandel," *Wochenbericht*, vol. 10, no. 43 (1937): 249ff.

19. League of Nations, *World Production and Prices 1925-1933* (Geneva: League of Nations, 1934), 6.

20. The case of Sweden in the 1930s has proven that it is possible.

21. Hans Kernbauer, *Währungspolitik in der Zwischenkriegszeit. Geschichte der Österreichischen Nationalbank von 1923-1938* (Vienna: Österreichische Nationalbank, 1991), 289.

22. According to my own calculations, based on *Volkseinkommen*, 42 and *Wochenbericht*, vol. 10, no. 26 (1937): 146. The 46.5% mark reflects the average taken from eleven industrialized European countries, as calculated by the German business cycle research institute.

23. The data for 1936 and 1928 is calculated from Brian R. Mitchell, *European Historical Statistics 1750-1970* (London: Macmillan, 1978), 295ff. and 407ff. The data for Austria is taken from *Volkseinkommen*, 41. The data for Belgium reflects the National Domestic Product of 1927. The export shares of the 1928 GNPs of Czechoslovakia and Germany are

at constant 1929 prices. The GDP growth rates for 1932-1937 are calculated according to data from Angus Maddison, "Measuring Long Term Growth and Productivity Change on a Macro-economic Level," in *Productivity in the Economies of Europe*, ed. Rainer Fremdling and Patrick K. O'Brian (Stuttgart: Klett-Cotta, 1983), 114-15. The GDP growth rate of Czechoslovakia is calculated from Mitchell, *Historical Statistics*, 410. The 1936 GNP of Germany is according to figures from Albrecht Ritschl and Mark Spoerer, "Das Bruttosozialprodukt in Deutschland nach den amtlichen Volkseinkommens- und Sozialproduktstatistiken 1901-1995," *Jahrbuch für Wirtschaftsgeschichte. Volkswirtschaftliche Gesamtrechnungen im internationalen Vergleich* 2 (1997): 44.

24. All values are in 1937 Schillings and are based on my own calculations from *Volkseinkommen*, 42.

25. Calculated from *Volkseinkommen*, 42.

26. Felix Butschek, *Die österreichische Wirtschaft im 20. Jahrhundert* (Stuttgart: Fischer, 1985), 60; and idem, *Die österreichische Wirtschaft 1938 bis 1945* (Stuttgart: Fischer, 1978), 57.

27. For a more complete analysis, see Jens-Wilhelm Wessels, "Economic Policy and Performance in Inter-war Europe and Micro-economic Development in Austria, 1918-1938," PhD. Diss., University of Innsbruck, 2001.

28. According to my own calculation from *Volkseinkommen*, 12; and Statistisches Reichsamt, *Statistisches Jahrbuch für das Deutsche Reich, 1938* (Berlin: Schmidt, 1938), 83 and 85 (international survey).

29. *Volkseinkommen*, 18-19.

30. Alois Mosser, "Wachstumsstrategie oder Krisenmanagement? Vom Investitionsverhalten der österreichischen Industrie in der Ersten Republik," in *Beiträge über die Krise der Industrie Niederösterreichs zwischen den beiden Weltkriegen. Studien und Forschungen aus dem Niederösterreichischen Institut für Landeskunde*, vol. 7, ed. Andreas Kusternig (Vienna: Selbstverl. d. NÖ Inst. für Landeskunde, 1985), 106-12.

31. See these issues of *Bilanzen. Beilage zum Österreichischen Volkswirt*: 21 October 1922, 25 November 1922, 20 January 1923, 29 December 1923, 17 January 1925, 28 August 1926, 4 June 1927, 5 May 1928, 24 August 1929, 14 June 1930, 4 July 1930, 14 June 1930, 4 July 1931, 28 May 1932, 15 July 1933, 19 May 1934, 16 February 1935, 13 May 1935, 4 April 1936, 30 January 1937, 15 May 1937.

32. Walter Hermann, *Der Magnesit in der Weltwirtschaft unter besonderer Berücksichtigung Österreichs. Eine wirtschaftsgeographische Untersuchung* (Vienna: Müller, 1937), 67.

33. Ibid., 71ff.

34. Friedrich Walter, *Veitscher Magnesitwerke Actien-Gesellschaft 1881-1951* (Vienna: Veitscher Magnesitwerke, 1951), 213ff.

35. Hermann, *Der Magnesit*, 74ff.

36. Ibid., 77.

37. Österreichisches Statistisches Zentralamt, *Der Aussenhandel Österreichs in der Zeit zwischen den beiden Weltkriegen. Beiträge zur österreichischen Statistik* (Vienna: Österreichische Staatsdruckerei, 1946), 49.

38. Walter, *Veitscher Magnesitwerke*, 208.

39. According to my own calculations from *Jahrbuch* (1938), 72 (international survey).

40. With a capital stock of one million or more.

41. Data for 1935. See Bundesamt für Statistik, *Statistisches Handbuch für den Bundesstaat Österreich*, vol. 17 (Vienna: Österreichische Staatsdruckerei, 1937), 85.

42. Walter, *Veitscher Magnesitwerke*, 217.

43. Ibid., 218.

44. See these issues of *Bilanzen. Beilage zum Österreichischen Volkswirt*: 1 August 1931, 4 June 1932, 24 June 1933, 16 June 1934, 30 June 1934, 1 December 1934, 28 September 1935, 11 April 1936, 27 June 1936, 1 August 1936, 5 September 1936, 2 January 1937, 20 March 1937, 17 April 1937, 12 June 1937, 3 July 1937, 7 August 1937, 25 September 1937, 25 December 1937.

45. *Aussenhandel*, 49.

46. *Jahrbuch* (1938), 72 (international survey).

47. *Aussenhandel*, 50.

48. See these issues of *Bilanzen*: 5 December 1925, 21 August 1926, 2 July 1927, 9 July 1927, 7 July 1928, 6 July 1929, 5 July 1930, 4 July 1931, 4 July 1931, 16 July 1932, 26 August 1933, 1 September 1934, 24 August 1935, 22 August 1936, 2 October 1937. In the late 1920s, Siemens Austria had between 6,000 and 7,000 workers and employees. Elin had between 1,500 and 2,000.

49. See these issues of *Bilanzen*: 24 July 1926, 10 September 1927, 19 May 1928, 25 May 1929, 14 June 1930, 4 July 1931, 14 June 1930, 4 July 1931, 23 July 1932, 16 September 1933, 18 April 1936, 5 September 1936, 9 October 1937.

50. See these issues of *Bilanzen:* 18 September 1926, 30 April 1927, 30 June 1928, 15 June 1929, 7 June 1930, 1 August 1931, 23 July 1932, 4 November 1933, 8 September 1934, 21 September 1935, 14 November 1936, 21 November 1936, 9 January 1937, 23 October 1937.

51. Wilhelm Heiße, "Die Energiewirtschaft der Welt in Zahlen," *Vierteljahreshefte zur Konjunkturforschung,* special issue 19 (1930): 40.

52. See the chart "Weltausfuhr von Elektrokraftmaschinen nach Ländern," ibid., 42.

53. The Austrian National Committee of the International Chamber of Commerce (Österreichisches Nationalkomitee der Internationalen Handelskammer), *Zollhöhe und Warenwerte. Eine vergleichende Studie über die Höhe der Zollbelastung für 402 Waren in 14 europäischen Staaten* (Vienna: Publication for the World Economic Conference, 1927), 3.

54. Harm Schröter, "Siemens and Central and South-East Europe between the two world wars," in *International Business and Central Europe, 1918-1939*, ed. Alice Teichova and P.L. Cottrell (New York: St. Martin's Press, 1983), 173-91.

55. See *Jahrbuch* (1938): 85.

56. Data for Austria calculated from *Aussenhandel*, 67. Austrian export value in Schillings converted into Reichsmark at current exchange rates according to Jürgen Schneider, Oskar Schwarzer, and Markus A. Denzel, eds., *Währungen der Welt II. Europäische und nordamerikanische Devisenkurse (1914-1951)* (Stuttgart: Steiner Verlag, 1997), 286. The decline of the value of Austrian exports in 1935 and 1936 was in reality not as pronounced as indicated here, because the Deutschmark appreciated against the Schilling in these years. Data for Germany from Länderrat des Amerikanischen Besatzungsgebiets, *Statistisches Handbuch von Deutschland 1928-1944* (Munich: Ehrenwirt, 1949), 302. Data for world development from "Der Welthandel in elektrotechnischen Erzeugnissen," *Wochenbericht*, vol. 12, no. 20 (1939): 126.

57. *Aussenhandel*, 67.

58. *Statistisches Handbuch von Deutschland*, 302.

59. Wilfried Feldenkirchen, *Siemens, 1918-1945* (Munich: Piper, 1995), 134 and 137-38.

60. Ibid., 328.

61. *Statistisches Handbuch für den Bundesstaat Österreich 1937*, 83. Including electrical supply companies, this sector's share of industrial stock amounted to 26% in 1935.

62. *Wochenbericht*, vol.12, no.20 (1939): 127.

63. The following information on this industry was taken from general reports in *Bilanzen*: 16 July 1932, 26 August 1933, 25 August 1934, 27 April 1935, 24 May 1935, 22 August 1936, 2 October 1937.

64. Feldenkirchen, *Siemens*, 327-28.

65. Gert Hautsch, "Der Elektrokonzern AEG-Telefunken. Untersuchungen zum Verhältnis von Wirtschaft und Politik am Beispiel eines westdeutschen Großunternehmens," PhD. diss., University of Bremen, 1982, 41.

66. See *Bilanzen*, 24 July 1926, 18 June 1927, 9 July 1927, 14 July 1928, 22 June 1929, 13 July 1929, 19 July 1930, 29 August 1931, 30 July 1932, 26 August 1933, 25 August 1934, 31 August 1935, 16 November 1935, 19 September 1936, 16 October 1937.

67. Franz Mathis, *Big Business in Österreich. Österreichische Großunternehmen in Kurzdarstellungen* (Munich: Oldenbourg, 1987), 92.

68. See "Das Rußlandgeschäft in der Weltwirtschaftskrisis," *Wochenbericht*, vol. 5, no. 28 (1932): 54. In fact, in 1931, the value of total Russian imports reached their peak. See The Scientific Department of the German Nitrogen Syndicate (Arbeit der wissenschaftlichen Abteilung des Stickstoff-Syndikates), *UdSSR. Struktur, Industrie, Verkehr, Außenhandel* (Berlin, 1939), 62.

69. "Das ist eine für das Jahr der Dollarabwertung bemerkenswerte Feststellung," *Bilanzen*, 25 August 1934.

70. "Der Auslandsabsatz der elektrotechnischen Industrie," *Wochenbericht*, vol. 9, no. 20 (1936): 77-78.

71. Statistisches Reichsamt, *Die Wirtschaft des Auslandes 1900-1927. Einzelschriften zur Statistik des Deutschen Reiches*, (Berlin: Hobbing, 1928), 248.

72. Svennilson, 150-51.

73. This included automobiles, trucks, motorbikes, engines, and parts for vehicles of all types. See *Aussenhandel*, 70.

74. The decline in prices is calculated from the numbers and value of cars exported; ibid.

75. Ibid.

76. All tariffs for 1927. See *Zollhöhe und Warenwerte*, 19.

77. This is evident when comparing the number of people per vehicle in different countries in 1929. Among developed countries, the Austrian per capita number was by far the highest with 200. In Portugal, it was 224 people per vehicle. Germany was also far below the average of industrialized European countries, with 111 people per vehicle. In France, it was only 23, in Britain 35, and in Belgium 66 people per vehicle. For comparison, in the United States, the number of people per passenger car was only 4.6. See Statistisches Reichsamt, *Statistisches Jahrbuch für das Deutsche Reich* (1930), 72 (international survey).

78. "Die Kraftfahrzeugsaison 1936," *Wochenbericht*, special issue, vol. 9, no. 34 (1936): 3.

79. The numbers in Mitchell, *European Historical Statistics*, 278-80, differ slightly.

80. Own calculation from "Die Kraftfahrzeugkonjunktur im vierten Aufschwungsjahr," *Wochenbericht*, special issue, vol. 9, no. 19 (1936): 2.

81. Albert E. Musson, *The Growth of British Industry* (Norfolk: Batsford, 1978), 346.

82. Ibid.

83. According to sources from Heidrun Edelmann, *Vom Luxusgut zum Gebrauchsgegenstand. Die Geschichte der Verbreitung von Personenkraftwagen in Deutschland* (Frankfurt a. M.: Schriftenreihe des Verbandes der Automobilindustrie e. V., 1989), chapter 5, footnote 113. The author estimates the German export rate to have ranged between 6.7% and 7.5% in 1935 and 1936, and the British rate was 17%.

84. See the following study by the German business cycles research institute: Deutsches Institut für Wirtschaftsforschung, "Untersuchungen zur Kraftverkehrsplanung im europäischen Großwirtschaftsraum. I. Die Ausrüstung des europäischen Großwirtschaftsraums mit Kraftfahrzeugen und die Triebkräfte der europäischen Kraftverkehrsentwicklung," unpublished manuscript, Berlin, 1941, 112.

85. "Die Kraftfahrzeugsaison," 4.

86. Edelmann, *Vom Luxusgut zum Gebrauchsgegenstand*, 165.

87. "Die Kraftfahrzeugsaison," 4.

88. Even in Germany, the output value of 1928 was only barely surpassed (+10.2%) in 1936. Own calculation from "Die 'jungen' Industriezweige," *Wochenbericht*, vol. 10, no. 7 (1937): 33.

89. Home market sales as "Kostenträgerin für die Exportverluste." Edelmann, *Vom Luxusgut zum Gebrauchsgegenstand*, 195.

90. Only Opel, as part of the foreign holding of General Motors, was able to profit from export sales. Edelmann, *Vom Luxusgut zum Gebrauchsgegenstand*, 170 and 194.

91. An average Austrian car came to 4,976 Schillings whereas an imported vehicle amounted to 3,558 Schillings. Own calculation according to figures from *Aussenhandel*, 70.

92. Ibid.

93. The number of licensed new vehicles per year was only 4,700 in 1936 and 5,700 in 1937. In contrast, most smaller countries had higher annual demand. For instance, in Norway and Switzerland it was between 6,000 and 12,000 vehicles per year. Even in underdeveloped Portugal, the number for annually licensed cars and trucks was up to 5,000. In the large developed countries figures ranged between 160,000 and more than 400,000 annually. See *Jahrbuch* (1937), 106 and *Jahrbuch* (1938), 114.

94. See these issues of *Bilanzen*: 5 March 1932, 3 December 1932, 17 December 1932, 7 January 1933, 25 February 1933, 17 June 1933, 23 September 1933, 20 October 1934, 20 January 1935, 20 July 1935, 8 August 1936, 24 October 1936, 26 June 1937.

95. See these issues of *Bilanzen:* 26 July 1930, 25 November 1933, 19 May 1934, 22 September 1934.

96. Total car output was 1,725. *Statistisches Handbuch für den Bundesstaat Österreich* (1937), 75.

97. Total number of exported Austrian cars was 432. Steyr must have sold the majority. *Aussenhandel*, 70.

98. *Statistisches Handbuch für den Bundesstaat Österreich* (1937), 123.

99. See Wessels, "Policy and Performance," chapters 2, 4, and 6.

100. For data on *Semperit* see these issues of *Bilanzen:* 14 November 1931, 8 October 1932, 21 October 1933, 27 October 1934, 25 January 1936, 26 September 1936, 6 November 1937.

Engelbert Dollfuss and Austrian Agriculture

James William Miller

Photo: Vogelsang-Institut, Vienna

Few figures in the history of the Austrian First Republic were so controversial, both during their lifetimes and after, as Chancellor Engelbert Dollfuss. All one needs to do to expose the continuing political divisions in the country between members of the three main camps (Christian Social, Social Democrat, and German Nationalist/ Liberal) is to begin a discussion of Dollfuss. Hailed as a political martyr by some within the Christian Social tradition, he is hated with equal passion by many Social Democrats and at least some followers of the Freedom Party, and this nearly seventy years after his assassination.

These divisions have colored the historical scholarship pertaining to Dollfuss. In the years immediately after his death, several right-wing authors wrote hagiographical accounts of his life, and, very much in the tradition of the medieval writers who extolled the virtues of the saints, they made their subject appear better fit for a halo than he was perhaps in real life.[1] Books much more critical of Dollfuss and his policies began to appear during World War II. One of the first was by an American leftist, Charles Gulick, who saw Dollfuss as a fascist dictator of a particularly Austrian stamp, different from Hitler and Mussolini in some ways, but a fascist nonetheless.[2] The interpretation of Dollfuss as an Austrofascist continues in much of the literature down to the present. It may be clearly found in Martin Kitchen's book *The Coming of Austrian Fascism* and, in a much more nuanced version, in one of the best books on the Dollfuss-Schuschnigg regime of the last two decades, namely that edited by Emmerich Talos and Wolfgang Neugebauer.[3] This view of Dollfuss as an Austrofascist was contested in the most recent publications on Dollfuss, four articles by R.

John Rath, which appeared in the *Austrian History Yearbook* just shortly before the author's death in 2001.[4] John Rath saw Dollfuss as a mixture of democrat and authoritarian, whose authoritarian tendencies became more pronounced as he struggled to deal with the economic, political, and social crises that mounted after his appointment as chancellor in 1932. Rath bases his argument at least in part on the fact that, before 1933, Dollfuss was actually viewed by leading Social Democrats as one of the most democratically-minded Christian Socials, and thus someone they could work with.

The curiously favorable light in which Dollfuss was viewed by Social Democrats before 1933 deserves closer examination. In 1964, Julius Deutsch, who headed the Social Democratic paramilitary organization *Republikanischer Schutzbund,* recalled encountering Dollfuss for the first time in a meeting of the parliamentary committee for housing and settlement policy:

> What struck me then was that Dollfuss appeared not to find it too important to follow the Christian Social party line consistently. For him it was much more important to find a consensus with his political opponents, and by this he made clear that practical solutions were more important to him than preconceived party positions. Nothing changed in this regard once he became minister of agriculture in early 1931 in the ministry of Dr. Ender. He managed to get along fine with social democratic members of Parliament, and no one at that time, himself included, thought that this expert minister would so soon be playing such a prominent political role.[5]

So what was it that transformed Dollfuss from apparently one of the more non-partisan, moderate leaders of the Christian Social party to an arch-enemy of both the National Socialists and the Social Democrats? Why did Dollfuss, of all people, ultimately become the gravedigger of Austrian parliamentary democracy?

There is no simple answer to this question, but at least a partial one may be found in the priorities that Dollfuss followed throughout his career. For him, the most important segment of society was the peasantry, and their survival was crucial to the survival of the state. All other considerations were secondary. In his view, the peasantry formed the economic foundation of the nation, and, consequently, the future of society as a whole depended on securing the well-being of the peasant population. To him, the peasantry was the "source of the rejuvenation of society, even in the cities, . . . so ensuring the economic survival of the peasantry is at the same time a matter of survival for our people as a whole."[6] This was because, for Dollfuss, the peasantry was the repository of a set of values upon which all of society depended: "Our struggle for [economic] existence would be for naught if the most important, indeed the only, basis for the state were lost, namely

German customs and the Catholic faith, which are most thoroughly anchored in the peasantry. If that were to happen, nothing could ensure the future of our people."[7]

Thus, any policy that disadvantaged the peasantry would ultimately undermine the state. While Dollfuss was willing to recognize that workers, too, had basic economic needs, and that ultimately the well-being of peasants as agricultural producers depended on the ability of proletarian consumers to buy the goods the peasants produced, meeting the needs of the peasantry was always the primary task of government for him, and he saw his life's work in protecting their interests. His identification with the peasantry and with their representative organizations was lifelong. A rather minor incident is telling in this regard. In 1932, as a consequence of having been appointed chancellor, he was invited by *Who's Who* to fill out a form so he could be included in their next volume. In the slot where he was asked to indicate his professional position, he wrote: "Director of the Lower Austrian Chamber of Agriculture. Presently chancellor of Austria."[8]

Setting the welfare of the peasantry at the top of his list of priorities meant that, if parliamentary democracy appeared to be an inadequate political tool in securing the peasantry's survival, then other, more effective methods would have to be tried. It is perhaps a bit too much of an over-simplification to say that Dollfuss's eventual rejection of democracy in favor of the more authoritarian *Ständestaat* essentially came down to the decision to protect the interests of the peasantry at all costs, but certainly this played a large role.

Another factor played a role in Dollfuss's ultimately ambivalent commitment to democratic institutions. His rather specific conception of democracy derived both from peasant tradition and from his own close study of agricultural cooperatives: an authoritarian, elitist conception of democracy that combined a system of political legitimization through elections with an authoritarian style of administration. In this concept of democracy, once elected, political officials were more or less free to do as they pleased, without much concern for the wishes of their constituents. Thus, to understand the events of 1933 and 1934 and Dollfuss's role in them, it is necessary to know about his career as an agricultural policy maker and about the values that shaped the policies he helped develop in the 1920s and early 1930s.

Dollfuss was born in Texing, Lower Austria, on 4 October 1892 as the illegitimate son of Josefa Dollfuss and Josef Weninger. Josefa was the daughter of a relatively comfortable, though by no means wealthy peasant. Josef Weninger was an orphan, apprenticed to a miller, with few prospects for acquiring wealth or status. Josefa's father accordingly refused to permit the two to marry, and instead arranged for his daughter to wed Leopold Schmutz, a peasant in the neighboring village of Kirnberg. The young

Dollfuss was then taken in by his somewhat miserly stepfather. Engelbert Dollfuss did well enough in school and as an altar boy in the local church to attract the attention of the village priest, who arranged a scholarship for him at the archiepiscopal school at Hollabrunn. The expectation was that Dollfuss would eventually study for the priesthood.[9]

Dollfuss completed his secondary education and entered the University of Vienna's theological seminary in 1913, when, after an intense period of soul-searching, he decided that he did not have the makings of a priest. He was particularly concerned that he would not be able to keep an oath of celibacy.[10] He still wanted to serve the peasantry—just not as a parish priest—so he turned instead to the study of law with the intention of pursuing a career in public service. While a student, he began to work in a network of Catholic social organizations founded by Karl Rudolf, which, among other things, provided job training to disadvantaged workers.[11] Dollfuss also joined the Catholic fraternity *Franco-Bavaria*, which would serve him as a vital social network for the rest of his life.

The *Franco-Bavaria* was part of the umbrella organization of Catholic fraternities, the *Cartellverband* (or CV for short), which was more pro-Austrian than the traditional German nationalist fraternities. The CV was an important key to future success in Catholic circles, because from it were recruited the officials who were to serve in various institutions and organizations dominated by the Catholic church and the Christian Social party. Not only did the fraternity help boost Dollfuss's career prospects, it also became an important recruiting pool for him once he began to hire staff, first in the Lower Austrian Chamber of Agriculture (*Niederösterreichische Landes-Landwirtschaftskammer*) and then later as minister of agriculture.[12]

Dollfuss's studies were interrupted by the outbreak of the First World War. He volunteered already in August of 1914 and went into training as commander of a machine gun platoon. He served with distinction on the Italian front, advancing to the rank of lieutenant by war's end. The front-line experience was important in building Dollfuss's abilities as a leader. Once in an administrative position, he demanded loyalty and attention to duty from his employees, just as he had from those under his command at the front; but he demanded no more than he himself gave.[13] Service in the military also cemented his loyalty to Austria as a nation, and, despite the demise of the monarchy in 1918, Dollfuss came home from the front committed to the new Austrian Republic.[14]

In 1918, Dollfuss returned to his legal studies and to his work with Karl Rudolph's social welfare movement. Some of the most important ideas to which Dollfuss was exposed during this period were the corporatist concepts of the philosopher Othmar Spann and the social gospel represented in the papal encyclical of 1891, *Rerum novarum*. Dollfuss visited

Spann's lectures at the University of Vienna, and his later actions as a Lower Austrian agricultural official and as chancellor suggest that he owed at least some of his ideas to Spann.

Spann rejected both liberalism and capitalism, objecting especially to their overemphasis on the rights of individual and free competition. Instead, Spann looked back at the medieval social order and saw in it a better way to secure social peace. Rather than regarding society as being first and foremost made up of individuals, Spann conceived of society as being divided up into professional estates along the lines of the medieval guilds. The interests of the individual would be represented and protected by the estate to which he or she belonged. Within the estate, however, the individual should subordinate himself to its leadership. The individual could then concentrate on going about his or her profession, while leaving politics to the leadership of the estate. The leaders of the estates would work together in a unified manner to secure the stability of the state as a whole, replacing political competition with cooperation. It was essentially an anti-democratic, authoritarian understanding of the role of the state.[15] Despite his rejection of liberal concepts regarding individual rights, however, Spann did not reject the notion of private property. In order for private property not to be used in ways that harmed society as a whole, however, its use had to be guided by ethical principles; its owners had to be forced to use their property in a way that benefited society as a whole, rather than just themselves as individuals. The state thus had not only the right, but also the responsibility to step in and guide the economy.[16]

The actions Dollfuss later took as an official of the Lower Austrian chamber of agriculture were clearly directed at creating a powerful institutional expression of the peasant estate. As minister of agriculture, he then set about creating the structures by which the state could direct the economy into socially desirable paths. As chancellor, in seeking an answer to the political crisis of 1933, he finally tried to take what he had learned in setting up the Lower Austrian chamber and apply it to an estate-based system of government for Austria as a whole—the *Ständestaat*.[17]

Perhaps even more important in the formation of Dollfuss's intellectual world than Spann was the reformist Catholicism that gained popularity in the late nineteenth and early twentieth century. Associated with individuals such as Bishop Emmanuel Ketteler from Germany and Karl von Vogelsang in Austria, this reformist Catholicism fed off the ideas expressed in Leo XIII's encyclical, *Rerum novarum*. The encyclical was also critical of liberalism and capitalism, arguing that they reduced the value of a human being to the wares he or she produced. Human labor, however, was not a commodity like any other, because there was a divine law that limited how it could be exploited. A worker was entitled to a just wage that would support him and his family in modest comfort—anything less was nothing short of sinful exploitation. If the market was unable to supply a worker with this living wage, then restrictions had to be placed on the market to ensure that it did.[18] Dollfuss later applied this principle to the agricultural economy, arguing for market controls to ensure peasants sufficient profit on their products so that they could survive.[19]

Dollfuss's world view was not only influenced by Spann and the Catholic reformist tradition. He spent 1920/21 at the University of Berlin under a scholarship from the Lower Austrian Peasant's League (*Niederösterreichischer Bauernbund*), taking coursework in economics, political and agricultural science. He attended lectures by Werner Sombart, Gerhardt von Schulze-Gävernitz, and Max Sering, and he made some of their ideas his own.[20] His benefactors at the Lower Austrian Peasants' League, Director Josef Sturm in particular, wanted him to gain an understanding of peasant cooperatives in Germany, so Dollfuss not only attended lectures in Berlin, but also worked in cooperative organizations, as, for example, the Prussian Central Cooperative Bank.[21] This background work was to be significant in his later activities as an agricultural policy maker in Lower Austria, where he paid particular attention to the expansion of the agricultural cooperatives.

Based on his experiences in Berlin, Dollfuss began work on a treatise that he intended to become his dissertation in political science. The manuscript is of interest because it provides insights into Dollfuss's ideological makeup.[22] He was convinced that unfettered capitalism would be the ruin of the Austrian peasantry and that cooperatives could provide a way for the peasants to compete successfully. Furthermore, the cooperatives were a way to infuse the marketplace with Christian values. Not competition was the guiding principle of cooperation, but mutual support. The cooperative movement valued the needs of the community over the desire of the individual for private profit and so embodied the principle of brotherly love that was so central to Christian ethics.[23]

This clearly Christian Social, anti-capitalist view of political economy was accompanied by another lesson that Dollfuss thought could be learned from the example of the cooperatives. When people joined a cooperative, they became responsible, not to one another as individuals, but to the cooperative as a whole. Though they were free to leave the cooperative at any time, they were bound to the leadership of the cooperative in a dependent relationship while they were members. Dollfuss understood the cooperative to be an ideal model of democracy in action, but his understanding of democracy was an elitist, rather than a populist, one. He had little sympathy for the grassroots democracy so typical of the populist forms of agrarian cooperation in the United States in their early stages.[24] While the members of a cooperative might freely elect their leadership, they were obligated to obey them once the leaders were in place. "In a cooperative members are not obligated to one another as individuals, but to the cooperative as a whole, in the form of its leadership."[25]

Dollfuss's emphasis on the obligations of the individual members to the cooperative's leadership, rather than the obligations of the leadership to the membership, has much to say about how he thought democracy should work. This sort of democracy shut the average citizen out of the formulation of policy. This was to be undertaken by the *experts*, by the leadership. As one of Dollfuss's elderly fraternity brothers put it in a conference sponsored by *Franco-Bavaria* in 1984, commemorating the fiftieth anniversary of his assassination, "The people's role is to vote for its leaders, and then to obey them."[26] This rather restricted conception of democracy was reflected in Dollfuss's groundbreaking work in the field of agrarian organization in the 1920s, and later in his actions as minister of agriculture, and subsequently as chancellor.

Dollfuss's career as an agricultural policy maker began immediately upon his return from Berlin in 1921. His benefactor, Josef Sturm, who was then director of the Lower Austrian Peasants' League, hired him as secretary of the organization. The Lower Austrian Peasants' League had been founded in 1906 as an arm of the Christian Social party. While the league officially represented only the peasants of Lower Austria, the fact that it had its offices in Vienna, close to the seat of government, meant that it played a disproportionately big role in the formulation of agricultural policy on the federal level.[27] Considering Dollfuss's later career path, it is worth looking at the decision-making patterns, administrative structures, and the system of political legitimization of the Lower Austrian Peasants' League. They reflect the authoritarian approach to democracy outlined above.

The Lower Austrian Peasants' League was structured hierarchically, which guaranteed the emergence of a powerful political elite insulated from the grassroots membership of the organization. The system worked as follows: Local peasants' leagues each elected a chairman for their respective county. The chairmen of these local organizations then constituted a county-wide peasants' league. The county league, in turn, elected a chairman. The county chairmen then made up the provincial peasants' league, and elected a chair from among themselves.[28] This gave the average peasant in Lower Austria no direct way to influence the political leadership of the organization—it was structurally too far removed. If the average peasant wanted something from the Lower Austrian Peasant League chairman, the only recourse was to petition him. One could not threaten him with a recall, or a grassroots campaign to remove him in the next election, because he did not directly depend upon the average peasant's vote for his power. Thus, there was a democratic legitimization process, but the structure of the organization helped to insulate the leadership from the rank-and-file members of the organization. Peasant leaders were able to consolidate power so thoroughly that they could do more or less as they pleased with relatively little concern for whether the policy direction they took had grassroots support.[29]

This consolidation of power can be seen very clearly in the career of Josef Reither, one of Dollfuss's most important mentors and his successor as minister of agriculture after Dollfuss's assassination in 1934. Reither served as mayor of his home village of Langenrohr in the Tulln basin for nine years before being elected to the provincial legislature as a peasant league candidate. In 1925, he became chairman of the league, and in 1928 he was elected president of the Lower Austrian Chamber of Agriculture. By 1931, he was also governor of Lower Austria. During this same period, he simultaneously held the following posts: vice-chairman of the Lower Austrian Central Cooperative Bank, member of the board of directors of the Association of Rural Cooperatives, chairman of the Lower Austrian Association of Dairies, chairman of the Lower Austrian Fire Insurance Company, chairman of the Provincial Association of Dairy Cooperatives, chairman of the Rural Cooperative of Tulln, and chairman of the Agrarian Publishing House of Lower Austria, to name just his most important positions.[30] Josef Reither held more posts simultaneously than probably any other single peasant leader in Austria, but the general pattern he set was by no means unusual. This meant that the peasant leadership of Austria made up a tightly woven fabric, and that the leaders were in a relatively sovereign political position. It meant that the average peasant really had no alternative but to elect and then obey.

The Lower Austrian Peasant League served as midwife to the organization in which Dollfuss was to make his career, the Lower Austrian Chamber of Agriculture. The league's leaders, especially Josef Sturm, were dissatisfied with the established system of support for agriculture. The Provincial Agricultural Council was a remnant of the monarchy and posed a problem for the Lower Austrian peasant leadership for several reasons. First, during the monarchy, it had been dominated by the aristocracy and was not viewed as particularly sympathetic to the needs of the peasantry. A certain aristocratic taint remained even after 1918. Second, the political restructuring that followed the creation of the First Republic brought with it the creation of two provinces, Lower Austria and Vienna, where previously there had been just one. This separation took place in stages between 1920 and 1922 and necessitated the creation of separate provincial organizations to promote agriculture (despite its urban character, Vienna did still have a small agricultural sector).[31]

If structural changes were necessary in any case, the peasant leadership of Lower Austria began to ask itself what particular form an institution should take to further agricultural interests in the province. A commission went to Bavaria to study the chamber of agriculture there, and upon its return, Dollfuss and Rudolf Fink, a Lower Austrian agrarian official, were put in charge of writing a draft law for the creation of a similar organization in Lower Austria. The bill was debated in the Lower Austrian legislature early in 1922 and then passed on 22 February of that year. Dollfuss became the new chamber's first secretary. The law defined the new organization's field of operations in fairly far-reaching terms, including: ". . . administration of agricultural matters, especially rural property valuation, housing, and settlement, the setting of prices for agricultural products; statistical studies of agriculture; collection of data on work-related matters; improvement of economic and social conditions for those engaged in agriculture; contributions to policy making and the drafting of legislation and regulations relating to agriculture."[32] In addition, the chamber was responsible for agricultural research, the creation of agricultural schools and other educational outreach programs, advising the rural population on matters relating to agricultural technology and agricultural economics, as well as providing legal advice relating to agricultural matters.

The law went beyond a mere reorganization of the tasks previously undertaken by the Provincial Agricultural Council. It actually assigned to the chamber several responsibilities that previously had been carried out by the ministry of agriculture.[33] The chamber, therefore, became a quasi-public institution, serving at once as a lobbying organization for agrarian interests and as an administrative organization that actually implemented policy. It was a very ambitious agenda, one that matched in scope the ambition of the law's author.

The ink was hardly dry on the paper before Dollfuss began putting the law to work. He quickly hired a staff of twenty, the higher-level positions being filled almost exclusively by members of the CV. The working climate in the chamber was by all accounts a good one, though it was very intense. Dollfuss was a man with a mission, and he expected his employees to put in the same long hours as he did. In 1927, when he was elevated to director of the chamber, he described the chamber's officials in these words:" We stick with the peasantry. We are not just bureaucrats who are content to put in our hours and punch the clock—we see our work as our life's purpose. The man who does not find fulfillment in his work, is a poor man indeed. A man must be filled by his profession. This is a personal code for me, and I will do all I can to make sure it continues to be the spirit that guides our officials in the future. My guiding principle is, 'The greatest honor is duty.'"[34] And for Dollfuss this was not empty rhetoric. He and his staff were true to this work ethic. The array of laws and initiatives that emerged from the chamber in the first years of its existence, especially given its relatively small size, is nothing short of amazing.

Only five days after the ceremony celebrating the official founding of the chamber, Dollfuss put forward the draft of a bill to create a national system of obligatory social insurance for all Austrians working in agriculture: peasants, their wives and children, as well as their employees. The process of getting the bill passed proved to be long and drawn-out, encountering stiff opposition, not only from the ranks of the Social Democrats, but also from within his own camp. The Social Democrats wanted to incorporate agricultural employees into the already existing system of insurance for workers. Class conscious as the Social Democrats were, they thought it unwise to have workers insured by companies that were likely to be controlled by employers. An additional consideration was political. If the agricultural workers were enrolled in an insurance system controlled by Social Democrats, then they might more easily be won over to actually vote according to their class interests, which is to say, Social Democratic.[35] On the other hand, many peasants were opposed to the bill because they did not want to pay premiums for their employees and family members, who they saw as cheap replacements for paid labor.[36] Peasant representatives from Salzburg, Upper Austria, and Styria were also opposed because they did not want to see their provincial insurance companies, which they controlled and which provided opportunities for political patronage, replaced by a federally-based insurance system.[37]

Against such widespread opposition, the bill made little progress, and in 1928 a much watered-down alternative bill, put forward by the Minister for Social Affairs Josef Resch, made it through Parliament. The crucial difference between Dollfuss's bill and the one that passed was that the latter created a voluntary system. Dollfuss was correct in assuming that if the system were made voluntary, too few people would join. The system would attract primarily those who already had high medical bills, and there would accordingly be an insufficient spreading of risk to make the system viable. He was right—the new system was almost completely ineffectual.[38] Dollfuss was forced to be satisfied with a thoroughgoing reform of the insurance system in Lower Austria and the neighboring provinces of Vienna and Burgenland. There, an obligatory system of insurance was put into place by 1929 that even included the family members of peasants. It was implemented despite widespread opposition from the peasants. On one occasion, Dollfuss was even forced to flee from an angry crowd of peasants in a village pub not far from his home village of Kirnberg.[39] Dollfuss, however, was convinced that making the system obligatory was the key to its success, and that ultimately all Lower Austrians involved in agriculture would benefit. As he put it in a speech on 11 September 1928: "Agricultural insurance is not only a purely humane, ethical problem, but also a fundamental economic problem. There will be no improvements in agriculture unless the social and economic condition of agricultural laborers improve."[40] The importance of the issue made it imperative to proceed despite the widespread opposition. The great power exercised by the Lower Austrian peasant estate in the form of the chamber of agriculture and the peasants' league meant that any opposition to the new legislation could be ignored. While Dollfuss was almost certainly right about the need for such a system of insurance and the need to make it obligatory, the way the system was implemented in Lower Austria reflected the patriarchal, authoritarian nature of the political system there.

Social insurance was by no means the only problem area of agricultural policy that Dollfuss and his team at the chamber took on. They also had considerable success in expanding agricultural production. After the war, Austria was in a very difficult position with regard to agricultural supply. Much of the beef and pork that supplied the Vienna market before 1918 had come from Hungary and the Carpathians, for example.[41] Austrian agriculture was also, by and large, not as progressive as that of Bohemia or Hungary. One of the great tasks facing Austrian agriculture in the postwar period was replacing the Hungarians and Czechs as far as possible with Austrian suppliers on the Vienna market.

The Lower Austrian chamber undertook a whole array of measures to increase production. At the end of the war, agricultural experts were convinced that the dairy sector offered significant growth potential. The climatic and geographic conditions in Lower Austria lent themselves well to dairy production. One of the chief problems was the lack of an adequate infrastructure to process milk products and get them to market efficiently. Dollfuss saw dairy cooperatives as the answer, and set about encouraging their growth in the province.

Financing for this expansion came from the League of Nations. According to the terms of the Geneva Protocols, the league provided Austria with a loan of 650 million gold crowns to create a new, stable currency, the schilling. After 1925, surplus funds from the loan, beyond what had been needed for currency stabilization, became available, and Dollfuss proposed that they be used to provide loans to peasant cooperatives for the expansion of dairy production. The league approved the proposal, and six million schillings were freed for this purpose, a whole third of which went to Lower Austria alone. In the following three years, new dairies sprang up very rapidly all over Lower Austria, with an associated increase in fresh milk processing. In 1927, the number of dairies in the province stood at thirteen; by 1930 there were twenty-one. Fresh milk production increased by 60%, and the annual amount of milk processed into butter and cheese in Lower Austrian dairies nearly trebled in that period. The chamber audited the dairies' books, created an umbrella organization to oversee them, and introduced a system of butter inspection to control quality, all during the years from 1926 to 1928.[42]

Dairy production was not the only agricultural sector to receive Dollfuss's attention, however. He also expended great energy in setting up distillery cooperatives to process potatoes into industrial alcohol. The type of potatoes needed for distillation was high in starch and grew well in some of the more economically depressed areas of Lower Austria, such as the Waldviertel along the border with Czechoslovakia. In 1926, Dollfuss worked successfully to change the law governing distilleries to make it easier for cooperatives to get into the business. The new law guaranteed the agricultural cooperatives 50% of the market. As a consequence, eighteen new distillery cooperatives were founded in the province, mainly at Dollfuss's initiative.[43]

Dollfuss's endeavor to expand the network of cooperatives had as its goal the increased economic independence of Lower Austrian peasants. The cooperatives freed the peasants from dependence on commercial middlemen, who stood between producer and consumer and profited from both. An initiative that was similarly intended to free the peasantry from economic dependence on other social groups was the creation of a mediation service housed in the chamber. Peasants could agree to mediation by the chamber and thus avoid the cost of going to court to settle a dispute. The legal profession, of course, saw this as an encroachment upon its territory and got the ministry of justice to rule that the chamber had overreached its charter. Dollfuss dealt with the matter by simply ignoring the objections of the minister of justice.[44] The mediation service was an interesting idea, especially since it was implemented by someone who himself held a law degree.

Dollfuss also began a number of initiatives in the public relations realm. One of the first steps in this direction was the creation of an agrarian news service, the *Agrarische Nachrichtenzentrale,* in 1926. Eventually, this agency was producing daily reports on agricultural matters, the most important of which were sent by telegram to the various Austrian newspapers, some of which reproduced them verbatim. This was followed in 1929 by the creation of the chamber's own publishing house, the *Agrarverlag*, which published not only practical guides to things like sugar beet culture or the newest agricultural machinery, but also informative brochures on social insurance or the organization of the chamber itself. The public outreach work of the chamber extended to a weekly radio program on agricultural matters broadcast over Austrian Radio.[45]

The diverse nature of the initiatives undertaken by Dollfuss and his staff in the 1920s demonstrates the energetic nature of the man, as well as his goal of creating an all-encompassing, powerful peasant organization that would be able to defend peasant interests. The chamber, together with the system of cooperatives and the political representation of the peasantry provided by the peasants' league, constituted a sort of corporate state in miniature within the established structure of democratic Austria. Given Dollfuss's background and beliefs, it should have come as no surprise that, as minister of agriculture, he would attempt to implement increased market controls to shield the peasantry from the effects of the worldwide agricultural depression and that, as chancellor, he would try to take the structure of peasant corporatism he had helped build in Lower Austria and apply it to the country as a whole.

Dollfuss became minister of agriculture on 18 March 1931, after a controversial six-month stint as president of the Austrian railway system (ÖBB).[46] Despite the difficult nature of the job at the ÖBB, the ministry of agriculture was a much tougher assignment. Since 1927, Austrian agriculture had faced an ever-deepening crisis. This was the result of world market forces, over which Austrian policy makers had very little control. The increase in Austrian agricultural production achieved since World War I had unfortunately been matched by similar increases elsewhere in the world. A global oversupply of agricultural goods, along with an associated decline in prices, was the result. The problem emerged first in grain prices but then spread to meat as well, as farmers world-wide attempted to deal with the erosion in grain prices by feeding their grain to cattle and hogs. Central European wheat prices dropped by two-thirds and beef prices by one-quarter between 1927 and 1931.[47] The situation was made worse for Austria by the disjointed nature of the trade treaties with its neighbors,[48] since, despite increases in production, Austria continued to be dependent upon them for a large portion of its food supply.[49]

As early as 1930, Dollfuss had advocated the creation of a unified, regulated market for Europe as a whole to address the agricultural crisis.[50] Failing that, he suggested that the "most-favored-nation system" should be replaced with what he called a neighbor regulation, which would permit neighboring countries to enter into special treaties that would grant them special treatment in matters of trade. Those privileges would not extend to all other nations who held the most-favored-nation status. The new system was to be accompanied by the establishment of a European system to store grain in times of overproduction and thus support prices. The system was to be run by a syndicate of agricultural cooperatives.[51]

Initially, this proposal won little support from the League of Nations, so once Dollfuss became minister of agriculture, he began to work on establishing a neighbor regulation for central Europe without the sanction of the League. This was to be accomplished by a series of special treaties with Austria's immediate neighbors. The first such treaty was concluded with Hungary in June of 1931, and similar treaties followed with Yugoslavia and Czechoslovakia in July. The treaties guaranteed Austria's partners a certain portion of the Austrian market under reduced customs duties but also introduced a quota system that limited the total export of agricultural goods to Austria. The net effect of the treaties was to control where Austrian imports were coming from, to the disadvantage of countries such as the United States, Germany, and Poland. Hungary, Yugoslavia, Italy, and Romania were the main winners—and of course Austria, as well, because it was able to reduce the total amount of agricultural imports.[52]

Of much less far-reaching import, but interesting nonetheless in the context of Dollfuss's single-minded attention to the needs of Austrian agriculture, were two incidents involving less-favored European trading partners. On 18 April 1931, Dollfuss banned the import of Soviet eggs. Soviet egg exports to Austria were practically negligible anyway, but Dollfuss found a way to ban them. He may have been experimenting in a small way with methods for reducing imports that could then have been applied elsewhere with more consequence. He based the ban on a veterinary ordinance of 1909 that permitted the government to ban imports of all agricultural products that had been in contact with fowl from countries where a poultry epidemic was known to exist. Now, it really was an incontrovertible fact that the eggs had been in contact with fowl, but it was not quite so clear that there was a poultry epidemic in the Soviet Union. The Soviets, in any case, took umbrage at this attack on their chickens' honor and declared that, if Austria was going to refuse to import Soviet eggs, then the Soviet Union could do without a rather large machine-tool contract of ten million schillings that was then pending between the two nations. Pressure from the Austrian industrial sector forced Dollfuss to retract the ban.[53]

A more significant attempt to reduce imports was a ban on Polish veal, which followed almost immediately on the heels of the Soviet egg ban. The ban singled out Polish calf carcasses of under fifty kilograms. The Poles raised cattle breeds that were, by and large, smaller than Austrian ones, so Polish calf carcasses generally ranged between forty-two and fifty kilos. Dollfuss argued that the small size of the carcasses pointed to a potential danger to public health.[54] Unfortunately for Dollfuss, he was able to produce no evidence that eating meat from small calves was a danger to health. He came closer to the truth when he admitted in a cabinet meeting that the import of cheap Polish calves had had a depressive impact on the price of Austrian veal. The Poles were singled out because at the time they were the source of 90% of the foreign veal on the Austrian market.[55] Particularly irritating to the Austrian companies engaged in importing the Polish veal was that the ban had been announced on 17 April with an implementation date of 26 April. Many of the companies had contracts for calves in hand that had been executed before the announcement, but for which they had yet to receive delivery. If left in place, the ban would have forced them to dump the calves on the already far overloaded European market at a horrendous loss. As was the case with the Soviet eggs, Dollfuss was forced to back down. He eventually had to be satisfied with a regulation that let the vast majority of Polish calves through to Austria.[56]

These two cases demonstrate Dollfuss's willingness to use all means at his disposal to reduce foreign market pressures on Austrian agricultural producers. The two cases also betray something about his administrative style. Dollfuss undertook these measures without prior consultation with his fellow ministers. Had he consulted them, he would, for example, have learned about the high-level negotiations with the Soviets, that could have been endangered by his actions. In addition, the haste with which these measures were put through was the result of a long-standing, pent-up impatience on the part of the Lower Austrian agrarians with the plodding way the agriculture ministry had gone about its business in the past. Indeed, one of Dollfuss's predecessors as minister of agriculture, Florian Födermayr, had lost his post in part because Josef Reither thought he had been too lackadaisical in pushing the bureaucracy to address the crisis in Austrian agriculture more aggressively.[57] Dollfuss took up his post in the agriculture ministry thinking that, finally, the time had come to get something done, and that it had to happen quickly because the peasant estate was bleeding financially. This sense of urgency then led to missteps such as those described above, and this same pattern would be repeated once Dollfuss became chancellor.

Despite the will to bring the peasantry rapid relief, the measures Dollfuss took early in 1931 did not lead to a dramatically improved situation in the agricultural markets. Dollfuss accordingly moved to more aggressive measures to support prices. The trade treaties proved inadequate to the task of reversing the downward trend in Austrian meat prices so, by the fall of 1931, Dollfuss pushed Parliament to pass a bill that would create a regulated livestock market in Austria. The provincial chambers of agriculture were pressed into service as the administrative apparatus of the new system. A central office in Vienna was set up to determine the number of cattle and hogs needed at the main slaughterhouses in a given week and to inform the provincial chambers of the quotas to be observed for that week. The chambers then distributed only enough sale permits to producers to meet the demand. Without a sale permit, livestock could not be sent to market. The approach assured that an excess of livestock on the market would not drive the price down.[58]

The second major market regulating initiative introduced by Dollfuss was in the dairy sector. One of the main problems in the domestic market for dairy products was the uneven nature of the market because of the huge concentration of consumers in Vienna. Peasants who lived far from Vienna were not in a position to sell fresh milk and so were forced to concentrate on butter and cheese production. The peasants close to Vienna in Lower Austria, on the other hand, concentrated on fresh milk production. They were particularly hard hit by the decline in fresh milk consumption in the capital city, a consequence of the depression. Faced with falling prices, peasants tried to produce more in order to maintain their previous incomes. This just made the price situation even worse, as the Vienna market was flooded with fresh milk. Dollfuss's solution, put forward in draft legislation on 15 May 1931, was to propose creation of a milk price fund to equalize the price for milk across the country, regardless of the form—fresh milk, butter, or cheese—in which the milk eventually made its way to the end-consumer. The fund was to be fed by a levy on fresh milk paid by producers and sellers, which would then be distributed among the producers of butter and cheese. This would eliminate the advantage of producing fresh milk for the Vienna market, and one could then hope that the fresh milk price would become more stable.[59]

Dollfuss's Milk Equalization Fund Bill unleashed a storm of controversy. Since the fund involved a levy on producers, Dollfuss did not see a reason why the body overseeing it should contain consumer representatives. Instead, it was to be made up only of representatives of the peasants and the sellers of milk. The Social Democrats and the chamber of labor did not see it that way.[60] Minister of Commerce Eduard Heinl, on the other hand, opposed it as yet another interference in the operation of the free market. Peasant representatives from western Austria also objected, fearing that the costs of the fund would be too great. To get the bill passed, Dollfuss was forced to write the western provinces out of the law and give the Social Democrat-dominated chamber of labor a seat on the governing board of the fund. The bill finally became law on 27 July 1931. Dollfuss, however, was by no means pleased with the compromise. A little less democracy would have yielded a better policy, according to him.

The regulatory measures taken by Dollfuss began to have their effect by the time he became chancellor on 20 May 1932. Grain and livestock prices had begun to stabilize, though, of course, at levels considerably lower than before the onset of the crisis.[61] The Milk Equalization Fund, however, had not managed to reverse the price decline in fresh milk. From 1931 to the end of 1933, the wholesale milk price fell by two groschen per liter per year, largely because of unregulated competition among the milk merchants in the larger cities. Though most of the cooperatives tried to stand shoulder to shoulder in maintaining a higher price, they were undercut by independent milk dealers and by a renegade cooperative in Schärding. After becoming chancellor, Dollfuss pushed for the establishment of a cartel to either shut down the dairies that were driving prices down, or force them to tow the line. Though he retained the post of minister of agriculture while chancellor, Dollfuss's other duties meant that he was unable to apply his considerable energies exclusively to agricultural matters, and the progress of this proposal suffered as a result. It worked its way through the bureaucratic maze much more slowly without the indefatigable nudging that Dollfuss normally devoted to such matters. Dollfuss was already in the grave before it was finally implemented in mid-August 1934.[62] It goes without saying that a cartel to keep milk prices artificially high did little to win Dollfuss points with consumers.

Consumers were also hard hit by a measure Dollfuss pushed through in 1933 to prop up rye prices. The initial success in stabilizing grain prices was reversed in 1933, and rye prices tumbled as a consequence of a record harvest that was 25% to 50% higher than in the previous year. Dollfuss met with officials of the agriculture ministry on August 7 to look for a solution. The millers had suggested that the government permit them to import wheat free of customs duties if they promised to buy more domestic rye. Since this would only have meant shifting the crisis from the rye to the wheat market, Dollfuss rejected this proposal out of hand. Instead, a combination of measures was put into action. Taxes were increased on sugar beets, the income from which was given to the cooperatives so they could buy up and store rye. Sugar beet prices had not fallen so dramatically as those for other agricultural goods, so Dollfuss and his advisors felt the tax would not harm the farmers who grew them too much. Dollfuss then met with the large Viennese bakers and promised them an increase in the bread price, if they agreed to use more rye in their bread. He also converted the subventions that were going to peasants in mountain regions from cash to in-kind payments—namely in rye. These measures quickly brought the price fall for rye under control.[63] Once again, however, stability was purchased at the expense of consumers, especially those in Vienna.

Such measures, as well as the trade treaties that included signifi-cant advantages for Austrian agriculture, led to a widespread belief that the Dollfuss government was robbing from already hard-pressed workers in order to give alms to peasants, and this helped harden already very tense relations between reds and blacks.[64] The charge that the government was following an "agrarian course" was nothing new—it had cropped up already when Dollfuss was only minister of agriculture.[65] The details of the agricultural policies outlined above should make it clear that there was more than a little truth to these charges. This pro-agrarian course was a natural consequence of Dollfuss's background and ideology. As he saw things, the way out of the general depression of the 1930s was first to stabilize and then to increase agricultural prices. If the free market had to be sacrificed in the process, it was no great loss. In fact, it needed reform anyway so that cooperative values could replace capitalistic ones. If authoritarian methods had to be employed to achieve this end, then perhaps that was the way political decision making should be structured anyway. In a reformed market, peasants would have higher incomes and would then be in a better position to buy industrially produced goods, and workers would, as a consequence, get their jobs back.[66]

Economic recovery would go hand in hand with a restructuring of the Austrian political system that would make similar crises in the future much less difficult to master, because control mechanisms would be in place to address them. The fact that the depression in agriculture began in the mid-1920s and then spread to other areas of the economy by the end of the decade was all the confirmation that Dollfuss needed for the wisdom of his course—if the crisis had begun in agriculture, that was where to seek its solution. For Dollfuss, it was a simple matter of putting first things first.

Notes

1. See, for example, Attilio Renato Bleibtreu, *Der Heldenkanzler: Ein Lied von der Scholle* (Vienna: Jung-Österreich Verlag, 1934); Dietrich von Hildebrand, *Engelbert Dollfuss: Ein katholischer Staatsmann* (Salzburg: Pustet, 1934); Hans Maurer, *Kanzler Dollfuss* (Graz: Styria Verlag, 1934); John Gregory, *Dollfuss and His Times* (London: Hutchinson, 1935); Johannes Messner, *Dollfuss* (Innsbruck: Tyrolia, 1935).

2. Charles Gulick, *Austria from Habsburg to Hitler*, 2 vols. (Berkeley: University of California Press, 1934).

3. Martin Kitchen, *The Coming of Austrian Fascism* (London: Croom Helm, 1980); Emmerich Talos and Wolfgang Neugebauer, eds., *Austrofaschismus: Beiträge über Politik, Ökonomie und Kultur1934-1938*, 4th ed. (Vienna: Verlag für Gesellschaftskritik, 1988).

4. R. John Rath, "Deterioration of Democracy in Austria, 1927-1932," *Austrian History Yearbook* 27 (1996): 213-60; "The Molding of Engelbert Dollfuss as an Agrarian Reformer," *Austrian History Yearbook* 28 (1997): 173-216; "The Dollfuss Ministry: The Democratic Prelude," *Austrian History Yearbook* 29.1 (1998): 161-94; "The Dollfuss Ministry: The Intensification of Animosities and the Drift toward Authoritarianism," *Austrian History Yearbook* 30 (1999): 65-102.

5. Julius Deutsch, *Forum* (June/July 1964): 298, quoted in Eva Dollfuss, *Mein Vater: Hitlers erstes Opfer* (Vienna: Amalthea, 1994), 72.

6. Dollfuss in an address on Radio Vienna, published in its entirety in *Agrarische Nachrichten Zentrale* (henceforth abbreviated *ANZ*), 28 December 1931, 2.

7. Dollfuss in a speech before the Lower Austrian Peasant League, *ANZ*, 25 November 1932, 19.

8. Dollfuss, *Mein Vater*, 55-56. Dollfuss remained director of the Lower Austrian chamber of agriculture until his assassination.

9. Gerhard Jagschitz, "Die Jugend des Bundeskanzlers Dr. Engelbert Dollfuss. Ein Beitrag zur geistig-politischen Situation der sogenannten 'Kriegsgeneration' des 1. Weltkriegs," PhD. diss., University of Vienna, 1967, 7-59.

10. Dollfuss, *Mein Vater*, 24-25.

11. Rath, "The Molding of Engelbert Dollfuss," 184.

12. Gerhard Popp, *CV in Österreich. Organisation, Binnenstruktur und politische Funktion* (Vienna: Böhlau, 1984); James William Miller, *Engelbert Dollfuss als Agrarfachmann. Eine Analyse bäuerlicher Führungsbegriffe und österreichischer Agrarpolitik 1918-1934* (Vienna: Böhlau, 1989), 75-76.

13. Jagschitz, "Die Jugend des Bundeskanzlers," 118.

14. Dollfuss, *Mein Vater*, 42.

15. Othmar Spann, *Der Wahre Staat. Vorlesungen über Abbruch und Neubau der Gesellschaft, gehalten 1920 in Wien* (Leipzig: Quelle und Meyer, 1921), 205-6, 232.

16. Ibid., 267.

17. Dollfuss was, however, by no means an unwavering disciple of Spann. They disagreed about the value of cooperatives, for example, of which Spann was skeptical. Dollfuss himself traced his ideas more to the Catholic social movement than to Spann. See Rath, "The Molding of Engelbert Dollfuss as an Agrarian Reformer," 182.

18. See §34 of *Rerum novarum,* in Anne Freemantle, ed., *The Social Teachings of the Church* (New York: Mentor-Omega, 1963), 46.

19. Engelbert Dollfuss, "Wie helfen wir der österreichischen Landwirtschaft," *ANZ,* 28 December 1931, 2.

20. In some of his speeches, for example, Dollfuss used ideas that almost certainly were derived from Sering. See Miller, *Engelbert Dollfuss als Agrarfachmann,* 33.

21. Dollfuss, *Mein Vater*, 50-51. It was at the Prussian Central Cooperative Bank that Dollfuss met his future wife, Alwine Glienke.

22. Surviving only in the form of an incomplete, very rough draft, the untitled, handwritten manuscript, written by Dollfuss in Berlin in 1921, is in the possession of the Dollfuss family. The author is grateful to Eva Nicoladoni-Dollfuss, the now deceased daughter of Engelbert Dollfuss, for permitting him to make a photocopy of it.

23. Dollfuss manuscript, 20-21, 68-71.

24. For American forms of cooperation see Lawrence Goodwyn, *The Populist Movement: A Short History of the Agrarian Revolt in America* (Oxford: Oxford University Press, 1978), 305-8.

25. Dollfuss manuscript, 73.

26. Comment at the conference, "Engelbert Dollfuss—Tyrann oder Märtyrer," sponsored by the fraternity *Franco-Bavaria* in Mödling, Lower Austria, on 27 July 1984.

27. In 1919, a federation of the provincial peasant leagues was formed, but it remained a rather loose organization. See Therese Kraus, "Der Niederösterreichische Bauernbund als Kern des Reichsbauernbunds 1918-1938" (Paper delivered at the Symposium der Wissenschaftlichen Kommission des Theodor Körner-Stiftungsfonds und des Leopold-Kunschak-Preises zur Erforschung der österreichischen Geschichte der Jahre 1918-1938, Vienna, 24 and 25 October 1983), 7-8.

28. Gavin Lewis, "The Peasantry, Rural Change and Conservative Agrarianism: Lower Austria at the Turn of the Century," *Past and Present* 81 (1978): 122.

29. This model of political leadership was also present on the local level. It is striking, for example, how frequently local peasant leaders from the period bragged about having had the political situation firmly in hand, and how they had not permitted dissent to raise its ugly head. See James William Miller, "Democracy and Rural Elites in Lower Austria, 1900-1938," in *Actors on the Changing European Countryside*, ed. Leo Granberg and Imre Kovach (Budapest: Institute for Political Science of the Hungarian Academy of Sciences, 1998), 44-74.

30. Miller, *Engelbert Dollfuss als Agrarfachmann,* 64-65.

31. Rath, "The Molding of Engelbert Dollfuss," 195.

32. Law of 22 February 1922 on the creation of chambers of agriculture, *Landesgesetzblatt* (Lower Austria), no. 59.

33. Josef Reither made it clear that this was not an accident. In the legislative debate over the law, he argued that the chamber was necessary because the ministry was so bureaucratic that it would never be able to address adequately the needs of Austrian agriculture. See the stenographic protocols of the Lower Austrian Provincial Legislature, 1st legislative period, 15th sitting of the 2nd session on 22 February 1922, 257.

34. Quoted in Edmund Weber, *Aus der Geschichte der Niederösterreichischen Landes-Landwirtschaftskammer. Eine Übersicht* (Vienna: Agrarverlag, 1932), 19.

35. Rath, "The Molding of Engelbert Dollfuss as an Agrarian Reformer," 200.

36. The bill required them to pay the full premium for their family members and 50% of the premium for their employees. The employees were to pay the other half of the premium.

37. For a detailed treatment of the social insurance question, see James William Miller, "*Bauerndemokratie* in Practice: Dollfuss and the Austrian Agricultural Health Insurance System," *German Studies Review* 11.3 (October 1988): 405-21.

38. Ibid.

39. Report of the Police Commando for Lower Austria, 19 March 1929, Bundesministerium für Land- und Forstwirtschaft, fasc. 317, no. 17.27 ex 1929, Allgemeines Verwaltungsarchiv, Vienna.

40. Quoted in Rath, "The Molding of Engelbert Dollfuss as an Agrarian Reformer," 200.

41. Approximately 77% of the beef and 87% of the pork that was processed at the central market of St. Marx in Vienna in the years from 1901 to 1913 came from these two areas. See Miller, *Engelbert Dollfuss als Agrarfachmann,* 44-45.

42. "Kundmachung betreffend die Übernahme der Revision der landwirtschaftlichen Genossenschaften durch die Niederösterreichische Landes-Landwirtschaftskammer," *Die Landwirtschaft,* 15 January 1926, 3; *50 Jahre landwirtschafliches Genossenschaftswesen in Niederösterreich* (Vienna: Niederösterreichische landwirtschaftliche Genossenschaftszentralkasse, 1936), 199-201; "Standardisierung der österreichischen Butterproduktion," *ANZ,* 23 March 1928, 8.

43. Emil Goldschmid, *Die Spiritusérzeugung in den landwirtschaftlichen Brennereien* (Vienna: Agrarverlag, 1930), 4-5.

44. Bundesministerium für Land- und Forstwirtschaft, Fasc. 340a, no. 18.465-2/8 ex 1927, Allgemeines Verwaltungsarchiv, Vienna.

45. Ibid., Fasc. 903, no. 31.946-6 ex 1928.

46. For the so-called Strafella affair, that led to Dollfuss's appointment as president of the railway system, see Ludwig Jedlicka and Rudolf Neck, eds., *Vom Justizpalast zum Heldenplatz. Studien und Dokumentationen 1927 bis 1938* (Vienna: Verlag der österreichischen Staatsdruckerei, 1975), 296-315. Dollfuss was appointed to the position so that he could appoint Franz Strafella as general director of the Austrian Federal Railway. Strafella, who had made a fortune as a profiteer during the great inflation of the early 1920s, had earned the enmity of the Social Democrats by breaking a strike of streetcar workers in Graz. In short order, Dollfuss and Strafella succeeded in greatly reducing the staff of the railway system and minimizing Socialist influence over it.

47. Miller, *Engelbert Dollfuss als Agrarfachmann,* 93.

48. Ulrich Kluge, *Bauern, Agrarkrise und Volksernährung in der europäischen Zwischenkriegszeit. Studien zur Agrarpolitik und Agrarwirtschaft der Republik Österreich 1918-1938. Ein Beitrag zur Strukturkrise des östlichen Mitteleuropa* (Stuttgart: Fritz Steiner Verlag, 1988), 357-8.

49. In 1930, Austria was only 42% self-sufficient in wheat, only 82% in rye, only 37% in beef, and only 13% in pork. These numbers were to improve dramatically by 1933, mainly because of a cut in both imports and consumption. See Miller, *Engelbert Dollfuss als Agrarfachmann,* 95.

50. "Feststellungen des Kammeramtdirektors Dr. Dollfuss im Expertenkomitee beim Völkerbund," *ANZ,* 7 January 1930, 2.

51. "Die Getreidebaukrise beim Völkerbund," *ANZ,* 8 January 1930, 1; see also Bundesministerium für Land- und Forstwirtschaft, fasc. 1004, no. 10.409-8 ex 1931, Allgemeines Verwaltungsarchiv, Vienna.

52. For a detailed treatment of these issues see Miller, *Engelbert Dollfuss als Agrarfachmann,* 98-109.

53. "Kleine Ursachen—Große Wirkungen," *Neue Freie Presse,* 18 April 1931, evening edition, 1; "Der Eierkrieg des Herrn Dollfuss," *Arbeiter-Zeitung,* 19 April 1931, 2; "Das Einfuhrverbot für russische Eier aufgehoben," *Neue Freie Presse,* 19 April 1931, morning edition, 8.

54. Ministerratsprotokolle, box 138, no. 686, 24 April 1931, § 5, 5-6, Allgemeines Verwaltungsarchiv, Vienna.

55. Ministerratsprotokolle, Box 138, no. 688, 8 May 1931, § 8, 15 and Appendix E; Bundesministerium für Land- und Forstwirtschaft, fasc. 761, no. 20.124 ex 1931, Allgemeines Verwaltungsarchiv, Vienna.

56. Bundesministerium für Land- und Forstwirtschaft, fasc. 761, no. 20.124 ex 1931, Allgemeines Verwaltungsarchiv, Vienna; "Die Verhandlungen über die Kälbereinfuhr aus Polen," *Neue Freie Presse,* 28 April 1931, morning edition, 12.

57. "Wie lange denn noch?," *Bauernbündler,* 29 March 1930, 1; "Der Bauer ist kein Spielzeug!," *Bauernbündler,* 5 April 1930, 1; "Zwei kleine Irrtümer," *Bauernbündler,* 19 April 1930, 1; "Der Kampf des Niederösterreichischen Bauernbundes gegen Auswüchse der Bürokratie im Landwirtschaftsministerium," *Neuigkeitsweltblatt,* 10 April 1930, 2; Sozialwissenschaftliche Dokumentation, Group 63 (Agriculture), "Bauernbund und Landwirtschaftsministerium," *Neues Wiener Tagblatt,* 12 April 1930, Kammer für Arbeiter und Angestellte, Vienna; ibid., "Gegen Bürokratismus als Selbstzweck im Landwirtschaftsministerium," *Reichspost,* 9 April 1930.

58. Miller, *Engelbert Dollfuss als Agrarfachmann,* 117-21.

59. Bundesministerium für Land- und Forstwirtschaft, fasc. 327, no. 20.576 ex 1931, Allgemeines Verwaltungsarchiv, Vienna.

60. For the debate over the makeup of the governing board of the fund see the speech by Social Democratic representative Emmy Freundlich on 19 May 1931, Nationalrat, Stenographic Protocols, vol. 1, 32nd Session, 907, Allgemeines Verwaltungsarchiv, Vienna.

61. Kluge, *Bauern, Agrarkrise und Volksernährung,* 388-89.

62. Bundesministerium für Land- und Forstwirtschaft, fasc. 329, no. 24.791-2a ex 1934, Allgemeines Verwaltungsarchiv, Vienna.

63. Bundesministerium für Land- und Forstwirtschaft, fasc. 914, no. 27.661-8 ex 1933, Allgemeines Verwaltungsarchiv, Vienna; Ministerratsprotokolle, box 165, no. 896, 1 September 1933, §20, 24-25, Allgemeines Verwaltungsarchiv, Vienna; ibid., box 167, no. 905, 3 November 1933, § 8, 35; "Neue Hilfsaktion für den Bergbauern," *ANZ,* 24 November 1933, 2.

64. See, for example, the impassioned speech of Social Democratic representative Viktor Stein on 14 July 1931, Nationalrat, Stenographic Protocols, vol. 4, 42nd Session, p. 1066-67, Allgemeines Verwaltungsarchiv, Vienna. See also Rath, "The Molding of Dollfuss as an Agrarian Reformer," 211.

65. Ulrich Kluge rejects this claim, basing his argument on the fact that the budget for the ministry of agriculture actually declined under Dollfuss's leadership. Despite that fact, the measures undertaken by Dollfuss in defense of agricultural interests in Austria clearly *did* come at the expense of other social groups. See Kluge, *Bauern, Agrarkrise und Volksernährung,* 394-6; Miller, *Engelbert Dollfuss als Agrarfachman,* 113-5.

66. See his speech in Haag, Lower Austria on 3 October 1932, quoted in Edmund Weber, ed., *Eines Mannes Wort und Ziel* (Vienna: Reinhold Verlag, 1935), 149-150.

A Chancellorial Dictatorship with a "Corporative" Pretext: the Austrian Constitution Between 1934 and 1938

Helmut Wohnout

Introduction

> "It was, however, essentially an authoritarian regime in fascist guise, a fascist impersonation; at best it was a semi-fascist authoritarian dictatorship."[1]

In this quotation, Ernst Hanisch sums up the political reality of Austria in the years 1933/34 to 1938. Scholars today no longer concentrate on the polemics of *Ständestaat* (corporative state) vs. "Austrofascism," which dominated—with varying political undertones—the discussion on the characteristics of the political system of the Dollfuss/Schuschnigg era in Austria until the 1980s.[2] Attention now focuses on other issues, including a question Ernst Hanisch has repeatedly raised: To what extent have a long tradition of etatism and the bureaucratic tendencies inherent in the history of the Austrian administration favored the elimination of parliamentarism and democracy, and what position was occupied by Austria among the burgeoning authoritarian and dictatorial regimes in Europe in the 1930s.

To answer these and other questions, it will be helpful to examine the Austrian Constitution of 1934 and constitutional reality leading up to the Anschluss. The Anglo-American reader, in particular, may be surprised to learn that, to date, this has been done only in a very cursory manner. The fact that the Austrian Constitution of 1934 has not received closer scientific scrutiny by historians or law scholars can probably be explained by its status as a document which temporarily suspended the constitution of 1920 and had no lasting consequences. To this day, analytical studies predominantly explore the circumstances surrounding the end of democracy in Austria and the establishment of the authoritarian regime, i.e. the period between 4 March 1933 (the day when the national council was dissolved after its three presidents had resigned from office) and the assassination of Chancellor Dollfuss on 25 July 1934.

The new constitution which entered into force on 1 May 1934 is rarely, if at all, part of the research, and its nature—depending upon the point of view of the scholar—is usually considered to lie somewhere between "corporative," "authoritarian," and "Austrofascist." As yet, no attempt has been made to draw a comprehensive map of the Austrian government system between 1934 and 1938 on the basis of historical, juridical, and political analysis.

This article highlights certain aspects of government practice in Austria in the 1930s on the basis of an analysis of both the written constitution of 1934 and the very different constitutional reality of the years leading up to 1938. The author deliberately avoids going over a discussion he considers more or less closed, i.e., how the constitution of 1934 came into being. He mentions but does not elaborate on the individual stages of the transition from the systematic elimination of political and legal safeguards after 5 March 1933 to the violation of basic rights, the use of military force, the ban on political parties, the attempt to create—in the form of the *Vaterländische Front* (Fatherland Front)—an omnibus political organization, and the establishment of detention camps. This study concentrates on how the semi-dictatorial phase was followed by an authoritarian regime installed on the basis of the *Kriegswirtschaftliches Ermächtigungsgesetz* (War Economy Empowering Act) and after quashing the uprising of parts of the *Schutzbund* (Republican Defense League) with the pseudo-legal enactment of the constitution in late April/early May 1934.

The Constitution of 1 May 1934

Generally speaking, the 1934 constitution was a deliberate and intentional break with the democratic constitution of 1920 and its underlying principle of vesting sovereignty in the people, a principle derived from the Age of Enlightenment, the French Revolution, and the process of democratization in Europe in the 19th century. In Article 1 the "Republic of Austria" was replaced with the "Federal State of Austria," which, as the pre-amble said, was defined as being "Christian," "German," and on a "corporative basis."[3] The two highest executive officials of the federal state, i.e. the federal president and the federal chancellor, had predominant status both within the context of state administration and in their relations with the legislative bodies. As this article will demonstrate, the ultimate decision-making power was vested in them, not only at the executive level but also at the legislative level. Even contemporary literature recognized that an authoritarian state rule was "therefore the main characteristic of the new form of state."[4]

Generally speaking, four "construction principles,"[5] according to the constitutional terminology of the time, were assigned to the new constitution: the Christian-German principle, the authoritarian state rule, the federal organization of the state, and the corporative principle.

The first of these construction principles, the Christian-German principle, should be considered more of a state policy guideline, albeit with tremendous material legal consequences within the context of the Catholic church. In the eyes of the political elites, at least those rooted in the Christian Social camp, Austria was to become a model Catholic state. This was symbolized by the fact that the constitution started out with an appeal to the Almighty, and it was deliberately enacted on the "Day of the New Austria," 1 May 1934, together with the concordat between the Holy See and Austria, which had been concluded in June 1933. This was an ostentatious way of manipulating the day the Social Democrats had marked as "Labor Day," transforming it into a public holiday associated with the foundation of the new, distinctly church-based state.

The Catholic church was accorded significant privileges both in matrimonial law and in education. The principle of religious freedom, however, still applied, and Catholics were not the only ones to enjoy recognized status under public law. The same applied to the Protestant church and the Jewish community.[6]

As already mentioned, the text of the constitution gave the "duumvirate" of federal president and federal chancellor a dominant constitutional status.[7] Political realities of the years up to 1938, which led to the "interim regulations," which will be discussed in greater detail elsewhere, meant that this power was in fact vested almost exclusively in the position of federal chancellor.

In the constitution of 1920, the position of chancellor was—from the point of view of constitutional law—relatively weak. In the context of the federal government he merely acted as "primus inter pares" (first among equals). Except for his function as presiding officer of the council of ministers he was no different from any other minister,[8] in the sense that he only had ministerial accountability for his own portfolio. He had no organizational authority over other federal ministries. In comparison, Article 93 of the new constitution explicitly accorded the chancellor a guiding function. The relevant article reads as follows: "The federal chancellor determines the political guidelines. Within these guidelines, each minister implements his portfolio independently."[9] This provision is modeled on Article 56 of the Weimar Constitution of 1919, which was rooted in the monocratic principle of Bismarck's constitution.[10] This meant that the chancellor enjoyed that share of autonomy of leadership which was also largely reflected by his factual position and is enshrined to this day in the Bonn Constitution, the *Grundgesetz für die BRD* (Basic Law for the Federal Republic of Germany).[11] Even more significant than this rather programmatic right to establish political guidelines were the comprehensive rights of appointment and direct intervention, which not only encompassed the state administration but also encroached upon legislative issues and those at the *Länder* (individual state within the federal state) level.

The function of federal president was also enhanced along similar lines—at least as far as the text of the constitution went. This was reflected by the completely restructured election mechanism and an extension of the term of office to seven years.[12] The president was elected by the mayor of each local authority on federal territory, who took a secret ballot on a triad proposal presented by the *Bundesversammlung* (federal assembly). Since, as will be shown elsewhere, the federal president had a decisive influence on the composition of parts of the *Bundesversammlung*, he was also indirectly involved in the mechanism of his own election or that of his successor. In addition, the accountability of the federal president had been reduced in scope in comparison to the 1920 constitution. There was no mechanism for any legislative body to remove the federal president from office and, unlike in the earlier constitution, re-election was admissible.

In the context of legislative bodies, the people as a single electoral body were replaced by cultural communities and occupational sections. Their representatives were joined by a number of appointed virilists. It must be noted that, compared to democratic parliamentary systems, they had only a limited right of participation in state decisions. The former *Nationalrat* (national council) and *Bundesrat* (federal council) were replaced by four advisory bodies, the *Staatsrat* (federal state council), the *Bundeskulturrat* (federal council of culture), the *Bundeswirtschaftsrat* (federal council of economics), and the *Länderrat* (council of the (several) states). The new decision-making bodies were the *Bundestag* (federal diet) and the *Bundesversammlung* (federal assembly).[13]

The *Staatsrat* (federal state council) was the most important advisory body.[14] It was designed to enforce the authoritarian element of the constitution and was required to submit mandatory opinions on all government bills which required the consultation of an advisory body. The *Staatsrat* was composed of between forty and fifty members. The federal president, who appointed the members of the council, had the right to determine the actual number within this range. He did not require a proposal from the government for the appointments, but he needed the countersignature of the federal chancellor. Membership in the council was for a term of ten years and re-appointment was possible.

The *Bundeswirtschaftsrat* (federal council of economics) and the *Bundeskulturrat* (federal council for culture) were designed to represent the corporative idea in national legislation, i.e., to represent the population which was organized in "corporations" according to occupation and cultural communities. During the deliberations on the constitution, the decision had been made that the corporative design itself was not to be an integral part of the constitution but was to be regulated by a separate law. Accordingly, the constitution provided only for the existence of the two corporative representative bodies and a framework of organizational provisions.

The duties of both bodies were limited to their advisory functions. The *Bundeswirtschaftsrat* submitted mandatory opinions on bills which the government deemed to be purely or predominantly of economic significance. The *Bundeskulturrat* submitted mandatory opinions on bills categorized as exclusively or mainly cultural in scope. Bills which the government considered to be of both economic and cultural significance received mandatory opinions from both advisory bodies. Both councils were free to participate in the legislative process on a voluntary basis, as they both were permitted to submit unsolicited voluntary opinions on bills which the government deemed not to need mandatory opinions. Even so, the voluntary opinions of the *Bundeswirtschaftsrat* were required to concentrate exclusively on economic aspects, those of the *Bundeskulturrat* exclusively on aspects of cultural interest.

The *Bundeswirtschaftsrat* consisted of between seventy and eighty members who were delegated by the seven main "professional corporations." The constitution specified these groups as follows:

- Agriculture and forestry
- Industry and mining
- Trade
- Commerce and traffic
- Finance and insurance
- Free professions
- Public service

The representation of the individual groups had to ensure a balance of its self-employed and employed members. Generally, the *Bundeswirtschaftsrat* was considered to uphold the democratic element in the constitution. Erich Voegelin, an expert on state law who taught in Vienna at the time and viewed the new constitution in a distanced, though ultimately positive manner, called the *Bundeswirtschaftsrat* "the constitutional concession to the element of mass democracy."[15]

The *Bundeskulturrat* consisted of thirty to forty representatives of three main groups: the legally recognized churches and religious communities, education and learning, as well as science and art. While in the case of the *Bundeswirtschaftsrat* the constitution spoke of "representatives delegated by the professional corporations," implying that elections were held within these "corporations," the constitution does not contain provisions on the mode of appointment to the *Bundeskulturrat*. A criterion that applied to members of both bodies stipulated that citizens were only eligible if they could be expected to be "loyal patriots," which, in plain language, meant they had to be members of the state party, the *Vaterländische Front* (Fatherland Front). Both the *Bundeswirtschaftsrat* and the *Bundeskulturrat* could be dissolved by the federal president upon a proposal by the federal chancellor, at any time, if they did not function as desired.

The fourth advisory body, the *Länderrat* (council of the (several) states), was designed to implement the federalist principle in matters of legislation. According to the principle that all nine *Länder* were equal, each land delegated its governor and the member of the land diet in charge of state finances to the *Länderrat*, which thus consisted of eighteen members. Some commentators on the 1934 constitution perceived the principle of arithmetic equality in *Länder* representation, which happened to be a longstanding claim of Christian Socialists that had already been voiced in the constitutional discussion of 1920, as an enhancement of the rights of the *Länder*. The *Länderrat* was obliged to render opinions on bills that touched upon *Länder* interests. Even if, at first glance, the *Länderrat* seemed to represent an enhancement of the federalist principle, the new constitution actually resulted in a "tremendous reversal of Austrian federalism."[16]

The main reasons for this were the changes in the way the members of the *Länderrat*, the state governors, and the members of the land diets were appointed. The state governors were appointed by the federal president, with the countersignature of the federal chancellor, on the basis of a triad proposal submitted by the respective land diet. The state governors could just as easily be removed from office at any time by the federal president upon a proposal from the federal chancellor and with the latter's countersignature. The governors, in turn, were free to appoint or remove the other members of the state government at their discretion.[17] The dominance of executive rights over the legislative bodies can also be seen in the fact that the chairman and the two vice-chairmen of the *Staatsrat* (federal state council) were appointed by the federal president upon a proposal from the federal chancellor and with the latter's countersignature. Although the two permanent corporative advisory bodies, the *Bundeskulturrat* and the *Bundeswirtschaftsrat* elected their chairmen from among their members, this election required the approval of the federal president, which was granted following a proposal from the federal chancellor and with the latter's countersignature.

The decision-making body in the new legislative system was the *Bundestag* (federal diet). It encompassed fifty-nine members and consisted of delegates from the advisory bodies elected by these bodies from among their membership. With the exception of bills pertaining to the budget, however, its participation in the legislative process was restricted to a power of veto. The *Bundestag* was authorized to decide whether bills presented by the federal government were to enter into force as laws, but it had no influence on the content of the bills and could not submit motions for amendments. This meant that it did not enjoy two rights typically held by a classical Parliament, i.e., initiating and determining the content of laws.

In addition, both the federal government and the federal president enjoyed comprehensive rights to issue emergency decrees which gave the government the possibility, under certain circumstances, to enact legislation without the participation of the advisory bodies.[18] The constitution also contained an element of plebiscite, which gave the government the option of submitting bills rejected by the *Bundestag* to the public vote in the form of a referendum. If the referendum approved of a law that had been rejected by the *Bundestag*, the latter's decision was automatically rescinded. The government was also entitled to refrain entirely from consulting the advisory bodies and submit a matter directly to a referendum, which, if approved, rendered superfluous deliberation by the legislative bodies.[19] This strong plebiscite element of the 1934 constitution is not unusual for authoritarian constitutions.

The seemingly strong focus on direct democracy in otherwise authoritarian systems always harbors the risk of autocratic decisions in a pseudo-democratic guise. The method of consolidating dictatorial autocratic power through (manipulated) popular decision is one that can be observed in the plebiscites of Napoleon Bonaparte, the reign of Napoleon III, and the totalitarian regimes of the 20th century. In this connection, let us recall a 1936 study by Karl Loewenstein on the dictatorship of Napoleon I. Although public-law expert Loewenstein wrote of Napoleon Bonaparte, he meant Adolf Hitler.[20]

Several other provisions in the 1934 constitution had a similar objective: The individual constitutional and administrative courts were replaced by a single body, the *Bundesgerichtshof* (federal supreme court).[21] Although the independence of judges was still enshrined in the constitution,[22] jury decisions were replaced by a system in which a professional judge was involved in the decision-making process together with the jurors, which represented a weakening of the lay element in the judiciary.[23] The "auditing department" (court of audit) also lost the greater part of its character of parliamentary body, even if the constitution referred to it as an "organ of the federal diet and of the land diets."[24] Its president, however, was no longer elected by the legislative bodies but appointed by the federal president.

What is remarkable, however, is that in its second division the constitution contained a catalogue of fundamental rights which was linked to the basic state law on the general rights of citizens in the 1920 constitution, even if certain items were modified to fit the new, non-democratic starting point.[25] This was especially true of the principle of equality, which was curtailed. The catalogue of general rights nevertheless ran counter to the authoritarian spirit that marked the rest of the new constitution. Adolf Merkl, Viennese professor for constitutional law, therefore appropriately described the catalogue of general rights in the constitution as "fundamentally, the most far-reaching concession to the political zeitgeist of the past century and thus to an individualistic view of the state and liberal thought."[26] The fact that such a catalogue was indeed part of the constitution, particularly one that tied in with the one of 1867, is one of the reasons why Othmar Spann, the founder of Universalism, was vehemently opposed to the Constitution, even though he had exerted considerable influence on it indirectly—via his students—and analogies to his universalistic theory are easily discernible. In allusion to the catalogue of fundamental rights, he condescendingly called the May constitution "a mix of principles from 1789 and corporative institutions that have no firm footing." He explicitly objected to the fact that it had "intellectually borrowed" from his theory.[27]

Finally, any analysis of the 1934 constitution must mention several provisions concerning federalism, explicitly stressed in the constitution by defining the country as the "Federal State of Austria." In practice, however, federalism was further curtailed. Apart from the afore-mentioned appointment of the governors, which involved considerable participation by the federal bodies, the federal chancellor also enjoyed the right to propose to the federal president the removal from office of a state governor.[28] The federal chancellor also had the right to approve or revoke the appointment of the highest civil servant in a State, the so-called government director, and this proposed appointment had to be submitted to him by the respective state governor.[29]

Moreover, the law resolutions of the land diets, which in their composition corresponded more or less to a combination of *Bundeswirtschaftsrat* and *Bundeskulturrat* at land level, had to be communicated to the federal chancellor and the competent federal minister, who had to give their explicit "consent" before these resolutions were promulgated.[30] This constituted an implicit right of approval, i.e., a material right of the federal government to intervene in *Länder* legislation.

The fact that what used to be "red" (i.e., Socialist) Vienna formally lost its status as a land and became a "federal city" had a certain symbolic value, even if this did not involve any substantive changes, as the status of the mayor of Vienna was equal to that of a state governor, the *Wiener Bür-*

gerschaft ("Vienna House of Burghers") to the land diet, and the "magistrat director" to the "government director."[31]

Constitutional Reality in Authoritarian Austria

The text of the constitution itself was characterized by a strong preponderance of the executive branch, and this tendency was further enhanced by the political reality of the 1934-38 period. The bipartite rule by the federal chancellor and the federal president provided for in the constitution was narrowed down to the dominance of the federal chancellor, who enjoyed tremendous power. This power had its positive law basis in the so-called *Ermächtigungsgesetz* (Empowering Act), which had been adopted, even before the new constitution entered into force, by the "truncated Parliament" that had been convened specifically for this purpose on 30 April 1934, and by the *Verfassungsübergangsgesetz* (Interim Constitutional Act) adopted on 19 June 1934 by the government.

The *Ermächtigungsgesetz* paved the way for the government to continue adopting material laws without any participation from the legislative bodies. Article III, para. 2 of the *Ermächtigungsgesetz*, whose actual title was *Bundesverfassungsgesetz vom 30. April 1934 über außerordentliche Maßnahmen im Bereich der Verfassung* (Federal Constitutional Act of 30 April 1934 on Extraordinary Measures in the Constitutional Sphere),[32] provided for the possibility of enacting government bills solely upon a decision by the council of ministers. The government made ample use of this option in the following years. In the period between the constitution of the legislative bodies in the autumn of 1934 and 11 March 1934, the ratio of laws adopted directly by the council of ministers and those adopted by the *Bundestag* was 69:31% in favor of the council of ministers.[33]

This situation seems all the more grotesque as the mechanisms for creating the advisory bodies stipulated by the constitution were ignored. Without exception, these advisory bodies were composed of members appointed directly by the federal chancellor rather than having been nominated through any form of election or a similar procedure.[34] This also applied to the members of the *Staatsrat*. It is therefore hardly surprising that the legislative bodies, even when they were indeed entrusted with discussing a bill, did not reject a single one.

What applied to the legislative bodies also applied to all other areas. The *Verfassungsübergangsgesetz* (Interim Constitutional Act) transferred virtually all rights of appointment from the federal president to the federal chancellor. Nor was any use made of the mechanism provided for in the constitution for the election of the federal president. His term of office was simply prolonged until the new constitution entered into force fully. Constitutionally speaking, this meant that the federal president in office continued to play a marginal role, as increasingly imposed on him by the government in the phase of transition from a democracy to an authoritarian regime from 5 March 1933. In fact, federal president Wilhelm Miklas was completely cut off from all state matters and a "living monument of a past political system."[35]

The federal chancellor was also responsible for police and security matters, which were centralized as early as 1933. Originally, the *Länder* had been responsible for issues relating to public security, i.e., maintaining public order and security, weapons-related issues, ammunition and explosives, as well as matters related to the press, associations, and public meetings. The bloodshed during a series of National Socialist terror attacks in late May/early June 1933 gave the government the opportunity to set up dedicated security bureaus which were directly answerable to the federal chancellor through the General Directorate for Public Security.[36] The constitution also reflected this circumstance. The security police was thus transferred to the direct control of the federal administration.

Once again, decision-making authority had been taken from the governors and entrusted to the federal chancellor's centralized administration. The *Verfassungsübergangsgesetz* unequivocally stipulated that the federal police was directly subordinate to the federal chancellor in all matters of organization and direction.[37] When the competencies of security directors were further enhanced in December 1934, the *Länder* put up some resistance.[38]

Although initially set up as temporary tools in the fight against National Socialist terrorism, the security directors and the General Directorate of Security (now part of the Ministry of the Interior) are enshrined in Austrian law to this day.

The independence of judges was restricted by the fact that judges could be transferred to other posts or made to retire "if their remaining in office or in the service of the law as such were seen to be obviously detrimental to the standing of jurisprudence."[39] The protection of basic rights was also restricted.

It has already been shown that the constitution restricted the federalist principle to a considerable extent. Now, with the interim regulations, the federal chancellor had an almost unlimited right of direct intervention. It culminated in the provision that enabled him to use his discretion in replacing state governors by any successor he deemed appropriate; a provision which Schuschnigg actually made use of.[40] Although, in keeping with the authoritarian guiding principle of the constitution, the governors were given more authority in their own sphere of action, especially in the area of *Länder* legislation, the power was effectively vested in the federal chancellor. Since the governors were appointed and removed by the federal chancellor, and the governors in turn enjoyed the same privileges with regard to the members of the *Länder* government, the *Länder* administration was almost completely dependent on the federal government. This represented a return to the principle of governorship as a "representative of the Crown" in the historical sense of the term, as it had been used in the Austro-Hungarian monarchy before 1918.[41]

In order to purge the administration, at all levels, of adherents of National Socialism, of Social Democrats, and—to a lesser extent—of Communists, the government established a Federal Commissioner for Personnel Matters in early 1934 and thus took over all staffing decisions at *Länder* and at local levels. Civil servants who were critical of the regime were now disciplined from a central federal office, which could dismiss them and even cancel or reduce their old-age pensions. The possibilities for intervention were gradually expanded in scope and the *Beförderungssperregesetz* (Promotion Ban Act), for instance, granted the federal chancellor the right of approval in all public-service promotions, including those at *Länder* and at local levels.[42]

Although in its propaganda the regime relied heavily on presenting the "corporative" reform of society as the programmatical anti-thesis to democratic parliamentarism, this restructuring process never got off the ground. Of the seven "professional corporations" provided for in the constitution, only two had been established by 1938: agriculture and forestry, politically probably the most homogeneous group, and public service, in which the employer's side—represented by the state—was not applicable. Otherwise, each of the workers' groups that were part of the Trade Union Federation had a counterpart on the employer's side. When the latter were created in 1934/35, great consideration was given to the particular interests of existing employers' associations, which made the resulting structure rather inhomogeneous.[43] This corporative scheme had been devised in a top-down approach aimed at uniting the members of a professional sector. In practice, however, especially after the assassination of Dollfuss, it enhanced the rigidity of the dividing line between the two sides of industrial relations rather than bring them together.

What the regime actually wanted to achieve through this social reform along corporative lines has never been quite clear: On the one hand, there was Fascist Corporationism as propagated by the *Heimwehr* (National Defense League), modeled on the Italian version and based on Othmar Spann's Universalism; on the other hand, there was the corporative theory of Catholic social doctrine as presented in the two encyclicals *Rerum Novarum* and *Quadragesimo Anno* and further developed in different variations by Catholic social teaching and the theoreticians in the Christian workers' movement. The encyclical itself referred to a model of society, not of state law. In a few paragraphs, it discussed the principles of a corporative social order and promoted the creation of corporative bodies with the aim of allowing members of the same professional sectors to associate freely for issues relating to their profession. The encyclical avoided any concrete references as to how such a system could be implemented in the sphere of the state. It had a neutral attitude with regard to the state system and the organization of the corporate states—"pro-vided," as it said, "that proper regard is had for the requirements of justice and of the common good."[44]

Ignaz Seipel was a man who knew how to interpret the Papal Encyclical to suit his policy objectives in Austria, and in the late 1920s and early 1930s, Seipel construed a new start for society and a corporative design to mean the elimination of the democratic state based on political parties.[45] In summary, it can be said that little of the corporative and the federalist elements of the new constitution were actually implemented in political reality. The removal of class differences by uniting workers and employers in any given professional sector remained fiction, and the relief of state administration through autonomous self-administration within the "professional corporations" never happened. What came in its stead was, again, centralized administrative power controlled by the federal chancellor.

As Martin F. Polaschek rightly observes, the "professional corporations" of the 1934 constitution—to the extent they existed at all—were delegated state bodies, which is actually diametrically opposed to the social-corporative theories of the church, since the latter had intended the corporative level to provide a counterbalance to the state, an autonomous self-administration in keeping with the subsidiarity principle, the second pillar of Catholic social teaching in addition to the corporative system.[46] There was, however, no complete concept, nor was there enough of a political will to consistently attempt a radical reform of society. This is why constitutional practice in these years lacked the intended sectoral involvement of the population, which would have given the new state system at least some semblance of legitimacy. Several representatives of the government were indeed aware of this deficiency.

In terms of federalism, the 1934 constitution lagged far behind the earlier constitution of the First Republic. This is all the more remarkable in view of the 1920 constitution and its subsequent amendments, where the Christian-Socialists in particular had claimed—often successfully—that the *Länder* should have more autonomy from the federal level. Ultimately, however, the "trend towards dictatorship in Europe in the 1930s" (Karl Dietrich Bracher) and the "traditions of a specifically Austrian authoritarianism" (Ernst Hanisch) proved to be stronger than the autonomy of the *Länder*, maintained only superficially and only to be re-enhanced after the new beginning in 1945.[47]

The Constitution as Reflected by Political Developments from 1934 to 1938

The first half of 1934, when the state structures of authoritarian Austria were formed, was part of the short period when the *Heimwehr* (National Defense League) had an effective and lasting influence on government action. It enjoyed a strong position, having been the main force in quashing the uprising of February and thanks to external support from Mussolini. The *Heimwehr* thus managed to gain acceptance for many of its claims regarding the representatives of the Christian-Socialist camp when the wording of the constitution was discussed. Thus, it is misleading for literature on this topic to describe Otto Ender, long-standing Christian-Socialist governor of Vorarlberg and the minister within the Dollfuss regime responsible for constitutional matters, as the "founder" of the constitution.[48] In keeping with his political socialization, Ender would have been content with giving the 1934 constitution a strong corporative and federalist element. In order to do so, he would have had to create a legislative body which was at least partially based on a public election. For Ender, whose opinions were rooted in the traditions of Catholic social reform, the term "corporative" referred primarily to the need to balance interests between employers and workers at the lowest level.

Although Ender was the person who edited the new constitution, the content was decided by other men from the government camp, in particular by someone working in the upper echelons of the *Heimwehr*, who today is largely forgotten: Odo Neustädter-Stürmer. Within an organization otherwise oriented along the lines of military categories, he was the only one capable of translating Mussolini's political demand for constitutional reform in line with the Fascist-corporative theory into political and constitutional reality. As early as 1930, the *Heimwehr* ideologist had published a draft constitution that was clearly influenced by Othmar Spann's Universalism.[49] He based his philosophy on an organic division of the state into three parts: state administration, the economy, and intellectual life. This was to form the basis for all legislation, administration, the judiciary, and the executive. Hence, he opted for three legislative bodies at federal level: the *Staatsrat* (federal state council), which would have been responsible for the sovereign sphere, i.e., legislation in all matters pertaining to domestic and foreign policy, as well as the military, judiciary, and constitutional policy; the *Bundeskulturrat* (federal council of culture), responsible for all legislation in cultural, educational, and scientific matters; and the *Bundeswirtschaftsrat* (federal council of economics), responsible for all matters pertaining to economic and social policy. A comparison between Neustädter-Stürmer's writings of 1930 and the 1934 constitution reveals striking similarities. The constitution not only uses the same terminology, it is based on the very structure the *Heimwehr* ideologist envisaged.

There was at least one issue where the committed federalist Otto Ender had been able to have his wishes heard: Neustädter-Stürmer's "three-pillar model" was complemented by a federalist chamber. But even in this respect, he had only moderate success. Although he had gained acceptance for the traditional Christian-Socialist demand for arithmetical equality between the individual *Länder* in the composition of the *Länderrat* (council of the (several) states), *Länder* legislation was still completely dependent on the federal chancellor's approval. As the latter also enjoyed comprehensive rights of appointment and approval, autonomous *Länder* policy was virtually non-existent. Neustädter-Stürmer was not exaggerating, when, at a *Heimwehr* event shortly before the new constitution was enacted, he referred to his study of 1930 and declared: "Today, our idea has become the idea of the state."[50]

However, after the assassination of Engelbert Dollfuss and the quashing of the National Socialist putsch attempt of July 1934, new Federal Chancellor Kurt Schuschnigg managed—more swiftly and efficiently than his domestic and international opponents had expected—to exploit the strong position the constitution gave him and to secure his status and gradually reduce that of the *Heimwehr*.

With his appointment to the post of federal chancellor on 30 July 1934, Schuschnigg had taken over a coalition government between the militant defense leagues and what little was left of the Christian-Socialist party.[51] Skillfully using the support of the Catholic church,[52] he pitied the rival forces within the government against each other. At the same time, he consistently repressed the illegal National Socialists, who were ailing after their defeat on 25 July, and was able to weaken their organization to such an extent as to exclude the possibility that they would revive the terror attacks that had increasingly destabilized the country before 25 July.[53]

One thing that the regime never managed to set up in any phase of the authoritarian rule was a grassroots basis for the *Vaterländische Front* (Fatherland Front), comparable to the Fascist mass organizations in Italy and Germany. On the contrary, the *Vaterländische Front* remained a bureaucratic organizational shell with no dynamic development or significance of its own.

In his foreign policy, Schuschnigg initially opted for a cautious rapprochement to the Western Powers without, however, renouncing the "Italian course" of his predecessor.[54] At the same time, during 1935, Schuschnigg undertook guarded attempts towards a reconciliation with the left wing. These were to remain without response, as he effected no changes in the state model or the political direction of his rule.[55]

What was more significant was that in the autumn of 1935, Schuschnigg managed to crowd the two *Heimwehr* leaders Odo Neustädter-Stürmer and Emil Fey out of the government. In May 1936, he also succeeded in getting rid of the chief *Heimwehr* leader, Vice-Chancellor Ernst Rüdiger Starhemberg, who had also directed the *Vaterländische Front* up until then. A short time later, the *Heimwehr* was dissolved and its militias merged with those of the *Vaterländische Front*. The latter was soon put under the army's control. Schuschnigg's strategic plan was to divest the *Heimwehr* of any political influence but still ensure government support for its policies by keeping in office several personalities selected from the dissolved organization.[56]

At the same time, in late March/early April 1936, conscription was reintroduced through a constitutional act "on general service obligation," as the act was officially designated for foreign policy considerations and in consideration of the peace treaty of Saint Germain.[57] This considerably strengthened the Austrian army. This time period also saw a modest effort to rearm the military, which was to be one of the most important pillars of the regime next to the security police and state bureaucracy, after the militias had successively been eliminated.[58]

With this development and initial cautious attempts to pluralize the regime and the above-mentioned guarded signals of reconciliation with the workers—albeit with no lasting impact—Gerhard Botz perceived a "partial reduction of the fascist element" in the authoritarian regime.[59] Contrary to this trend, there were increasing signs of "imitatory fascism" engendered by the historical context. For instance, the leadership principle was clearly given more prominence as soon as Schuschnigg took over the *Vaterländische Front*, and, as stressed by Ernst Hanisch and Dieter A. Binder, the authoritarian-etatistic element in particular made an increasing impact from 1936 onward.[60] Although Schuschnigg skillfully cemented his domestic position, his foreign relations became more and more precarious as of the spring of 1936. After having tried unsuccessfully to keep several options open, the only option left to him was to play for time. This resulted in the agreement of July 1936, which gave the nationalist opposition the leeway the National Socialists needed in order to gradually undermine the power structures and the state apparatus. This way, the constitutional practice of authoritarian Austria was eroded from within.

Only much later, very much later in fact, towards the end of February 1938, did Schuschnigg endeavor to break away from his image of cool, calculating power player with no emotional ties to the people, and seek to be a charismatic leader to mobilize the general public for the cause of independence. But neither the state system nor the constitutional context lent themselves to these tactics, nor was the political platform of "corporative" Austria appealing enough to achieve this aim.

Conclusions

What Erich Voegelin so rightly noted in his 1936 analysis of the constitution from the perspective of public-law would be valid until 1938[61]: Owing to the *Verfassungsüberleitungsgesetz* (Interim Constitutional Act) of 18 June 1934 and the *Ermächtigungsgesetz* (Empowering Act) of 30 April 1934, the constitution remained largely a piece of paper with very limited practical impact. The federal chancellor's position was dominant and even further enhanced, while the corporative element was a truncated structure not greatly appreciated by the general public. This emphasized the deeply authoritarian character of Austria in the period from 1934 to 1938. The legislative power had to a large extent been vested in the government and the system exhibited many of the characteristics of a dictatorial government. In view of the substantive power concentration in the hands of the federal chancellor, which also corresponded to factual power relations, especially after the *Heimwehr* had been eliminated, the system can more accurately be described as a "chancellorial dictatorship."

In its dealings with the Western Powers, however, Austria ostentatiously tried to differentiate itself from the totalitarian German Reich and from the dictatorial regimes around Austria by highlighting the existence of the catalogue of fundamental rights and federal structures—even if they were in most cases no more than an empty shell. In official rhetoric, the corporative elements were used to support the claim that Austria had actually designed a completely new state system. This claim, however, remained fictional and was easily unmasked by the manner in which the regime implemented its rule. In its self-presentation, authoritarian Austria proved to be increasingly unable to avoid the European trend and so it began, with the help of the *Vaterländische Front*, to elevate the late Chancellor Engelbert Dollfuss to the rank of martyr and to develop a veritable "Führer myth" around Federal Chancellor Schuschnigg. This myth was not only grotesque in many of its manifestations, but also emulated German fascism, as can be demonstrated by the often quoted creation of a *Sturmkorps* (storm troops) for the *Vaterländische Front* in imitation of the German SS.

Just like other authoritarian regimes of the interwar period, the Austrian government under Dollfuss and Schuschnigg thought that the 1934 constitution would allow them to go a "third way," avoiding both liberal democracy and totalitarian dictatorship.[62] This "third way," however, was to remain a theoretical construction, which the government only implemented in rudimentary form and which received hardly any support from the general public.

This is also why Schuschnigg, when his foreign policy designs failed, did not receive the domestic support which would have made it possible—even as late as in March 1938—to offer, or at least attempt to offer, some resistance to National Socialist pressure and preserve Austria's independence.

Notes

1. Ernst Hanisch, *Der lange Schatten des Staates. Österreichische Gesellschaftsgeschichte im 20. Jahrhundert* (Vienna: Ueberreuter, 1994), 313.

2. In a recent essay, Dieter A. Binder critically comments on the historiography of the 1970s and early 1980s, which was both oriented on party-politics and institutionalized according to a grand-coalition mindset: "Upon a suggestion by Kreisky, the interaction between the 'Theodor-Körner-Stiftungsfonds' and the 'Leopold-Kunschak-Preises' had resulted in that kind of 'scientific commission' which ostentatiously promoted an approach to history oriented on social partnership and grand coalition, while being for a long time marked by a strange co-existence of scientific research and the aging representatives of Austro-Marxism and Social Democrats, Christian Socialists and Austro-Fascism, viz. Austrian National Socialists." Dieter A. Binder, "Populismus zu allen Jahreszeiten," in *Gestörte Identitäten? Eine Zwischenbilanz der Zweiten Republik. Ein Symposium zum 65. Geburtstag von Moritz Csäky*, ed. Lutz Musner, Gotthart Wunberg, and Eva Cescutti (Innsbruck, 2002), 72-85, here 78.

3. The oft-quoted original text of the pro-oemium ran as follows: "In the name of almighty God from whom all justice emanates, the Austrian people receives for its Christian, German Federal State on a corporative foundation this constitution." The Constitution of the Federal State of Austria, Bundespressedienst, Vienna, 1934 (Engl. version).

All quotations and the majority of constitutional terminology have been taken from this "official" contemporary English translation. However, there are a number of omissions in the English version. Moreover, the English is full of grammatical mistakes and inconsistencies, which is why the author has exercised his discretion as to which terms and phrases could not be used because they are in crass contravention of current English usage.

4. Ludwig Adamovich and Georg Froehlich, eds., *Die neue österreichische Verfassung samt Ausführungs- und Nebengesetzen* (Vienna, 1934), 2.

5. See Georg Froehlich, *Die "Verfassung 1934" des Bundesstaates Österreich. Systematisch als Leitfaden dargestellt* (Vienna, 1936), 98 pp., 140-42; Ludwig Adamovich, "Die Baugesetze der neuen österreichischen Verfassung: Das föderalistische Prinzip," *Juristische Blätter Vereinigt mit Gerichtszeitung* 64 (2 February 1935): 55-57; Adolf Merkl, "Die Baugesetze der neuen österreichischen Verfassung: Das berufsständische Prinzip," ibid. 64 (16 February 1935): 76-80.

6. Constitution of 1934, Art. 29, Para. 1.

7. Wilhelm Brauneder, *Österreichische Verfassungsgeschichte*, 8th ed. (Vienna: Manz, 2001), 241.

8. B-VG 1920, Art. 69, Para.1.

9. Constitution of 1934, Art. 93. Author´s note: This article is missing in the "official" English translation from 1934!

10. Article 56 read: "The Reich chancellor determines the political guidelines and is responsible for them to Reichstag. Within these guidelines, each Reich minister implements his portfolio independently, and is responsible to Reichstag." Die Verfassung des deutschen Reiches vom 11. August 1919, Art. 56; see also Gerhard Anschütz, *Die Verfassung des Deutschen Reiches vom 11. August 1919*, 14th ed. (Bad Homburg, 1969), 326-29.

11. Grundgesetz für die Bundesrepublik Deutschland vom 23. Mai 1949, Art. 65.

12. Constitution of 1934, Art 73, Para. 1-5.

13. For a detailed description of legislation see Helmut Wohnout, *Regierungsdiktatur oder Ständeparlament? Gesetzgebung im autoritären Österreich,* no. 43 of *Studien zur Politik und Verwaltung* (Vienna: Böhlau, 1993), 160-78.

14. For the following see the 4th division (the federal legislation) of the constitution: Constitution of 1934, Art. 44-72.

15. Erich Voegelin, *Der autoritäre Staat. Ein Versuch über das österreichische Staatsproblem* (Vienna, 1936), 229; Voegelin's views on the period 1934-38 remained benevolent even after his emigration in 1938. Looking back, he credited the Schuschnigg government with the fact "that an authoritarian state that would keep radical ideologists in check was the best defense of democracy." Eric Voegelin, *Autobiographical Reflections*, edited, with an introduction by Ellis Sandoz (Baton Rouge: Louisiana State University Press, 1989), 40.

16. Adolf Merkl, *Die ständisch-autoritäre Verfassung Österreichs. Ein kritisch-systematischer Grundriss* (Vienna: J. Springer, 1935), 76.

17. Constitution of 1934, Art. 114, paras. 4-5.

18. Ibid., Art. 177-178.

19. Ibid., Art. 65, Para. 1-6.

20. Loewenstein wrote: "It is this application of democratic techniques for which the French writers have coined the expression of a 'Cesarean regime,' if a dictatorial government purports to act on the wishes of the population expressed in plebiscites. . . . The referendum gained an importance going far beyond the adoption of an abstract constitution. It became a new organizational principle by including a personal plebiscitarian acclamation in favor of a particular leader. . . . The plebiscite thus conferred to the new Cesar the label of one 'chosen by the nation,' with a spiritual power equal to that of a monarch reigning by God's grace. And every subsequent plebiscite confirmed him as the exclusive representative of the nation. A new mythology had been created, which gave him—by law as well as de facto—the moral prerequisites to wield absolute power. The imitations of the Cesarean plebiscite that followed in the time of Napoleon III and at present very clearly reflect this mythological function of a perverted idea of democracy." Karl Loewenstein, "Über die Diktatur Napoleons I," *Österreichische Zeitschrift für öffentliches Recht* 16 (1936): 619-51, here 637f; reprint in idem, *Beiträge zur Staatssoziologie* (Tübingen: Mohr, 1961).

21. The president, vice-president, and the other members of the *Bundesgerichtshof* were appointed by the federal president upon a proposal by the federal government. If the court sat as a constitutional court, i.e., decided on whether a point of legislation or administration was in line with the constitution, the decision was taken by a permanent constitutional council, which was reinforced by four additional members. These members were appointed by the federal president on the basis of a triad proposal for two members each from the *Staatsrat* and the *Länderrat*. Ibid., Art. 177, Para. 1; Art. 179, Para. 1-2.

22. Ibid., Art. 101, Para.1.

23. Ibid., Art. 106.

24. Ibid., Art 149, Para. 2.

25. Ibid., Art. 15-33.

26. Merkl, *Verfassung*, 35.

27. Othmar Spann, *Kämpfende Wissenschaft*, vol. 7 of *Gesamtausgabe*, 2nd ed. (Graz: Akademische Druck- und Verlagsanstalt, 1969), 5. For a comprehensive study of Spann's corporative theory see Helmut Wohnout, "Verfassungstheorie und Herrschaftspraxis im autoritären Österreich. Zu Entstehung und Rolle der legislativen Organe 1933/34-1938," PhD. diss., 1990, 12-16.

28. Constitution of 1934, Art. 114, Para.4.

29. Ibid., Art. 115, Para. 2.

30. Ibid., Art. 111, Para. 2.

31. Ibid., Art. 136-137.

32. *Federal Legal Gazette* 255/I 1934, 30 April 1934.

33. Wohnout, *Regierungsdiktatur*, 305pp.

34. *Federal Legal Gazette* 75/II 1934, 19 June 1934, Art. 21.

35. Gerhard Jagschitz, "Theorie und Praxis des österreichischen Ständestaates 1934-1938," *Zeitgeschichte. Beiträge zur Lehrerfortbildung* 22 (Vienna,1982): 122. Hilde Verena Lang, "Bundespräsident Miklas und das autoritäre Regime 1933-1938," PhD. diss., University of Vienna, 1972.

36. Martin F. Polaschek, "Der Föderalismus in der Verfassung 1934," *Geschichte und Gegenwart. Vierteljahresschrift für Zeitgeschichte, Gesellschaftsanalyse und politische Bildung* 12 (3/1993): 141-78, particularly 167.

37. *Federal Legal Gazette* 75/II 1934, 19 June 1934, Art. 14, Para. 1.

38. Polaschek, "Föderalismus," 144.

39. *Federal Legal Gazette* 75/II 1934, Art. 28, Para. 1.

40. Ibid., Art. 32, Para. 2.

41. Adamovich, "Baugesetze," 57.

42. Polaschek, "Föderalismus," 156.

43. Helmut Wohnout, "Programmatischer Anspruch vs. politische Realität. Anmerkungen zu Theorie und Praxis der Katholischen Soziallehre in Österreich," in *Was bleibt an sozialer Gerechtigkeit? Gesellschaft und Katholische Soziallehre im neuen Jahrtausend*, ed. Matthias Tschirf, Helmut Wohnout, and Karl Klein (Vienna: Verlag Österreich, 2000), 21-37, here 28.

44. Papal Encyclical Quadragesimo Anno (Pius XI., 1931), Section 86, www.vatican.va (website of the Holy See).

45. Wohnout, *Regierungsdiktatur*, 49-53.

46. Polaschek, "Föderalismus," 149.

47. Karl Dietrich Bracher, "Eine düstere Erfahrung: Der Zug zur Diktatur in Europa der dreißiger Jahre," in *Demokratie und Geschichte. Jahrbuch des Karl von Vogelsang-Instituts zur Erforschung der Geschichte der christlichen Demokratie in Österreich*, vol. 1, ed. Helmut Wohnout (Vienna: Böhlau, 1997), 107-23; Hanisch, *Der lange Schatten*, 315.

48. See Helmut Wohnout, "Politisch-juristische Kontroversen um die Verfassung 1934 im autoritären Österreich," in *Justiz und Zeitgeschichte. Symposionsbeiträge 1976-1993*, vol. 2, ed. Erika Weinzierl et al. (Vienna: Jugend & Volk, 1995), 833-48, particularly 837-40.

49. Odo Neustädter-Stürmer, *Der Ständestaat Österreich. Dem jungen Österreich gewidmet* (Graz, 1930).

50. *Der Heimatschützer. Offizielles Organ des Österreichischen Heimatschutzes*, 28 April 1934, 7.

51. Dieter A. Binder and Helmut Wohnout, "Das autoritäre Regierungssystem und der Versuch ständischer Vertretungskörperschaften 1933/34–1938," in *Parlamentarismus in Österreich*, vol. 64, *Schriften des Instituts für Österreichkunde*, ed. Ernst Bruckmüller (Vienna: Öbv & Hpt, 2001), 145-68, particularly 156.

52. For the interrelations between the Catholic church and the authoritarian regime see Dieter A. Binder, "Der 'Christliche Ständestaat' in Österreich 1934-1938," in *Österreich im 20. Jahrhundert. Ein Studienbuch in zwei Bänden*, vol.1, ed. Rolf Steininger and Michael Gehler (Vienna: Böhlau, 1997), 203-56, here 207f.

53. Georg Kastner, "Die Opfer des NS-Terrors in Österreich von 1933 bis 1938," in *Demokratie und Geschichte. Jahrbuch des Karl von Vogelsang-Instituts zur Erforschung der Geschichte der christlichen Demokratie in Österreich*, vol. 5, ed. Helmut Wohnout (Vienna,

2002, not yet released).

54. For foreign policy between 1934-38 see Gerald Stourzh, "Die Außenpolitik der österreichischen Bundesregierung gegenüber der nationalsozialistischen Bedrohung," in *Österreich, Deutschland und die Mächte. Internationale und österreichische Aspekte des Anschlusses*, ed. Gerald Stourzh and Birgitta Zaar, vol. 16, *Österreichische Akademie der Wissenschaften. Veröffentlichungen der Kommission für die Geschichte Österreichs* (Vienna, 1990), 319-46.

55. Binder and Wohnout, "Regierungssystem," 156-60.

56. Wohnout, *Regierungsdiktatur*, 285f.

57. *Federal Legal Gazette* 102/1936, 1 April 1936.

58. For an overview of Austria's military potential between 1934-1938 see Binder, "Ständestaat," 228f.

59. Gerhard Botz, *Gewalt in der Politik. Attentate, Zusammenstöße, Putschversuche, Unruhen in Österreich 1918-1938* (Munich: W. Fink, 1983), 235.

60. Hanisch, *Der lange Schatten*, 311-15; Binder talks about an equation of "absolutist power conferred by God's grace" and "state-upholding bureaucracy" which had been "intended as a leitmotif." Binder, "Ständestaat," 211.

61. Voegelin, *Staat*, 251.

62. Karl Dietrich Bracher, "Autoritarismus und Totalitarismus. Die deutsche Diktatur und Österreich im Spannungsfeld der europäischen Nationalismen," in idem, *Wendezeiten der Geschichte. Historisch-politische Essays 1987-1992* (Stuttgart: Deutsche Verlags-Anstalt, 1992), 145-72, particularly 152; Bracher, "Eine düstere Erfahrung," 114-18.

The Foreign Policy of the Schuschnigg Government 1934-1938: The Quest for Security

Alexander Lassner

Kurt Schuschnigg (left)
Theodor Hornbostel (above)

Photos: Vogelsang-Institut, Vienna

In Austria, few subjects can provoke more heated debate than the Anschluss. Over the last fifty-six years, manifold works relating to it, mostly in German and English, have been published in an extensive array of fields: literary examinations, socio-cultural histories, military studies, photographic compilations, biographies, memoirs, and traditional political accounts. Yet, despite the extensive coverage that has been given to the field of Austrian foreign policy from 1934 to 1938, there are compelling reasons for renewed study: the distortions by Kurt Schuschnigg, his colleagues, and their international counterparts, in their numerous *ex post facto* apologiae (Schuschnigg himself misleadingly wrote that his government was not and could never be "anti-German"[1]); scholars' general acceptance of the view that Schuschnigg's failure to embrace parliamentary democracy contributed decisively to the successful Anschluss; the failure of many historians to undertake the kind of exhaustive research, in the required languages and from a broad international perspective, that would bring us closer to the truth of what the chancellor and his colleagues believed, and what they sought to do from 1934 to 1938; the release of tens of thousands of documents over the last two decades in American and European archives; and, finally, the failure of many scholars to see the enormous degree of deceit present in the European diplomatic record in general, and, above all, to recognize the perversion of language and of argument by the Nazis and their agents (especially in conversation with one another).[2]

This essay, based upon portions of the author's dissertation, seeks to shed new light on the foreign policy of the Schuschnigg government, which was part of a more expansive strategy designed to prevent the conquest of Austria by Nazi Germany.[3] Specifically, this paper charts the efforts of the Schuschnigg government to procure a politico-military guarantee of Austria from Britain, France, and Italy (later Britain and France) between 1934 and 1937. Such a guarantee, the members of the Schuschnigg government correctly understood, was absolutely essential to provide Austria the necessary security against the Nazi Reich.

The Murder of Dollfuss and the Quest for Security

Despite the neutrality that had been officially espoused by the Austrian government of Johannes Schober in 1929, an important shift in Austrian neutrality had already taken place under the subsequent leadership of Chancellor Engelbert Dollfuss. Due to the *de facto* war with the Third Reich, the Austrian government undertook two international protests against state-sponsored terrorism and subversion by Nazi Germany (July 1933 and January/February 1934), received economic support from Britain and France, and, from 1932 to 1934, expanded existing cooperation with Italy. This cooperation included the creation of the Roman Protocols (a politico-economic grouping of Austria-Hungary-Italy), the purchase of Italian military equipment, and the securing of oral promises of military intervention in the case of a German invasion. Such associations were assuredly less than neutral. Though Dollfuss did not renounce the policy of neutrality (a policy explicitly opposed by Italian dictator Benito Mussolini and Hitler in private), he used Britain, France, Hungary, and Italy as a means to stop the Reich's attempts to destabilize and overthrow his government. This established a credible and necessary military deterrent since the *Bundesheer* and other paramilitary and auxiliary formations were too small and poorly equipped to stop an outright German attack.[4]

After the failed Nazi putsch of 25 July 1934 (which was approved by Hitler and during which Dollfuss was murdered), Schuschnigg became chancellor. Schuschnigg was aware of the danger in which Austria found itself in the wake of the Nazi uprising. Furthermore, he was greatly concerned about the inaction of France and Great Britain and the unilateral Italian deployment of already mobilized troops to the Austro-Italian border.[5] The new chancellor realized that an effective protection of Austria was necessary, in addition to existing guarantees as provided in article 88 of the Treaty of St. Germain, Articles 10 and 16 of the Covenant of the League of Nations, and the 1922 Geneva Agreement.[6] This was necessary, he understood, above and beyond the Nazi Reich forswearing interference in Austria and recognizing its independence. Thus, the Schuschnigg government set about creating an "Austrian Pact": a politico-military guarantee of Austria by Britain, France, and Italy, existing outside of the League of Nations.

In order to do so, Vienna first sought proof of Germany's complicity in recent terrorism in Austria, on the Austro-German border, and in the July putsch. In June, approximately six weeks before the murder of Dollfuss, the *Ballhausplatz* had recommenced collecting evidence of the Reich's involvement in the support of terrorism in Austria. Dollfuss and his colleagues believed that the acts were centrally directed by Germany.[7] Throughout August and into the first days of September 1934, the *Ballhausplatz* assembled that evidence.

This evidence included, but was far from limited to, such documents as the so-called *Kollerschlager Dokument*, and the minutes from a meeting of Nazi group leaders in Leipzig, Germany on 18 August 1934. The *Kollerschlager Dokument*, purportedly found on a courier infiltrating the border from Germany near the town of Kollerschlag on 25 July 1934, was a detailed how-to list for a putsch against the Austrian government. The copy of the minutes from the Nazi group leaders' meeting on 18 August, purloined by Austrian agents and believed authentic by the Austrian government, showed that the Nazi leadership had changed means but had not altered its goals. Schuschnigg and then-Foreign Minister Egon Berger-Waldenegg confided to American Ambassador George Messersmith that these and other reports together revealed "that while certain surface measures may be taken to reassure public opinion and to indicate that action against Austria has ceased, the real action is to be carried through." It was clear to the Austrians that "so far as possible the direction was to be from within Austria rather than from Germany, and to cover up so far as possible the German connection and direction of these efforts against the [Austrian] Government."[8]

On 28 August 1934, Schuschnigg let London, Paris, and Rome know of his intention to pursue the Austrian Pact at Geneva that September. Over the next fortnight, Vienna supplied preliminary details as to what the pact would entail. First and foremost, the *Ballhausplatz* wanted the great powers—Britain, France, and Italy—to "ensure [the] independence of Austria and non-interference with Austrian internal affairs especially by Germany." Should another German threat materialize, the great powers would "intervene immediately as soon as the Austrian government notified everyone that it felt threatened" in order "to make the exterior cause of the threat disappear." Both the request for action and a precise determination of countries from which military aid might come were to be left to the discretion of Vienna.[9]

Schuschnigg rejected attempts by Mussolini to conclude a bilateral pact of joint military assistance between Italy and Austria, which, only at some later date, could have been opened to British, French, and German participation.[10] But the Austrian chancellor accepted the British and French demand that Germany be asked to grant the same guarantees to Austria as to Britain, France, and Italy.[11] This was done in order to expose the true intentions of Germany, since nobody at the *Ballhausplatz* believed that Germany had altered its goal of conquering Austria.[12]

On 12 September 1934, Schuschnigg, Berger-Waldenegg, and Political Director Theodor Hornbostel arrived in Geneva at the head of the Austrian delegation in order to craft the politico-military guarantee. The Austrian Pact, as presented by Hornbostel that same day, contained three articles: First, any threat to Austria was contrary to the interests of the contracting parties (France, Italy, and, if possible, Great Britain and Germany); second, "in the case that the independence of Austria is threatened by acts of interference coming from outside and directed against the internal order or stability of its government, the signatories promise to give Austria their aid in order to make the external cause of the threat disappear[;]" and third, the pact would subsequently be open to membership by countries beyond the original contracting signatories.[13]

Later that day, Schuschnigg and Berger-Waldenegg met with French Foreign Minister Louis Barthou. The Austrian chancellor informed the French foreign minister that the situation in Austria was "calm" and that it would remain so "until Berlin or Munich send a different order." But it was "urgent to take measures on the international level that, politically and economically, can assure the independence of Austria." Thereafter, Hornbostel gave the French assistant director and head of the League of Nations Division at the *Quai d'Orsay*, René Massigli, evidence of Germany's involvement in terrorism in Austria and in the assassination of Dollfuss, as well as a first draft of the Austrian Pact. The British received the same communications.[14]

But the result of Austria's effort at Geneva was failure: A British refusal to take part in guarantees of any sort, the national security concerns and obstructionism of Czechoslovakia and Yugoslavia, France's desire to defend its allies' interests, and the suspicion of Italian intentions towards the Little Entente together created insurmountable obstacles. Nor were Italian leaders even willing to consider the interests of the Little Entente.[15] All that could be agreed upon by British, French, and Italian officials was to reiterate, on 27 September, a slightly elaborated version of the 17 February 1934 declaration, which stressed the "necessity of maintaining Austria's independence and integrity in accordance with the relevant treaties."[16]

No sooner had Schuschnigg returned to Vienna, than the newly appointed German Ambassador to Austria, Franz Papen, went on the offensive. Papen had arrived in Vienna in August 1934, full of friendly protestations to the effect that the Nazi Reich had not been involved in the failed 25 July putsch, while proclaiming that the issue of the Anschluss was not "actual." But Papen was sufficiently indiscreet at that time as to admit to leading members of the Schuschnigg government and foreign diplomats that the Austrian people would eventually find a way to "satisfy their desire for union with Germany." Indeed, Schuschnigg initially refused to accept Papen as ambassador, backing down only after being threatened by German officials with a "diplomatic war."[17] But the Austrian leaders—above all President Wilhelm Miklas, as well as Schuschnigg and Berger-Waldenegg—were right to treat Papen with deep suspicion and mistrust from the very beginning.[18]

Now, at the end of the first week of October 1934, Papen accused the Schuschnigg government of attacking the Reich. Schuschnigg and Berger-Waldenegg prevaricated, denying that such was their intent. And while the Austrian statesmen negotiated briefly with Austrian "Nationals" (i.e., individuals with Pan-German and/or pro-Nazi views who supposedly were not members of the Nazi party and who purportedly disagreed with the terroristic policies pursued by the Nazis), they informed Messersmith that, based on the most recent information collected by the *Ballhausplatz*, "the German Government has not given up its pretensions in any sense against Austria[;] it is not the intention of the highest powers in the German Government and in the National Socialist Party that overt acts against Austria should be undertaken in the near future.... [T]hese higher placed persons are endeavoring [merely] to exert a positive influence to prevent any action against Austria for the present in order that the German Government may have a freer hand in other directions [i.e., the upcoming plebiscite in the Saar for reunion with Germany]."[19]

In the wake of Austria's failure at Geneva that September, however, both the French and Italian governments recognized that the Austrian state did indeed require an effective guarantee in order to be protected from the Reich. Thus, from October to December, proposals and counterproposals passed between Paris and Rome. Although the deliberations were part of the general and ongoing Franco-Italian rapprochement and covered a wider scope than the subject of Austria, the focus on Austria was unmistakable.[20] In mid-November, Mussolini proposed joint military conversations on Austria to the French military attaché to Rome, General Henri Parisot.[21] But the new French Foreign Minister, Pierre Laval, was determined to make a guarantee of Austria contingent on three conditions, and in harmony with Barthou's previous representations. First, it should take place in the League. To this end, Prague and Bucharest, too, applied pressure on Rome.

Second, Laval stipulated that the Little Entente (Czechoslovakia, Romania, and Yugoslavia) be included in any agreement as equal members. Third, and most problematic for Rome (and ironically for Paris as well), Laval desired that any guarantee of Austria, as well as the Franco-Italian rapprochement itself, should depend on an Italo-Yugoslav accord.[22]

By early December, with no agreement yet reached, Schuschnigg and his colleagues began to worry about whether or not they could obtain a satisfactory Franco-Italian agreement of guarantee.[23] Laval notified Schuschnigg that he preferred the formula of reciprocal general convention under the auspices of the League, in which all the countries bordering on Austria, together with France and Britain, would agree to respect the independence and integrity of each other. Within such an agreement, countries could assume specific obligations for purposes of enforcing the general convention.[24] While the *Ballhausplatz* was sympathetic to the idea, Berger-Waldenegg emphasized that this pact should remain separate from a guarantee of Austria, "which dealt with a clearly articulated problem: the defense of Austrian independence. The [Austrian] Federal government asks that in 'practical' terms the defense is assumed by France and Italy *only* and in agreement with Austria."[25] The Austrian foreign minister further indicated that a pact of guarantee "which deals practically with the eventual safeguard of Austria . . . is not mutual [and] cannot involve the adhesion of other neighbors, because the pact is limited to the measures of security to be taken eventually by France and Italy for the independence of Austria." The Schuschnigg government would not compromise on Austrian security. Nor did it trust the "territorial pretensions" of Czechoslovakia, Yugoslavia, or Hungary.[26] Laval thereupon reassured the *Ballhausplatz*, and Berger-Waldenegg informed Puaux that Laval's formula seemed acceptable.[27] In response, officials at the *Quai d'Orsay* notified Vienna that Laval would visit Rome to help formulate an effective protection of Austria.[28]

As part of the Rome Accords in early 1935—which covered numerous contentious issues between Italy and France—Laval and Mussolini formally agreed to consult in case of a threat to Austrian independence while allowing for the creation of "specific engagements" in order to ensure the protection of Austria.[29] Schuschnigg, for his part, believed that the Rome Accords were also significant since they not only showed the interest of France and Italy in maintaining Austrian independence, but also that of Britain, which approved of the accords.[30] The Austrian government nevertheless continued to stress its desire for a guarantee from France and Italy, in which those countries alone would provide Austria with immediate military aid in case of need, and in agreement with Vienna.[31] However, the *Ballhausplatz* showed itself willing to accept that the Franco-Italian consultation on Austria within the Rome Accords be paralleled in Laval's reciprocal general convention (by February alternately termed the

"Austrian Pact," the "Central European Pact," or the "Danubian Pact," and hereafter referred to as "Central European Pact" (CEP) to distinguish it from Schuschnigg's Austrian Pact of September 1934 and Czechoslovakia's proposed Danubian Pact of 1936-37). This promised the non-interference, mutual assistance, and respect of the territorial integrity of states amongst all the countries bordering on Austria, as well as France and Britain. The CEP, in turn, would be created in harmony and association with the League.[32]

But there were limits to the kind of action that the Austrian government was willing to take vis-à-vis the Third Reich, as Schuschnigg made clear before and during his trips to London and Paris from 21 to 26 February 1935. Austria was on the defensive and wished to avoid taking part in bloc building aimed explicitly against Germany, as indeed did Laval. Austria was also vulnerable to German retribution. The archival evidence shows that Schuschnigg's wish to avoid an obvious anti-German stance—which actually conformed to the views of his colleagues including Vice-Chancellor Ernst Rüdiger Starhemberg, Foreign Minister Egon Berger-Waldenegg, Political Director Theodor Hornbostel, State Secretary for Defense Wilhelm Zehner, and Chief of the General Staff Alfred Jansa among others—did not stem from Germanic feelings of brotherhood that overrode thoughts of preparing Austria for resistance to Germany.

Rather, this desire arose from far more rational, calculated, and defensive motives: The Nazi Reich was dangerous and economically, politically, and militarily too strong for Austria to provoke or even ignore. There were also Germanic sympathies within the Austrian population, which the Nazis and their agents exploited at every turn. Schuschnigg did not want to aggravate these sentiments or provide Nazi propagandists with ammunition. Yet, from August 1934 to March 1935, he repeatedly accused the German government on the international stage and implicated it in the support and employment of terrorism and coercion against the Austrian state. And although the Austrian government declared itself unwilling to take part in provocative bloc building aimed against Germany per se, it continued to desire the protection of the Rome Accords, the creation of a Franco-Italian guarantee of Austria (derived from Schuschnigg's Austrian Pact proposal of August/September 1934 and amounting to a de facto Austro-French-Italian defensive military alliance to protect Austria against poten-tial German aggression), and the conclusion of the CEP. In addition, in August 1935, operational planning began within the *Bundesministerium für Landesverteidigung* (Federal Defense Ministry or BMfLV), which envisio-ned an attack on Austria by the Reich. These plans were formulated bet-ween Jansa, the operations department of Section III of the BMfLV, and the commanders of the 4th and 6th Infantry Divisions.[33] Speaking about an unwillingness to take an "anti-German" stance in the face of this evidence is to deprive the term of much significance. What Schuschnigg and his colleagues were always mindful of was not to be perceived as the accusers of Germany.

Although, during the Stresa Conference in April 1935, British Prime Minister Ramsay MacDonald and Foreign Secretary John Simon explicitly refused to take measures to defend Austria (agreeing only to what they understood was a meaningless "consultation" on Austria in the case of a threat to its independence),[34] the Austro-French-Italian discussions on a guarantee of Austria made real progress in May and June. This was especially due to the improved relations between Rome and Belgrade. As Schuschnigg noted during talks in Venice with Mussolini in May, "the big concern for Austria up to now has been that of having to face not only an attack from Bavaria but also from Yugoslavia. If Italian troops would have had to come to the aid [*soccorso*] of Austria, they could have faced a Yugoslavian penetration in Carinthia. So the Italian-Yugoslav agreement avoids this." At the same time Schuschnigg prudently rejected Mussolini's offer—made during the same meeting—of unilateral Italian aid to Austria in the case of German aggression, correctly understanding that "... in this case [of a German attack] there are only two choices: to submit or to rely on European aid. The first choice is out of the question, so in this scenario we are compelled to put forward a claim for help. Thus we are of the view that, with respect to the current foreign political situation, [Austria] cannot rely on unilateral Italian assistance. The other powers also [would] have to stand up for the territorial status quo in central Europe directly and immediately."[35]

On 2 July 1935, the Austrian government received good news. Schuschnigg's efforts to obtain a guarantee of Austria, as envisaged in the August/September 1934 Austrian Pact, had been realized in a different form. Thus, Italian Undersecretary for Foreign Affairs Fulvio Suvich informed the Austrian chancellor that, in agreement with the Roman Accords of 7 January 1935, a Franco-Italian engagement had been concluded at last, namely the Franco-Italian Military Accords of 27 June 1935.[36]

The Military Accords dealt exclusively with mutual Franco-Italian military assistance in case of a German attack on either country and with the defense of Austria by French and Italian troops (the accords even contemplated forces from Yugoslavia and Czechoslovakia participating in the defense of Austria, though this remained problematic). Although the Military Accords were never officially ratified, both Laval (later Pierre-Etienne Flandin and, briefly, Léon Blum) and Mussolini considered them operational. But Austrian civil and military authorities refused French requests that troops be permitted to transit Austria in order to reinforce the states of the Little Entente, while reiterating that they would not take part in offensive operations against Germany.[37] Short of a direct attack on Austria, which the Danubian state would resist, officials at the *Ballhausplatz* still hoped to avoid being dragged into war.

Security Falls Apart

From March until September 1935 talks surrounding the possibility of the CEP also continued. Unfortunately for Vienna, despite the seriousness of the negotiations, multiple quarrels impeded progress. Berlin manufactured issues in order to hamper negotiations and objected to a pact of mutual assistance and a detailed definition of non-interference (notwithstanding Hitler's declared willingness to define the term in his 21 May speech); London categorically refused to defend Austria, agreeing only to "consult" in case of a threat; Budapest wanted to make an agreement for a CEP contingent on equality of rights, specifically as applied to armaments, and insisted that Vienna follow suit; Prague doubted the wisdom of any engagements of assistance beyond Articles 10 and 16 of the League Covenant; Bucharest feared taking any action for Austria that would expose it to German hostility; and Belgrade desired that any agreement be subject to an Italian guarantee of Yugoslavia and to limits on Austrian and Hungarian rearmament.[38] Further, all three members of the Little Entente desired to regulate any possible restoration of the Habsburgs in Austria as an international question and as part of the CEP conversations.[39]

In the matter of the CEP, Vienna, too, had a variety of interests and aims. Primary among them was not to appear as the "special object" of the CEP, which would make Austria look as if under an international "protectorate," with all that would entail for Nazi propagandists and Austrian pride; the assistance clauses of the CEP, therefore, should be reciprocal. Equally important, and as Hornbostel reiterated to the French *Chargé d'Affairs* Hugues Barthon Montbas, there had to be a very explicit definition of non-interference. This was essential since anything omitted by the definition would be interpreted by the Nazis as authorized behavior.[40]

To make matters more difficult, by early summer 1935 the buildup of Italian forces in Africa and growing tension between Rome and London threatened European peace and any furtherance of the CEP. In June, the foremost question at the *Ballhausplatz* was what would happen if Italian prestige became bound up in Abyssinia, especially if military operations commenced.[41] But Anglo-Italian friction continued to increase, becoming the leading foreign political focus of the 28 August cabinet meeting in Vienna. Berger-Waldenegg stated that a peaceful solution to the crisis in Abyssinia was unlikely; one "could only hope that Italy had success, and [that] the affair remain localized and be ended swiftly."[42] In September, however, British leaders took the lead in advocating sanctions against Italy should it commence hostilities against Abyssinia, which posed a threat to British Imperial lines of communication. Consequently, an Anglo-Italian war threatened.[43]

For the *Ballhausplatz* this posed a significant and multifaceted hazard. First, sanctions against Rome could encourage an Italo-German rapprochement, thereby calling into question Italy's commitment to Austrian independence. Second, the commencement of sanctions would jeopardize three more immediate issues: the admittedly weak Stresa front; the 27 June 1935 Franco-Italian Military Accords; and Italian membership in the League altogether. In light of the deteriorating situation, Berger-Waldenegg, before leaving for Geneva in mid-September, informed Messersmith that one of the principle objectives of his trip was to see how far Laval, Aloisi, and the newly appointed British Foreign Secretary, Samuel Hoare, were prepared to go in supporting Austria if it came to a confrontation in Europe over the Abyssinian crisis.[44]

Unfortunately, the British refused to offer effective aid to the Austrian government should it alienate Italy, even as Hoare unequivocally insisted that Austria support the sanctions. By the end of September 1935, the members of the Schuschnigg government correctly understood that Anglo-Italian antagonism had led to the *de facto* collapse of the Stresa front, and that any prospects for the CEP had also declined precipitously. Thankfully—from the perspective of Vienna—Franco-Italian relations, although strained, persevered with Laval seeking to mediate between London and Rome. Thus, throughout October and November, the Schuschnigg government engaged in a diplomatic balancing act aimed at preserving Italian support, avoiding British hostility, and maintaining recourse to aid from the League against German aggression. While this maneuver proved overall successful, Austria's international position continued to degenerate. A plan to settle the Abyssinian conflict at the cost of Ethiopia (the Hoare-Laval Plan) collapsed in mid-December, and Anglo-Italian animosity surged. Vienna was thrust into a constricting international position in which Italy stood defiantly against the League, and a furiously rearming Nazi Reich loomed ominously. Officials at the *Ballhausplatz* viewed this circumstance with great trepidation and hoped, along with leaders at the *Quai d'Orsay*, for an early end to the Italo-Abyssinian conflict. But war in Africa continued into the spring of 1936. And on 7 March 1936, Germany remilitarized the Rhineland in contravention of the Versailles and Locarno Treaties. Panic gripped the *Ballhausplatz*.[45]

On 8 March, a deeply troubled Schuschnigg told Puaux, "now that the treaty of Versailles is abolished the Führer will execute his pan-German program." The chancellor indicated to Puaux, Hungarian President Gyula Gömbös, and Foreign Minister Kálmán Kánya who would be the next victim: Austria. In conversation with Messersmith on 11 March, Berger-

Waldenegg, too, agreed that, Austria "will be next" and that, while the German move had not been unexpected, it had nevertheless come as a surprise with serious implications.[46]

Thus, in March, with Austrian security at stake and the CEP on indefinite hold, leaders at the *Ballhausplatz* decided to accept Mussolini's offer to strengthen the Roman Protocols. This, they believed, would help stabilize the situation in the short term. More significantly, leaders at the *Ballhausplatz* worked to promote Franco-Italian reconciliation, since relations between Paris and Rome had continued to degenerate after Laval's fall from power in January. They further attempted to forge anew security for Austria with France, Italy, and, if possible, Britain; poor relations between the French and Italians necessarily threatened the 27 June 1935 Franco-Italian Military Accords.

But, as is frequently the case, the Austrian cabinet records omit much, and they do not tell the story of Vienna's proposal for a reworked politico-military guarantee; more seriously, neither does the evidence uncovered by historians at the state archives in Vienna over the last sixty years.[47] During the 19 March 1936 cabinet meeting, Minister of Social Welfare Josef Dobretsberger highlighted that, although there was at present no other political possibility than a strengthening of the Roman Protocols, a tightening of that group could produce an adverse effect in France and Britain.[48] Such was also the concern of Schuschnigg, Berger-Waldenegg, and Hornbostel, since Italy did not represent a sufficient military guarantee of Austria.

Consequently, on 20 March, the Austrian government contacted the French government to solicit, in strictest secrecy, the creation of a "system of collective security" through a "pact with the western Powers [i.e., Britain, France, and Italy]." This would be built upon the already existing and still functional, if endangered, 27 June 1935 Franco-Italian Military Accords. Vienna informed Paris that, after Germany's remilitarization of the Rhineland, "[the] next time it is our turn. Germany needs our electricity and our iron; we can be sure that at the smallest international complication we will be invaded without having the opportunity to defend ourselves given our current weakness." Now, the Schuschnigg government sketched the "pact with the western Powers." In a manner fundamentally similar to the views expressed by Jansa to the French in August and October 1935, it outlined two "psychological" difficulties that would limit Austria's role within the pact:

> [O]n the one side it would be better if the Austrians did not feel very openly the 'object' of a 'protection' that would put them in a state of inferiority. On the other side, the feelings of Germanic solidarity [in the citizenry] are still very powerful, even in the patriotic milieu, and [this] makes it difficult to ask the army to have an offensive attitude against Germany.... [I]n order to avoid those difficulties Austria should enter

> this prospective group [i.e., Britain, France, Italy] as equal to the others, and, in case of an attack by Germany against one of this group [other than Austria], Austria should remain passive; Austria should be asked no more than to defend its own frontiers against any aggression by the Reich.

As French officials succinctly noted in their reports regarding the Austrian appeal,

> [y]ou will observe that the Austrians propose their entry into a pact with the western Powers. This might well be a solution; but, as you will also see, *one must not count on dragging Austria into offensive operations against Germany*. If we can get Austria to defend its own frontiers that would already be a lot. The issue of penetrating the Austrian [frontier] with the justification of helping her is a point that the Austrian military never want to deal with openly.[49]

And no one at the *Ballhausplatz* was fooled by Hitler's offer of European non-aggression pacts, which were made immediately after the remilitarization of the Rhineland in March but would only officially recognize Germany's western boundaries. Schuschnigg told Mussolini on 21 March 1936 that the offer was "not important" and would not guarantee Austria, while Berger-Waldenegg and Hornbostel notified Puaux on 3 April that "[t]he offer of non-aggression to the neighbors of southeastern Europe is not explicit [with regard to boundaries] in contrast to western frontiers. This is revealing of German plans which [are to] neutralize western powers and gain a free hand to the south and east." Both Austrians asserted that the only effective counter to Hitler's maneuvers would be "not to let the problem of security in central Europe become distinct from that of security on the Rhine." Berger-Waldenegg was even more candid with Messersmith stating that

> Austria had no intention of attacking Germany and under no circumstances could or would think of such a thing. On the other hand, the intentions of the present German Government with respect to Austria were already too well known and aggressive action was within those intentions and no one could tell when such action would be taken .... [E]ven if [Vienna] had a letter from Mr. Hitler directly offering ... a non-aggression pact, the situation had now become such that Austria would have to show all lack of interest unless there were proper guarantors of the pact to whom [Austria] could look to see that Hitler kept his word.

Given the gravity of the situation, and in order to promote the "pact with the western Powers," the *Ballhausplatz* asked—even begged—the *Quai d'Orsay* at the end of March and repeatedly throughout April to begin a rapprochement with Italy. On 2 April, Berger-Waldenegg and Hornbostel together begged Puaux for a "reestablishment of the Franco-Italian front for the defense of Austria." On the 17th Berger-Waldenegg stated to Montbas that his "last hope" was that Franco-Italian solidarity could be maintained in central Europe since "Italy, by itself, is today, more than ever, an insufficient state." Showing just how serious the level of fear in Vienna had become he bluntly declared, "[i]f [France] allows the Reich to fortify the area of the Rhine we are lost. In that case we may as well go to Berlin and ask for forgiveness." A week later, Schuschnigg confided to Puaux that "[t]he German threat would disappear if France and England, or even France alone, solemnly let Germany know that their armed aggression against Austria would meet armed French resistance."[50]

Dobretsberger made the case even more explicit in his conversation with Messersmith. He hoped that "Italy and France would soon make up their differences" so that "France might join Italy as an active guarantor of Austrian independence" since the aid of Italy alone would not suffice: "[F]or Italy and Austria to hold out for any length of time, France would have to create a diversion in the Rhineland and thus occupy the attention of large bodies of German troops, otherwise Austria would be completely overrun." If Britain could be added to this combination then "the safety of Austria would be complete." But French and Italian cooperation was "indispensable."[51]

With reason, Schuschnigg, Berger-Waldenegg, Dobretsberger, Zehner, and Jansa believed that talks between Italian and German diplomats, as well as Rome's estrangement from London and Paris, were conditioned primarily by Italy's war in Africa and the League sanctions, and not due to designs of far more ambitious nature. Once the sanctions were lifted, Austrian leaders reasoned, Anglo-French-Italian relations could be restored, and Italy would become less interested in conversations with Berlin. Berger-Waldenegg highlighted Austrian perceptions when he told Messersmith, after the March 1936 Roman Protocols meeting, that "as long as sanctions were being applied against Italy, and the Abyssinian question was not liquidated, Mr. Mussolini would continue conversations with Berlin." But, he continued, the conversations

> had no real significance provided the Western Powers could arrange matters. Mr. Mussolini had no confidence in Mr. Hitler and no confidence in any arrangements with the present government in Germany. [Mussolini] was, however, a realist and had to face situations as he found them.... [Mussolini] understood the situation in Germany thoroughly and the menace which Hitler and Hitler Germany were to Europe. It was necessary, however, for the Abyssinian question to be settled, in order that Franco-Italian cooperation could be put on a proper basis with English support.... [E]fforts were being made to settle the Abyssinian problem directly between Paris and Rome, and that... was something very much to be desired. The League prestige would suffer

> further, but after all one must recognize that unfortunately League prestige is gone already. The English position and the English press . . . could not [be] underst[ood], for it seemed to show a lack of appreciation of the fact that England was as definitely threatened [by Germany] as the rest of Europe.

Mussolini did everything within his power to encourage this conviction in Rome, Paris, and Vienna for the time being. In fact, however, in the wake of the Abyssinian crisis the *Duce* steered Italy hence-forth—slowly and secretly—towards alliance with Nazi Germany. Overall, Berger-Waldenegg described the European situation as "very critical," and deduced correctly that "it was only determined action by the Western Powers which could avoid a great war." Vienna would now have to wait and see if appeals met with a positive response.[52]

Unfortunately, no response from Paris was forthcoming. For complex domestic and foreign politico-military reasons, the transitory government of Albert Sarraut permitted the matter to languish. Moreover, in April the Italians began hinting to Vienna that they desired a settlement of the Austro-German conflict, while, at the same time, they repeatedly assured the Austrians that this would in no way change Italian support for Austria. Italian civil and military authorities followed up these assurances by collaborating with the Austrians militarily. Thus, by the end of April 1936, Schuschnigg began to consider the necessity of reaching a *modus vivendi* with Germany in consideration of a confluence of factors: the immediate threat of a German attack, as suggested by Austrian intelligence reports; the risks implied by potential League oil sanctions against Italy and the ongoing Italo-German conversations; no response from Paris to Vienna's proposal for "a pact with the western Powers"; the lack of Franco-Italian rapprochement; massive German rearmament; and the categorical British unwillingness to participate in any guarantee of Austria.[53] The Austrian chancellor therefore asked Guido Schmidt, who was a longtime friend and the liaison between the office of the president and the chancellery, to select names of supposedly moderate Nationals that might be brought into the government. Among the names were those of Arthur Seyss-Inquart and Edmund Glaise-Horstenau.[54] On 4 May 1936 Schuschnigg suggested to Papen that they discuss "the possibility of a German-Austrian reconciliation" and that he, Schuschnigg, was prepared to consider representatives of the Nationals for a position in the government.[55] Over the next two months, Austrian and German statesmen debated the contents of an Austro-German settlement.

From *Abkommen* to Invasion

Sporadic negotiations for an Austro-German settlement had begun in early 1935, but had failed to develop into anything serious, since Schuschnigg and his colleagues were profoundly suspicious of Papen and uninterested in any settlement with Nazi Germany without a great power guarantee of Austria. Moreover, after his arrival in Vienna in August 1934, Papen had spent his time lying ineptly to the Austrians and being repeatedly caught; trying to sew discontent and uncertainty among Austrian civil authorities in the provinces; and regularly attempting to threaten and intimidate Schuschnigg and his associates. Indeed, the degree of Papen's sinister, if ludicrous, incompetence in the service of Hitler was well reflected during a tirade in spring 1935, after the return of Schuschnigg and Berger-Waldenegg from Paris and London: Arriving at the Foreign Office, Papen began to issue demands of and threats against Schuschnigg, while protesting against the "Jewish press of [Eduard] Ludwig." (Ludwig was Chief of the Austrian Press Bureau and a Catholic. Standard Nazi linguistic perversion described acts of resistance as "poisonous" or "Jewish.") When General Secretary of the Foreign Office Franz Peter confronted him with evidence of his subversive activities, Papen became increasingly nervous and upset. Dismayed at his failure and not thinking clearly, Papen carelessly blurted out: "[Y]es you have your French and English friends now and can have your independence a little longer." Unsurprisingly, given Papen's frequent and inept duplicity, Schuschnigg well understood the Nazis *modus operandi* and goals, telling Czechoslovak foreign minister Milan Hodza in January 1936 that

> the expansionist push of the Third Reich is not to be overlooked. The [German] rearmament that is being pursued with the greatest intensity will need an escape valve one day, and it will vent itself, predictably, in the direction of least resistance. There is no question of surrender for us and we would in this case [of a German attack] be forced to take corresponding measures. Every German avowal about a *desinteressement* in Austria is useless and is not believed. The ruling principle [*Leitsatz*] in the Reich is [that] one may say anything at all in politics and must hold to nothing [*man dürfe in der Politik alles sagen und müsse nichts halten*]. As a result of that it is only too evident that one is dubious in Austria about assurances from Berlin.

Schuschnigg and his colleagues were not, as a rule, honest and forthright in their talks with Papen and his collaborators but, rather, wily and deceitful—downplaying issues, omitting key proceedings, feigning goodwill, playing linguistic games, and often mixing truth and falsehood in order to misdirect the Nazis.[56]

In their negotiations for an Austro-German settlement, Schuschnigg and his colleagues acted with cold calculation and with the knowledge that the Nazis and their agents were pathological liars. The 11 July 1936 Austro-German *Abkommen* (hereafter referred to as *Abkommen*) was a carefully constructed piece of writing, in which clarity deliberately alternated with vagueness and which represented the centerpiece of Schuschnigg's second strategy of resistance to Nazi Germany from May 1936 to September 1937, that of feigned friendship. Making full use of the wording that he, Berger-Waldenegg, and Hornbostel had helped to draft (wrangling with Papen), Schuschnigg waged battle with Hitler by means of the spoken and written word. In this way, Schuschnigg tried to buy time for a reconstitution of the Franco-Italian front with whatever British support could be garnered, or, at least, to avoid the armed German expansion, which, as he believed, would undoubtedly come. In the ensuing battle of wits, the Austrians repeatedly proved themselves superior to the Nazis and their agents.[57]

The conclusion of the *Abkommen* did not stop Schuschnigg's appeals for guarantee, which he again undertook in July 1936 and April/May 1937 (prior to foreign secretary Guido Schmidt's trip to London and Paris). And at the same time as the Austrian chancellor made his penultimate appeal for guarantee in April/May 1937, Schuschnigg acknowledged to the French that he could no longer depend upon Mussolini to oppose Germany with force; the best that could be hoped for was to keep Hitler and his cronies guessing as to Italy's attitude.

In what was by now an established pattern, neither of Schuschnigg's appeals to London and Paris produced results. The French Popular Front government of Léon Blum became suspicious of Vienna after seeing portions of the *Abkommen* communiqué, especially in light of Austria's membership in the Roman Protocols. In addition, they hoped to revitalize the League and procure the cooperation of Britain, Italy, and the U.S.S.R. in establishing collective security. (Contrary to established myth, Blum and his foreign minister, Yvon Delbos, made a concerted, and secret, effort at Franco-Italian rapprochement in June and July 1936 explicitly for purposes of security against the Third Reich. Mussolini ignored these appeals.) Finally, Blum and Delbos were still not convinced that they could not strike a deal with Germany.

But by April 1937, Blum and Delbos' views had undergone a drastic revision in favor of Schuschnigg and in comprehending German intentions of aggression. Thereafter, until the destruction of the Austrian state, Delbos in particular did all that he could to aid Schuschnigg, while showing great admiration and understanding for Austria's resistance. Unfortunately, by April 1937 it had also become apparent to French civil and military leaders that they could only take forceful action on behalf of Austria—or indeed Czechoslovakia—if they had the absolute support of Britain. This, the British had no intention of providing, believing that central Europe was not a vital interest for the British Empire and could, therefore, be given to Germany irrespective of any obligations or the will of its inhabitants.[58]

Indeed, with regard to this latter issue, Schuschnigg's most ambitious aim in order to generate assistance for Austria, beginning in spring 1936, was to try to convince the British, French, and Italian elite that the overwhelming majority of Austrians did indeed desire their independence. He believed that this knowledge would help to bring effective support for Austria. Schuschnigg and his colleagues therefore informed London and Paris directly that the Nazis in Austria formed a small minority and that the overwhelming majority of Austrians would vote for independence if permitted to do so freely. In July 1937, the chancellor further indicated his desire to hold a plebiscite for this purpose but that, before he would consider it safe to do so, he must be relieved of the menace of Nazi Germany. Schuschnigg's plan to hold a plebiscite was in direct opposition to the propaganda of Hitler and his collaborators, who vehemently maintained, on the international stage, that precisely the opposite was true.[59]

Here, Schuschnigg scored what must be judged as his most spectacular success: By late 1937, the senior leadership of Britain, France, and Italy *believed* that the Nazis were a minority of somewhere between 10 and 30 percent (with 20 percent being the accepted statistic in the British and French foreign office), that a majority of Austrians were likely to vote for independence if permitted to choose freely, and that an Anschluss could only be brought about by force. Unfortunately, these assessments were either ignored or dismissed by Mussolini and by British Prime Minister Neville Chamberlain, since the issue of national self-determination was, in fact, irrelevant to their calculus. (Indeed, it was Chamberlain who was most anxious that this not become public knowledge.)

The *Duce*'s plans for empire and for aggression alongside Germany, and Germany's clear intention not to abide by the *Abkommen* but, instead, to take control of Austria, forced Mussolini to make a decision. In November 1937, he chose to allow the Nazis in Berlin to continue their tactics of strangulation with the expectation that they would be able to Nazify Austria, or worse.

The Chamberlain government, understanding that Austria was now on the German menu, to be followed by Czechoslovakia, rejected any involvement on the continent except to promote German aggression and, in a calculating and brutal manner, to purchase peace at Hitler's price.[60] Thus, after receiving two appeals for aid against Nazi German aggression from Schuschnigg in mid-February 1938, the British, French, and Italian governments abandoned Austria (though for very different reasons), beginning with Britain on 19 February and ending with Italy on 27 February.[61]

By 1 March 1938, Schuschnigg grasped, quite accurately, that he had been deserted, but his options were now limited. The domestic situation was collapsing. Although he now accepted the support offered from the disaffected Left (including members of the SDP), which was necessary if he were to challenge the Reich with a war, he remained unwilling to take the measures necessary to take firm control of Austria, by decapitating the Nazi party in Austria through ruthless police strikes, followed by military and para-military actions, and placing the *Bundesheer* on a war footing.

Instead, on 4 March Schuschnigg initialized steps for a plebiscite, which became public knowledge on 9 March. In doing so, he surely realized that he would provoke Nazi action against him: Schuschnigg was convinced that a plebiscite would result in a large majority in favor of Austrian independence, and he knew that Hitler's "claims" to Austria abroad had always been based on the premise that the Austrians would overwhelmingly vote to join the Nazi Reich. Moreover, Schuschnigg had contemplated holding a plebiscite for at least ten months but avoided doing so precisely out of fear of a German invasion. It was self-evident in March 1938 that the risk of a German invasion was far greater. Still, in a desperate gamble, he pressed ahead.

When faced with a mobilizing *Wehrmacht* on 10-11 March, accompanied by German demands to cancel the plebiscite, and, finally, an ultimatum for his resignation, Schuschnigg sent out final requests for foreign help. When no aid was proffered, at 3:30 p.m., he submitted again to force and resigned. Later that evening, at 7:47 p.m., he announced his departure in a radio address, concluding with the words "God protect Austria." Early the next morning, the *Wehrmacht* invaded; no organized resistance took place and no foreign government raised a finger.[62]

Notes

1. Kurt Schuschnigg, *Ein Requiem in Rot-Weiß-Rot*, foreword by Stephan Verosta (Vienna: Amalthea, 1978), 267.

2. I use the term Nazi to denote the Nazis in Austria *and* in Germany. In the case where one or the other group is meant it is preceded by its modifier, e.g., German Nazis.

3. For a full treatment of Schuschnigg's strategic aims, European politics towards Austria at the time, and an in-depth discussion of the foreign political and security issues dealt with in this essay see Alexander N. Lassner, "Peace at Hitler's Price: Austria, the Great Powers, and the Anschluß, 1932-1938," Ph.D. diss., Ohio State University, 2001.

4. Lassner, "Peace at Hitler's Price," 17, 24-39, 43. American, British, French, and (of particular note) German officials described the conflict between Austria and Germany as a "battle" and as a "war." For examples of the term "war" see *Documents on British Foreign Policy* (hereafter *DBFP*), 2, VI, 563, Selby to Simon, 3 August 1934; *DBFP*, 2, XII, 102, Vansittart to Selby, 20 September 1934; National Archives and Records Service (hereafter NARS), M1209/4/0070, Messersmith to Hull, 17 August 1934. See especially the response of leading members of the German Foreign Office to the international protests by Austria in July/August 1933 against German terrorism and subversive activities, stating that Germany's "battle with Austria, which already has lasted much longer than we had expected, costs us exceptionally [*sic*]." NARS, T120/2838/E453718, German Foreign Office to Legations in London, Paris, and Rome, 26 July 1933.

5. Contrary to popular myth, Italian troops were already mobilized and on maneuvers at the time of the 25 July 1934 revolt.

6. Article 88 of the Treaty of St. Germain stated that the independence of Austria was inalienable except by consent of the Council of the League of Nations. Articles 10 and 16 of the Covenant of the League of Nations provided for collective defense of states against unprovoked aggression. See Avalon Project/Covenant of the League of Nations (hereafter, AP/CLN), retrieved from the world wide web on 28 June 2001, <http://www.yale.edu/lawweb/avalon/leagcov.htm#art10>; AP/CLN, <http://www.yale.edu/lawweb/avalon/leagcov.htm#art16>. The 1922 Geneva Protocol provided for unconditional maintenance of the independence of Austria in agreement with the League of Nations. See League of Nations, *The Restoration of Austria: Agreements Arranged by the League of Nations and Signed at Geneva on 4 October 1922, with Relevant Documents and Statements* (Geneva: 1922).

7. *Akten zur Deutschen Auswärtigen Politik 1918-1945* [hereafter, *ADAP*], C, II, 501, Reith to Bülow, 12 June 1934.

8. NARS, M1209/3/0504, No. 77, Messersmith to Hull, 3 August 1934; NARS, M1209/3/0654, No. 117, "Further Alleged Attempts to Organize a Movement to Overthrow the Austrian Government," Messersmith to Hull, 30 August 1934; *I Documenti Diplomatici Italiani* (hereafter, *DDI*), 7, XV, 727, Preziosi to Mussolini, 24 August 1934. See also, *ADAP*, C, III, 174, Bülow to Lammers, 22 August 1934; *ADAP*, C, III, Erbach to Foreign Ministry, 30 August 1934.

9. *DBFP*, 2, XII, 56, Selby to Simon, 29 August 1934; *DBFP*, 2, XII, 74, Clerk to Simon, 4 September 1934; *Documents Diplomatiques Français* (hereafter, *DDF*), 1, VII, 249, Puaux to Barthou, 6 September 1934; *DDF*, 1, VII, 204, Puaux to Barthou, 31 August 1934; *DDF*, 1, VII, 293, Massigli to Barthou, 11 September 1934; *DDF*, 1, VII, 303, Hornbostel to Massigli, 12 September 1934; *DDI*, 7, XV, 740, Preziosi to Mussolini, 29 August 1934; *DDI*, 7, XV, 776, Preziosi to Mussolini, 6 September 1934; *DDI*, 7, XV, 844, Preziosi to Mussolini, 20 September 1934.

10. *DDI*, 7, XV, 783, Aloisi to Mussolini, 8 September 1934; *DDI*, 7, XV, 788, Suvich to Mussolini, 9 September 1934.

11. *DBFP*, 2, XII, 70, Clerk to Simon, 2 September 1934; *DBFP*, 2, XII, 74, Clerk to Simon, 4 September 1934; *DBFP*, 2, XII, 102, Vansittart to Selby, 20 September 1934; *DDI*, 7, XV, 798, Aloisi to Mussolini, 11 September 1934; NARS, M1209/3/0622, telegram [conversation Straus and Léger], Straus to Hull, 7 September 1934

12. Lassner, "Peace at Hitler's Price," 55-59, 65.

13. *DDF*, 1, VII, 303, conversation Hornbostel and Massigli, 12 September 1934; *DBFP*, 2, XII, 102, Vansittart to Selby, 20 September 1934.

14. *DDF*, 1, VII, 302, Note de la délégation Française à la Société des Nations, 12 September 1934; *DDF*, 1, VII, 303, conversation Hornbostel and Massigli, 12 September 1934; *DDF*, 1, VII, 343, [detailed summary of events at Geneva 12 – 19 September], memorandum by the French Delegation to the League of Nations, 19 September 1934.

15. Lassner, "Peace at Hitler's Price," 68-76, 526-27, 631-33.

16. *DBFP*, 2, VI, 288, Simon to Drummond, 17 February 1934; *DBFP*, 2, VI, 290, Drummond to Simon, 17 February 1934; *DBFP*, 2, XII, 124, Phipps to Simon, 28 September 1934.

17. *ADAP*, C, III, 146, memorandum Bülow, 3 August 1934; NARS, M1209/4/0039, Messersmith to Hull, 1 August 1934; NARS, M1209/4/0069-0070, Messersmith to Hull, 17 August 1934.

18. Ibid., NARS, M1209/4/0051-0059, Messersmith to Hull, 9 August 1934; *ADAP*, C, III, 167, Papen to Hitler, 19 August 1934; NARS, M1209/4/0075-0076, Messersmith to Hull, 23 August 1934; *DBFP*, 2, XII, 10, Selby to Simon, 10 August 1934. The two most recent biographies of Papen, one in English and one in German, are unsatisfactory in a vein similar

to Papen's memoirs. Both biographies seek to excuse Papen's collusion with the Nazis while ignoring incriminating evidence. See Franz von Papen, *Memoirs*, trans. Brian Connell (New York: Dutton, 1953), passim; Joachim Petzold, *Franz von Papen: Ein deutsches Verhängnis* (Munich: Buchverlag Union, 1995), 239, 250-51, passim; Richard W. Rolfs, *The Sorcerer's Apprentice: The Life of Franz von Papen* (New York: 1996), 342, 354, passim. A far more accurate metaphor for the Hitler-Papen relationship than sorcerer's apprentice would be "the devil's toady." Although Papen may not have joined the Nazi party formally, he was decidedly philo-Nazi in his actions. Rolfs goes so far as to argue, quite stupefyingly, that Papen was a misguided but decent man and a good Catholic.

19. NARS, M1209/4/0198-0199, Messersmith to Hull, 19 October 1934.

20. Other pivotal issues concerned, for example, the settlement of still unresolved territorial disputes in Africa.

21. *DDF*, 1, VIII, 88, Parisot to Gamelin, 18 November 1934; *DDI*, 7, XVI, 199, conversation Suvich and Chambrun, 27 November 1934; *DDI*, 7, XVI, 200, Chambrun to Suvich, 27 November 1934; *DDI*, 7, XVI, 214, conversation Suvich and Chambrun, 29 November 1934; *DDI*, 7, XVI, 230, memorandum by Suvich, 3 December 1934; *DDI*, 7, XVI, 231, conversation Suvich and Chambrun, 3 December 1934; *DDI*, 7, XVI, 323, Suvich to Chambrun, 22 December 1934.

22. *DDF*, 1, VII, 492, Naggiar to Laval, 19 October 1934; *DDF*, 1, VIII, 235, Chambrun to Laval, 12 December 1934; *DDF*, 1, VIII, 246, Chambrun to Laval. 13 December 1934; *DDI*, 7, XVI, 108, Aloisi to Mussolini, 5 November 1934; *DDI*, 7, XVI, 171, conversation Pignatti and Léger, 21 November 1934; *DDI*, 7, XVI, 246, conversation Suvich and Lugosianu, 5 December 1934; *DDI*, 7, XVI, 247, Aloisi to Mussolini, 6 December 1934; *DDI*, 7, XVI, Aloisi to Mussolini, 11 December 1934; *DDI*, 7, XVI, 288, Pignatti to Mussolini, 14 December 1934.

In May, Barthou made it clear that a Franco-Italian rapprochement would not be concluded without an Italo-Yugoslav accord of some sort. *DBFP*, 2, XII, 311, Résumé of Conversation at the *Quai d'Orsay* . . . ., 22 December 1934; *DDF*, 1, VI, 209, Barthou to Naggiar 15 May 1934. Laval suspected that Vienna and Rome would resist Czechoslovak and Yugoslav participation, and he therefore insisted on the involvement of the entire Little Entente, which had "a soul of its own" and was more difficult to ignore. *DBFP*, 2, XII, 288, Clerk to Simon, 13 December 1934.

23. *DDI*, 7, XVI, 161, conversation Suvich and Berger-Waldenegg, 18 November 1934; *DDI*, 7, XVI, 269, Preziosi to Mussolini, 10 December 1934; *DDI*, 7, XVI, 270, Aloisi to Mussolini, 10 December 1934; *DDI*, 7, XVI, 300, Colonna to Mussolini, 16 December 1934; NARS, M1209/4/0334, No. 252, Messersmith to Hull, 20 December 1934.

24. *DDF*, 1, VIII, 337, Laval to Puaux, 28 December 1934.

25. Italics in original. *DDF*, 1, VIII, 354, Puaux to Laval, 30 December 1934. See also the *DDI* for the November representations of then Austrian Ambassador to Rome Alois Vollgruber: *DDI*, 7, XVI, 199, conversation Suvich and Chambrun, 27 November 1934.

26. *DDF*, 1, VIII, 355, Puaux to Laval, 30 December 1934. See also the reservations and observations of Schuschnigg and Berger-Waldenegg in *DDF*, 1, VIII, 344, Puaux to Laval, 29 December 1934. Specifically, both men inquired about France and Italy's declaration "that the consultation [about what steps to take for Austria] would be open to other powers." The Austrian statesmen wanted to know "could one derive from this that certain countries could, from now on, adhere to the Franco-Italian consultative pact and through that be associated with eventual military measures?" Such a possibility was not acceptable. Schuschnigg and Berger-Waldenegg expressed to Puaux "with force" that the Austrian government "cannot accept" that kind of protection and that while "they trust France and Italy entirely they cannot consider Czechoslovakia, Yugoslavia, or Hungary because of the territorial pretensions of each of these countries [to Austrian territory]."

27. *DDF*, 1, VII, 371, Puaux to Laval, 2 January 1935. Laval did not, however, renounce to the participation of the Little Entente in the matter of a guarantee to Austria and he informed Austrian permanent delegate to the League, Emmerich Pflügl, that France simply

could not ignore the interests of the Little Entente and that "for an eventual intervention of troops in Austria one can not expect that all the states that are party to the consultations should send their own troops, but France and Italy in agreement could designate for that goal [of military intervention] some other countries which would intervene materially;" *DDI*, 7, XVI, 365, Pignatti to Mussolini, 1 January 1935.

28. *DDF*, 1, VIII, 402, Puaux to Laval, 5 January 1935.

29. *DDF*, 1, VIII, 402, Puaux to Laval, 5 January 1935; *DDI*, 7, XVI, 403, Accordi Italo-Francesi i Declaration Generale, 7 January 1935.

30. NARS, M1209/4/0487-0489, No. 287, Messersmith to Hull, 16 January 1935; NARS, M1209/4/0435, memorandum by U.S. Department of Western European Affairs, 8 February 1935.

31. *DDI*, 7, XVI, 380, Suvich to Pignatti, 3 January 1935.

32. *DDF*, 1, VIII, 436, Puaux to Laval, 10 January 1935; *DDF*, 1, IX, 149, Puaux to Laval, 4 February 1935; *DDI*, 7, XVI, 432, Suvich to all ambassadors, 11 January 1935. For examples of terminology regarding the CEP and the guarantee of Austria from January to June 1935—variously designated as "pact," "convention," "security pact," "political pact," and "Austrian Pact"—see *ADAP*, C, III, 167, Papen to Bülow, 17 August 1934; *DBFP*, 2, XII, 104, Patteson to Simon, 23 September 1934; *DBFP*, 2, XII, 378, Simon to Clerk, 28 January 1935; *DDF*, 1, VII, 249, Puaux to Barthou, 6 September 1934; *DDF*, 1, VII, 302, Note de la délégation Française à la Société des Nations, 12 September 1934; *DDI*, 7, XV, 776, Preziosi to Mussolini, 6 September 1934; *DDI*, 7, XV, 798, Aloisi to Mussolini, 11 September 1934.

33. Lassner, "Peace at Hitler's Price," 89-94, 97-99, 101-4, 112, 161-63.

34. *DBFP*, 2, XII, Anglo-French-Italian Conversations . . . ., 11-14 April 1935; *DDI*, 7, XVI, 902, Preziosi to Mussolini, 11 April 1935; *DDI*, 8, I, 7, Preziosi to Mussolini, 15 April 1935.

35. Archivio Storico Diplomatico al Ministero degli Affari Esteri, Rome [hereafter MAE/R], fondo lacellotti, #11, "Colloquio fra il Capo del Governo ed il Cancelliere Federale Schuschnihh [*sic*], presente il Sottosegretario di Stato, On. Suvich," conversation Schuschnigg and Mussolini, 11 May 1935; Österreichisches Staatsarchiv, Archiv der Republik, Bundesministerium für Äußeres, Neues Politisches Archiv, Vienna [hereafter, ÖStA/AdR, BMfA/NPA], #414, 2799, "Der Herr Bundeskanzler hat am 11. d.M. . . . ," conversation Schuschnigg and Mussolini, 14 May 1935. See also *DDF*, 1, X, 119, Monicault to Laval, 5 April 1935; *DDF*, 1, X, 155, Gamelin to Flandin, 8 April 1935; *DDF*, 1, X, 358, Chambrun to Laval, 12 May 1935; *DDF*, 1, X, 404, Parisot to Maurin, 17 May 1935; *DDF*, 1, X, 487, Dampierre to Laval, 31 May 1935; *DDF*, 1, XI, 179, Gamelin to Maurin, 24 June 1935; *DDF*, 1, XI, 179, Gamelin to Fabry, 29 June 1935; *DDF*, 1, XI, 189, Laval to Chambrun, 2 July 1935; *DDI*, conversation Piccio and Flandin, 13 April 1935; *DDI*, 8, I, 180, conversation Mussolini and Schuschnigg, 11 May 1935; *DDI*, 8, I, 469, Suvich to Colonna and Preziosi, 2 July 1935; *DDI*, 8, I, 480, Suvich to Mussolini, 3 July 1935; William I. Shorrock, *From Ally to Enemy: The Enigma of Fascist Italy in French Diplomacy, 1920 – 1940* (Ohio: Kent State University Press, 1988), 129-32.

36. *DDI*, 8, I, 469, Suvich to Colonna and Preziosi, 2 July 1935; NARS, M1209/4/1017-1031, Messersmith to Hull, 8 July 1935; ÖStA/AdR, BMfA/NPA, #411, 204/pol., 36.593-13/35, "Militarische Besprechungen im Zusammenhang mit dem Besuche Generals Gamelin in Rom," Vollgruber to Berger-Waldenegg, 24 July 1935.

Virtually every European and American historian to examine the genesis and development of what became the 27 June 1935 Franco-Italian Military Accords misses the Austrian initiative and conceptions for such an accord during the September 1934 meetings at Geneva (the Austrian Pact) and the *Ballhausplatz*'s pursuit of this politico-military guarantee afterwards. Among the accounts which suffer from the striking omission are Shorrock, *From Ally to Enemy*, 118-29; Jonathan Ders, "French Military Intelligence and the Franco-Italian Alliance, 1933-1939," in *The Historical Journal* 29 (1985): 143-68; Salvatore Minardi, "L'accordo militare segreto Badoglio-Gamelin del 1935," *Clio* (April

– June 1987): passim; Robert J. Young, "Soldiers and Diplomats: The French Embassy and Franco-Italian Relations 1935-1936," *The Journal of Strategic Studies 7* (1984): passim; Geoffrey Warner, *Pierre Laval and the Eclipse of France* (New York: Macmillan, 1968), 131-33.

37. Lassner, "Peace at Hitler's Price," 92-93, 93 n. 18, 160-63, 161 n. 60, 479-80, 538-39, 543-44, 547-48, 550-51.

38. *DBFP*, 2, XII, 355, Phipps to Simon, 19 January 1935; *DBFP*, 2, XII, 358, Phipps to Simon, 21 January 1935; *DBFP*, 2, XII, 361, Phipps to Simon, 22 January 1935; *DBFP*, 2, XII, 362, Phipps to Simon, 23 January 1935; *DBFP*, 2, XII, 363, Phipps to Simon, 23 January 1935; *DBFP*, 2, XII, 364, Phipps to Simon, 23 January 1935; *DBFP*, 2, XII, 397, Notes of Anglo-French Conversation, 1 February 1935; *DDF*, 1, VIII, 436, Puaux to Laval, 10 January 1935; *DDF*, 1, VIII, 437, Puaux to Laval, 10 January 1935; *DDF*, 1, IX, 374, François-Poncet to Laval, 13 March 1935; *DDF*, 1, 326, Chambrun to Laval, 5 March 1935; *DDF*, 1, XI, 49, "Pacte de l'Europe centrale. Dispositions des gouvernements intéressés. Possibilités. Propositions," note by Massigli, 10 June 1935; *DDF*, 1, XI, 140, Naggiar to Laval, 25 June 1935; *DDF*, 1, XI, 189, Laval to Chambrun, 2 July 1935; *DDF*, 1, XI, 192, Laval to Naggiar, 2 July 1935; *DDF*, 1, XI, 225, Chambrun to Laval, 8 July 1935; *DDF*, 1, XI, 310, Naggiar to Laval, 19 July 1935; *DDF*, 1, XI, 435, Laval to [European Legations], 10 August 1935; *DDF*, 1, XI, 391, Note by Charvérait, 1 August 1935; *DDI*, 7, XVI, 121, conversation Hassell and Suvich, 8 November 1934; *DDI*, 7, XVI, 385, Cerruti to Mussolini, 4 January 1935; *DDI*, 7, XVI, 393, Cerruti to Mussolini, 5 January 1935; *DDI*, 7, XVI, 422, Preziosi to Mussolini, 9 January 1935; *DDI*, 7, XVI, 518, conversation Mussolini and Hassell, 31 January 1935; *DDI*, 7, XVI, 886, Butti to Mussolini, 8 April 1935; *DDI*, 7, XVI, 854, Pignatti to Mussolini, 3 April 1935; *DDI*, 7, XVI, 856, Pignatti to Mussolini, 3 April 1935; ÖStA/AdR, BMfA/NPA, #608, 44/pol., 35.360 13/35, "Haltung Deutschlands zur Romkonferenz; . . .," Schmidt to Berger-Waldenegg, 12 June 1935; NARS, M1209/5/0034-0053, No. 554, "Developments in the Austrian Internal and External Position," Messersmith to Hull, 20 September 1935. See especially Laval's comments during the Stresa conference during which he told Simon that "[b]oth the French and Italian Governments had sent suggested definitions [regarding non-interference] to Berlin. The German Government would never come to agreement on the point. They always wished to ask fresh questions. They would multiply questions in order to create delay." *DBFP*, 2, XII, 722, Notes of Anglo-French-Italian Conversations . . . ., 11-14 April 1935.

39. *DDF*, 1, XI, 246, Naggiar to Laval, 10 July 1935; ÖStA/AdR, Österreichische Vertretungsbehörden im Ausland, Belgrad [hereafter ÖVB/Belgrad], #7, Z. 60/Pol., "Sitzung der Kleinen Entente in Bled," Schmidt to Berger-Waldenegg, 7 September 1935.

40. *DDF*, 1, XI, 317, Montbas to Laval, 20 July 1935; *DDF*, 1, XI, 390, Montbas to Laval, 1 August 1935; NARS, M1209/5/0034-0053, No. 554, "Developments in the Austrian Internal and External Position," Messersmith to Hull, 20 September 1935; Gertrude Enderle-Burcel, ed., *Protokolle des Ministerrates der Ersten Republik* [hereafter *PMER*], vol. 3 (Vienna: Verlag der Österreichischen Staatsdruckerei, 1995), 1007, 8. "Außenpolitische Lage," 28 August 1935. See also *DDI*, 8, I, 180, conversation Mussolini and Schuschnigg, 11 May 1935; *DDF*, 1, XI, 397, Montbas to Laval, 2 August 1935.

41. *DDF*, 1, XI, 52, Puaux to Laval, 11 June 1935; *DDI*, 8, I, 456, Preziosi to Mussolini, 28 June 1935; *DDI*, 8, I, 495, Viola to Mussolini, 5 July 1935; NARS, M1209/4/0927, No. 448, Messersmith to Hull, 5 June 1935; NARS, M1209/4/0946, No. 461, Messersmith to Hull, 21 June 1935; NARS, M1209/4/1015-1016, No. 2241, Bullitt to Hull, 21 August 1935.

42. *PMER*/3, 1007, 8. "Außenpolitische Lage," 28 August 1935.

43. Giorgio Rochat, *Militari e politici nella preparazione della campagna d'Etiopia: Studi e documenti, 1932-36* (Milan: F. Angeli, 1971), 265-69; Robert Mallett, *The Italian Navy and Fascist Expansionism 1935 – 1940* (London: Frank Cass, 1998), 31, 79; Reynolds M. Salerno, "The Mediterranean Triangle: Britain, France, Italy and the Origins of the Second World War, 1935-1940," Ph.D. diss., Yale University, 1997, 74-86.

44. *British Documents on Foreign Affairs* [hereafter *BDFA*], 2, F, XI, 215, Selby to Hoare, 4 October 1935; *DDI*, 8, II, 194, Preziosi to Mussolini, 27 September 1935; *DDI*, 8, II, 267, conversation Suvich and Berger-Waldenegg, 7 October 1935; NARS, M1209/5/0174-0175, Messersmith to Hull, 12 September 1935; NARS, M1209/5/0034-0053, No. 554, "Developments in the Austrian Internal and External Position," Messersmith to Hull, 20 September 1935; NARS, M1209/5/0034-0053, "Memorandum of Conversation with the Foreign Minister Baron Berger-Waldenegg," Messersmith to Hull, 20 September 1935; *PMER*/3, 1008, 6. "Außenpolitische Lage," 18 September 1935.

45. Lassner, "Peace at Hitler's Price," 133-41, 145-49, 158, 177-78, 542.

46. *DDF*, 2, I, 332, Puaux to Flandin, 8 March 1936; *Diplomáciai Iratok Magyarország Külpolitikájához* [hereafter, *DIMK*], I, 62, conversation Schuschnigg, Berger-Waldenegg, Gömbös, and Kánya, 14 March 1936; NARS, E-2050, RG 84, #11, No. 725, Messersmith to Secretary of State, 13 March 1936. The judgement that Germany was now on the offensive was not confined to the *Ballhausplatz*. *Foreign Relations of the United States*, [hereafter, *FRUS*], I, 1936, memorandum of comments by Antonescu, Harrison to Hull, 9 March 1936.

47. This omission from the cabinet records is significant, as it represents an important example of what is a pattern of increasingly rare conversations of substantive issues with regard to Germany in the transcripts of the cabinet meetings 1934-1938. This is true both in the published *PMER* and the unpublished ÖStA/AdR, MRP1. The causes are twofold: First, the records of the cabinet were taken by the Germans after the Anschluss and suffered from the ravages of the war; and, second, and more importantly, as German pressure on the Schuschnigg regime increased from 1935 to 1938, the government became less and less willing to discuss substantive issues "on the record" for fear of German espionage. This is especially revealed by non-Austrian documents 1935 – 1938 from archives located around Europe, but also by evidence contained at the ÖStA. The last valuable cabinet transcript for 1937—which omits much that is important to understand Schuschnigg's objectives—is from 27 May. Jansa, in his postwar testimony was speaking truthfully—and, though he may not have known, far more broadly—when he stated that he gave orders for the most sensitive discussions and plans for defense against Germany to be transmitted and discussed orally.

Because of missing evidence, the scholarship of highly influential Austrian historian Ludwig Jedlicka inverted agency as between Austria and France at the end of March 1936, making it seem as though Jansa alone reacted noncommittally to an approach by the French military attaché to Austria, C. R. Salland, which was made solely for purposes of closer Austro-French military cooperation. For Jedlicka's misguided interpretation, based upon a note by Jansa to the Foreign Ministry, see ÖStA/Kriegsarchiv [hereafter KA], Nachlässe und Sammlungen [hereafter NLuS], Emil Liebitzky, B/1030, Nr. 46., Ludwig Jedlicka, "Ein Österreichischer Militärdiplomat in Rom 1933-1938: Oberst des Generalstabes Dr. Emil Liebitzky," 198-99; Ludwig Jedlicka, "Die Ära Schuschnigg," in *Österreich 1927 bis 1938. Protokoll des Symposiums in Wien 23. bis 28. Oktober 1972* (Munich: R. Oldenbourg Verlag, 1973), 199-200. Note should be made that a mistake exists in this latter work. Jansa's conversation with Salland—as Jedlicka identifies correctly in his article on Liebitzky—took place on 21 March 1936 and not on 11 March 1936. For this error see ibid., 199.

48. ÖStA/AdR, *Ministerratsprotokolle* [hereafter, *MRP*1], 1025, "Geheimprotokoll zu Punkt 4 des Verhandlungsprotokolls . . . .," 19 March 1936.

49. Lassner, "Peace at Hitler's Price," 159-63, 180-86, 204-5, 545-46. Quotes in ibid., 185-86.

50. Ibid., 188-92,

51. Ibid., 190-91.

52. Ibid., 187, 215, 455-61, 473-74, 547-48, 556-59. Quotes in Ibid., 191.

53. Ibid., 141-59, 163-77, 179-217, 215 n. 76, 223, 463-67, 546-49, 634-42.

54. *ADAP*, C, V, 294, Papen to Hitler, 24 April 1936.

55. *ADAP,* C, V, 304, Papen to Foreign Ministry, 4 May 1936.

56. Lassner, "Peace at Hitler's Price," 57, 62, 77-78, 85-87, 95, 97-98, 101, 121-25, 141-43, 146, 155, 157, 166-67, 198, 219. Quotes in ibid., 98, 172.

57. Ibid., 151-54, 226-45, 249-66, 283-85, 293-94, 315-21, 333-41. Note should be taken that in autumn 1935 Schuschnigg and Berger-Waldenegg concluded a press *Abkommen* with Germany, which, however, the Germans contravened in January 1936.

58. Ibid., 247-48, 277-82, 285-87, 558-59, 560-63, 569-76, 626-29, 630-34, 636-42, 653-97, 707-18.

59. Ibid., 32-4, 62-3, 294-96, 443, 478, 633, 657, 669 n. 41, 684.

60. Ibid., 89-90, 245-46, 279, 328, 580, 583, 685-89, 695.

61. Ibid., 501-02, 604-10, 681-82.

62. Ibid., 342-54. For two different interpretations of the performance of the *Wehrmacht* during the invasion of Austria compare the work of Lassner and Williamson Murray with that of Erwin Schmidl. Alexander N. Lassner, "The Invasion of Austria in March 1938: Blitzkrieg or Pfusch*?*," in *Contemporary Austrian Studies*, Günter Bischof, Anton Pelinka and Dieter Stiefel eds., vol. 8, (New Jersey, 2000), 447-467; Williamson Murray, "May 1940: Contingency and fragility of the German RMA," in *The Dynamics of Military Revolution 1300-2050*, MacGregor Knox and Williamson Murray eds., (Cambridge: Cambridge University Press, 2001), 154-74, 161-62; Erwin Schmidl, *Der "Anschluß" Österreichs: Der Deutsche Einmarsch im März 1938* (Bonn: Bernard and Graefe Verlag, 1994), passim, 254, 208.

NON-TOPICAL ESSAY

Right-Wing Movements in the European Union: A Case Study of the Austrian Freedom Party (FPÖ) and the Lega Nord (LN)

Megan Greene

Introduction

When the Austrian People's Party (ÖVP) formed a coalition government with the Austrian Freedom Party (FPÖ) on 4 February 2000, alarm bells rang throughout Austria and the international community. Mindful of Austria's collaboration with Nazi Germany during the Third Reich and disturbed by some of the Freedom Party's right-wing proposals, Austrians and foreigners alike feared that the new government represented the emergence of a neo-fascist, extreme right political movement in Austria.[1] Austria's fourteen fellow European Union (EU) member states immediately imposed diplomatic sanctions on Austria to protest the FPÖ's inclusion in the government. Over the course of the following year, however, the perceived threat that the Freedom Party posed to the democratic principles of the European Union diminished. At the recommendation of the "three wise men," commissioned to report on the nature of the FPÖ, the "EU fourteen" dropped their diplomatic sanctions against Austria in September 2000.[2]

There is currently a debate among scholars whether the inclusion of the Freedom Party in a ruling coalition is a European issue or whether it is merely an Austrian phenomenon. Many academics attribute the Freedom Party's success to Austria's failure to come to terms with its National Socialist past.[3] The Freedom Party has its roots in the National Socialist German Worker's Party (NSDAP); it grew out of the *Verband der Unabhängigen* (Association of Independents, VdU), a party created in 1949 and largely comprised of old Nazis, neo-Nazis, and Pan-Germans.[4] Additionally, several Freedom Party leaders have made comments expressing sympathy for the policies of Nazi Germany. According to academics such as Walter Manoscheck, "National Socialism is responsible for the fact that the Haider-FPÖ . . . has not been stigmatized and excluded from the democratic political arena, but has rather increased its support for almost fifteen years."[5] Austria's failure to deal with its past has hindered the development of an Austrian national identity, thereby enabling a right-wing party with apparent ties to National Socialism to gain popularity.[6]

Although the Freedom Party's success can be partly attributed to Austria's unique history, the ideologies and policies of the FPÖ are not merely an Austrian phenomenon. As Hans-Georg Betz argues, "Much of the concrete program [of the FPÖ] was not all that different from the projects adopted by a growing number of center-right... parties in Europe and elsewhere."[7] With right-wing parties promoting programs comparable to those of the Freedom Party throughout Europe, EU member nations feared that the electoral success of the FPÖ would spread to their own countries (see Table 1: Right-wing Movements in Europe). According to many experts, this fear of a contagious "Haider effect" was the primary reason EU member states imposed diplomatic sanctions on Austria.

One European Union member state in particular had cause to suspect that the "Haider effect" was invading its borders; on 13 May 2001, a center-right coalition comprised of *Forza Italia* (FI), *Alleanza Nazionale* (AN), and the *Lega Nord* (LN) won a majority of the seats in both the upper and lower houses of the Italian Parliament. The policies of the Lega Nord in particular have frequently been likened to those of the Freedom Party in Austria. Suspecting that a precedent had been established by the European Union with the imposition of sanctions on Austria, many experts predicted that similar measures would be taken in Italy. The political leaders of the European Union, however, accepted the outcome of the Italian elections and many of them promptly congratulated the center-right coalition on its victory.

That the European Union reacted vehemently in the Austrian case and comparatively mildly in the Italian case raises several questions about the significance of the EU's diplomatic sanctions. Where on the political spectrum can the Freedom Party and the Lega be placed, both as campaigning parties and as members of coalition governments? Are the programs of one party more extreme than those of the other? If not, what explains the inconsistency in the EU's response to the Austrian and the Italian elections? Were the Austrian sanctions "useful," as argued by the French presidency of the EU in September 2000, or was Jörg Haider correct in claiming they were a complete "debacle"?[8] In order to answer these questions, it is first necessary to delineate the criteria used to determine the parties' respective places along the right wing of the political spectrum. By applying this framework to the FPÖ and the LN, it becomes possible to examine the degree to which these organizations have affected their governments as both campaigning parties and as coalition members.

In doing this, one can determine the legitimacy and success of the diplomatic sanctions against Austria as well as the lessons learned from them.

Table 1: Right-wing Movements in Europe

Country	Right-Wing Movement
Austria	Freedom Party
Belgium	Agir Front National Front National Belge Parti des Forces Nouvelles Vlaams Blok
Denmark	Dansk Folkeparti Fremdskridtspartiet
France	Alliance Populaire Front National Front National-Movement National Mouvement pour la France Parti des Forces Nouvelles
Germany	Deutsche Volksunion (-Liste D) Nationaldemokratische Partei Deutschlands Die Republikaner
Greece	Chryssi Avghi Ethniki Politiki Enosis Enomeno Ethniko Kinema
Italy	Alleanza Nazionale Lega Lombarda Lega Nord Lega Veneto Movimento Sociale Italiano (-Destra Nazionale) Movimento Sociale Italiano-Fiamma Tricolore
Luxembourg	Nationalbewegong
Netherlands	Centrumpartij Centrumdemocraten Centrumpartij'86 (Nationale Volkspartei) Nederlandse Volks-Unie
Norway	Fedrelandspartiet Fremskrittspartiet
Portugal	Força Nacional-Nova Monarquia Partido da Democracia Crista Partido de Solidariadade Nacional
Spain	Allianza por la Unidad Nacional Alternativa Democratica Nacional Falange Española Autentica de las JONS Falange Española Independiente Fuerza Nueva/Frente Nacional Union Nacional
Sweden	Ny Demokrati Sverigedemokraterna

Country	Right-Wing Movement
Switzerland	Freiheitspartei der Schweiz Lega dei Ticinesi Nationale Aktion für Volk und Heimat Schweizer Autopartei/Parti Suisse des Automobilistes Schweizer Demokraten/Démocrates suisses Schweizerische Republikaner Bewegung/Mouvement Républicaine Suisse Vigilance
United Kingdom	British National Party National Front

Political Party Classification: The Extreme Right, Libertarian, and Conservative Party Families

The terminology commonly used to characterize the various shades of the political spectrum is highly contested and, therefore, must be clearly understood and defined before it can be applied to specific parties. To date, no single, dominant theory has emerged to delineate between the different shades of right- and left-wing movements. As Cas Mudde argues, "There is a wide variety of definitions [of political parties], based on an almost as wide variety of criteria, but none can claim general acceptance in the field."[9] It is particularly difficult to distinguish between party families along the right wing of the political spectrum: "The more closely the data relating to the European right are scrutinized, the more lines stubbornly refuse to be drawn or, when drawn, to remain straight and motionless; exceptions disprove more rules than they prove."[10] While scholars have found it difficult to define the political right wing, they can usually agree on which parties fit into this category; scholars can identify *who* the right wing is even if they cannot determine exactly *what* it is. Although several professionals classify right-wing political parties according to "gut feeling" and intuition, this method is insufficient in an academic setting. In order to place political parties in their respective categories along the political spectrum, it is important to consider both the ideologies and the political platforms of the parties: "Ideology and program are . . . a convenient vehicle for bringing some kind of intellectual order out of what would otherwise be the chaos of competing political groups."[11] Using these criteria, right-wing parties can be placed into three primary political party families: the extreme, the libertarian, and the conservative movements.

Extreme right-wing movements

The most thorough definition for the extreme Right is presented by Cas Mudde. Mudde considered twenty-six different definitions of the extreme Right proposed by as many different authors of varying nationalities. In the twenty-six definitions, only five of the features were introduced by more than half of the authors: nationalism, racism, xenophobia, a strong state, and anti-democracy. In addition to these fundamental characteristics, the extreme Right is also distinguished by its promotion of economic nationalism,[12] its belief in a naturally hierarchical society, and its use of violence to achieve political, social, and economic goals.

The western media has commonly depicted both the Freedom Party and the Lega Nord as members of the extreme right-wing party family. According to the characteristics typical of radical right-wing parties, however, this portrayal is incorrect. Both the FPÖ and the LN exhibit a degree of nationalism and xenophobia. However, the Austrian FPÖ and the Italian Lega Nord contradict extreme right-wing ideals in their conception of the role of the state. Whereas right-wing extremists endorse a strong state, members of the Freedom Party and the Lega support a small government. Additionally, these two political parties oppose the radical Right's belief in economic nationalism; the FPÖ and the Lega Nord promote the principles of capitalism and the free market and reject national protectionism. These parties also refute the extreme right wing's notion of the natural hierarchy of society. This idea is manifested in both parties' programs to improve gender equality.

The Freedom Party and the Lega Nord also belong to more moderate party families than the extreme Right because they reject the use of physical violence to achieve their political, social, or economic goals; the FPÖ and the Lega are committed to democratic ideals. Proof of the Freedom Party's belief in the rule of law lies in former FPÖ leader Jörg Haider's signing of the "Declaration: Responsibility for Austria—A Future in the Heart of Europe" when his party entered the Austrian coalition government. The FPÖ also exhibited dedication to democratic principles when Haider repeatedly apologized for apparently National Socialist comments that he made. The Lega Nord displayed a commitment to constitutional procedures throughout its participation in the Italian government in 1994.

Libertarian movements

Libertarian movements comprise a slightly more moderate strain of the right wing than the extreme Right. Libertarians share some fundamental ideologies with extreme right-wing radicals; both party families express a degree of nationalism, racism, and xenophobia. However, libertarian movements place less of an emphasis on these elements than radical right-wing parties do. Furthermore, the libertarian party family contradicts some extreme right ideals. Whereas right-wing extremists believe in the supremacy of the state over the individual, libertarians endorse the exact opposite; they give higher priority to individual liberty than they do to a hierarchical authority. According to libertarians, the political framework most conducive to establishing individual responsibility is that in which governmental regulation is minimized. For libertarians, governments serve to establish the infrastructure necessary for individuals to exercise their personal freedom: "The role of the state is to provide stable legal institutions to enable people to make their own plans and conduct their own lives."[13]

Libertarian movements also contradict extreme right-wing party ideals in their enthusiasm for capitalism and the free market. Whereas radical right parties believe that national politics are superior to economics, libertarians promote the primacy of economics in their party programs.[14] Libertarians argue that the free market protects the individual rights of citizens by undermining authoritarian regimes.[15] The libertarian party family also differs from extreme right-wing movements in its commitment to democracy; libertarian parties feel bound by constitutional procedures and, therefore, do not invoke violence to promote their ideologies. Although libertarians reject the use of physical violence, however, they frequently express xenophobia and racism by launching verbal attacks on foreigners and immigrants.[16]

Conservative Movements

Conservatives lie closer to the center of the political spectrum than libertarians do. Like the other shades of the political Right that I have examined, conservatives express nationalist, racist, and xenophobic sentiments. Of the three right-wing party families, however, conservative movements place the least emphasis on these elements. Furthermore, several of their ideological themes differ from those of the libertarians and the right-wing extremists. Whereas libertarians believe in the common good of man, for example, conservatives insist that mankind is inherently selfish and greedy. As a result, conservatives prefer limited forms of government to mass democracy.[17]

Although conservatives agree with the libertarian notion that freedom is essential to human dignity, they think that libertarians have taken this idea to an extreme. As Robert George has asserted, libertarians "take an important truth and stretch it to a falsehood ... [Freedom] has degenerated into license and no longer serves human dignity."[18] Conservatives do not view freedom as being an end in itself. Rather, they consider it to be a condition necessary for the flourishing of traditional virtues such as self-reliance and personal responsibility.[19] While they are generally opposed to a large government, conservatives believe that a small but strong state is required for freedom; a limited government promotes and protects the family, the most critical institution in society. Conservative movements also differ from the other strains of the political Right in their conception of the free market. Whereas libertarians are absolutely committed to capitalism, conservative parties tolerate some governmental intervention in the nation's economy.[20]

Table 2: Right-wing Party Families

Right-wing Party Family	*Defining Characteristics*
Extreme-right movements	Nationalism
	Racism
	Xenophobia
	Support of strong state
	Anti-democratic
	Economic nationalism
	Naturally hierarchical society
	Promotion of violence
Libertarian movements	Nationalism
	Racism
	Xenophobia
	Support of individual liberty
	Democratic
	Belief in capitalism and the free market
	Faith in the common good of man
	Commitment to rule of law
Conservative movements	Nationalism
	Racism
	Xenophobia
	Support of small state
	Democratic
	Tolerance of governmental interference in nation's economy
	Belief that man inherently selfish and greedy
	Commitment to rule of law

Like the libertarians, conservatives are committed to democracy and to the rule of law. Conservative democratic principles are entrenched in the political movement's belief in tradition. As its name indicates, the conservative party family defends existing institutions and behavior; it frequently embraces controls to safeguard traditions and customs. Conservatives trust customs because they believe that traditions reflect "the accumulated wisdom of the past."[21] As Charles Funderburk and Robert Thobaben argue, conservative movements believe that "today is the product of thousands of yesterdays."[22] Because of their support of traditional institutions, conservatives uphold democratic principles and constitutional procedures. As a result, they reject the use of violent measures to achieve their political, economic, and social goals. (For a summary of the primary characteristics of the extreme right, libertarian, and conservative movements, refer to Table 2: Right-Wing Party Families.)

Impact on National Politics as a Campaigning Party

During their campaigns, political parties may have a great impact on national politics. As opposition organizations, parties can make promises that citizens are eager to hear without actually being held immediately accountable for fulfilling their vows. Political parties already in government, on the other hand, are met with skepticism when they promote programs that they have not yet implemented. In countries which have been governed by the same political forces for several years, protest parties may have particular impact. This was the case in the most recent Austrian and Italian elections. Between the end of World War II and 1999, the Austrian Social Democratic Party (SPÖ) and the Austrian People's Party (ÖVP) either ruled Austria as a coalition or assumed alternating responsibility for the nation. During the same time period, Italy was run by the Christian Democratic Party (DC), either on its own or in collaboration with smaller parties.[23] In part because of the stagnant nature of Austrian and Italian domestic politics, the Austrian Freedom Party and the Italian Lega Nord both had considerable clout over their respective governments during the election campaigns.

Austrian Freedom Party

As it geared up for the Austrian general elections in October 1999, the Freedom Party delineated its platform in party documents such as the "Austria First" initiative and the "Contract with Austria." Several of the programs that the FPÖ suggested in these documents initially faced vehement opposition from the established ÖVP-SPÖ government. The primary reason for this was the unpopularity of the leader of the Freedom

Party, Jörg Haider. Haider became a "black sheep" in Europe partly because of his controversial statements hinting at FPÖ sympathies for the ideas and strategies of Nazi Germany during World War II. In 1991 and 1995, for example, Haider declared that the Third Reich had an "orderly employment policy" and that the Waffen SS "deserves all the honor and respect of the army in public life."[24] The former Freedom Party leader's apparently National Socialist comments prompted many of Haider's political opponents to adopt a policy to "Stop Haider."[25] Despite this policy, however, the campaigning FPÖ managed to influence the immigration and welfare ideologies and policies of the Austrian government.

Immigration proposals

The Freedom Party's ideological motivations for reforming Austria's immigration policies stemmed from the party's concept of *Heimat*, or cultural identity. According to Haider, order in a state requires a general consensus on basic rights and values. When immigrants entered Austria, they brought with them their own values that sometimes conflicted with those already established in the country. With unlimited immigration, it became impossible to assimilate all of the foreigners and, as a result, these foreign values allegedly overwhelmed the Austrian cultural identity. Rather than being anti-foreigner, racist, or xenophobic, the FPÖ, as Haider insists, is merely pro-Austrian: "My friends and I are not obsessed with power. We have something that matters to us, and that is Austria!"[26]

While the Freedom Party's objectives to protect Austria's *Heimat* were initially rejected, several of them were later adopted by the leading parties in the government. A primary example of this was the Freedom Party's 1993 "Austria First" initiative aimed at reforming the nation's immigration policies. Although this document received widespread popular support in a referendum in 1993, it was immediately defeated by the SPÖ-ÖVP coalition.[27] Shortly thereafter, however, the Austrian government passed new immigration laws reminiscent of those proposed in the "Austria First" initiative. Six months after the "Austria First" initiative was defeated, for example, the existing coalition demanded that all foreigners carry identification cards with them.[28] Once instituted, the policies from the "Austria First" initiative were widely accepted by politicians and the Austrian public alike.

The Freedom Party's concept of guest worker family reunification also had an impact on several government officials' stances on immigration. In 1996, the new ÖVP-SPÖ coalition designed an integration package allowing children and dependents of guest workers to join their families in Austria. The Freedom Party harshly criticized the integration package, insisting that immigrants should be sent back to their native countries instead of bringing their children and other dependants to live in Austria. The FPÖ argued that Austria did not have the necessary infrastructure to cope with an influx of immigrant family members and warned that slums would develop as a result. The coalition partners decried the Freedom Party for being "alarmist," but in Vienna some of the local governmental officials agreed with the FPÖ. These politicians proposed measures to spread guest workers and their families throughout the city to diffuse the impact of immigrant family reunions on the capital.[29] Although none of the politicians' measures were actually implemented, the concern of these officials prompted the ÖVP-SPÖ coalition to withdraw its integration package just months after proposing it.

The Freedom Party also influenced the ruling government's policies regarding financial assistance to immigrants. Prior to the 1995 general elections, the FPÖ called for the repatriation of immigrant workers. The Freedom Party believed that unemployed immigrants who wanted to return to their native countries should be given some financial incentive to leave Austria. This proposal was immediately condemned by the more moderate Austrian parties as being "racist." A few months later, however, Chancellor Klima announced that the government would provide financial assistance to enable refugees to return to their home countries. The coalition partners also adopted the FPÖ proposal to abolish family allowances for children of guest workers in their native countries; the government implemented the FPÖ's proposal, for which the political party had been deemed "xenophobic" only a few months earlier.

Compared to the political spectrum, the campaigning Freedom Party's immigration ideologies had some conservative characteristics. Driven by the notion of *Heimat*, the Freedom Party sought to protect the cultural values and the identity of the Austrian people through its immigration policies. Libertarians would reject this idea of the government protecting certain ideals and values. The immigration programs that the campaigning FPÖ endorsed were also conservative in nature. The Freedom Party supported active government regulation of immigration, a policy that libertarians would have repudiated.

Welfare proposals

The ruling government's welfare policies were also greatly influenced by the Freedom Party. As a campaigning party, the FPÖ warned against cultivating an overactive welfare system. According to the FPÖ, too much welfare would cause a citizen's responsibilities and rights to be usurped by the government. As Haider stated, "in a complete welfare state, freedom and independence of people are forfeited to the 'nanny state'."[30] The Freedom Party believed that those who were genuinely in need of welfare benefits should be granted them, but that those who made no effort to help themselves should not enjoy social benefits funded by the state. As the FPÖ's program of 1985 stated, "Social welfare institutions must ensure that anyone in need is guaranteed at least a minimum level of care. On the other hand, abuse of welfare institutions must be prevented."[31]

In order to achieve this, the Freedom Party sought to reform the Austrian welfare state indirectly by reducing the role of the government. The ÖVP-SPÖ coalition adopted the campaigning Freedom Party's tenor by discouraging the dependence of beneficiaries on the state and by encouraging self-help.

Again, in regard to the political spectrum, the ideologies the FPÖ used to justify its welfare reforms were primarily conservative in nature. The Freedom Party's encouragement of self-dependence complied with the conservative ideal that individuals should be rewarded according to their efforts and achievements. Libertarians would have rejected such ideology, maintaining that the government's influence should remain outside of the realm of an individual's morality. The welfare policies the FPÖ promoted also had conservative undertones; the Freedom Party sought to reduce the size of the government but recognized that some governmental presence was necessary to provide for those citizens who were unable to provide for themselves.

Italian Lega Nord

Like the Freedom Party in Austria, the campaigning Lega Nord also initially faced vehement opposition to its ideologies and policies. One of the reasons for this was the unpopularity of the LN leader, Umberto Bossi. Bossi has made several controversial statements in the past conveying xenophobic sentiments that outraged the Italian government and public alike.[32] As a result, many have compared Bossi with Austria's Jörg Haider. According to some, however, Bossi's views are not as intelligent or well thought-out as those of his Austrian counterpart. As Klaus Wölfer has claimed, "Haider is very well-educated and speaks fluent English. As for Mr. Bossi, he cannot even speak proper Italian."[33] Despite the widespread disregard among Italian citizens and politicians for Bossi, the campaigning LN managed to impact its country's immigration and welfare ideologies as well.

Immigration Proposals

The ideological motivations for the Lega's immigration proposals are manifested in the LN's concept of regional identity. According to the Lega, the regions of northern and central Italy in particular had tremendous cultural assets. The LN believed that Italian culture was undermined because it was treated as a single identity rather than as a "kaleidoscope of cultures different among themselves."[34] The Lega therefore maintained that Italian culture in general could only be developed by embracing the country's local traditions; the culture of each region should be protected from "massification and . . . ideological or religious fanaticism."[35]

The LN's immigration ideologies also stemmed from the impact of guest workers on Italy's economy. The influx of immigrants into Italy distorted the labor market by creating an excess supply of workers. As the Lega argued, "Even the most enthusiastic pro-immigration policy-makers realize that Europe will never be able to create enough new jobs to relieve the pressures of the growing populations of North Africa."[36] The excess of workers in Italy aggravated the country's chronic problem of structural unemployment. Additionally, the Lega believed that the migration of workers impeded the economic development for all of Europe: "The League is opposed to mass migration... not for reasons of racial prejudice: what needs to be avoided is the uprooting of people from their fathers' lands and traditions, an achievable result only through balanced economic development in each area. We want mobility of capital, not of people."[37]

In order to protect local Italian cultures, the campaigning Lega Nord insisted that immigrants in Italy assimilate into their new communities. The ruling center-left Italian coalition quickly adopted the Lega's tenor on this issue and called for the complete integration of foreigners into society. According to the government, the assimilation of migrants was necessary to avoid "conflicts of insertion" and to guarantee the protection of individual foreigners.[38] To help immigrants adapt to their communities, the government established an institute for job placement designed specifically for migrants. The center-left coalition also created programs to improve the education of immigrants, especially in terms of Italian language instruction.

Seen on the political spectrum, the Lega Nord's immigration ideologies were both conservative and libertarian in nature. The Lega displayed conservative characteristics by seeking to protect its various regional cultures from the influence of foreigners. Libertarians would have rejected this idea because it involved the state's defense of specific values. In this sense, the Lega's ideologies were comparable to those of the Austrian Freedom Party. However, the Lega Nord's ideologies were somewhat more extreme than those of the FPÖ because of the Lega's emphasis on the economic effects of immigration. The LN's preoccupation with the mobility of capital and its effects on the free market is a libertarian notion.

Although the Lega's immigration ideologies had some libertarian characteristics, the campaigning LN's immigration policies were primarily conservative. Like the Freedom Party, the Lega supported an active governmental role in the assimilation of immigrants into Italian culture. Such "social engineering" on the part of the government would have been opposed by libertarians.

Welfare proposals

The Lega Nord believes that the family is the primary institution through which anti-social behavior can be combated. Because of the important role of the family in social affairs, the LN supported the granting of welfare in appropriate situations. However, according to the Lega, southern Italy has developed a welfarist culture that is addicted to the guarantees of the Italian bureaucracy.[39] This addiction tied up federal resources that might otherwise have been invested in the private sector to foster economic development. The Lega Nord argued that granting welfare benefits to unworthy candidates in southern Italy resulted in a country of "the producer . . . [and] the parasites."[40]

During its electoral campaign, the LN sought to reform the Italian welfare state in large part by revising Italy's tax system. The Lega suggested that tax money be used for initiatives to reduce unemployment instead of for welfare handouts from the state. In January 2001, the ruling Italian coalition reduced its monetary grants to welfare beneficiaries and expanded its programs for benefits in kind. For example, the center-left government established programs to integrate disabled people into society and to provide home care for older citizens who were no longer self-sufficient.[41]

The ideologies motivating the Lega Nord's welfare proposals had both conservative and libertarian characteristics. The Lega believed that those who deserved welfare benefits should be granted them. Bossi's party, therefore, promoted conservative ideals by advocating some governmental presence in the social fabric of daily Italian life. In this respect, the welfare ideologies of the LN were similar to those of the Austrian Freedom Party. The Lega's ideologies also had some libertarian undertones when the LN sought to minimize welfare payments based on their impediments to economic development; unlike the Freedom Party, the Lega Nord displayed libertarian characteristics in its strong belief in the free market and the private sector.

The campaigning Lega's strategies for welfare reform were primarily libertarian in nature. By insisting that the Italian government redirect public funding from welfare benefits to employment initiatives, the LN displayed libertarian characteristics; libertarians believe that the free market can protect citizens more effectively than a strong welfare state can. As a result, the Lega Nord's welfare proposals were more extreme than those of the Austrian Freedom Party.

Impact on National Politics as a Member of the Ruling Coalition

Although political parties may influence ruling coalitions during election campaigns, their influence on national politics is usually enhanced once they become members of the government themselves. Opposition parties are often able to impact their governments because they have more room to maneuver than coalition members; outside parties can promote policy changes without having to implement them immediately. However, coalition partners have direct access to the infrastructure and resources needed to implement governmental programs; it is easier for members of the government to put new policies into effect. When the FPÖ and the LN were incorporated into their respective governments, therefore, the influence of their ideologies and policies on Austrian and Italian national politics was magnified. As coalition members, the Freedom Party and Lega Nord had particular impact on their nations' immigration and employment ideologies and programs.

Austrian Freedom Party

Immigration proposals[42]

One immigration issue that particularly concerned the Freedom Party was the high degree of foreign students in Austrian elementary and vocational schools. In its "Austria First" initiative, the FPÖ sought to limit the percentage of foreign pupils in these schools to thirty percent. When the Freedom Party entered the government, this proposal was included in the new ÖVP-FPÖ coalition program: "In each class, the proportion of pupils in need of special assistance in the area of linguistic and socio-cultural integration should not exceed a limit of roughly one-third."[43] Another policy promoted in the "Austria First" initiative was the improvement of language instruction for foreign school children. The new ÖVP-FPÖ government made German language instruction a central component of its active integration program for immigrants. The government also made "veritable proof of German language skills" a requirement for Austrian citizenship.[44]

Looking at the political spectrum, the FPÖ's strategies for immigration policy reform were primarily conservative in nature. The Freedom Party encouraged the government to play a large role in the regulation of foreign pupils in Austrian schools; libertarians would have rejected such an active role for the government. The language programs and requirements promoted by the Freedom Party also had conservative characteristics. By insisting that foreigners develop a certain capacity for the German language, the government actively sought to integrate foreigners into Austrian society. Libertarians would have denounced these policies as "social engineering" on the part of the state.

Employment proposals

The Freedom Party's employment ideologies stemmed primarily from the system of *Proporz* that has dominated Austrian politics and economics since the end of World War II. According to this system, the ÖVP and the SPÖ divided employment opportunities in the government, bureaucracy, public sector, semi-public sector, and corporate bodies according to the parties' representation in Parliament.[45] As a result, politicians were granted inflated incomes, severance payments, and pensions for work that they completed inefficiently or ineffectively. The squandering of public funds in state-run industries cost Austria thousands of jobs annually. Recognizing the harm that the system of *Proporz* caused to the Austrian economy, the Freedom Party insisted that this system be abolished.

In order to undermine the *Proporz*, the FPÖ proposed that government and companies hire employees based on their personal skills and talents. At the FPÖ's suggestion, a clause was included in the ÖVP-FPÖ coalition program to implement this proposal. The clause stipulates that recruitment for general staff and management positions within the federal government's sphere of influence must be based on an applicant's personal merit rather than on his or her party affiliation.

According to the Freedom Party, one of its greatest achievements as a governing party has been to implement the child benefit scheme, an employment policy geared towards families. On the FPÖ website, the party declares this new program to be "[t]he most important electoral pledge of the FPÖ fulfilled."[46] As part of the child benefit scheme, the government provides parents with ATS 6,000 (EUR 436) per month for up to three years for each child to which they give birth after 1 January 2002.[47] Mother and father can alternate as recipients of the *Kindergeld* ("children's money"). By granting more financial support to families with very young children, the child benefit program allows both parents to reconcile their family and professional lives.

Another employment policy that the Freedom Party prompted the Austrian government to adopt involves the promotion of skilled worker training. The FPÖ believes that, by encouraging apprenticeships, Austria can develop its high-technology sectors and, therefore, can attract more investors. In order to achieve this, the ÖVP-FPÖ coalition modernized existing apprenticeships and promoted apprenticeship training in new sectors such as information technology (IT) and communications. The government also fostered learning in the IT and communications industries by creating special technology focuses in Austrian schools.[48] Furthermore, the ÖVP-FPÖ coalition highlighted specifically targeted training as a component of its unemployment benefit programs; rather than providing general skills, the *Arbeitsmarktservice* (Public Employment Service) now trains the unemployed for occupations in high demand, such as information technology.[49]

Along the political spectrum, the ideologies driving the Freedom Party's employment reforms were primarily conservative in nature. Although the FPÖ sought to disentangle the government from the country's economy, it also recognized that the government had some role in Austrian economics. Libertarians would have rejected this notion, insisting that the government should be prohibited to interfere with the free market at all. Like the FPÖ's ideologies, the party's employment policy proposals were also conservative in nature. The Freedom Party's desire to hire new employees according to personal merit sought to minimize unwarranted benefits for public officials. This notion complied with the conservative idea that individuals should have to work for what they receive. The *Kindergeld* initiative was also conservative in nature because it actively promoted full-time child-rearing. In doing so, this new program endorsed the conservative ideal that the family should be protected and supported as the primary building block of society. Additionally, both the *Kindergeld* program and the FPÖ's support of apprenticeships involved a degree of social engineering on the part of the government; libertarians would have rejected such proposals.

Italian Lega Nord

Immigration proposals

Like the Austrian Freedom Party, the Italian Lega Nord was concerned about its citizens becoming "foreigners in their own land."[50] The Lega was particularly wary of the influences of Islamic cultures on Italian regional identities.[51] In the wake of the 11 September 2001 terrorist attacks on the United States, the center-right coalition in Italy adopted the LN's anti-Islamic sentiments. In an interview with reporters, Prime Minister Berlusconi claimed, "We should be confident of the superiority of our civilization, which consists of a value system that . . . guarantees respect for human rights and religion . . . This respect certainly does not exist in Islamic countries . . . .[The West] is bound to occidentalize and conquer new people." The prime minister went on to insist that "Europe must reconstitute itself on the basis of its Christian roots."[52]

The center-right Italian government also adopted LN proposals to limit immigration to Italy. During its election campaign, the Lega Nord endorsed a "vigorous control of immigration" and encouraged the government to expel immigrants.[53] When the center-right government came into power, one of the first bills it passed sought to address these issues. According to the new legislation, illegal immigrants may be jailed for up to four years if they do not leave Italy within one week of receiving an expulsion order.

Additionally, legal immigrants are only permitted to bring their offspring under eighteen years of age and their spouses to Italy.[54] The government also adopted LN ideals when it developed legislation to punish those who smuggle immigrants into the country; Berlusconi's government hopes to give prison sentences of up to eighteen years for anyone encouraging illegal immigration.[55]

Both the Freedom Party and the Lega Nord sought to protect their national cultures by restricting immigration. By insisting that the government expel and punish immigrant smugglers, the Lega encouraged the state to take a large role in Italy's social fabric. This reform was conservative in nature; libertarians would have rejected such an active role for the government. In this sense, the Lega Nord's immigration proposals were comparable with those of the governing Freedom Party in Austria. However, some of the LN's immigration policies also had libertarian undertones. By specifically targeting Islamic cultures instead of seeking to exclude foreigners in general, the Lega displayed an intensified degree of xenophobia. Overall, therefore, its immigration proposals as a member of government were more extreme than those of the Freedom Party.

Employment proposals

The Lega Nord's employment ideologies, like those of the Austrian Freedom Party, were largely motivated by the "rule-by-kickback regime" that has dominated Italian politics since the end of World War II.[56] According to this system, the Italian government has controlled the nation's credit system as well as its banking, insurance, electronics, steel, chemicals, construction, transport, and food industries. Additionally, political parties have distributed jobs based on political loyalties instead of the proven abilities of potential employees. This system of providing employment wasted federal resources and reinforced criminal activities instead of promoting an entrepreneurial spirit.

Recognizing the negative economic effects of the "rule-by-kickback regime" on Italy, the Lega Nord sought to disentangle the government from the nation's economy. The center-right coalition adopted the Lega's tenor in May 2001 when Berlusconi vowed to slim down the public sector. In order to achieve this, the prime minister proposed that his government institute a hiring freeze in the public sector and train existing staff so they might gain employment with private corporations.

The center-right coalition also sought to diminish the government's role in the economy by adopting the LN proposal to reform Italy's labor laws. Under the "free labor contract," it became easier for Italian corporations to take on and release employees as they saw fit. This policy ensured that workers were hired and fired according to their personal merit and not according to their political affiliations.

Perceived within the political spectrum, the motivations for the Lega Nord's employment reforms were primarily conservative in nature. The Lega Nord sought to decrease the government's involvement in the economy without eliminating the hand of the state altogether. This notion would have been rejected by libertarians who believe that the free market reigns supreme.

While the Lega's ideologies had mainly conservative characteristics, its employment policies were both conservative and libertarian in nature. By prompting the center-right coalition to decrease the size of the government, the LN displayed conservative ideals. However, the Lega Nord's proposal to transfer hiring and firing powers from the government to the private sector had some libertarian undertones. Whereas conservatives believe that the government should play some role in a nation's socio-economic fabric, libertarians believe in the primacy of the free market and capitalism.

The Significance of the EU Sanctions

Application in Italy

In general, the Lega Nord has prompted its government to adopt more extreme right-wing ideologies and policies than the Freedom Party has in Austria, both before and after the parties' incorporation into their respective national governments. (For a summary of the parties' impact on their national policies see Table/Diagramm 3: Comparison of the Ideologies and Policies of the Freedom Party and the Lega Nord.) If the Austrian diplomatic sanctions were an established precedent for how the EU should respond to extreme elements in its member nations, therefore, one would have expected a similar quarantine on Italy. Why, then, did the European Union merely administer Italy a warning: ". . . given what this country [Italy] represents in Europe we [the leaders of EU member states] will be very attentive to the way in which the government will be made up and to its policies. Attentive, and if need be vigilant."?[57]

One explanation for the inconsistency in the European Union's reactions to the composition of the Austrian and Italian governments is that Italy has more clout in the EU relative to Austria. According to Haider, for example, the EU did not impose sanctions on Italy because "Italy is a powerful country and Austria is a small country. That is the explanation."[58] Whereas Italy was one of the founding members of the original European Community (EC), Austria did not join the European Union until 1995. Additionally, Italy has more than four times the number of representatives in the European Parliament (EP) than Austria has.[59] Finally, Italy's GDP is significantly larger than that of Austria; in 2001, for example, Italy's GDP was USD 1.16 trillion,[60] compared with Austria's USD 255 billion.[61]

Diagram 3: Comparison of the Ideologies and Policies of the Freedom Party and the Lega Nord

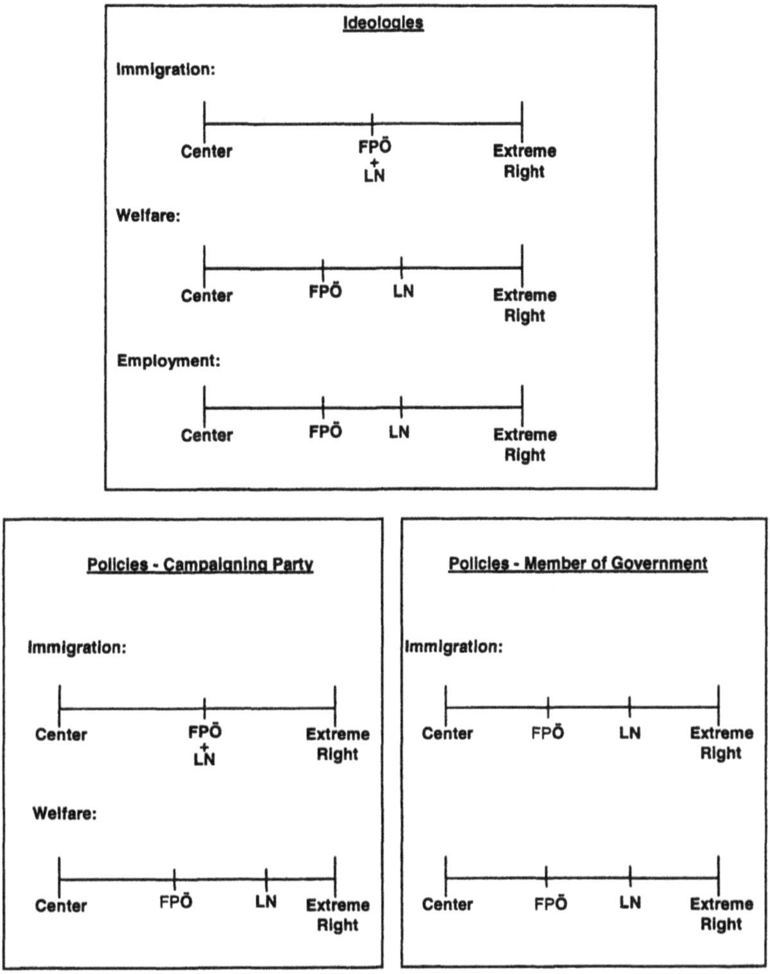

This diagram is intended to display the relative positions of the FPÖ and the LN along the political spectrum; the exact spacing between the parties does not reflect the degree to which one is more extreme than the other.

Some experts claim the European Union did not impose sanctions on Italy because of personal factors. Hannes Androsch, for example, attributes the EU's relatively harsh reaction in the Austrian case to personal insults made by the former FPÖ leader. Just after the formation of the ÖVP-FPÖ coalition, for example, Haider called French President Jacques Chirac a failure and claimed that Belgium was run by corrupt pornographers. Of all the EU member states, France and Belgium were the most enthusiastic about imposing diplomatic sanctions on Austria.[62]

Failure of the sanctions

According to most experts, the primary reason the European Union did not impose sanctions on Italy is that "you only make the same mistake once, and the sanctions against Austria were a big mistake."[63] Austrian Ambassador Michael Breisky described Austria's diplomatic quarantine as being "[poorly] drafted, ill-conceived, and exaggerated."[64] Although the Austrian sanctions were largely unsuccessful in achieving their intended purpose, the EU's actions did have some value. The Austrian quarantine highlighted the European Union's need for an institutionalized, consistent response to the emergence of extreme elements within its borders. In a way, the sanctions were successful specifically because they were such a failure. As Alexander van der Bellen, the head of the Austrian Green Party, has claimed, "This [the sanctions] cannot be allowed to happen again and the EU needs a procedure based on legal values."[65]

The members of the European Commission have recognized the need for such a procedure. At the Intergovernmental Conference (IGC) in October 2000, they proposed to amend Articles 6 and 7 of the *Treaty on European Union* (TEU). The reforms agreed upon by the European Commission granted a legal basis for *preventing* a violation of EU ideals; a surveillance mechanism was established to enable the member states to detect a breach of fundamental principles before a punishable violation had actually occurred.[66]

Conclusion

The Austrian Freedom Party and the Italian Lega Nord have influenced their national politics both as campaigning parties and as members of ruling coalitions. Almost without exception, however, the Lega has prompted its government to adopt more extreme ideologies and policies than the FPÖ has in Austria. When the Freedom Party was incorporated into the Austrian government, the European Union immediately imposed diplomatic sanctions on the alpine nation. Upon inclusion of the Lega Nord in the Italian government, therefore, many experts expected the EU to adopt similar measures in Italy. In reality, however, the European Union merely administered the Italian center-right coalition a warning that the new government would be closely monitored for breaches of fundamental EU values. Austrian and international experts alike have criticized the European Union's reaction to the formation of the ÖVP-FPÖ coalition government, arguing that the diplomatic sanctions were exaggerated and useless. The failure of the sanctions, however, has intrinsic value; it has alerted the European Union to the need for a consistent, institutionalized response to the emergence of extreme elements within its borders.

Although the European Union has already begun to create such a reaction to radical elements within its borders, additional measures must be taken. One reason the EU should continue to expand its policies to combat political extremism is that right-wing movements are currently emerging all over Europe. Additionally, the European Union is seeking to expand its membership. As the EU enlarges and the member states represent a greater degree of political, economic, and social differentiation, the potential for a breach of the European Union's fundamental rights is augmented.

The most effective way to combat extreme political mobilization in the EU is to prevent it from occurring in the first place. When the "three wise men" submitted their report on Austria to the European Union, they suggested that ". . . a system of prevention should be put in place which would react through information and education measures to any forms of direct or indirect discrimination or xenophobia."[67] In order to create such a system of prevention, the European Union must establish *continuous transparency* among its member states.

Although establishing continuous transparency might enable countries to detect and prevent radical political mobilization in the European Union, it could also serve to cultivate extreme elements. When the Freedom Party gained enough Austrian popular support to place it on the radar screen of the European Union, for example, the EU member states reacted by publicly denouncing the party and its leaders. Although Haider is sometimes deserving of criticism, the Austrian and international community's obsession with the FPÖ politician's quips may have done more harm than good. Right-wing political leaders throughout Europe have noticed that Haider's controversial leadership style has drawn attention to the Freedom Party and, therefore, has provided the FPÖ with a platform on which to gain political ground. As a result, several of these leaders have used Haider as a model for their own political maneuvering.

In addition to spreading the tactics of political leaders transnationally, increased transparency between the member states may also serve to radicalize political parties. If the Austrian and international communities continually criticize Haider and denounce him as a neo-Nazi, for example, he may eventually come to fulfill their accusations. Like several right-wing leaders, Haider has the "ability to change, or seem to change, his politics as often as he changes his clothes."[68] As a result, Haider may adopt whichever ideologies and policies he believes will bring his party attention; the constant negative reinforcement of a political party may turn into a self-fulfilling prophecy.

The risks involved in establishing continuous transparency among the European Union member states are substantial. However, they are not as dangerous as the potential implications of failing to establish this transparency. Without the implementation of a forum for open dialogue among its member states, the EU may grossly over- or under-react to radical political mobilization in the future. If the European Union responds too extremely to the emergence of a radical political party within its borders, it risks compromising the democratic ideals on which it was founded. If this supranational body does not react strongly enough, however, a radical party could be democratically elected into the government of an EU member state. The European continent already experienced the horrific results of such an occurrence with the emergence of Hitler's NSDAP during the interwar period. In the 1970s, former Austrian Federal Chancellor Bruno Kreisky urged the citizens of his country to "do [their] history lessons."[69] To those who have heeded this advice, the necessity for a new method for handling extreme elements in the European Union is evident.

Notes

1. In this study, I use the phrases "extreme right" and "radical right" interchangeably. Some authors distinguish between these two terms; see, for example, Cas Mudde, *The Ideology of the Extreme Right* (Manchester: Manchester University Press, 2000), 12-13.

2. The "three wise men" chosen by the European Union for the investigation were Martti Ahtisaari (former prime minister of Finland), Mercelino Oreja (former foreign minister and EU commissioner from Spain), and Jochen Frowein (German legal scholar).

3. For an analysis of Austria's efforts to come to terms with its past, see Günter Bischof, "'Experiencing a Nasty Fall from Grace:' Austria's Image in the United States after the Formation of the New ÖVP/FPÖ Government," in *Austria, the European Union, and the United States*, ed. Wolfgang Danspeckgruber (Princeton: Princeton University Center for International Studies, 2002), 112-17.

4. For a history of the VdU see Brigitte Bailer and Wolfgang Neugebauer, "Die FPÖ: Vom Liberalismus zum Rechtsextremismus," in *Handbuch des österreichischen Rechtsextremismus*, ed. Stiftung Dokumentationsarchiv des Österreichischen Widerstandes (Vienna: Deuticke, 1994), 357-94.

5. Walter Manoschek, "The Freedom Party of Austria (FPÖ)—an Austrian and European Phenomenon?," in *Contemporary Austrian Studies*, vol. 10, *Austria in the European Union*, ed. Günter Bischof, Anton Pelinka, and Michael Gehler (New Brunswick: Transaction Publishers, 2002), 14.

6. From 1804 until 1945, Austria was the head of an empire, part of a transnational community, a "second German state," and, finally, an independent nation; see Anton Pelinka, "Die FPÖ im internationalen Vergleich," *Conflict and Communication Online*, vol. 1, no. 1, 2002, 7; retrieved from the world wide web 5 February 2002, http://www.cco.regener-

online.de. As a result, this alpine state was late to develop national emotions and loyalties; Austria did not begin to develop its own national identity until after World War II.

7. Betz continues to argue that the Freedom Party was distinct, however, in its frontal attack against Austria's stagnant centers of political power as well as in the degree of radicalism of its tone. See Hans-Georg Betz, "Haider's Revolution or The Future Has Just Begun," in *Contemporary Austrian Studies*, vol. 10, *Austria in the European Union*, ed. Günter Bischof, Anton Pelinka, and Michael Gehler (New Brunswick: Transaction Publishers, 2002), 13.

8. Stephen Castle, "Haider All Smiles as EU Lifts its Sanctions," *Independent* (London), 13 September 2000, 13.

9. Mudde, *The Ideology of the Extreme Right*, 1.

10. Martin Blinkhorn, "Introduction: Allies, Rivals, or Antagonists?," in *Fascists and Conservatives*, ed. Martin Blinkhorn, (London: Unwin Hyman, 1990), 2.

11. R.J. Alexander, *Latin American Political Parties* (New York: Praeger, 1973), xix, qtd. in Mudde, *The Ideology of the Extreme Right*, 5.

12. According to radical right extremists, the nation is the most important facet of a community and the economy functions to serve the nation. Although extreme right movements that have arisen since World War II are committed to capitalism, they fear that free trade may undermine their country. See Cas Mudde, "The War of Words Defining the Extreme Right Party Family," *West European Politics* 19, no. 2 (April 1996): 189.

13. Starobin, "Right Fight," *The National Journal* (9 November 1995): 3025.

14. Mudde, *The Ideology of the Extreme Right*, 178.

15. "A History of 'Libertarian'," retrieved from the world wide web 1 April 2000, http://www.libertarian.org.

16. Reinhold Gärtner, "Right-Wing Press in Austria," in *Contemporary Austrian Studies*, vol. 4, *Austro-Corporatism: Past, Present, Future*, ed. Günter Bischof and Anton Pelinka (New Brunswick: Transaction Publishers, 1996), 305.

17. Brian Girvin, *The Right in the Twentieth Century*, ed. Roger Eatwell (London: Pinter Publishers, 1994), 20.

18. Qtd. in Starobin, "Right Fight," 3023.

19. David Frum, *Dead Right* (New York: BasicBooks, 1994), 202.

20. Andrew Heywood, *Political Ideologies*, 2nd ed. (London: MacMillan Press Ltd., 1998), 68.

21. Ibid., 70.

22. Charles Funderbunk and Robert G. Thobaben, *Political Ideologies: Left, Center, Right*, 2nd ed. (New York: Harper Collins College Publishers, 1994), 124.

23. The exception to this assertion is 1994, when a center-right coalition briefly controlled Italy.

24. "Profile: Controversy and Jörg Haider," 29 February 2000, *BBC News*, retrieved from the world wide web 4 march 2000, http://news.bbc.co.uk.

25. Melanie Sully, *The Haider Phenomenon* (New York: Columbia University Press, 1997), 200.

26. "The State of the Republic and the Situation of the FPÖ," retrieved from the world wide web 1 March 2000, http://www.fpoe.at/englisch/images/republic.pdf.

27. Sully, *The Haider Phenomenon*, 79.

28. Jörg Haider, *The Freedom I Mean*, trans. Hans Janitschek (Pine Plains, NY: Swan Books, 1995), 37.

29. Sully, *The Haider Phenomenon*, 83.

30. Haider, *The Freedom I Mean*, 51.

31. Sully, *The Haider Phenomenon*, 47.

32. James Blitz, "The Premier's Men: James Blitz Looks at Some of the Politicians Who Will Be Holding Power Within the New Government Coalition," *The Financial Times*, 5 June, 2001.

33. Klaus Wölfer, interview with author, tape recording, Rome, Italy, 31 October 2000.

34. Umberto Bossi and Daniele Vimercati, "The Revolution," ed. Sperling and Kupfer, 1993, 40, retrieved from the world wide web 20 November 2000, http://www.leganord.org.

35. Ibid., 42.

36. "Padania: The Foundations of a Nation," retrieved from the world wide web 11 November 2000, http://www.leganord.org/eng/remake.htm.

37. Bossi and Vimercati, "The Revolution," 37.

38. "Le politiche del governo sull'immigrazione," retrieved from the world wide web 15 May 2001, http://www.governo.it/sez_dossier/immigrazione/presentazione.html, trans. by author.

39. Bossi and Vimercati, "The Revolution," 42.

40. Ibid., 20.

41. "Economic Survey of Italy, 2000," Policy Brief OECD, June 2000, retrieved from the world wide web 15 May 2001, http://www.oecd.org/publications/Pol_brief.

42. As I argued in the beginning of this piece, it is important to explore both the ideologies and the policies of political parties to determine where they fall along the political spectrum. In this case, however, the immigration ideologies of the FPÖ and the LN did not change when the parties were incorporated into their ruling governments; the Freedom Party's immigration ideologies remained primarily conservative while those of the Lega Nord contained both conservative and libertarian undertones. Instead of comparing the parties' immigration ideologies and programs after they became government members, therefore, I will only examine the FPÖ and LN's strategies for immigration policy reform.

43. "A New Governance for Austria," 3 February 2000, retrieved from the world wide web 15 May 2001, http://www.austria.gv.at.

44. Ibid.

45. Max Riedlsperger, "The FPÖ and the Right," in *Contemporary Austrian Studies,* vol. 4, *Austro-Corporatism: Past, Present, Future*, ed. Günter Bischof and Anton Pelinka (New Brunswick: Transaction Publishers, 1996), 353.

46. "Minister Herbert Haupt: The most important electoral pledge of the FPÖ fulfilled," retrieved from the world wide web 15 May 2001, http://www.fpoe.at.

47. "Child Benefit—a milestone in family policy," retrieved from the world wide web 15 May 2001, http://www.fpoe.at.

48. "Implementation Report 2000 on the National Action Plan for Employment," Federal Ministry for Economic Affairs and Labour, 1 May 2000, retrieved from the world wide web 21 December 2001, http://europa.eu.int/comm/employment_social/empl&esf/naps00/napau_en.pdf.

49. "Labour Market," retrieved from the world wide web 15 May 2001, http://www.reformmonitor.org/index.php3?mode=reform.

50. "Padania: The Foundations of a Nation."

51. Bossi and Vimercati, "The Revolution," 42.

52. John Hooper and Kate Connolly, "On the Brink of War: Berlusconi Breaks Ranks Over Islam," *Guardian* (London), 27 September 2001, 3.

53. Hans-Georg Betz, "The Two Faces of Radical Right-Wing Populism in Western Europe," *Party Politics* 55, no. 4 (Autumn 1993): 682.

54. This is in contrast to the previous law allowing legal immigrants to bring their parents, siblings, and cousins into the country. See John Follain, "Italy Threatens Migrants with Four-Year Jail Terms," *Sunday Times* (London), 29 July 2001, retrieved from the world wide web 1 October 2001, http://www.lexis-nexis.com.

55. John Follain, "Berlusconi under Pressure to Get Tough on Migrants," *Sunday Times* (London), 20 May 2001, retrieved from the world wide web 1 October 2001, http://www.lexis-nexis.com.

56. Bossi and Vimercati , "The Revolution," 23.

57. "Cautious response from world leaders," 14 May 2001, retrieved from the world wide web 15 May 2001, http://www.cnn.com/2001/WORLD/europe/5/14/italy.election.reaction/index.html.

58. Dr. Jörg Haider, interview with author, tape recording, Klagenfurt, Austria, 30 July 2001.

59. European Commission, "Who's Who in the EU: What difference will the Treaty of Nice Make?," Luxembourg, Office for Official Publications of the European Communities, 2001, 8.

60. "Index of Economic Freedom: Italy," retrieved from the world wide web 14 February 2002, http://cf.heritage.org/index/country.cfm?ID=72.0.

61. "Index of Economic Freedom: Austria," retrieved from the world wide web 14 February 2002, http://database.townhall.com/heritage/index/country.cfm?ID=7.

62. For a more detailed explanation of the discrepancy between the EU's response to the Austrian and Italian cases, refer to Chapter 3 in Megan Greene, "Combating Right-Wing Extremism in the European Union: A Case Study of the Austrian Freedom Party and the Italian Lega Nord."

63. Ian Black, "EU Ready to Grit Teeth and Shake Hands," *Guardian* (London) 12 May 2001, 16.

64. Ambassador Michael Breisky, interview with author, tape recording, Vienna, Austria, 28 June 2000.

65. Vaiju Naravane, "Vienna Smarting under Sanctions," *Hindu,* 20 June 2000, retrieved from the world wide web 4 October 2001, http://www.lexis-nexis.com.

66. "Intergovernmental Conference: the Commission Proposes an addition to Article 7 of the Treaty on Respect for Democratic Values," Brussels, 4 October 2000, retrieved from the world wide web 21 December 2001, http://europa.eu.int/rapid/start/cgi/guesten.ksh?p_action.gettxt=gt&doc=IP/00/1116|0|RAPID&lg=EN.

67. M. Ahtisaari, J. Frowein, and M. Oreja, "Report," Paris, 8 September 2000, 34, retrieved from the world wide web 20 March 2001, http://www.austria.gv.at/e/bundesreg/Report.pdf.

68. J.S. Marcus, "Shadows on the Danube," *The New York Review of Books,* 14 March 2001, 65.

69. Hannes Androsch, "The State of Affairs" (Revised version of the speech held at the opening session of the third International Theodor Herzl Symposium, Vienna, Austria, 13 March 2000).

FORUM

Commissioning History: Austria and World War II Restitution and Reconciliation[1]

Günter Bischof

When the cold war ended, in the course of the 1990s, Europeans—East and West—discovered the old verity that you cannot escape history. The post-cold war era has brought a major upsurge of serious historical inquiry into World War II related war crimes such as Nazi plunder of "Holocaust era assets" and Nazi slave labor utilization. Germany, Austria, and many nations that had been occupied and had collaborated with Nazi policies and plunder saw a last chance for making good for their collaboration with the Nazis during World War II and paying restitution for property theft ("Aryanizations," art theft, life insurance policies, dormant bank accounts, etc.).

American historian Elazar Barkan sees the cumulative effect of these restitution settlements in a larger international context. He posits that "the need for restitution to past victims has become a major part of national policy and international diplomacy." He adds: "Interaction between perpetrator and victim is a new form of political negotiation that enables the rewriting of memory and historical identity in ways that both can share." Such negotiated justice, often coming late, amounts to a new "*moral economy*" (my emphasis). Barkan asserts that "moral issues came to dominate public attention and political issues and displayed the willingness of nations to embrace their own guilt." Such "national self-reflexivity" amounts to a "new *guilt of nations*" (my emphasis).[2] Whether justice and morality will replace realpolitik in international diplomacy remains to be seen.

This new interest in World War II restitution and reconciliation, the negotiated rewriting of national history and memory, and the willingness to admit one's historical guilt and apologize for past misdeeds was related to a number of factors. First, the end of the cold war did not only open massive archives full of new evidence on World War II, Nazi oppression, and occupation in Eastern Europe but also gave back the peoples of formerly Communist Eastern Europe their long suppressed recent history. The reawakened interest in Nazi occupation practices brought the gargantuan use of slave labor by the Nazis out into the open again. It egged on the governments of new states like Belarus and Ukraine, as well as Russia, Poland, the Czech Republic, and Hungary to negotiate settlements with Germany and Austria on behalf of these former victims of labor exploitation in the industries of the Third Reich.

Second, the newly democratic nations of Eastern Europe also have been forced to confront their own unmastered World War II pasts, which have been lying dormant for half a century. A surfeit of memory broke loose that had been in hibernation for two generations as a result of Communist suppression of historical memory. Like the Germans and Austrians before them, the newly independent nations of Eastern and Southeastern Europe have been finding plenty of skeletons in the closet too. After the break-up of the former Yugoslavia, Croats and Serbs began to settle unresolved World War II accounts (Chetnick vs. Ustaše). The Czechs are forced to confront the expulsion of their German population and the forced property seizures after the war ("Beneš decrees"). In fact, in these two cases little willingness surfaced to admit guilt or to apologize. The ghastly story of the Jedwabne progrom is catching up with the Poles, a location where they became "willing executioners" of the local Jewish population for the Nazis.[3]

Third, the avalanche of class action suits produced enormous hype. American lawyers like Ed Fagan aggressively began class actions on behalf of Jewish and other victims against Swiss banks as well as German and Austrian financial institutions and private industries for restitution of World War II accounts and assets. These high profile suits produced negative publicity and pressured Central European corporations doing business in the United States to work towards quick settlements so as not to affect their current business.

Fourth, these suits produced an avalanche of settlements often coupled with the establishment of *historical commissions* for a thorough scholarly investigation of the nature of property transfers of "Holocaust era assets." They not only probed fairness of the court or diplomatic settlements but also produced the evidence necessary for nations to confront their pasts and clear their consciences by confronting past injustices. Due to the nature of thorough scholarly investigations in obscure archives, and if possible through direct communication with the victims, the reports of these commissions were years in the making and often came after the restitution settlements. The Swiss banks were the first to set up a special audit of their accounts ("Volker Commission") in 1996. As a result of the audit, they established a seven-billion Swiss franks solidarity fund for Jewish victims.[4] The "Bergier Commission" was set up by the Swiss Parliament in December 1996. It delivered its final report after six years of investigations in April 2002.

Fifth came the rippling effect. The swift Swiss bank settlement put massive pressure on the German and Austrian governments and private corporations to follow suit. Numerous private corporations such as German and Austrian banks and insurance companies set up their own private historical commissions to probe the extent of their companies' World War II collaboration with the Nazi regime, the utilization of slave labor, or the hiding of ill-gotten gains from forced property transfers of victims. The German government initiated an investigation into the utilization of slave labor under former Finance Minister Count Lambsdorff. A five-billion German mark compensation fund was set up with public and private industry funds in February 1999 and endorsed by the German Parliament in July 2000. The German investigations and settlements put further pressure on Austrian corporations and the government to act and address Austrians' involvement in Nazi victimization and exploitation. Pressured by the intense public interest in the Swiss settlement and the German effort, the government of Viktor Klima set up the Austrian Historical Commission in November 1998, to broadly investigate these World War II related issues of forced property transfers in the broadest historical context.

In this FORUM, *Brigitte Bailer-Galanda* and *Eva Blimlinger*, who work for the Austrian Historical Commission, summarize the multiple efforts of this state-sponsored group of some 140 researchers who have been working on 45 different projects related to World War II property issues and forced transfers. At the same time, private banks, the Austrian insurance industry, and public corporations privately commissioned their own historical expertise to comb through elusive company archives to understand the extent of their own involvement in Nazi criminal activities. In their FORUM essays, *Oliver Rathkolb*, *Dieter Stiefel*, and *Margit Reiter* respectively present summaries of the findings of their commissioned work on the Austrian postal savings bank, the life insurance industry, and the massive electrical power plant of Kaprun.[5] Kaprun constitutes a fascinating case study of both the use of massive slave labor (some 6,000 foreign workers from 20 different nations) in the construction of a Nazi hydroelectric power project. Kaprun, a kind of oversized Austrian Tennessee Valley Authority "New Deal" project, was finished after the war with American Marshall Plan funds by many former Nazis that found employment in this project high up in the Salzburg Alps. Kaprun became an important part of the myth of Austrian reconstruction, where the Nazi beginnings and the postwar American financial contribution have been conveniently purged from the Austrian postwar memory!

In February 2000, the conservative People's Party (ÖVP) formed a surprise coalition with the right-wing Freedom Party (FPÖ) under the leadership of Chancellor Wolfgang Schüssel (starting what seems to amount to a current trend in Western Europe of *center-right coalitions*). This new Austrian government came under massive pressure from the European Union[6] and the entire international community due to the leadership of Jörg Haider in the FPÖ. The xenophobic and anti-EU Haider sported a long record of anti-immigration policies and pro-Nazi statements.[7] Even though he had no cabinet position, the "EU-14" levied sanctions against the new Schüssel government. These were eventually lifted in September 2000.[8] An unspoken part of this isolation of the Schüssel government was the charge that Austria had done a lousy job of mastering its World War II past. With the right-wing FPÖ in the coalition, the fear abroad was that matters would get worse rather than better in terms of Austria facing its deficient World War II related record. The frequent charge of Austria's "unmastered past" in the international media was coupled with the assertion that Germany had a much better record in confronting its World War II past.[9]

This charge was off the mark: Ever since the "Waldheim affair" of 1986 Austria had engaged in many efforts to finally cast its favorite notion over board that Austrians had been victims of Hitler rather than frequently overeager perpetrators.[10] Throughout the 1990s, Austria made numerous efforts to develop a more open mindset over its World War II involvement in Nazi war crimes. President Waldheim made a speech about Austrian "victims and perpetrators" during the 50th anniversary commemoration of the Anschluss in 1988. Chancellor Franz Vranitzky and Waldheim's successor President Thomas Klestil gave celebrated speeches in Jerusalem in 1991 and 1994, making similar statements of Austria's complex World War II past. The Austrian Parliament set up a "Reconciliation Fund" (*Versöhnungsfonds*) in 1995 to pay restitution to Jewish victims. And, as mentioned above, the late 1990s saw a spate of new investigations unleashed by the new international climate militating for restitution and reconciliation (Barkan).[11]

The new Schüssel government had to operate in a unique pressure-cooker environment of intense international scrutiny. On the one hand Schüssel and his coalition partner had no choice but continue previous Austrian efforts to make amends—at last—for its long record of procrastinating its confrontation with the unsettled World War II past. On the other hand, it had to respond to the hostile international climate. Schüssel chose the *Flucht nach vorne*. He vigorously confronted Austria's difficult World War II record from day one. In the preamble of the ÖVP/FPÖ government declaration of February 4, the government announced to assume its part of responsibility for the "unspeakable crimes of the National Socialist regime" as well as for the light and dark chapters of Austria's World War II history. Five days after the formation of his government, Schüssel appointed Maria Schaumayer as chair of a task force investigating slave labor utilization on Austrian territory during World War II. As a result of Schaumayer's negotiations, the Austrian government set up a reconciliation fund to pay restitution to some 150,000 former slave laborers still alive in Eastern Europe. In his FORUM essay, *Martin Eichtinger*, who had acted as Schaumayer's chief of staff, summarizes these complex negotiations with various Eastern European and the American governments. They were completed in October 2000 and a fund of 3,7 billion Austrian schillings was constituted in December. Payments amounting up to US $7,000 each were started to some 50,000 former slave laborers in the course of 2001.[12]

But the slave labor reconciliation fund was not all. In May 2000, Schüssel appointed the Viennese diplomat Ernst Sucharipa as special ambassador. He was to establish—both with the American government's representative Undersecretary of the Treasury Department Stuart Eizenstat and with class action lawyers—what "gaps and deficiencies" still existed in Austria's postwar restitution efforts. In other words, were there still Jewish victims that had not received any or insufficient restitution payments for property losses they incurred during World War II ("*Wiedergutmachung*")? In October 2000, at a time when Schaumayer concluded her negotiations, Sucharipa's parallel efforts reached a first framework agreement on these "gaps and deficiencies." After around-the-clock negotiations, an agreement was reached in mid-January 2001. The Austrian Parliament passed the necessary legislation by the end of the same month. A 400-million dollar fund was set up to compensate victims of "Aryanizations." In return for Austria's willingness to finally cover all "gaps and deficiencies" in restitution payments, the American government guaranteed that no further class action suits could be launched on behalf of former victims.[13]

One may cautiously hypothesize today that, ironically, the center-right Schüssel government accomplished more in confronting the unsettled World War II agenda than any of the previous Austrian governments did after World War II. We do not know much about the possible opposition inside the governing coalition in arriving at these dramatic concessions to finally achieve historical justice vis-à-vis the victims; nor is the FPÖ's specific stance inside the cabinet, or its possible role as a reluctant ally, clear to the outside observers. What we do know that is that, in this case, being under the intense scrutiny of the international community was a good thing to produce quick results. We do know the reconciliation-friendly international climate of the 1990s, when "restitution provide[d] a beacon of morality" in a morally flawed and unjust world got Austria out of its deep rut of ignoring its responsibility for World War II related in justices.[14]

Notes

1. Two of the essays (Stiefel and Eichtinger) in this FORUM were first delivered in a panel of the same title during the 25th anniversary meeting of the German Studies Association in October 2001 in Washington, D.C. Two of the scheduled papers (Rathkolb and Bailer-Galanda/Blimlinger) fell victim to the 9/11 terrorist attacks and were not delivered but later written for this FORUM. We would like to thank Kurt Tweraser from the University of Arkansas for his incisive commentary at the GSA-panel. Reiter had presented her paper in the October 2000 GSA meeting in Houston, Texas.

2. Elazar Barkan, *The Guilt of Nations: Restitution and Negotiating Historical Injustices* (Baltimore: Johns Hopkins University Press, 2001), xv-xli (quotations xvi, xviii, xl).

3. Ibid., 112-56.; Jan T. Gross, *Neighbors: The Destruction of the Jewish Community in Jedwabne, Poland* (Princeton: Princeton University Press, 2001).

4. Barkan, *Guilt of Nations*, 88-111.

5. Rathkolb et al.'s study on the *Hermann Göring Werke* and Stiefel's life insurance report are published; both are reviewed by Hermann Freudenberger in this volume.

6. For insightful discussions of the deeper roots of Austria's relationship with Europe see the essays in Thomas Angerer, ed., *Österreich in Europa*, in *Wiener Zeitschrift zur Geschichte der Neuzeit* 1 (2000).

7. See also the non-topical essay by Megan E. Greene in this volume.

8. The best summary of the EU-14 "sanction measures" is Michael Gehler's essay in Günter Bischof, Anton Pelinka, and Michael Gehler, eds., *Austria in the European Union*, vol. 10, *Contemporary Austrian Studies* (New Brunswick: Transaction Publishers, 2002), 223-70; on the nature of Haider and the FPÖ see the essays by Hans-Georg Betz and Walter Manoschek, in ibid., 118-60; see also Anton Pelinka and Ruth Wodak, eds., *The Haider Phenomenon in Austria* (New Brunswick: Transaction Publishers, 2002).

9. Günter Bischof, "'Experiencing a Nasty Fall from Grace...'? Austria's Image in the U.S. after the Formation of the ÖVP/FPÖ Government," *Diplomatische Akademie Wien Occasional Paper* 2/2000, 7-33. For the larger context of public opinion on Austria and National Socialism see Heinz P. Wassermann, *Naziland Österreich?: Studien zu Antisemitismus, Nation und Nationalsozialismus im öffentlichen Meinungsbild*, vol. 2, *Schriften des Centrums für jüdische Studien* (Innsbruck: Studienverlag, 2002); for a recent comparison of Austria's and Germany's postwar restitution record see David Forster, *Wiedergutmachung in Österreich und der BRD im Vergleich* (Innsbruck: Studienverlag, 2001).

10. See, for example, Heidemarie Uhl, "Nur jener, der mit seiner Vergangenheit im Reinen ist, hat die Hände frei für die Zukunft. Zur Frage der Instrumentalisierung von 'Vergangenheitbewältigung'," in *Gestörte Identitäten? Eine Zwischenbilanz der Zweiten Republik*, ed. Lutz Musner, Gotthart Wunberg, and Eva Cescutti (Innsbruck: Studienverlag, 2002), 10-26.

11. The argument that Austria has vigorously confronted its World War II past ever since the Waldheim fiasco of 1986 is being made in detail and with further evidence by Günter Bischof, "'Watschenmann der europäischen Erinnerung'? Internationales Image und Vergangenheitspolitik der Schüssel/Riess-Passer ÖVP/FPÖ Koalitionsregierung," in *Österreich in der EU*, vol. 5, Institut für Zeitgeschiche der Universität Innsbruck, Arbeitskreis europäische Integration, ed. Michael Gehler, Anton Pelinka, and Günter Bischof (Vienna: Böhlau, 2003 forthcoming).

12. For the most thorough analysis of the work of the Schaumayer commission see Martin Eichtinger, "Der Versöhnungsfonds: Österreichs Leistungen an ehemalige Sklaven- und Zwangsarbeiter des NS-Regimes," *Österreichisches Jahrbuch für Politik* (2000): 193-242.

13. For the best summary of these restitution negotiations see Ernst Sucharipa, Die Rückkehr der Geschichte, *Europäische Rundschau* 29 (2001): 71-80; idem, Austria s Measures and Compensation for Holocaust Victims: Recent Negotiations and Their Background," *Österreichisches Jahrbuch für Internationale Politik* (Vienna, 2000): 75-95; idem, "Revisiting the National Socialist Legacy. Restitution: Why Now? The Austrian Experience," *Georgetown Journal of International Affairs* (Summer/Fall 2002): 97-104; for the international legal perspective see also Hans Winkler, "Österreich – die völkerrechtlichen Aspekte," in *Die politische Ökonomie des Holocaust: Zur wirtschafllichen Logik von Verfolgung und "Wiedergutmachung,"* ed. Dieter Stiefel (Vienna: Verlag für Geschichte und Politik/R. Oldenbourg, 2001), 259-88.

14. Barkan, *Guilt of Nations*, xli.

The Austrian Historical Commission: International Background, Motives, Results, and Impact

Brigitte Bailer-Galanda and Eva Blimlinger

1. International Background

At the end of December 1997 the *New York Times* charged the art collector Rudolf Leopold with having at least four pictures with a "difficult history" in his famous Schiele-Collection.[1] Before 1938, the works of art in question had been owned by people later persecuted by the Nazis. In his first statement, Rudolf Leopold explained to the Austrian Press Agency (APA) that these reproaches were absolute lies and that he considered suing.[2] To this day, one of the four pictures—*Bildnis Wally*—is still confiscated and the object of a law suit.

The article in the *New York Times* marked the beginning of an extensive discussion about restitution and compensation after the Second World War in Austria. In February 1998, the Secretary of State for Education and Cultural Affairs Elisabeth Gehrer established a commission to research the provenance of works of art that belong to the Republic of Austria and are exhibited and stored in public museums. In some cases, looted works of art had simply been kept by museums; in other cases, formally restituted pieces were held back as a sort of "price" the owners had to "pay" for being allowed to export the rest of their collection, as is known of the Rothschild Collection. The commission should establish who the owners before, during, and after National Socialism were, and which of these works of art the Republic of Austria had just kept and which of them the former owners had to "donate." The Leopold Foundation,[3] which unleashed the debate, refuses to do research concerning the provenance of its works of art. Its homepage reveals that many gaps in the history of the pictures still exist.[4]

In autumn 1998, Parliament passed a law about the restitution of works of art from Austrian federal museums and collections.[5] In the meantime, a lot of collections and art pieces have been given back to the original owners, as for example the Rothschild Collection.

While in Austria the discussion started with four pictures, in Switzerland the debate was triggered by dormant bank accounts. Until the 1990s, the Shoa had not really been an issue in Switzerland. There was some research, some discussion, as for instance about the film *Das Boot ist voll.*[6] The Bergier Commission was established in December 1996 by an unanimously approved resolution of the Swiss Federal Assembly. Its mandate was to investigate the volume and history of assets moved to Switzerland before, during, and immediately after the Second World War. The final report was finished in April 2002. On 2 May 1996, the Swiss Bankers Association, the World Jewish Restitution Organization, and the World Jewish Congress (representing the Jewish Agency and allied organizations) agreed to the so-called Memorandum of Understanding and established the "Independent Committee of Eminent Persons" (the Volcker Commission). The committee was mandated to conduct an investigative audit to determine whether there were any dormant accounts, financial instruments, or any other assets of the victims of Nazi persecution that had been deposited in Swiss banks before, during, or immediately after the Second World War. In January of 1997, this investigative audit was designated as a special audit by the Swiss Federal Banking Commission, giving it the force of law in Switzerland. In December 1999, the reports were presented.

Forced labor was another crucial element in the system of the National Socialist exploitative war economy.[7] In Germany, the intensive discussion about compensation for forced labor started after 1989, when the German Democratic Republic collapsed and the formerly Communist states in Eastern and Eastern-Central Europe were democratized. Immediately after the Second World War, forced laborers had tried to get compensation. They usually received the same answer: Compensation would only be possible if a German peace treaty was signed. However, this did not happen until the "2+4 Treaty" of 12 September 1990. In the years following, German elite companies such as *Volkswagen* and *Daimler Benz* were confronted with class-action lawsuits of former slave laborers. In 1999, the German industry founded the *Stiftungsinitiative der deutschen Wirtschaft*, and most of the forced laborers have received their compensation by now. Following these events, commissions and research groups have been established all over Europe and in the United States. The French commission and the commission of the United States have already finished their work.

These changes in the international arena, then, put pressure on Austria to initiate a serious historical investigation of its own. In the 1990s, the political and legal environment has changed dramatically in Austria. Domestic restitution has become an international issue. The class action suit approach of U.S. attorneys may appear strange to Europeans, but its effectiveness and accelerating impact on the restitution debate cannot be denied.

2. Motives for Establishing the Historical Commission of the Republic of Austria

In November 1998, the government of Viktor Klima established the Historical Commission of the Republic of Austria. Beside the international context discussed above, a number of decisive factors were in play. First, there appears to be a basic trend bringing Austria into the new millennium with a comprehensive clarification of her World War II past. Perhaps as a consequence of the "Waldheim affair" and many historians' debates, the general attitude towards Austria's way of dealing with the Nazi period has changed. At least the intellectuals, parts of the political establishment, and especially the younger generation have opened up to a candid debate. This perceptible process was a main precondition for a positive working atmosphere of the Historical Commission. It seems to be largely accepted now that Austria's complex international legal status between 1938 and 1945 bears no relation to her moral responsibility after the war.

Nevertheless, the widespread view that Austria has previously done nothing in the field of restitution and/or compensation is incorrect. It is true, however, that the restitution measures were often half-hearted, inconsistent, and too late. Most of the problems only come to light in the details. Inevitably, the poorest victims got the least from the restitution and compensation system because their meager property had not been formally "Aryanized." They did not get any compensation if they had been lucky enough to escape to another country, had taken foreign citizenships, and had not come back because they had no money to start all over again.

Another important factor for the establishment of the Austrian Historical Commission emanated from the progress of contemporary and economic history. A new generation of historians and researchers benefiting from a more open access to the archives has been producing important work. Only now are we aware of the whole complexity of expropriation during the Third Reich. While Nazi crimes have dominated the scholarly as well as the public debate, property transfer has so far not been at the center of international research. One more factor is the noticeable change within the Austrian Jewish community in recent years. The older generation was either glad to have survived the Nazi horrors or did not want to be reminded of Austria, if they had stayed abroad. They abstained from putting pressure on Austria, above all for fear of reawakening Austria's notorious anti-Semitism. The second and third generations after the Shoa do see the conspicuous danger of anti-Semitism, but do not overestimate it and will not be deterred. Austria's anti-Semitism always finds opportunities to articulate itself. It has been visible in recent years but has not been intensified by the work of the Historical Commission and the negotiations concerning restitution and compensation. Also other groups of former persecutees such as Roma und Sinti or homosexuals have found the courage to demand restitution and compensation from Austria.

3. The Mandate of the Commission

On 1 October 1998, Austria's federal chancellor, the vice-chancellor, the speaker of the national assembly, and the speaker of the federal council jointly appointed the Historical Commission. The commission works on their behalf but is autonomous and independent. The commission's mandate is to research and report on the looting of property in the territory of the Republic of Austria during the Nazi years as well as to probe the acts of restitution and/or compensation (including economic and social benefits) by the Republic of Austria after 1945.

In contrast to the Swiss Bergier Commission, the Austrian commission has no magisterial power. Special legal provisions apply to the work of the Swiss commission. In Austria, the commission and all its researchers are bound by data protection laws and the Official Secrets Act. Generally speaking, the cooperation with all the authorities has worked very well, and it was possible to secure new documentation during the last years.

The commission consists of six members: Chairman of the Historical Commission is the president of the Austrian Administrative Court, Clemens Jabloner, vice-chairpersons are the director-general of the Austrian State Archives, Lorenz Mikoletzky, and the historian and social scientist Brigitte Bailer-Galanda (*Dokumentationsarchiv des Österreichischen Widerstandes*, DÖW). The other members are the British expert Robert Knight, a specialist on Austrian postwar history; Bertrand Perz, respected for his work about Mauthausen; and Roman Sandgruber, professor for social and economic history at the University of Linz in Upper Austria. During the constituent session, a number of permanent experts were commissioned to complete the Historical Commission's extensive work program. More expertise on economic and civil law aspects was needed and was provided by Georg Graf, professor for civil law at the University of Salzburg, Alice Teichova, professor for economic history at the University of Cambridge, and Karl Stuhlpfarrer, professor for contemporary history at the University of Klagenfurt, Carinthia.

The Historical Commission submitted its work program to the government on 16 March 1999 and then published it. In April 1999, the sponsors approved the projected research program, the time frame, and the budget—ATS 88 million/ EUR 6,395,209.40—without alterations. The commission's budget was passed by Parliament, and a secretariat was established at the Austrian State Archives. The Historical Commission advertised its detailed projects in spring 1999 and winter 2000. Some three hundred and fifty scholars from nine countries applied for research contracts. Since then, about forty-five research projects have been commissioned and one hundred and thirty researchers have been working on behalf of the Historical Commission. The members of the commission meet regularly. Some members are carrying out their own research projects for the commission. But the main work of the commission is to supervise all projects, to read all interim reports, and to provide feedback to the researchers. The members also take the opportunity to present their work and plans in lectures at international conferences, advanced education programs for teachers, the diplomatic corps, etc. Together with the secretariat, the commission organizes talks, workshops, and seminars with the researchers. The secretariat coordinates the researchers, looks up new sources, collects and distributes the sources from archives all over the world, tries to establish good and effective cooperation with archives, chambers, authorities and companies, prepares drafts for statements to bills, and sends out a daily press review and a regular electronic mailing, among other tasks.

4. The Work of the Historical Commission

The Historical Commission is working in an extraordinarily complex field. Its challenges, therefore, are easily discernible. It is an insoluble dilemma that the commission was set up so late. More than fifty years after the war, most of the victims are dead or quite elderly. The commission's mandate is far-reaching and time-consuming because it has to work properly and according to international scholarly standards. Thus, from the very beginning, the commission has been confronted with the reproach that it was being used as an instrument for gaining time. The commission has been conscious of these difficulties from the very beginning. Its members, therefore, clearly pointed out that in various fields the legal-political process was not dependent on the research results.

To find a way out of this dilemma, the Historical Commission decided to give immediate attention to the question of forced labor. As a first step, the commission appointed reports about the number of forced laborers who worked in the territory of the Republic of Austria between 1939 and 1945,[8] as well as a reevaluation of survivors.[9] These reports were handed over in January 2000, and the following month Maria Schaumayer, special representative of the Austrian Federal Government, started negotiations for a wholesale compensation for all slave and forced laborers still alive. Some six months later, the Austrian Parliament passed the Reconciliation Fund Law. About fifty thousand people have already received their payments. Secondly, the commission issued two reports—one historical and one legal-historical—about the Aryanization and non-restitution of rented apartments.[10] During the 1950s, a draft restitution law for rented apartments reached the stage of a government bill but was not passed as law. In autumn 2000, this second report was handed over, and in January 2001, the amendment to the national fund and the federal law on the general settlement fund was passed by the Austrian Parliament.

In light of the general agreement reached in Washington on 17 January 2001, and the resulting Austrian legislation, the Historical Commission is confronted with two questions. From the victim's point of view, one may ask whether the agreement was signed too early, since the commission is still working. Given these circumstances, the question arises whether the commission is still needed at all.

The relatively rapid agreement was surely beneficial to the victims and their heirs but perhaps ambivalent for the Austrian Jewish communities, which were partners to the settlement of the agreement. The problem of the damage suffered by the Jewish community is marginalized. But it may have been necessary in the framework of these negotiations. Moreover, many victims abroad are still waiting for the payment of social benefits.

Yet, nothing in the mission of the Historical Commission has changed as a result of these agreements. The research projects are proceeding with all possible energy. Inevitably, the January 2001 agreement will be measured against the results of the Historical Commission. But in principle, it must be noted that the work of the commission will serve the purpose of making some difficult and sensitive issues of recent Austrian history comprehensible to as many people as possible. Such broad transparency is the real intended purpose of the commission. In this sense, the Historical Commission of the Republic of Austria has a historic mission to fulfill, one long overdue.

It should be underlined that the commission is neither a restitution court nor a restitution or compensation office of Nazi era assets. Therefore the commission is not in the position to deal with restitution or compensation claims. Furthermore, the commission will not make direct recommendations on any legal or political action programs. But the facts will speak for themselves. The commission cannot investigate thousands of individual cases. This is sometimes difficult to understand for the victims. Nor will the commission just focus on spectacular individual cases. As important as the return of works of art is, the commission has to be just as careful to elucidate the untold misery produced by the Nazis. The fate of tens of thousands of ordinary people needs to be told.

5. Research Program

The details can be found in the commission's work program, the interim reports, press releases, and other details dispersed through the Internet.[11]

The current state of research in the commission's various fields of investigation, as reflected in the literature and available sources, varies enormously. So far the commission has not been able to do all the necessary research. It has had to rely also on the results of other commissions. Valuable work has been commissioned by the private sector, such as the recently published study edited by Oliver Rathkolb about forced and slave labor at the *Hermann Göring Werke* (*Voest*),[12] the research by Dieter Stiefel on life-insurance policies,[13] the research on the Dorotheum auction house, and the investigations into the role of political parties after 1945. Nevertheless, the commission reserves the right to decide for itself whether these studies address the issues under review fully and finally. If this is the case, the commission will formally endorse these reports and make appropriate reference to them.

The first chapter of the Historical Commission's work program is intended to throw light on the various phenomena of the looting of property under the Nazi regime, especially Aryanization, forced labor, and the areas of compensation and restitution. This is reflected in the concrete research themes. The Aryanization issue, for example, is divided into several smaller projects. The calculation of the monetary value of Aryanized assets will be made on the basis of the files of the *Vermögensverkehrsstelle*. In examining the Aryanization of immovables and subsequent losses, researchers look at the land register and at selected districts in Vienna in an attempt to highlight typical examples. Changes in the property situation of banks, industrial companies, and small businesses will also be examined to determine whether there were expropriations during the war and actual measures to restitute looted property after the war. A short study will focus on the role of the market inspectorate as an Aryanization authority and will show how Aryanizations were carried out in Vienna's open markets, such as the *Naschmarkt*, what type of property was confiscated, and whether it was restituted. Another project will examine the dismissals and exclusion from the labor market of Jewish civil servants, lawyers, workers, and employees, and the financial losses resulting therefrom.

Research work on the *Zentralstelle für jüdische Auswanderung* and the *Gildemeester-Aktion*, which was launched to speed up forced emigration, focuses on the structure and functions of these Nazi institutions as looting instruments. A comprehensive study will examine forms of Aryanization, confiscation, restitution, and compensation in the provinces of Upper Austria, Salzburg, and Burgenland; a regional study will examine these forms also in Lower Austria. Regarding the confiscation of property owned by national minorities and the ensuing questions of restitution and compensation, studies will focus on Slovenes, Roma and Sinti, Czechs, Hungarians, and Croats. Concerning the victims of political persecution, the experts' research focuses on expropriation, forfeiture of expectancies, and the compensation of resistance fighters. Another study examines the dispossession and compensation of male and female homosexuals.

The dissolution of associations, foundations, and funds leading to property confiscation, constitutes an important part of the research work. Taking the files of the "*Stillhaltekommissar*" as a point of departure, a survey and evaluation will be carried out on a sample basis. From a regional perspective, a complete population survey will be made in respect of Jewish clubs, foundations, and funds also for the province of the Tyrol. As regards the complex issue of restitution and compensation, researchers will analyze the (hitherto poorly investigated) history of restitution and compensation legislation and relevant measures taken by Austrian authorities, the Allied forces, and Austro-Jewish exile organizations. The practical application of restitution legislation is looked at from a legal and historical point of view. Legal experts will, for example, examine the question as to who benefited from the discretion defined by law and exercised by the Restitution Commission. They will also look at the definition of the concept of "fair earnings" and its impact on restitution proceedings. Another legal research project will examine the obligations of the Republic of Austria under international law with regard to restitution and compensation after 1945 and the relevance of the "victim compensation doctrine."

Furthermore, there will be analyses of the practical application of the relevant provisions of the social welfare law, a legal and a historical study on the meaning of citizenship, a study on the *Sammelstellen* for heirless assets, a calculation of deprived and restituted assets, and research on the policies of the *Finanzprokuratur*, the official attorney of the republic. According to the federal law on the establishment of a general settlement fund, the Historical Commission now has a completely new task. As mentioned in the settlement between Austria and the United States, the "Austrian federal government will undertake its best efforts to identify publicly owned property" which was Aryanized and not returned, for which the restitution treatment was extremely unfair, or which was owned by the republic on 17 January 2001. The Historical Commission will develop a database and documentation on all public property, which will be accessible on the one hand for the arbitration panel and on the other hand for the claimants. This project was only initiated in November 2001.

In the above-mentioned work program, the commission promises the final report—including the results of all projects—for the early autumn of 2002 and seems to be able to meet this deadline. According to the agreement with the sponsors, the report will first be submitted to them. Four weeks later—by this time the politicians will have had a chance to prepare their proper responses—the commission will publish the final report on the Internet and later on in the Oldenbourg publishing house. Thereafter, it will be the task of politicians, researchers, teachers, journalists, and other authorities to transmit the results to a wider public. The members of the commission are aware that their work and results are primarily for a very specific audience. It is inherent in the object of the commission's mandate that the final report will be ambiguous in some respects. Open questions will remain, and scholarly work always needs to be verified or refuted in the long run. But the commission is trying very hard to shed light on a somewhat confusing situation. And the results of the research initiated by the commission will close many gaps in contemporary historical research.

In conclusion, the members of the commission would like to point out that they are conscious of the deep emotions involved in this matter. If the commission succeeds in bringing this enormous and difficult research project to a successful conclusion, truth will break through as a matter of fact. The commission will be able to confront many of the frequently repeated legends and myths concerning the involvement of Austrians in the lootings of the years 1938-1945. The Historical Commission will also broadly address Austria's dealing with her National Socialist past and present the historical reality of these years.

Notes

1. Judith H. Dobrzynski, "The Zealous Collector. A Special Report; A Singular Passion For Amassing Art, One Way or Another," *New York Times*, 24 December 1997.

2. "*New York Times* wirft Leopold unrechtmäßigen Besitz von Bildern vor;" 1 *APA* 193, 26 December 1997.

3. The Collection of Rudolf Leopold was bought by the Republic of Austria and donated to the Leopold Foundation. Rudolf Leopold is one of the members of the foundation. Since September 2001 the collection is displayed at the Museum Leopold in the Museumsquartier (MUQUA) in Vienna, Austria.

4. See www.leopoldmuseum.org.

5. Federal law of 4 December 1998 concerning the return of works of art from Austrian federal museums and collections; Federal Law Gazette 1998/I/181.

6. *Das Boot ist voll*, Markus Imhoof, Switzerland 1981. The film is about Switzerland's policy of turning Jews, who had fled Nazi Germany, away from Swiss borders.

7. The term slave labor was established in the negotiation about compensation for forced labor and is a political but not a scholarly term.

8. Florian Freund und Bertrand Perz, "Die Zahlenentwicklung der ausländischen Zwangsarbeiter und Zwangsarbeiterinnen auf dem Gebiet der Republik Österreich 1939 – 1945," ed. Historikerkommission, Vienna 2000; see http://www.historikerkommission.gv.at/

9. Historikerkommission, ed., Mark Spoerer, "Schätzung der Zahl, der im Jahr 2000 überlebenden Personen, die auf dem Gebiet der Republik Österreich zwischen 1939 und 1945 als Zwangsarbeiter und Zwangsarbeiterinnen eingesetzt waren," ed. Historikerkommission; see http://www.historikerkommission.gv.at

10. Georg Graf, "Der Entzug von Mietrechten. Ein rechtshistorischer und rechtsdogmatischer Bericht unter besonderer Berücksichtigung der Entwicklungen nach der Wiedererrichtung der Republik Österreich," ed. Historikerkommission, Vienna 2000; Brigitte Bailer-Galanda, Eva Blimlinger, and Susanne Kowarc, "'Arisierung' und Rückstellung von Wohnungen in Wien. Die Vertreibung der jüdischen Mieter und Mieterinnen aus ihren

Wohnungen und das verhinderte Wohnungsrückstellungsgesetz," ed. Historikerkommission, Vienna 2000.

11. See homepage at www.historikerkommission.gv.at

12. Oliver Rathkolb with Karl Fallend, et al., *NS-Zwangsarbeit: Der Standort Linz der "Reichswerke Hermann Göring AG" Berlin, 1938-1945*, 2 vols. (Vienna: Böhlau, 2001); see also the review of this work by Hermann Freudenberger in this volume of *CAS*

13. Dieter Stiefel, *Die österreichischen Lebensversicherungen und die NS-Zeit. Wirtschaftliche Entwicklung. Politischer Einfluß. Jüdische Polizzen*, (Vienna: Böhlau, 2001); see also the review of this work by Hermann Freudenberger in the this volume of *CAS*.

The Austrian Reconciliation Fund: Austrian Payments to Former Slave and Forced Laborers of the NS Regime[1]

Martin Eichtinger

In only seventeen and a half months—from February 2000 to July 2001—Austria proceeded from merely announcing the appointment of a special representative for the negotiations about the forced and slave labor related issues of the Nazi era to actually disbursing the first payments to former victims of the NS regime. Why, though, did it take almost fifty-five years until the payments were made? Why did it happen now? And how was it possible to establish a fund so quickly and to get the necessary funds? And finally what was the reaction of the Austrian public to this effort?

Let us turn back to the year 1946, when Simon Wiesenthal, who at the time was president of the Jewish Central Committee in the American zone of occupation in Linz, acted on behalf of former slave laborers and contacted Austrian companies in order to get compensation payments for the victims. The companies declared that, during the NS regime, they had already paid wages to the SS and would not pay a second time. A similar request was filed in 1966 by the *Comité International des Camps* and was also rejected on the same grounds. Though legally correct, the companies' stand was not satisfactory from a humanitarian perspective.

Only after the fall of the Iron Curtain could the former victims of slave and forced labor make their voices heard all over Central and Eastern Europe. It became known that these victims had generally not received any compensation, neither by their national authorities, nor by Germany or any other country. In the course of German re-unification the German government established foundations for mutual understanding and reconciliation in Warsaw, Moscow, Kiev, and Minsk. The foundations received DM 1,5 billion, which were distributed over the following years to more than one and a half million victims of the Nazi regime, among them some, though by far not all, victims of slave and forced labor. The payments averaged

DM 1,000. This was certainly not nearly enough for the victims to feel adequately compensated and for their sufferings to be truly recognized.

During the years 1997 through 1999, the issue increasingly gained momentum and caught the attention of German media, politicians, companies, and the public. Courts pronounced judgments. In one case, the Federal Republic of Germany was sentenced to pay a compensation of DM 15,000—an amount which eventually became the accepted compensation for all slave laborers. The forced and slave labor issue also came up in Swiss negotiations for a settlement after American lawyers had filed class action suits against Swiss banks and insurance companies at the end of 1996 and the beginning of 1997.

The Volkswagen company announced the creation of an aid fund in July 1998. Other companies deliberated similar solutions. In August 1998, American class action lawyers filed a series of lawsuits against German companies. In October 1998, lawsuits against Austrian companies followed, but they were not successfully served to the companies until the spring of 1999. Several other lawsuits followed during the year of 2000.

Austrian companies have always rejected the idea of being legal successors to any of the companies of the Nazi era. In many instances, this lack of continuity to the then German companies on Austrian territory did not hold true in Germany proper. Most of the large Austrian companies which had been taken over by the Nazi regime or were founded by the Nazis were nationalized by Austria after World War II and remained state enterprises for decades. In the 1970s and 1980s, they were finally reorganized, split up, privatized, and run by new managements. This made it particularly difficult for the management of what had now become Austrian share-holding companies to agree to any payments since they would have to be justified to their shareholders. Austrian companies which had been sued before U.S. courts began to engage in expensive legal defense actions. They also funded historical research in their companies' archives to obtain a better understanding of what had happened in their plants during the Nazi regime. A core group of Austrian companies began deliberations about a broad national solution for slave and forced labor claims.

When Germany started to negotiate a settlement in February 1999 and announced the intention to establish a German compensation fund, Austrian companies discussed the idea of joining the German efforts. There seemed to be no intention of the grand coalition of Social Democrats and Christian Democrats in Austria to get involved in any compensation efforts. Federal Chancellor Viktor Klima stated on 3 September 1998 that it was the obligation of Austrian companies, not of the Austrian state, to deal with the problem of forced and slave labor.[2] However, the Austrian Historical Commission, which had been officially established by the Austrian government on 1 October 1998, included research on former forced and slave laborers in its work program and eventually delivered two reports in February 2000.[3]

When the new Austrian government composed of members of the Christian Democratic People's Party and the Freedom Party took office in February 2000, the fourteen other European Union Member States imposed so-called sanctions on Austria, thus protesting the inclusion of the Freedom Party in the Austrian government. (The so-called sanctions were eventually lifted on 12 September 2000.) However, the new government's program contained a provision that the search for a solution to the slave and forced labor issue should be initiated immediately. With only five days in office, Austrian Federal Chancellor Wolfgang Schüssel announced in his inaugural speech to the Austrian Parliament that the former president of the Austrian National Bank (the Austrian Central Bank), Maria Schaumayer, had agreed to act as special representative for these negotiations.

When she officially began her work on 15 February 2000, Dr. Schaumayer announced that she would like to find a genuinely Austrian solution, which would take into account the specificities of the Austrian situation. She said that it would be her intention to suggest to the Austrian federal government and the Austrian Parliament the creation of an Austrian fund which would make disbursements directly to the victims and would seek to ensure that the payments reach the victims in full. Given the provisions of the Austrian State Treaty of 1955, which relieved Austria of all future reparations, as well as the lack of continuity between Austrian companies and the enterprises of the Nazi regime, Schaumayer also declared that future payments by the envisaged Austrian fund would be made as a voluntary gesture and not out of legal obligations.

At this point, the German chief negotiator Count Otto Lambsdorff had already reached an agreement between the United States, Germany, Central and Eastern European countries, lawyers, companies, and victims' foundations. A foundation would be created which would deal with slave and forced labor as well as restitution issues and which would receive contributions of DM 5 billion each from the German government and German industry. Although the agreement was reached on 17 December 1999, it took until July 2000 for the relevant law to pass the German Parliament.

Meanwhile, the so-called "sanctions" on Austria did not make the task of Dr. Schaumayer any easier. Her activities were under constant scrutiny by the media and by the international community. Very quickly, though, everybody who saw her at work became convinced of the integrity and seriousness of her intentions. Dr. Schaumayer was certainly the ideal choice for the position of Austria's chief negotiator. Her own family was a victim of the Nazis. In addition, she enjoyed an extraordinarily high reputation within the Austrian business community and in the Austrian public.

Although she never left any doubt about her party affiliation with the Christian Democratic People's Party, she was highly esteemed by all political parties in Austria.

However, there were a series of difficulties which Dr. Schaumayer had to overcome at the outset. Most of all, it was necessary to communicate to the Austrian public and to the business community why Austria should eventually make payments to the survivors of slave and forced labor. In a recent article, Ambassador Ernst Sucharipa, Austria's special envoy for restitution issues, stated: "The unifying element after 1945 was to have survived the National Socialist regime and to be able to build a free and independent state. The responsibility for the crimes committed were entirely attributed to the 'Third Reich,' which had perished. Furthermore, not all who were spared persecution by the Nazis were on the side of the perpetrators; many rightfully saw themselves as victims of a war for which they were not guilty."[4] Present-day Austrian companies, as mentioned before, felt even less responsible for the crimes committed by the Third Reich.

On the other hand, Austria as a nation had embarked on a major *soul-searching effort* in the course of and after the presidency of former U.N. Secretary General Kurt Waldheim. In several speeches Austrian leaders—most notably Chancellor Franz Vranitzky in 1991, Federal President Thomas Klestil in 1994 and Chancellor Wolfgang Schüssel in 2000—officially acknowledged Austria's active involvement in the Nazi regime. As President Klestil said in his historic speech in Jerusalem, "we Austrians recognize that an acknowledgment of the full truth was long overdue. We know full well that all too often we have spoken of Austria as the first state to have lost its freedom and independence to National Socialism and far too seldom of the fact that many of the worst henchmen in the Nazi dictatorship were Austrians."[5] As a result of several years of debate, public opinion swayed. An ever-increasing number of Austrians were prepared to support additional restitution and compensation efforts. A majority also spoke out in favor of payments to former slave and forced laborers.

Let me now turn to the negotiating process for Austrian payments to former slave and forced laborers, which showed a number of peculiarities: From the outset, Dr. Schaumayer had insisted that the slave and forced labor issue should be kept separate from the more complex restitution efforts. This approach was only logical, given the fact that Austria had already carried out a large number of restitution measures in the years and decades immediately following World War II, among them seven restitution laws and other measures, such as pension payments and health programs for former victims. This is why U.S. Deputy Secretary of the Treasury Stuart Eizenstat rightly spoke of "gaps and deficiencies in restitution laws,"[6] which should be finally settled in the Austrian restitution negotiations. Also, Secretary Eizenstat was disturbed by eleven transatlantic plenary sessions during the German negotiations, which had resulted in controversies between the organizations representing restitution claims and those who spoke on behalf of victims of slave and forced labor, since the German foundation covers both issues.

One should not underestimate the role of U.S. class action lawyers in bringing about the negotiations on compensation for slave and forced laborers in the first place, particularly in Germany. However, some—and especially one of them—certainly overstretched their demands vis-à-vis Austria and Austrian companies, which was not helpful in the long run, resulting in adverse reactions by an otherwise favorably disposed Austrian public. Other lawyers, though, were constructive in their approach and were helpful in the search for legal solutions to class actions pending in U.S. courts, paving the way for quicker payments to the victims.

A great asset for the Austrian negotiations was the good will which Dr. Schaumayer had created from the first moment of her work in her relationship with the governments of the Central and Eastern European countries from where the majority of slave and forced laborers originated. They were soon convinced that Dr. Schaumayer was ready to make an extra effort to meet most of their demands and to quickly reach a conclusion in the negotiations for bilateral agreements, which should form the basis for the payments by Austria. The Central and Eastern European countries consider the Austrian Reconciliation Fund Law to be fair and generous. Austria included not only forced laborers in industry, but also those who had to work in agriculture. In addition, Austria decided to make payments to children who were deported onto the territory of present-day Austria along with their parents and to mothers who were forced to give birth under most horrible conditions in so-called maternity homes. As soon as a victim's application for compensation has been approved, Austria's one-time payments are disbursed at once and in full. Victims who are already registered in partner organizations of the Austrian Reconciliation Fund do not have to apply again. Applications from the partner organizations of the fund in Belarus, the Czech Republic, Hungary, Poland, Russia, and Ukraine are approved according to lists which the partner organizations submit to the fund in Vienna.

Whereas legal closure has not yet been reached in the field of restitution (there are still two lawsuits pending in U.S. courts), the Reconciliation Fund has already made payments to more than 28,000 slave and forced laborers of a total estimated number of 150,000. Again, the separation of the forced labor and restitution issues proved positive as the payments to the victims of slave and forced labor were not held up. Nevertheless, some restitution payments are already being disbursed. The Austrian National Fund has been entrusted to make lump sum payments to surviving victims whose apartments, small business leases, household property, and personal valuables and effects had been Aryanized. The fund has started its payments earlier this year, with each victim receiving US $7,000.

The speedy conclusion of the negotiations on the bilateral agreements with the United States and the Central and Eastern European countries would certainly not have been possible without negotiators on each side who were very much aware of the historic dimension of the undertaking. Deputy Secretary of the Treasury Stuart Eizenstat played a very important role as a mediator between all sides. In Austria, the passing of the Reconciliation Fund Law by unanimous vote in both houses of Parliament was proof of the broad national consensus on this issue. The highest representatives of Austria, Austrian Federal President Thomas Klestil, the President of the Austrian Parliament, Heinz Fischer, Austrian Federal Chancellor Wolfgang Schüssel and Vice-Chancellor Susanne Riess-Passer all contributed to this national effort. Last but not least, Austrian companies have to be commended for their contributions to the Reconciliation Fund. A considerable number of companies, which had not existed during World War II, affiliated themselves with the fund in a gesture of solidarity.

Dr. Schaumayer summed up the ratio of the Austrian Reconciliation Fund when she stated at the concluding ceremony of the negotiations on 24 October 2000 in Vienna:

> The establishment of the Austrian Reconciliation Fund is also an act of historical accountability. The twentieth century was one of deep division, fraught with horrors, but in its later second half also filled with hopes which opened up the prospect of a peaceful future. It is within this perspective that we must consider the question why there should be voluntary payments from an Austrian Reconciliation Fund although, indisputably, an Austrian state did not exist during the years of National Socialism. The conviction that, even though Austria does not bear attributable responsibility as a state for the blatant injustice committed during those times, it is befitting for us to assume moral responsibility as a consequence of these events, is shared by a large majority of the Austrian population. . . .
>
> Not only in Austria, but also in other countries, the following question has been and still is raised: What does the generation of today have to do with the horrors of the past? I believe that this generation should keep in mind that it is a generation of heirs—heirs of good as well as of evil. Without forced laborers in agriculture, there would have been far greater hunger during the years of the war and many a child would not have been born or have survived. Without the former forced laborers, Austria would have lacked the preconditions for spurring a boom in its tourism industry soon after it had regained its freedom. Even the Nazi armaments industry, though focused on destruction, left not only ruins in its wake, but also propelled Austria forward in its development into an industrialized country, so that with peace regained and the help of the U.S. Marshall Plan, we were able to achieve prosperity more rapidly.[7]

With the creation of the Reconciliation Fund, the Austrian government, Austrian businesses and industry, and the Austrian people have righted a wrong at the end of a century which saw the horrors of two world wars: the victims of forced and slave labor, who had to work on the territory of today's Austria, finally received appropriate compensations for their sufferings.

Notes

1. This statement is based on a comprehensive article published by the author in May 2001: "Der Versöhnungsfonds – Österreichs Leistungen an ehemalige Sklaven- und Zwangsarbeiter des NS Regimes," in *Österreichisches Jahrbuch für Politik 2000* (Vienna: Verlag für Geschichte und Politik, 2001); (Munich: Oldenbourg Wissenschaftsverlag, 2001), 193 – 242.

2. Statement to the Austria Press Agency on 3 September 2001 (APA report # 0468).

3. Florian Freund und Bertrand Perz, "Die Zahlenentwicklung der ausländischen Zwangsarbeiter und Zwangsarbeiterinnen auf dem Gebiet der Republik Österreich 1939 – 1945," Gutachten im Auftrag der Historikerkommission der Republik Österreich, Vienna, 24 January 2000; Mark Spoerer, "Schätzung der Zahl, der im Jahr 2000 überlebenden Personen, die auf dem Gebiet der Republik Österreich zwischen 1939 und 1945 als Zwangsarbeiter und Zwangsarbeiterinnen eingesetzt waren," Gutachten für die Historikerkommission der Republik Österreich, Stuttgart, 23 January 2000; available only in German on the website of the Austrian Historical Commission at www.historikerkommission.gv.at.

4. Ernst Sucharipa, "Die Rückkehr der Geschichte," in *Europäische Rundschau, Vierteljahreszeitschrift für Politik, Wirtschaft und Zeitgeschichte*, 29.3 (2001): 72 – 73; translation by the author.

5. Speech by Austrian Federal President Dr. Thomas Klestil before the Knesset on 15 November 1994, published in *Austrian Information*, newsletter of the Austrian Press and Information Service, Washington, D.C., vol. 47, no. 11 (1994): 2.

6. See remarks of Stuart E. Eizenstat, deputy secretary of the treasury and special representative of the president and secretary of state for Holocaust issues at the signing ceremony of the Austrian Reconciliation Fund, Vienna, 24 October 2000; published by the U.S. embassy in Vienna at http://www.usembassy-vienna.at/rest2.html.

7. Unpublished English translation of the remarks by Dr. Maria Schaumayer at the signing ceremony of the Austrian Reconciliation Fund, Vienna, 24 October 2000; see Eichtinger, "Der Versöhnungsfonds."

The Austrian Life Insurance Sector and the Nazi Regime

Dieter Stiefel

Generally, businessmen are not very interested in history. This is also true for Austria. Especially in the last decade, its business world was preoccupied with the future: with the developing markets in the former Eastern bloc countries, with globalization and the challenges of the new economy, with the integration into the European Union and the preparation for a common currency. Thus, many Austrian companies were more than surprised when all of a sudden, like a ghost out of the grave, they were confronted with financial claims of sixty years ago.

For future historians it will be most exciting to look at the protocols of board meetings of our time. Generally, the leading management did not really know how to handle the political as well as moral questions that arose from such claims. The term *morality* cannot be found in a business administration textbook. This does not mean that business management is immoral, but morality is seen as a function of the political and legal framework in which business activities are embedded. Business administration itself deals with efficiency, productivity, and profit, with the economic functioning of a company and not with ethical questions. It was not even clear which department had to deal with this matter of financial claims and in most cases the responsibility remained with the head of the company. Thus, it is not surprising that various European companies reacted quite differently: some asked historians to look into their past, opening their archives to historical research and—like the *Allianz* company in Munich—even creating a new archive; others engaged business consultants and lawyers and spent a lot of money to find out if there were any legal obligations or financial consequences of such claims; others simply wanted "to wait and see" or to know how much it would cost to get rid of the problem.

One question keeps recurring in the discussion about the role of big business during the Nazi regime: How free were leading businessmen in their decisions and actions? In fact, this question can also be asked in view of the recent compensation payments. Alfred D. Chandler characterizes today's market-system as "managerial capitalism."[1] In most companies, ownership and management are not identical any more. The managers, even if they understand themselves as entrepreneurs, are simply salaried employees. They do not work with their own money, but with that of other people. They are not allowed to make large payments out of moral considerations. The shareholders and the customers—if they participate in the success of the company, as in the insurance business—could hold the managers legally responsible if they exceeded their competence. The current shareholders, who are usually not the same as those of sixty years ago, did not understand that they should be held financially responsible for someone else. The argument that it was still the same company could not be accepted, because all legal claims had been taken care of. Austrian Holocaust claims either had lapsed or had been settled in one way or the other a long time ago. In addition, the business world shared the widespread feeling that the claims against the companies were quite unfair. After all, the injustices were done by the Nazi state and if there was still some responsibility, it should be one of the general public and not of the private industry. The managers would have agreed that, as part of the public and as tax payers, they might still have an obligation, but not as leaders of their companies.

Naturally, a company deals with a problem within the logic of business administration, and Holocaust claims are no exception. To begin with, Holocaust claims could affect a firm's business with the United States; in general, though, they were seen as a matter of public image and public relations. For Austria, the first argument should not be exaggerated: There are only a few companies, as for example the *Creditanstalt*, for which the American market is of considerable importance. Generally, 40% of Austrian products are exported to Germany and only 4% to the United States. In the context of Austrian-German business relations the question of Holocaust claims becomes even more complicated since a good part of Austrian industry is owned by German companies and the headquarters already negotiated a general solution. In the insurance business this was true for *Allianz* and *Generali*, which were part of the "International Commission on Holocaust Era Insurance Claims" (ICHEIC). This commission tried to find a solution for the entire German insurance sector, including its Austrian subsidiaries, which were expected to pay their share. Thus, since business relations with the United States and Germany could be disregarded in this matter, the argument of the public image was decisive. The government—and the media—wanted Austrian businesses to be involved in the final settlement of restitution and compensation. Even if Austria was legally accepted as the first victim of Nazi Germany, it was politically not possible to ignore its historical obligation after Germany and other countries accepted the necessity of additional payments. It was the pressure of the government on the industry, either directly or through the chambers of commerce, which convinced Austrian companies that they, too, had to do something.

In this context, the Association of Austrian Insurance Companies acted in the interests of its members and initiated a historical study—conducted by the author—about the Austrian insurance industry during the time of National Socialism. The initiative of the Association had the advantage that the research did not concentrate on one company alone but included all Austrian insurance companies which had been active in 1938. The main question, of course, was what happened with the life insurance policies of the Jewish population. For a better understanding of this question it was necessary to look at the economic, political, and legal framework of the insurance industry between the 1930s and the 1960s. The question of Jewish life insurance policies had to be embedded into the dramatic development of this sector, starting with the Great Depression and the breakdown of the *Phoenix Life Insurance* in 1936, then the takeover of Austrian life insurance companies by their German competitors in 1938 and the losses during the war, and finally the reconstruction and restitutions after1945. The study had to consider the general economic and political development of the insurance industry and the way discrimination, confiscation, and restitution was practiced during that period of time. As life insurance is always a standardized mass product—which is why statistics play such an important role—it was not the aim of the study to look at specific insurance policies or companies. This had to be done by the individual insurance companies themselves, but the study would give them a profound background about what generally happened in their field of business during the Nazi era.

Before the start of this project, there were long discussions between the author, the Association, and the different insurance companies involved. The companies were more or less in the same situation as a person consulting a doctor. Of course, they wanted to hear the good news that they were absolutely healthy and in good condition. On the other hand, they also wanted to hear the truth. It was not possible to hide the troubles forever and it was better to get a clear picture in time to solve the problem. Thus, the companies finally agreed to cooperate, to open their archives, and to take no influence at all on the outcome of the study.

The practice of using historical research for private industry has been much criticized and the objectivity of the outcome often doubted. We know that in legal disputes every side has its experts who seek to prove the validity of their arguments. One of the lawyers involved in the Holocaust negotiations said to the author that he knew no objectivity, only arguments which strengthened his case. This cynical argument did not take into account that the independence of the historical research about the insurance companies was not only guaranteed by contract, but also by the conditions in which this work had to be done. The first control mechanism was the academic standing of the researcher. His work had to meet the standards of the scholarly community, of which he wanted to be a respected member. In addition, several other researchers were working more or less on the same topic. These control mechanisms held true not only for insurance commissions in different European countries like the Netherlands, France, or Switzerland and for companies like *Allianz* or *Volksfürsorge*, but also for the research which was initiated by the "International Commission on Holocaust Era Insurance Claims" (ICHEIC), which included Austria as well. The study also profited from the help and criticism by the members of the Austrian Historical Commission. The work was intellectually quite satisfactory because it led to a professional discussion and cooperation, which normally is quite rare among Austrian historians. Thus, the way to an independent and objective research study was paved, eased by the cooperation with other historians and the research already conducted by the organizations of Jewish claimants.

Still, the study was a commissioned work, based on a contract (which is published in the annex of the book that contains the findings of this study[2]). This had several consequences. The positive ones were that not only was the author paid for his work, but there were also sufficient financial means for a research team to look for documents in archives all over the world. Thus, the research included not only archives in Austria and Germany, but also in London, Washington, and Moscow. In addition, whenever a technical or legal question arose, a leading insurance mathematician or lawyer was at hand to give the necessary professional information. It was also of tremendous help that a leading member of the Association with profound historical knowledge was available, who acted as a contact person and "buffer" between the research team and the insurance companies. These resources made for a working condition to which historians are generally not accustomed. The greatest disadvantage or challenge was the pressure of time, another condition with which historians are normally not confronted. The "customer" wanted results as soon as possible, but historical research is very time consuming. Nevertheless, a compromise was found: the manuscript for this project was to be finished within two years. The positive side of this time pressure was that it reflected the general interest in the outcome of the work. People were impatiently awaiting the results, which is not always the case with historical research. The short time period had also the advantage that a first draft of the manuscript could be presented in the final phase of the negotiations on Holocaust era assets between Austria and the United States. The author had the honor to give a summary of the study on two occasions during the negotiations: to the representatives of the governments in attendance, as well as to the Jewish organizations and the lawyers. One walks a thin line presenting a historical work when a dispute like the one on Holocaust era assets is going on. There was criticism, of course, as there were different points of view, but generally it was quite satisfactory to see that the quality of the historical work was accepted by every side.

Finally, the study—a short summary of which follows below—formed the basis on which the Austrian insurance industry decided to participate in the payments for the restitution of Holocaust era assets. The German saying "*Der Teufel liegt im Detail*" ("The devil hides in the detail") is particularly true for this subject. Everyone interested in the topic should have a closer look at the publication of the study, which includes a thirty-page summary in English.[3] The historical research made quite clear that by far the greatest part of Jewish life insurance policies in Austria had been settled and that the number of unclaimed policies could only be small. Still, the Austrian insurance industry has contributed $25 million to the Austrian Compensation Fund (*Entschädigungsfonds*). This is regarded as an act of solidarity and even insurance companies which were only founded in the 1980s have paid their share into the fund.

The Jewish Life Insurance Policies

The confiscation of life insurance policies during the Nazi regime was only one aspect of the persecution of Jews, other minorities, and opponents of the regime. In order to enable the Third Reich to take economic action against Jews and "mixed-blood Aryans" (*versippte Arier),* all who had assets of more than 5,000 Reichsmark (RM) were obliged to submit a "List of assets held by Jews as of 27 April 1938" to the Property Office (*Vermögensverkehrsstelle*) before 30 June 1938. This obligation to register their assets applied to all Jews in the Third Reich. In Austria, 47,768 registrations were submitted. The number of life insurance policies registered in this way was 20,815, valued at RM 50,656,800, of which RM 49,142,100 were registered by Jews and RM 1,514,700 by "mixed-blood Aryans." Accordingly, life insurance policies made up 2.48% of the total assets registered. 90% of these life insurance policies were registered in Vienna, 2% were accounted for by Austrian Jews who lived abroad or in the Old Reich, and 8% by Jews living in the Austrian federal provinces.

Total population of Austria in 1934	6,759,062
Jewish population in 1934	191,481
Percentage of Jewish citizens	2.8%
Number of life insurance contracts:	
Total number for Austria in 1936	1,472,184
Jewish-held policies in 1938 (Property Office, 1938)	20,185
Share of Jewish-held policies	1,4%
Jewish-held policies in 1938 (ICHEIC, 2000)	14,562
Jewish-held policies in 1938 (Collection Agency, 1958)	14,886
Share of Jewish-held policies	1.0%
Total amount of life insurance contracts:	
Total number for Austria in 1936	RM 1,222.1 million
Average amount of a life insurance contract per person:	
Total for Austria in 1936	RM 830
Total for Austria in 1939	RM 867
Average cash surrender value per life insurance policy:	
1936 – Austrian portfolios	RM 235
1937 – *Österreichische Versicherungs AG* (former *Phoenix Life Insurance* company)	RM 739
1938 – Jewish-held policies acc. to ICHEIC	RM 2,769
1938 – Jewish-held policies acc. to calculations of research study	RM 2,735
1938 – Jewish-held policies acc. to Property Office	RM 2,434

In 1938, in the wake of persecution of Jews, two major changes in life insurance contracts occurred:

- changes initiated by Austrian Jews themselves, as a consequence of political and economic discrimination (surrender, exemption from contributions, policy loans, and cessions);
- changes made directly by the German Reich authorities.

From 1938 onwards, cash surrender was by far the most frequent way to terminate life insurance contracts held by Austrian Jews. In most cases, the Jews were no longer in a position to pay their insurance premiums on account of economic discrimination, revocation of professional licenses, and so on. In many cases—especially in the case of Jewish emigrants—cash surrender was necessary to pay discriminatory taxes such as the Flight Tax (*Reichsfluchtsteuer*). In Germany, 67% of Jewish life insurance policies were redeemed, and in only 17% of the cases premium payments were suspended.[4] Ultimately, however, most of these policies were redeemed as well. Since 67% of the Jewish population of Austria emigrated and their life insurance contracts were all terminated, this percentage of redeemed life insurance policies seems to be the same for Germany and Austria. The second kind of change in insurance contracts held by Jewish policyholders was direct confiscation by the state authorities. In practice, the attachment of endowment insurances in connection with compulsory execution to meet tax liabilities was of considerable importance. The Nazi regime did not, at first, dare to pass a law which would terminate all Jewish insurance contracts, since it feared that foreign courts would then attach German assets abroad.

The peak of discriminatory legislation in respect of Jewish assets in the Third Reich was reached with Regulation Number Eleven (*11. Verordnung zum Reichsbürgergesetz*), which took effect on 11 November 1941. It determined that Jews who had their ordinary residence abroad were deprived of their German citizenship and their assets reverted to the German Reich. This measure did not only apply to emigrants but also to concentration camps deportees. Regulation Number Thirteen (*13. Verordnung zum Reichsbürgergesetz*) of 1 July 1943 further provided that after the death of a Jew his assets also reverted to the Reich. In keeping with Regulation Number Eleven, Jewish assets had to be reported, on pain of punishment, to the *Oberfinanzpräsident* Berlin within six months of the forfeiture. The insurance company owed the Reich the cash surrender value as determined at the stipulated time, plus 4% interest on arrears, calculated from 31 December 1941. The insurance companies did, however, not receive any lists of deported persons. All in all, Austrian insurance companies thus paid an amount of RM 7.917 million for seized policies directly to the German Reich.

Considering the circumstances created by the persecution, cash surrender was the most favorable solution for the insurance companies although it did not offer them any advantages. Since Jewish Austrians generally held insurance policies that exceeded the Austrian average by three to four times, the insurance companies lost their best clients. It is evident that insurance contracts that run, without interruption, for an entire life are of greatest advantage, both to the company and to the policyholder. Cash surrenders, though, at least resulted in a "withdrawal profit." The withdrawal profit is regulated by the terms and conditions of a specific insurance contract, as approved by the supervisory authority; it may differ considerably from company to company. It does not constitute a directly distributable profit but a surplus in the final account, which is entered as earnings in the final account pool. On the other hand, a cash surrender also generates expenses and lapse losses because:

- the costs of the conclusion of the contract are calculated over the entire life of the contract;
- a premature termination changes the risk distribution and the life of portfolio investments;

- and a premature termination involves additional work, which has to be remunerated.

Nevertheless, an unequivocal answer to the question of withdrawal profits is impossible. While it may be possible, in spite of the differences between the many contractual terms and conditions of the individual insurance companies, to roughly determine the withdrawal profit, it is impossible to say precisely whether and to what extent the insurance companies made a profit on the mass terminations of Jewish insurance policies. Too many different costs were incurred depending on the type and life of the insurance contracts and too many different insurance companies were involved.

Profits may also have been generated if the policies, seized according to Regulation Number Eleven, were not paid out before the end of the Nazi era. In such cases, the premium reserves of these policies were left with the enterprise, which could use them for their operations, at least up to 1945. Since all Jewish policies were generally deemed terminated by Regulation Number Eleven as of 31 December 1941, they involved no further risk and thus no further activity on the part of the insurance company. After the war, these reserves were lost, by and large. In order to determine a company's liabilities, Jewish insurance claims had to have been filed by 1955, when the Insurance Reconstruction Act came into existence; otherwise they were forfeited. The adoption of the Insurance Reconstruction Act, however, meant that the Republic of Austria committed itself to replenish the reserves for the insurance portfolios. "Unclaimed" insurance policies were therefore not profitable for the insurance companies but rather constituted a saving on the part of the public authorities, since the insurance companies were entitled to government compensation for claimed insurance policies, but not for unclaimed ones.

The restitution measures for life insurance policies depended on the history of these policies before 1945.

- Extant Jewish policies: Domestic insurance portfolios continued to be recognized after 1945, albeit with a 60% devaluation, similar to the arrangements made for cash and bank deposits. In principle, the same practice was adopted with regard to still existing Jewish-held policies. Jewish policies which had been seized but not yet paid out were honored if a restitution order issued by the *Finanzlandesdirektion* (fiscal authority) could be presented. Originally, applications for this had to be filed before 1 March 1948, but the deadline was repeatedly extended. This restitution order lifted the stoppage of payment resulting from the seizure by the German Reich and gave the policyholder an actionable claim. In all cases, however, Jewish claimants had to file an application for restitution.

- Redeemed Jewish policies: Insurance policies for which Jewish policyholders had received payments by way of cash surrender were deemed expired. This was ultimately also accepted by the Jewish organizations.
- Jewish policies surrendered to the German Reich: Similarly, insurance policies which had been seized and paid out individually or collectively in keeping with Regulation Number Eleven were deemed expired, since the insurance companies could not pay twice for a single insurance policy. Even though the laws of the German Reich were contrary to all principles of law, they were enforceable, and indeed enforced, during the Nazi era. The Ministry of Finance expressly stated the following: "In order to forestall any possible doubts, it is herewith stated that the repeal of the Nuremberg Laws does not mean that seizures of life insurance policies by public authorities, in particular seizures in keeping with Regulation Number Eleven, implementing the Reichsbürgergesetz of 25 November 1941, DRGBl [*Deutsches Reichsgesetzblatt*, Reich Law Gazette] I, page 722, are deemed to have been cancelled. Accordingly, payments in respect of such policies are not feasible now and will only become feasible once the relevant legislation has been passed."[5] As early as 1945/46, the Association of Insurance Companies stated that compensation was not to be required from the insurance companies, which were bound by the law at all times, thus also by the laws of the German Reich. Since the injustice had been done by the public authorities, which had also received the money, material and moral responsibility for restitution rested with the public authorities.

A general and definitive solution for all policyholders was found in 1955. In the wake of the Austrian State Treaty, which also resulted in a first settlement of property relations with the Federal Republic of Germany (FRG), the Insurance Reconstruction Act of 1955 was passed. It instructed the insurance companies to draw up, with the financial support of the federal government, a reconstruction balance sheet for the years 1945-54. For this purpose, it was necessary to clarify the question of existing claims. Life insurance contracts concluded before 1 January 1946 were devaluated by 60% and the policyholders had to notify the insurance companies about these contracts. While the Third Restitution Act had expressly suspended prescription for victims of political persecution, the Insurance Reconstruction Act of 1955 envisaged a two-year time limit for all extant insurance claims, which would otherwise be forfeited. This preclusive period was not to be annulled by the Restitution Act. After the expiry date, all rights would be "destroyed" so that nothing of them remained. In order to preclude difficulties, the insurance companies, of their own accord, reserved the right to honor delayed registrations without asking for compensation by the government.

A solution had to be found for the life insurance policies confiscated by the German Reich and paid out to it, especially because the Committee for Jewish Claims against Austria as well as the United States and the United Kingdom exerted pressure in this matter. This was particularly urgent since, under the Hague Programme, the FRG had already concluded an agreement with the Committee for Jewish Claims against Germany. In addition, Article 26 of the 1955 Austrian State Treaty envisaged this type of property settlement. In 1958, thirteen years after the end of the Third Reich, the Federal Act Governing Compensation for Life Insurance Policies Confiscated by the German Reich *(Entschädigungsgesetz)* was adopted. This law did not provide for a revival of claims but rather released the insurance companies of their financial burden, which was now borne by the federal government. The basic idea was that policyholders who had lost their insurance claims through the measures of the German Reich should finally be reinstated in their rights. Individuals whose policies formed part of the domestic portfolio of an insurance company had to notify this provider of their claims, in writing and before 30 June 1959, to the exclusion of further claims. The insurance company then sent a statement of the facts to the appropriate *Finanzlandesdirektion*, which decided the case and issued a notice thereon. The insurance benefit payable to the policyholder was calculated up to the end of premium payments and the subsequent period was regarded as a premium-exempt period; the benefit due was then diminished by 60%, according to the provisions of the Insurance Reconstruction Act.

After the end of the notification period, the Ministry of Finance—in its capacity as supervisory authority—called upon the insurance companies to determine how many applications had been received and what amounts had been approved. By September 1959, 456 of a total of about 1,000 claims had been processed with a positive result, and an amount of 1.4 million Austrian Schillings (ATS) had been paid out. The average amount per policy was thus ATS 3,086. What is most interesting is not the total amount that was restituted, which more or less corresponded to expectations, but the small number of claims actually made. The average surrender values indicate that most of the Jewish victims who took the trouble to file their applications for restitution were those with large amounts insured. The average surrender value according to the property registration of 1938 amounted to RM 2,434 per policy, while the average surrender value paid out under the Indemnification Act (after a 60% devaluation) was more than three times as high, and in the case of some insurance companies, even much higher.

On the basis of the State Treaty of 1955 the Republic of Austria passed the Collection Agencies Act (*Auffangorganisationsgesetz*) of 13 March 1957, which established collection agencies for unclaimed or "heirless" Jewish property claims. The measures taken under the Insurance Reconstruction Act and the Insurance Indemnification Act as well as the activities of the collection agencies legally, and from a statutory viewpoint, put an end to the issue of Jewish-held life insurance policies. The Jewish side was at that time also satisfied with what had been achieved. This was borne out by the much cited statement of the chairman of the Committee for Jewish Claims against Austria, Dr. Nahum Goldmann, and by the approval of Dr. Charles Kapralik of the Jewish Trust Corporation for Germany, who had detailed knowledge of the situation in Austria and found the solutions largely satisfactory.

We based our considerations on the fact that 67% of all Austrian Jews emigrated after the Anschluss of 1938 and most probably terminated their insurance policies themselves. It can, however, be assumed that the number of redeemed policies was even higher. On the one hand, Jews who could afford to emigrate were on the average better off than the overall Jewish population and their wealth also determined the number of life insurance policies held and the amount insured. On the other hand, Jews who were not able to leave the country had to terminate their policies because of economic discrimination. We can thus assume that 70% to 80% of the Jewish-held policies were actually redeemed. In addition, some 15% of the Jewish policies were directly looted by the German Reich, either individually or under Regulation Number Eleven, so that 85% to 95% of Jewish life insurance contracts had been terminated by the end of the war. After 1945, payments were made pursuant to the Restitution Acts. The sum total of these repayments is, however, unknown. Furthermore, payments were also made to the collection agencies so that it cannot be assumed that much was left. Whether there are still "unclaimed" Jewish policies and, if so, how many, cannot be determined with any amount of certainty. What can be determined, however, are individual claims against individual insurance companies.

The payments to Jewish policyholders were in accordance with the changes to which life insurance contracts were generally subject after 1938. In general terms, restitution measures were therefore based on first determining the amount of the property held in 1938, then applying to that amount the general currency measures of the Nazi era, and finally taking into account the effects of the currency and insurance laws after 1945. As a matter of principle, no valorization of restitutions was contemplated. In the case of real property, such as land, buildings, and business enterprises, this was frequently advantageous to the injured party; in the case of assets in the form of bank deposits or insurance contracts, though, the effect was disastrous due to the depreciation of the currency.

Notes

1. Alfred D. Chandler, *The Visible Hand. The Managerial Revolution in American Business* (Cambridge: Harvard University Press, 1977).

2. Dieter Stiefel, *Die österreichischen Versicherungen und die NS-Zeit: wirtschaftliche Entwicklung, politischer Einfluß, jüdische Polizzen* (Vienna: Böhlau Verlag, 2001).

3. Ibid.

4. Gerald Feldman, *Die Allianz und die deutsche Versicherungswirtschaft 1933-1945* (Munich: Beck, 2001), 301; also published in English as *Allianz and the German Insurance Business, 1933-1945* (Cambridge, U.K.: Cambridge University Press, 2001).

5. Schreiben des Bundesministeriums für Finanzen (Dr.Hartenau) an den Verband der Versicherungsanstalten Österreichs, 10 January 1946, *Der Anker* archives.

Private Commissions

Oliver Rathkolb

Private Industry and Banking Commissions and the Holocaust Era Assets Debate

After a few years time lag, the end of the cold war in 1989/1990 initiated a boom of historical commissions and projects conducting new and extensive research on forced and slave labor during the Nazi regime as well as on the role of banks and insurance companies in Nazi looting of property owned by Jews and other victims of the Nazis. Legal debates concerning restitution or compensation payments (including heirless assets) of European firms ended, however, in only two court settlements—the large Swiss Bank and the small Bank Austria settlements, the latter being finalized as late as 2001. These settlements were made in addition to three significant bilateral agreements between the U.S. and Germany, Austria and France, which were concluded in 2000 during the last days of the Clinton administration and concerned both forced labor issues as well as non-restituted or non-compensated Nazi looted property. They were designed to settle a number of class action lawsuits against the *Deutsche Bank* and the *Dresdner Bank*, as well as Austrian companies like *Voest Alpine Stahl AG* in Linz and Steyr and other German, Austrian, and French banks and companies.

Since the 1996 class action lawsuit against the Swiss banks by New York lawyer Ed Fagan, both state and corporate resources were made available in order to finance large-scale historical accounts and studies. This unexpected boom for public and private funding of historical research started with a public initiative, the establishment of a nine-member "Independent Expert Commission on Switzerland in the Second World War," headed by Jean-François Bergier and institutionalized by the Swiss Parliament in late 1996. Altogether, fifty researchers worked for this commission, which finalized its work in late 2001.

This prototype of a commission—handling "hot historical topics from the Nazi past"—soon multiplied into eighteen state-funded commissions. They were established in late 1998 in Austria as well as in France, the

Netherlands, Sweden, Norway, Spain, Estonia, Lithuania, and other countries outside Europe such as the United States, Argentine, and Brazil in order to analyze the value of looted property from 1938-1945 and the amount of restitution and compensation after 1945. In Germany, only company-funded commissions were engaged in research (among others *Bertelsmann* Publishers, *Commerzbank*, *Deutsche Bank*, *Dresdner Bank*, *Degussa* (precious metals), *Allianz* (insurance),[1] *BASF* (chemicals), *Diehl* (mechanical engineering), *Ford* (automobiles), *Hochtief* (construction), *Höchst* (chemicals), *Friedrich Krupp* (coal mining), *Lufthansa* (civil aviation), and *General Motors* (automobiles). In Austria, historians worked on the savings bank *Postsparkasse*, the steel combine *Voest Alpine Stahl AG Linz*, *Verbund* (a state-owned Austrian electrical utility holding company), and the *Lenzing AG* (viscose and paper). The Austrian insurance industry commissioned the economic historian Dieter Stiefel to investigate wartime insurance activities on Austrian territory.[2] Research on the *Dorotheum*, the state-owned traditional Austrian auction house, is still being conducted by Stefan Lütgenau and Alexander Schröck, since a previous report by an inexperienced historian was not accepted by the Austrian Historical Commission. The *Dorotheum* had whitewashed a huge amount of assets of Jewish owners in 1938-1945. Lütgenau and Schröck, who published the first empirical study on slave labor in the construction industry of *TEERAG ASDAG (Asphalt und Dachdeckungs AG)*,[3] have been commissioned to produce a completely new study to be finished in March 2003.

Austria has been very active, particularly in the field of looted art, and even passed laws—both on the national and provincial level—allowing for the restitution of state-owned art and the establishment of an expert advisory commission. From time to time, media reports as well as detailed unpublished reports appear, but no academic results have been published yet. (Recently, at the request of the Green party in the Vienna provincial government, a report concerning looted artwork in the *Historisches Museum der Stadt Wien* was declassified).

New Sources and Hidden Company Archives

Already at this point it is fair to argue that a significant number of primary sources has been discovered in the semi-archival deposits of banks and companies as well as museums. Although these sources are in many cases highly fragmentary, in total they constitute much more than what has previously been available for historical research. In addition, archives in Eastern Central Europe and Russia, which had been closed or had limited access, were found to contain materials from the Nazi period. Due to general disinterest in thorough historical documentation, combined with underlying fears of facing the "truth" with respect to the Nazi period, most of the banks and companies involved in the recent legal disputes rarely established professionally structured archives that also contained materials from outside sources. The *Creditanstalt-Bankverein*, for instance, has a particularly fragmentary collection because, in the mid-1970s, it destroyed a large portion of its documents. In the 1980s, the bank even discontinued an academic research project, started by Eduard März in 1973, and never approached a professional archival solution beyond the level of board meeting minutes. The former *Österreichische Länderbank*'s documentation is even more fragmentary, whereas the former *Zentralsparkasse* in Vienna, now part of the *Bank Austria* group, still has a large deposit of archival documentation. The *Voest Alpine Stahl AG* in Linz forgot about the existence of the largest collection of documents that was stored in the cellar of an anti-aircraft tower and contained more than thirty thousand personnel records of forced labor and German workers. The personnel records of the *Volkswagen AG*, on the other hand, have been completely destroyed, as were those of most Austrian and German companies.

An important issue that needs to be discussed publicly concerns the future availability of these sources for further research and whether the companies and banks involved will keep a historical department after research for the legal battles has been completed. The director of the Austrian State Archives, Lorenz Mikoletzky, used the new Archival Law (which was a first result of the Holocaust Era Assets Debate) and decreed more than seventy-four private and public company, banking, and insurance archives as *denkmalgeschützt*, which means that the companies are not allowed to destroy documents from the period of 1933-1967.

The author himself headed three commissions in Austria (*Postsparkasse, Verbund*—the latter together with Florian Freund—and *Voest Alpine Stahl AG* Linz) and is a member of the three-member committee (together with Gerald Feldman and Theodor Venus) nominated by a U.S. court for the settlement with the *Bank Austria* group of *Creditanstalt*, former *Länderbank*, and *Zentralsparkasse*. In the following, I shall try to compare the approaches used in these commissions.

An open research effort was designed in 1998 in order to begin a concentrated study of the Nazi past of the Austrian Postal Savings Bank, which had been absorbed by the German Postal Service in 1938. Former clients initiated this research by requesting detailed information about their pre-1945 accounts. They were assisted by both the Wiesenthal Center in Los Angeles and Lord Janner of Braunstone, a former British Labor politician active in Jewish affairs. Max Kothbauer, who then was the CEO of the *Postsparkasse*, was much more interested in an open debate than many other bank managers since he was Chancellor Franz Vranitzky's chief of cabinet during the Waldheim affair.

It seemed appropriate to publish the intermediary research findings online as soon as possible in order to initiate communication with former clients and their heirs. As a result of the publication of the first intermediary report in December 1998—published both in German and English and containing a list of seven thousand names of former account holders (mostly small amounts)—nearly four thousand requests for information have been handled by the *Postsparkasse* and the research team. A second report, again in German and in English, followed in January 2000.

Thus, classical historical research both contributed to the public debate about Holocaust era assets and was, at the same time, transformed by public pressure for more information and transparency. New structures emerged that had to be included in the analysis. The research, which is scheduled for publication in late 2002, represents the first Savings Bank study for the Nazi period in Austria that contains a detailed analysis on the transformation of the continuous expropriation orders after 1938 on the bank and client level, focusing on accounts, security deposits, saving accounts, and blocked accounts. It covers the Nazification of the Savings Bank and the Denazification after the war, as well as the accounts of forced laborers, the "Aryanization" of buildings, and postwar restitution issues surrounding this property.

This approach was the only one in the private sector in Austria that used the Internet and included victims' memories in the research and analysis structure. In general, the small dormant accounts that were looted by the Nazis prior to 1945 and restituted by the *Postsparkasse* (which also contributed a considerable amount to the Austrian Restitution Fund), were not really so important for the surviving clients and their heirs. The documentation of a large correspondence file and the candid historical analysis of the circumstances of Nazi looting and compensation and/or non-compensation after the war were much more important in their symbolic role.

As a result of the *Postsparkasse* study, the *Voest Alpine* asked the author of this article to lead a historians' commission from 1998-2001 to analyze the issue of forced and slave labor. It was clear from the beginning that this independent study would be published, but due to the rather intensive documentation and research work, a more classical communication structure was chosen. Oral history as performed in previous German industry studies seemed insufficient to produce usable results. Therefore, psychologist Karl Fallend was asked to conduct a number of long and intricate narrative interviews with former forced and slave laborers—mostly in the Czech Republic, Poland, the Ukraine, Italy, and Moldavia—in order to obtain subjective viewpoints that would illuminate certain typical personal experiences in a biographical context. These individual life stories, recollections, and insights of Austrians, forced laborers, and concentration camp survivors of the Linz *Hermann Göring Werke* could only be told by means of such interviews. The interviews do not contain random biographical details nor heroic tales, but rather experiences that have long been taboo and extremely traumatic in nature. These are memories that have been buried for more than fifty years, and many of the stories were uttered and heard for the first time, particularly in this amount of detail. The stories address suppression, humiliation, injury and subsequent shame, as well as the different forms of individual and social assimilation.[4]

In addition to a detailed economic historical review, volume I of this study also deals with the economic significance of forced labor under the National Socialist regime and the responsibility of the management. Comprehensive case studies about foreign workers—in particular women, who made up some 10% of the foreign labor contingent, their children, already born in Linz, and the many Greek workers—reconstruct the fate of these workers and deepen the extensive evaluation of the statistics, which contain biographical and work-related information on the twenty-two thousand foreign civilian workers among the forty thousand workers of the Nazi period. The slave labor contingent in the Austrian concentration camp Mauthausen consisted of more than seven thousand people. It is also important to point out that these histories do not end abruptly in 1945, but also deal with the postwar stigmatization in the former Soviet Union and the war crime tribunals against the perpetrators.

A similar report is supposed to be published in 2002, which will contain the results of a smaller study on forced labor and electric power plants, now owned by the *Verbund*. Studies were conducted about the plant of *Ybbs-Persenbeug* in Lower Austria (Christine Örtel and Oliver Rathkolb), the *Draukraftwerke* in Carinthia (Markus Purkhart), the *Ennstalkraftwerke* in Upper Austria (Florian Freund), and the plant of Kaprun in Salzburg (Margit Reiter).[5] This is the first study on the use of forced labor in the building of electric power plants which is based on primary sources. Although the wartime story of Kaprun was known, many significant details have recently been unearthed, and a database has been established to document individual life stories. Previous work on forced and slave labor relied exclusively on statistics and/or individual case studies; this new approach aims at considerably enlarging the empirical base. It is interesting to note, for instance, that *Ybbs-Persenbeug*'s wartime history seemed to be completely forgotten, even though the project was pushed by Adolf Hitler himself due to the location of the power plant near the town of Pöchlarn, which played a role in the Nibelungen saga. *Ybbs-Persenbeug* is a good example of how the Austrian postwar reconstruction covered up this first phase of construction and the use of forced labor during World War II.

The first study on the role of the wartime construction industry, conducted by Stefan Lütgenau and Alexander Schröck, was originally commissioned and financed by *TEERAG ASDAG*.[6] It aimed at reconstructing the fate of Jewish slave laborers, concentration camp inmates, and other forced laborers in the construction industry—both in the *Alpen- und Donaugaue* and outside the country in the German Reich and occupied territories. It makes an important contribution since all studies commissioned by the publicly sponsored Historical Commission will be limited to research about events and activities on current Austrian territory only.

Scholarly Independence and Research Standard

Can these commissions and experts work outside of a contested public, of political or legal pressures? This revises the issue of scholarly independence and research standards, which has even been discussed in the international news media (e.g. *Financial Times*, 22 February 1999; *International Herald Tribune*, 19 February 1999). In Austria, the weekly *Profil* debated the issue as well (22 March 1999).

Because private funds are a significant financial source, efforts to exclude privately-funded research from the scholarly discourse have not been successful. In Austria, only the *Bank Austria* Commission has been criticized—despite the fact that it is the only privately funded commission established by a court decision as a completely independent committee with a fixed budget. In Great Britain and the U.S., the political scientist Michael Pinto-Duschinsky has received much media attention with his attacks on what he calls the "Selling [of] the Past,"[7] even though his own research on the topic is extremely meager (he has one unpublished paper on "Slave Labor" to his name).

Recently the issue of scholarly independence came up again in the first English publication of the Office of Military Government (OMGUS) Reports on "War Crimes of the *Deutsche Bank* and the *Dresdner Bank*," which have been available in German since 1986. Although these reports contain important but rather incomplete documentation gathered in the first years after 1945, the editor Christopher Simpson praises them as the only purely historical accounts. He thereby tries to minimize the importance of previous historical scholarship published by independent historians from the *Deutsche Bank* and *Dresdner Bank* commissions. Simpson clearly overstates this case.[8]

There are crucial methodological issues at stake here. Are the scope and analytical depth of research in these projects limited by the special court related questions and by the narrow focus on individual businesses, or do they contribute to the advancement of historiography?[9] Here, both the field of economic and that of political contemporary history need to be extensively covered. As far as political history is concerned, the empirical research is "contra-cyclical"—it favors applied history. Trendy gender studies and cultural studies can contribute as well if they abandon their specialized discourse of academic debates inside the ivory tower.

As Gerald Feldman has recently pointed out, "the goal must be to understand how business organizations deal with the problems of political risk and the public sphere cannot be separated from their inner economic logic."[10] Feldman refers again to the example of *Daimler*'s management, which increasingly used forced labor in order to reduce investments in machinery that could be lost during or immediately after the war. This focus on the postwar beginning dominated the decision to use large pools of manpower.

Such a postwar perspective is important—both with regard to methodology and the availability of postwar sources such as investigations and trials, and with regard to continuity. In the case of the former *Hermann Göring Werke* in Linz it should be noted that the German top management was dismissed; on the management level and on the worker level, *Sudetendeutsche* refugees were integrated. One of the inventors of the world famous new LD (*Linz-Donawitz*) production was Herbert Trenkler, a Sudeten German steel expert. The post-1945 workers were partly Volks- and Sudeten Germans forced out of their home territories in 1944/1945. They took over the jobs of the forced laborers who were repatriated.

Business history needs still more research to analyze companies as social organizations in the WWII situation on the national, European, and global level. Here, the new and more empirical studies on forced labor and Aryanization have produced hidden sources that could be used for further analysis.

In order to compare the results of World War II forced labor research in Austria, all privately commissioned studies ought to be published—especially the studies of teams supervised by the economic historian Roman Sandgruber on the *Lenzing Zellwolle AG* (which used female concentration camp inmates from the subcamp of Mauthausen, with a capacity of 565 women at the most) and on the *Böhler Stahl Werke*. By comparing the empirical data, the social dimension can be analyzed more effectively. The percentage of female workers in the steel industry and the number of and reasons for abortions are still being debated.

The use of oral history as a research method has to be reexamined, too, since many projects base some of their analyses on "mass" interviews. A *Daimler-Benz* project by Barbara Hopman and others, for example, has conducted nearly two hundred interviews with surviving forced/slave laborers but gained practically no new information or insights that could not be gathered from primary sources. To be effective, oral history needs to combine intensive interviews with few, carefully selected interviewees and archival research. Personal memories are only reproductions of completely individual perceptions formed in order to cope with a traumatic situation (e.g., deportation and forced labor, often under the age of 18) and to continue a "normal" life after 1945. Business history should abandon the case study approach and place individual analysis in the framework of social, economic, and political history.

Reevaluation of the Decision Making and Responsibility Structure

The documentation and analysis of the Nazi expropriation and looting policies on the "executive" (working) level will lead to a more precise picture of the decision-making process on all levels of business. It will show who, from the CEO on down to the company foreman, dealt with forced laborers and made the day-to-day decisions on how to execute the racist orders from the Nazi regime. We can already recognize a rather large group of managers that were well within the limits of the Nazi orders, albeit their room to maneuver was much larger than previously assumed. As a result of the earlier studies we already know much about the *Überbau* (superstructure) of the Nazi regime concerning Holocaust era assets and forced/slave labor. However, we still need more empirical data on the execution of these policies by "experts" and "administrators." Here, the individual project studies will make a considerable contribution.

An interesting issue is the *continuity of elites* from the Nazi period after 1945—both in banking and industry in Germany and Austria (but also in other European countries, like France). Many business leaders had important executive positions or were CEOs during the war. In Austria, Josef Joham, the CEO of the *Creditanstalt-Bankverein*, continued in his job when the German Bank took over in 1939 and was given considerable power. He had first been installed as CEO by the Christian-Socials in 1936. After the war he was allowed to continue in his job since he had secretly cooperated with the Office of Strategic Services (OSS) and turned over plans and information to prepare for the bombing of industry owned by the *Creditanstalt*. Unlike in Germany, the Allies never thoroughly investigated the Nazi past in Austria. During the Allied administration, Joham was under the special protection of the U.S. government. When he was "interviewed" for the Nuremberg Trial the whole court came to Vienna!

Another example is Walther Kastner. As head of Department C of the *Kontrollbank*, he "administered" more than one hundred of the largest companies looted from their Jewish owners and sold them before 1942. The profit was transferred to the *Reichshauptkasse* in Berlin. After 1945, Walther Kastner became one of the most important "hidden" decision makers and legal experts in banking and industry and even managed some restitution cases. What effect did "continuity" of this type have on historical documentation from the Nazi period and professional research on business history? What effect did a business leader's professional socialization in the Nazi economy have on his peacetime role? In the 1960s, then CEO of the *VÖST Alpine* Walter Hitzinger (who later worked for *Mercedes Benz* in Germany) was a business expert with a Nazi Party background. His first experience as a CEO in wartime industry was to prepare the "centralization" of nationalized state industry in Austria. This proved to be a failure in the late 1970s. Was this decision to centralize in the 1970s influenced by the centralization mania of the Nazi period?

Still, only few experts realize how strong the impact of legal norms from the Nazi area continued to be in Austrian business life after 1945. Other issues are the transformation and continuity of decision-making processes, the control of institutions and culture from the Nazi period into the postwar era, especially in the nationalized industries (many of which were former "German property"). How strongly did these social continuities in the business community influence and change the emerging social partnership in the Second Republic?

To conclude, during recent years a large number of sources and studies focusing on the Nazi period have been introduced into the historical debate of the Austrian economy and business during the 1930s and 1940s. It is now up to the research community to continue and push these new insights into the postwar period. This will deepen our understanding of the social structure of companies during World War II. The business community and business schools have not yet realized how important a deeply rooted knowledge of the past is for modern companies. If nothing else, the Holocaust Era Assets Debate has shaken perceptions such as Henry Ford's idea that "History is bunk."

Notes

1. Gerald Feldmann, *Die Allianz und die deutsche Versicherungswirtschaft 1933-1945* (Munich: C. H. Beck, 2001).

2. Dieter Stiefel, *Die österreichischen Lebensversicherungen und die NS-*Zeit (Vienna: Böhlau Verlag, 2001). For a review of this published report see Hermann Freudenberger's essay in this volume. See also Dieter Stiefel, ed., *Die Politische Ökonomie des Holocaust. Zur wirtschaftlichen Logik von Verfolgung und "Wiedergutmachung,"* (Vienna: Verlag für Geschichte und Politik, 2001).

3. Stefan Lütgenau and Alexander Schröck, *Zwangsarbeit in der österreichischen Bauindustrie: Die Teerag-Asdag AG 1938-1945* (Innsbruck: Studienverlag, 2001).

4. Oliver Rathkolb, ed., *NS-Zwangsarbeit am Standort Linz der Hermann Göring AG Berlin, 1938-1945*, 2 vols. (Vienna: Böhlau, 2001), esp. vol 2. For a review of this study see Hermann Freudenberger's essay in this volume.

5. On Kaprun, see the essay by Margit Reiter in this section of this volume.

6. Lütgenau and Schröck, *Zwangsarbeit.*

7. *Times Literary Supplement*, 23 October 1998.

8. Christopher Simpson, ed., *War Crimes of the Deutsche Bank and the Dresdner Bank. Office of Military Government (U.S.) Reports* (New York: Holmes & Meier, 2002).

9. See the rather "eager" methodological debate on this issue in Lothar Gall and Manfred Pohl, eds., *Unternehmen im Nationalsozialismus* (Munich: Beck, 1998).

10. Gerald Feldmann, "Holocaust Assets and German Business History: Beginning or End?," *German Studies Review* 25 (February 2002): 23-34.

The "Myth" of Kaprun: Forced Labor at the Tauern Power Plant in Kaprun and How Postwar Austria Dealt With It

Margit Reiter

The hydroelectric power plant Kaprun is located amid the massive peaks of the *Hohe Tauern* range of the Austrian Alps in the tiny community of Kaprun in Salzburg. The imposing works that were built at Kaprun in the 1950s were considered in Austria to be *the* symbol of the country's postwar economic and political reconstruction, emblematic of the victory of technology over nature and a source of patriotic pride. The "dark side" of Kaprun, however, has long been ignored in Austria's account of its own history. Only in recent years, first steps have been taken to confront and come to terms with this history, and to begin to deconstruct the "myth" of Kaprun. Thus, individual historians and journalists have shed light on the postwar era,[1] and in February 1999 the *Verbundgesellschaft* (the organization with authority over Austrian electricity production) convened a historical commission to investigate the forced labor used to construct power plants during the Nazi era.[2] The designated subjects of research were those power plants (*Kraftwerke*) that were built during the Nazi era and are today mostly owned by the Austrian *Verbundgesellschaft*: the *Tauernkraftwerk Kaprun* (Salzburg), the *Ennskraftwerke* (Upper Austria, Styria), the *Draukraftwerke* (Carinthia) as well as the *Ypps-Persenbeug* facility, and the *Ernsthofen Transformer Station* (Lower Austria). The Kaprun Power Plant, the focus of my research work for the commission, played a key role in two respects. First, the power plant construction project in the *Hohe Tauern* was quantitatively speaking—both with respect to the size and duration of the project as well as the number of workers it employed—by far the largest undertaking by the energy sector of the so-called *Ostmark*. Furthermore, the project's enormous importance and highly symbolic impact and resonance during the postwar years additionally underscore the significance of Kaprun.

Besides providing an account of the construction project's history, the research work of the commission's staff members was to focus above all on the number of foreign workers employed in Kaprun between 1938 and 1945. Thanks to files coincidentally discovered in the archives of the Salzburg Regional Health Insurance Plan (by which some of the foreign laborers had been covered) as well as material found in the basement of the Kaprun Village Hall, I was able to achieve most of the research objective. The registration data filed with the Community of Kaprun—the project's most basic source material—prove that the number of foreign workers in Kaprun was several times larger than the number employed in other power plant projects. The commission was able to gather the names of over six thousand foreign workers and enter them into our data bank. Besides laborers' names, these sources also provide information on their nationality, age, and, in some instances, the duration of their employment, the name of their employer (construction firm), where they were housed, etc. On the other hand, highly elaborate efforts to reconstruct the actual working and living conditions of the foreign laborers in Kaprun yielded scant success due to the difficult nature of the source material.

The following summary account of forced labor in Kaprun is based on the results of my research in conjunction with the *Verbund* Historical Commission.[3] I have fleshed this out with a brief description and analysis of the political, cultural and symbolic significance of the Kaprun Power Plant in postwar Austria and the "myth" of Kaprun, which is, in my opinion, inseparably connected with the dark history of that undertaking.

Kaprun has a past that goes all the way back to the interwar years. Since the mid-1920s, there had been numerous plans—including some on a truly gargantuan scale—to exploit the hydroelectric potential of the *Hohe Tauern*. Due to the economic crisis of the 1930s, though, none of the competing projects ever came to anything, and it was not until the advent of the National Socialists in 1938 that the idea was taken up again. Immediately following the Anschluss in March 1938, Göring, in a programmatic speech on the economic development of the *Ostmark*, announced the construction of a mighty power plant in the *Hohe Tauern*.[4] Göring did not miss the opportunity to personally preside over the ground-breaking ceremony of the Tauern Power Plant on 16 May 1938. Nazi propaganda provided the following account of the day that was so momentous for the tiny mountain community: Göring entered the village of Kaprun "amidst the crowd's resounding shouts of '*Heil*.'" He "strode to the construction site as the cannon-fire salute reverberated, sirens wailed, and the narrow-gauge railway train moved forward. Then, Hermann Göring took spade in hand and set to work, accompanied by the jubilant cheers of the assembled multitude. A resounding '*Sieg Heil*' to the *Führer* and the songs of the nation ended the impressive commencement of work on the Tauern Power Plant."[5]

This sense of urgency with which the Nazis pressed to get the job underway reveals their great political and economic interest in the Tauern Power Plant, which was conceived as a project that would garner them tremendous prestige. As Göring frankly acknowledged in his speech that day in Kaprun, the interests of the National Socialist economy focused on the *Ostmark*'s unused energy reserves, including unexploited hydroelectric power. The Nazi rulers left no doubt that the Austrian energy sector would be subordinated to the requirements of the German armaments industry and an economy on war footing. In concrete terms, this meant that the planned Tauern Power Plant would be utilized first and foremost to provide energy for the *Altreich*. Despite the fact that plans for the Tauern Power Plant had still not been finalized, the *Alpen-Elektrowerke AG (AEW)*, the corporation created especially to manage the project, was ordered by Göring to get to work "immediately and without delay."[6] According to the construction program, the plant was to be in partial operation within three years, and the time to complete the entire job was estimated at about ten years.

Once the war began, though, the ambitious, large-scale project soon got bogged down and it became impossible to even come close to keeping construction on schedule. The reasons for this delay included the scarcity of building materials, a series of weather catastrophes, and, above all, a shortage of labor. Furthermore, following the outbreak of World War II, when a majority of the male population was called up for service in the *Wehrmacht*, this labor shortage became even more acute. During the entire time construction was underway, the engineers in charge complained about receiving an inadequate contingent of workers from the local labor board because the Kaprun construction project had not been classified as sufficiently "critical to the war effort." As early as February 1939, the director of the Tauern Power Plant, Hermann Grengg, stated that one had to "accept whatever was sent over."[7] Despite tremendous ideological reservations, the prospect of employing foreign laborers was raised at this time. At first, management wanted to take on workers only from Italy and the *Protektorat*, whereby the Italian workers were regarded as the lesser of two evils.

Nevertheless, the percentage of foreign workers rose dramatically, and they soon made up over 90% of the entire Kaprun workforce. In the final analysis, thousands of foreign workers were on the job at this enormous construction site between 1939 and 1945. The actual numbers fluctuated sharply, averaging between 500 and 1,800 workers (depending on the time of year) and reaching a climax in 1944, when approximately 4,000 laborers worked in Kaprun. The data bank of the Historical Commission includes the names of approximately 6,200 foreigners who worked there. Early on, many of them came voluntarily; they believed the promises of the Nazi propaganda and expected good working conditions and high wages. Once the war broke out, though, many of the foreign workers were no longer volunteers; they had been deported from their homelands or were forced to work as POWs.

Over the course of the war, about 20 different nationalities were accounted for:

- a strikingly high number of Poles, Italians, and Frenchmen (approximately 1,000-1,200 each)
- approximately 800 so-called *Ostarbeiter* (Russians and Ukrainians)
- many laborers from Belgium, Slovakia, the *Protektorat* of Bohemia and Moravia, and Yugoslavia (between 200 and 500)
- and approximately 30 (presumably Austrian) Jews, a small number of Bulgarians, Greeks, and Hungarians, and even a handful of Spaniards, Turks, and Armenians.

Among these diverse national and ethnic groups, there was a strict hierarchy that was oriented on the Nazi's racist ideology. Not all foreign workers were treated equally, and they did not all have the same working conditions. On the lowest rung of this ladder were the laborers from Eastern Europe—the so-called *Ostarbeiter*—who were classified as "racially inferior." Russian, Ukrainian, and Polish men—some of them still quite young—had been rounded up and transported from their homelands to do forced labor under unimaginably harsh working conditions in Kaprun. Their average workday was ten to twelve hours long; they were ill-fed and inadequately clothed, had virtually no days off, and received no wages. In contrast to forced laborers in the agricultural sector, for instance, they had hardly any contact with the local populace since they were housed in remote camps, which made it almost impossible for them to leave on their free days. Moreover, they faced many dangers on the high dam construction sites, and many of them were fatally injured on the job. Our sources provide concrete evidence of a total of fifty-six deaths among the foreign workers at the dam construction site in Kaprun from 1939 to 1945; however, the number of unrecorded cases of fatally injured laborers is presumably much higher. The so-called Russian Memorial in Kaprun commemorates some of them: the "87 deceased Soviet citizens," who, according to its inscription, "were driven into suffering and privation by the fascist aggressors, and died far from their native soil."[8] The Russian POWs' situation was, for the most part, even worse; they lived in camps surrounded by barbed wire fences, and Austrian soldiers kept them under strict surveillance while they worked. It was only the liberation by the U.S. Army in May 1945 that put an end to their suffering.

After the war, the American military government took over the AEW as "German property" and placed it under public administration. Some of the Nazi site engineers were fired on the spot, arrested, and sent to American internment camps. Only a couple of years after the end of hostilities, work was resumed and, with financial assistance from the United States, the power plant was completed in the 1950s. The most intensive building phase at Austria's largest construction site was between 1947 and 1955. After three years of work, the massive vaulted wall of the Limberg dam was completed in 1951, and was formally opened with a ceremony attended by President Theodor Körner and many other prominent Austrians. The monumental 120-meter high wall was, at the time, the world's third highest dam. The tremendous publicity campaign surrounding it made Kaprun the optimistic symbol of the economic and political rebirth of Austria from the wreckage of war. In August 1955—the year of the Austrian State Treaty—the work at Kaprun was officially declared to be complete.

At this time—the early 1950s—the "myth" of Kaprun was born. In politics, the media, film and literature, Kaprun was stylized as the symbol of the "reconstruction" of Austria, as an example of the taming of nature by technology, and as a patriotic Austrian community effort. Austrian postwar politicians, like Chancellor Karl Renner, celebrated the power plant as an "accomplishment of the entire people, as an emblem epitomizing the Austrian economy," and proudly took official state guests on tours of this "marvel of mastery over nature."[9] At the site itself, a regular tourist industry developed. Whole busloads of curious sightseers from all over Austria flocked to Kaprun. To this day, it remains an attractive and popular destination for family outings.

In the media, there was ongoing coverage of the progress and special features on the daily life of the workers of Kaprun and the dangers they faced. Special commemorative postage stamps were issued, ad agency copywriters got into the act, and the market was flooded with Kaprun novels and films.[10] These often bore highly evocative, archaic sounding titles as *The Men of Kaprun*, *Kaprun – Tamed Force*, *The Song of Kaprun*, *High above Kaprun*, and *White Gold*.[11]

The image of Kaprun created in literature and the media displayed the following essential features:

1) Kaprun was a man's world—pure and harsh with a distinctly military character—in which women had no place. These "Men of Kaprun," hermetically isolated in the high Alps and facing tremendous dangers, performed hard work for the good of the Austrian people and for the sake of progress.
2) In this male world of Kaprun, there were purportedly no social, regional and political differences or opposing interests. Whether a man was an engineer or a ditch digger, did not matter; all were "comrades." The novel *The Men of Kaprun* by Othmar Lang contains the following passage: "In Kaprun, there weren't any workers who were Carinthians, Styrians, Burgenlanders, Upper Austrians or Salzburgers. No. In Kaprun, there were only Kapruners. . . . Even a man's occupation had

hardly any meaning. Everybody, the masons, the electricians, the engineers . . . the carpenters, the truck drivers, and the mechanics, they were all simply Kapruners. The plant was so powerful that it gave its name to everyone, so powerful that it created a new type of worker."[12] Among this "new type of worker" were the so-called *Baraber* (as the workers in Kaprun were also known), who were proud to be employed as "tiny gears" in a "big operation." Especially because these images were being circulated so shortly after the end of the Third Reich, reference could be made to an extension of the *Volksgemeinschaft* (national community), which was now channeled into an Austrian patriotic collective "We."

3) A third aspect of the Kaprun image was that the war was ever-present. References were continually being made to the war, and war-based metaphors were a staple. The Kaprun construction site became a "theater of battle." Here is another passage from the novel *The Men of Kaprun*: "Kaprun was the scene of a struggle, Kaprun was nearly a war. It wasn't a war between different groups of men. . . . No, here human beings attacked nature, the mountainous landscape, hard rock. With no let-up, the assault persisted and pressed forward. And of course, sometimes the mountains struck back, killing and wounding. It was a struggle, but not a senseless struggle."[13]

These literary examples as well as the detailed and comprehensive media coverage of the time show how the work at Kaprun was portrayed as the continuation of war on a different level. Instead of fighting other human beings, a struggle against nature was now being waged. Finally, one emerges from this conflict as the "victor," since the construction of the power plant is successfully moving forward. In this context, it is also no coincidence that those workers who suffered fatal injuries on the job were sometimes characterized as "fallen" and—similar to the soldiers of the *Wehrmacht*—as having died a "heroic death." On the other hand, the fatalities among the forced laborers were long ignored by the accident statistics.

The "Myth of Kaprun" was a two-fold myth. First of all, the Nazi era was completely ignored for a long time in the Austrian postwar success story of Kaprun. It went unmentioned that construction had already begun during the time of National Socialism and that it was, by no means, necessary to start from scratch; nor was there any mention of the fact that the symbol of Austrian reconstruction had been built on the basis of forced labor and the oppression of thousands of foreign workers. Even when the period of construction during the Nazi era was mentioned, this time was invariably depoliticized or—as, for example, in the novel *Kaprun. Tamed Force* by Kurt Maix—portrayed as a conflict between the "bad Germans" and the "good Austrians."[14] Thus a "re-patriotization" of Kaprun could ultimately take place.

Secondly, the postwar myth of Kaprun did not completely square with the facts. The stylization of Kaprun as a patriotic masterwork was highly questionable due to the fact that key preparatory work had already been done during the Nazi era, which provided the basis to build on after the war. Furthermore, the speedy completion of Kaprun would not have been possible without American economic assistance and the Marshall Plan, since Kaprun was largely financed from Counterpart Funds provided by the European Recovery Program.[15] For a long time—despite this important financial aid from abroad—Austria has had no problems in including the Kaprun Power Plant on the positive side of the ledger in accounting for its own postwar reconstruction.

Nor did the reality of Kaprun have much in common with the idyllic clichés of *The Men of Kaprun*. Particularly in the immediate postwar period, the composition of the workforce was heterogeneous to the extreme. It included released Austrian POWs and returned war veterans, "incriminated" Nazis forbidden to practice their professions and thus unable to find any other kind of work, as well as Socialists and Communists who had survived the concentration camps, and, for a short time, Jewish DPs as well. In those days, Kaprun became a catchment basin for human beings who, for one reason or another, had difficulties reintegrating themselves into postwar society. Once denazification measures had been relaxed, even more Nazis came to Kaprun after being released from the American internment camp in Glasenbach, but the leftist parties also made the effort to mobilize their rank-and-file members and their youth organizations for work in Kaprun.[16] Thus, it certainly comes as no surprise that—in stark contrast to the harmonious, idealized picture that has been painted—there were numerous social and political conflicts in Kaprun. There were wage disputes and strikes, many fatal accidents as a result of inadequate safety precautions, as well as corruption.[17]

From a political perspective, too, the situation was highly explosive; the upshot of the heterogeneous composition of the workforce was political polarization. On the one hand, the leftist parties, and especially the Communists, had tremendous power in Kaprun; on the other hand, the Association of Independents (VdU), whose membership consisted chiefly of former Nazis, was able to achieve major successes at the polls there. In December 1949, the VdU even won the election for seats on the works committee, and in 1951, a VdU member briefly served as chairman of the works committee.[18]

It was not only due to the strength of the VdU that Kaprun was considered a "Nazi stronghold." As a matter of fact, according to police reports, approximately 80% of the workforce in Kaprun in 1948 were former Nazis, although most of them had not been political activists.[19] However, there were also occasional reports in the media about National Socialist intrigues among the engineers and workers, for example, it was claimed that Nazi songs were being sung at the construction sites, or that men would greet one another with "*Heil Hitler*."[20] There is no doubt that Kaprun offered many "incriminated" Nazis the opportunity to reintegrate themselves into postwar Austrian society, and perhaps even to rehabilitate themselves through their work on a shared undertaking for the good of Austria as a whole. The cultural historian Wolfgang Kos has spoken of Kaprun in this context as a "red-white-red purgatory" from which former Nazis could emerge "purified."[21]

I regard Kaprun as a reflection, as a microcosm of postwar Austrian society, and as one single example of the problematic way Austria has dealt with its Nazi past. This also explains why, for decades, the "dark side" of Kaprun—above all, the forced labor during the Nazi era—had no place in the success story of the Second Republic. Hopefully, the commission's research results will facilitate the long-overdue material compensation for those former forced laborers who are still alive.

Notes

1. Wolfgang Kos, *Eigenheim Österreich. Zu Politik, Kultur und Alltag nach 1945* (Vienna: Sonderzahl, 1995); Georg Rigele, "Kaprun. Das Kraftwerk des österreichischen Wiederaufbaus," *Inventur 45/55. Österreich im ersten Jahrzehnt der Zweiten Republik*, ed. Wolfgang Kos and Georg Rigele (Vienna: Sonderzahl, 1996), 311-28; Clemens Hutter, Kaprun. *Geschichte eines Erfolges* (Salzburg: Residenzverlag, 1994); Elfriede Jelinek, *In den Alpen. Drei Dramen* (Berlin: Berlin Verlag, 2002).

2. *Verbund* Historical Commission, "Einsatz von Kriegsgefangenen, 'ausländischen zivilen Arbeitskräften,' sowie Häftlingen aus Konzentrationslagern im Rahmen der Alpen-Elektrowerke AG (AEW) 1938-1945." The project leaders were Oliver Rathkolb and Florian Freund, the staff members included Margit Reiter, Markus Purkhart, and Christine Oertel.

3. For more information on this issue see the article of Margit Reiter in *NS-Zwangsarbeit in der Elektrizitätswirtschaft der "Ostmark" 1938-1945*, ed. Florian Freund and Oliver Rathkolb (Vienna: Böhlau, [projected publication date]: 2002).

4. Ernst Kropatschek, *Geschichte der Tauernkraftwerke AG. Eine Dokumentation* (Salzburg: Tauernkraftwerke AG, 1978), 9f.

5. *Salzburger Volksblatt*, 17 May 1938.

6. AEW-Geschäftsbericht 1938.

7. Salzburger Landesarchiv, Landesregierung, Tauernkraftwerk, Box 7, Ministerium für Landwirtschaft, Zl. 13819-V/1-1939.

8. Hutter, *Kaprun*, 121.

9.Quoted. In Kos, *Eigenheim Österreich*, 131.

10. Ibid., 131ff.

11. Wolfgang Straub, *Willkommen. Literatur und Fremdenverkehr in Österreich* (Vienna: Sonderzahl, 2001), 147-63.

12. Othmar Franz Lang, *Die Männer von Kaprun* (Vienna: Österreichischer Bundesverlag 1955), 166.

13. Ibid., 94.

14. Kurt Maix, *Kaprun. Bezähmte Gewalten* (Vienna: Wollzeilen Verlag, 1964), 250ff.

15. Georg Rigele, "The Marshall Plan and Austria's Hydroelectric Industry: Kaprun," *Contemporary Austrian Studies*, vol. 8, *The Marshall Plan*, ed. Günter Bischof, Anton Pelinka, and Dieter Stiefel (New Brunswick: Transaction Publishers, 2000), 323-56.

16. Rigele, "Kaprun," 318f.

17. Rigele, "Kaprun," 318f.

18. Rigele, "The Marshall Plan," 355.

19. Rigele, "Kaprun," 319.

20. *Österreichische Volksstimme*, 18 October 1949.

21. Kos, *Eigenheim Österreich*, 138.

REVIEW ESSAYS

New Literature on Nazi Austria and the Holocaust

Emmerich Tálos, Ernst Hanisch, Wolfgang Neugebauer, and Reinhard Sieder, eds., *NS-Herrschaft in Österreich. Ein Handbuch* (Vienna: övb & hpt, 2000)

Dieter Stiefel, ed., *Die politische Ökonomie des Holocaust. Zur wirtschaftlichen Logik von Verfolgung und "Wiedergutmachung"* (Vienna: Verlag für Geschichte und Politik, 2001)

Doran Rabinovici, *Instanzen der Ohnmacht. Wien 1938-1945. Der Weg zum Judenrat* (Frankfurt am Main: Jüdischer Verlag, 2000)

Evelyn Adunka, *Die vierte Gemeinde. Die Wiener Juden in der Zeit von 1945 bis heute* (Vienna: Philo Verlagsgesellschaft, 2000)

Evan Burr Bukey

Shortly after Jörg Haider's Freedom Party entered a governing coalition with Chancellor Wolfgang Schüssel's People's Party on 4 February 2000, the Austrian government stepped up efforts begun by the previous administration to redress the material injustices of the Anschluss era. It focused particularly on the return of stolen artworks and the settlement of survivors' claims against Austrian companies, banks, and insurance firms. The imposition of diplomatic sanctions by the European Union, devised to chastise the new right-wing regime, evidently accelerated the process. On 24 October 2000, Schüssel's government signed a landmark settlement, which would provide restitution, compensation, and social welfare benefits to the victims of Nazi slave labor. Among those present at the ceremony was Stuart Eizenstat, the American deputy secretary of the treasury. In his brief remarks he applauded the agreement but prodded Austria to complete the "unfinished moral business" of coming to terms with its Nazi past. His words did not go unheeded. On 17 January 2001 Austria and the United States set up a General Settlement Fund to disburse reparations to survivors of the Holocaust.[1] Precisely because both diplomatic settlements include provisions that dismiss class-action suits against Austrian companies and call for "legal closure" of outstanding claims, a fierce debate erupted in the media as to whether the country had at last made a clean break with Hitler's legacy or only just begun to confront it.[2] Judging from the volumes under review, the answer seems to be a mixture of both. The appearance of a new edition of *NS-Herrschaft in Österreich*, originally published in 1988, suggests that Austrians have been wrestling with their traumatic past longer and more systematically than commonly believed. The revised study consists of thirty-nine interpretative essays, including eighteen up-dated articles and thirteen entirely new pieces, each of which contains useful bibliographic and historiographic data. The compendium remains the most authoritative work on the Anschluss era yet published.

The individual contributions to this volume address a variety of themes arranged in six sections: 1) the organization and structure of the Anschluss regime, 2) regional developments, 3) socio-economic changes, 4) educational and cultural trends, 5) the persecution of the Jews, and 6) denazification and the impact of Nazism on the Second Republic. While the essays are based on documentary research, some of them are summaries of larger works, some preliminary studies, and some declarations of intent. Among the best original essays are Emmerich Tálos' piece on Nazi social policy, Gerhard Jagschitz's on the post-Anschluss NSDAP, and Wolfgang Neugebauer's on Hitler's terror apparatus and the problem of resistance. Wolfgang Sauer's critical assessment of the "church struggle" also deserves mention, although in places it is unduly harsh. And while Fritz Weber's excellent summary of the Nazi economic system remains worthwhile, it has been superseded by Kurt Tweraser's exhaustive study of the structural transformation of production in Linz and Upper Austria.[3] Among the new essays in *NS-Herrschaft in Österreich*, Ingrid Bauer's plea for a gendered study of the Nazi period stands out as a sophisticated analytic model. Relying on her mastery of the existing literature, Bauer interprets National Socialism as a coherent response to the disruptions in family structures following World War I. She stresses both the reactionary and revolutionary aspects of Hitler's movement, a system that excluded women from political power, expected them to produce 'designer children,' and offered unparalleled opportunities for career advancement. Bauer and her colleague,

Johanna Gehmacher, have many interesting things to say about the experience of Austrian women, especially the activist role of the "illegal" female militants in subverting the Dollfuss-Schuschnigg regime. Both authors also provide arresting examples of the relationship between sexuality and racialism. On the other hand, they offer little in-depth information about the lives of wives and mothers and prefer to ignore the sensitive subject of Hitler's psycho-sexual appeal. They do reveal, however, that there is still much to learn about the role of women in Nazi Austria. A number of other, supplementary articles also represent works in progress. These include a short piece on eugenics and euthanasia by Peter Malina and Wolfgang Neugebauer, a longer essay on exile politics by Peter Schwarz and Siegwald Ganglmair, and a survey of the literary scene by Klaus Amann. The most informative essay is Winfried Garscha's pioneering study of the Second Republic's judicial confrontation with the legacy of Hitlerism. Based on thousands of obscure transcripts and government documents, it makes a convincing case for the Austrian approach to denazification. Garscha shows that as early as 28 June 1945, Vienna had enacted legislation to prosecute individuals for crimes against humanity, political denunciation, and "Nazi atrocities." During the course of the next two-and-a-half years, Austrian courts processed 108,000 cases, convicted 10,649 defendants, and sentenced 43 persons to death; they also levied fines and dismissed thousands of Nazis from office. Since most of the legal proceedings took place in the shadow of the International Military Tribunal at Nuremberg, they have been largely forgotten. Nevertheless, Garscha argues, Austria's initial *épuration* was no less lenient than that of other European countries. He might have added that, as in France, the purge of selected offenders served to undergird the myth of national resistance.

That said, the judicial procedures provoked such widespread resentment that by 1948 most ex-Nazis were free or had been amnestied. And as Austrian authorities grappled to overcome the challenges of foreign occupation, economic impoverishment, and the cold war, it seemed best to put the past behind them. Not until the 1960s did scholars begin to examine the Anschluss era, especially the role of Austrians in the Holocaust. Analyses of this complex and painful subject have been mixed, but Florian Freund and Bertrand Perz provide a superb summary of both the existing literature and their own prodigious research.

Also impressive are the highly specialized essays in Dieter Stiefel's *Die politische Ökonomie des Holocaust*. Here, the frequent use of the term "reappraisal" (*Aufarbeitung*) suggests years of careful thought and deliberation. Furthermore, the inclusion of articles on German banks and insurance companies reveals a refreshing willingness to consider the history of Nazi Austria as inseparable from the history of the Third Reich itself.

It is unfortunate, however, that Stiefel's anthology is poorly organized. While the articles deal with the despoliation of Central European Jewry, they are not connected topically or chronologically. The editor, in his introduction, does provide background information on the sudden interest in the disposition of Nazi loot, but throughout the volume he intersperses case studies—including his own—with more general accounts.

Readers seeking logical coherence may wish to begin with Gerhard Botz's excellent summary of "Aryanization" in Hitler's homeland. While the essay provides little new information, it does cast light on the multifarious wave of spontaneous and official theft unleashed by the Anschluss. The enormous extent of individual larceny makes it impossible to determine how much property actually changed hands. Official data reveal that within two months "provisional managers" had seized twenty-six thousand Jewish enterprises, but the fate of stolen household goods, art objects, musical instruments, jewelry, cash, and other valuables still remains largely unknown. And while Reich Commissioner Josef Bürckel quickly put an end to "wild Aryanization," turf wars and property disputes persisted for years. Botz's emphasis on the "greatest revolution in Austria since the Counterreformation" (p. 52) does not overlook the subsequent "legal" expropriation of Jewish assets—which he describes in meticulous detail—but his interpretation certainly provides one explanation for the half-hearted attempts of postwar Austrian governments to compensate Holocaust survivors and their heirs.

Another reason for inaction, of course, lay in the "founding myth" of the Second Republic. Each of the essays in this anthology stresses that the half-truth embedded in the Moscow Declaration of 1943 that Austria was "the first free country to fall victim to Hitlerite aggression" had multiple consequences for those seeking restitution. First, it meant that the victorious Allies assumed the burden of locating and returning looted properties, $198 million of which had been recovered by 1949; the problem was that 90% of the assets, most notably artworks, went to the Austrian government. Second, the victim myth enabled the founders of the Second Republic to stonewall on reimbursement to individuals. State Chancellor Karl Renner, for example, in his proclamation of 27 April 1945 deliberately incorporated axioms to woo Hitler's supporters and to slight the real victims of the Anschluss, especially resistant fighters and Jews. As a consequence, Günter Bischof and Brigitte Bailer-Galanda contend, Renner and his successors carefully crafted restitution laws to placate both the Allies and ex-Nazi voters. This is not to imply that payments were not made in subsequent decades, but those entitled to them—especially after the Third Restitution Law of 1947 had been passed—invariably encountered bureaucratic obstructionism, recovered only a pittance, or came away empty-handed. The much-discussed "gaps and deficiencies" in Austrian restitution legislation can thus be attributed to the inability or unwillingness of policy makers to confront the legacy of the Holocaust as a moral issue, preferring instead to engage in what today would be called "triangulation."

Finally, one should not overlook the impact of the cold war. In Austria, the East-West conflict reinforced the victim myth, reduced pressure to compensate Nazi victims, and made it impossible for Eastern Europeans to seek restitution. It also concealed the immense contribution of foreign and slave labor to the economic modernization of the Alpine Republic. Florian Freund and Bertrand Perz document this process utilizing newly-gathered data and precise figures on the exploitation of foreign workers, prisoners of war, concentration camp inmates, and Hungarian Jews, nearly all of whom were imported to meet a wartime labor shortage. Of those assigned to the *Ostmark*, it was Poles, Serbs, and French POWs who initially worked in agriculture or in construction projects underwritten by the Four Year Plan. After the failure of Hitler's Moscow campaign, they were joined by an enormous influx of *Ostarbeiter*, including many women, and in 1943 by thousands of Italian "military internees." The conscripts toiled in the new industrial enterprises and armament factories under such appalling conditions that 23,039 of them perished in accidents, died of disease, or fell victim to Nazi overseers. At the end of the war, Austrian men and women constituted only 39% of the total workforce.Freund and Perz also provide new data on the number of concentration camp inmates and Hungarian Jews forced to excavate underground factories, clear rubble, or engage in other odious tasks in Nazi Austria. Although they fail to mention Gordon Horwitz's important study of the 1945 "death marches" and the immediate postwar reactions to them,[4] the authors take pains to stress the disappearance of slave labor from Austria's collective memory. This particular cloud of amnesia, though abetted by the victim myth, seems to have arisen in inverse proportion to the descent of the Iron Curtain. While multiple factors subsequently contributed to Austria's astonishing economic growth, Freund and Perz make us painfully aware of the role of chattel slavery in the country's industrial and infrastructural development. The most important articles in Stiefel's collection tackle the daunting problem of insurance and banking claims. Because middle-class Jews tended to invest in life insurance companies and those with lesser means in postal savings banks, it was easier for the emigrants to monetize or repurchase policies than to liquidate fixed assets. And since the Nazis initially targeted shops, businesses, or real estate, Jewish investors retained relatively free access to their money. But within months of the Anschluss, they had to register their possessions, pay "flight taxes" and "atonement fees," and transform their liquid assets into "blocked emigrant accounts." Thereafter, the financial authorities imposed such strict currency controls that Jewish monetary resources fell prey to what Gerald Feldman calls "indirect and direct confiscation."[5] The sheer scale of larceny explains why in the postwar period so many "dormant accounts" and "heirless assets" were difficult to locate or to identify.

In two impressive essays, Stiefel examines the "economics of discrimination." Following the pioneering works of Gerald Feldman and Harold James,[6] he meticulously shows how "Aryanization" warped Austrian business culture and stripped Jewish victims of their property, dignity, and very existence. Within eighteen months of the Anschluss, for example, the Nazis replaced half of the country's corporate managers and three-quarters of its supervisory personnel. While the administrative shake-up produced enormous inefficiencies, it also raised the value of "Aryan" assets and provided openings for younger employees. The response of corporate elites was mixed: Some accepted the changes; others kept Jewish employees on the payroll or posted them abroad.In the case of the insurance industry, German Reich executives scrambled to take over Austrian companies, eventually gaining control of 56% of the total share capital. However, neither they, nor their Austrian colleagues, or the Nazi government were eager to break insurance contracts or become involved in legal disputes abroad. As a consequence, at least two-thirds of Jewish policies were redeemed. Not until 1941 did the financial authorities seize the remaining premiums. Stiefel calculates that between 1938 and 1945 Austrian insurance companies paid Berlin 7.17 million Reichsmark (RM) in confiscated assets but never received lists of deported policy holders or their assets. The firms thus lost their best clients and found themselves largely destitute at the end of the war. The charge that Austrian insurance companies profited from the Holocaust does not, in other words, hold true.

Oliver Rathkolb's study of the Viennese Postal Savings Bank parallels Stiefel's work. Managed before 1938 by appointees of the Dollfuss-Schuschnigg regime, this financial institution had long been the bank of small depositors. It employed few Jews, but held the assets of over six thousand "non-Aryan" customers. Immediately following the Anschluss, it became a branch of the *Deutsche Post*. The new management, Rathkolb reveals, did not discriminate against Jews, allowing them until 1940 to retain checking and savings accounts. Nor did it attempt to interfere in over-the-counter transactions. On the other hand, the regime converted the bank's assets of RM 224.4 million to government securities and left it with just over RM 1 million in working capital. And while Jewish customers continued to make small transactions, Nazi restrictions, taxes, and fines severely limited access to their money. The collapse of the Third Reich left the Postal Savings Bank with assets of RM 1 million in largely worthless passbooks. Three years later an official audit assessed the worth of extant Jewish accounts at 251,512 Schillings (ATS).As both the Austrian insurance industry and the Postal Savings Bank were now bankrupt, the

Second Republic assumed the burden of replenishing the coffers of these and other private institutions. Renner's government recognized the *diplomatic* necessity of making restitution, but refused—for reasons discussed by Bischof—to distinguish between Jewish claims and those of other victims. While Stiefel makes no apologies for these and other insensitive policy decisions, he reminds readers of the many tribulations confronting Austria in the immediate postwar period. Even so, between 1946 and 1958, the Parliament did pass seven restitution laws, two Insurance Reconstruction Acts, and other statutory measures to provide partial indemnification or "assistance" to the victims of Nazism.

The problem was that registration and residence requirements caused a number of Jewish survivors and their heirs to fall through the cracks. And those who recovered their monetary assets received benefits that were devalued by 60%. The failure of successive Austrian governments to provide full restitution to those dispossessed by the Holocaust had many causes, though most can be attributed to Renner's mean-spirited priorities and the country's bizarre status as a "guilty victim." The record shows that Vienna did pay considerable sums. However, official unwillingness to confront the legacy of Nazi anti-Semitism inhibited the development of the sort of "proactive" approach taken by Stiefel. Even after the Eichmann trial in 1961, there was little incentive for the establishment of something like a "truth and reconciliation commission." A decade later Bruno Kreisky, relishing his position as the "Jewish leader of a former Nazi state,"[7] squelched the judicial investigation of eight hundred Austrian war criminals. Not until the Waldheim affair would a significant change in attitudes take place.

And what of the Jewish victims? Had Austrian politicians fully grasped both the enormity of their suffering and the complicity of their countrymen in the Holocaust, they might have been more sympathetic to the pleas of postwar survivors and their heirs. In this regard, Doron Rabinovici's impressive study of the Viennese Community Council (*Israelitische Kultusgemeinde*) offers a profusion of painful new information. It represents both a worthy sequel to Harriet Pass Freidenreich's *Jewish Politics in Vienna, 1918-1938* and a welcome companion to Herbert Rosenkranz's *Verfolgung und Selbstbehauptung. Die Juden in Österreich, 1938-1945.*[8] Rabinovici's book approaches the subject from the perspective of Jewish history and the Holocaust. It also provides detailed information on Nazi policies in Austria, the Jewish response to persecution, and, above all, the interaction of the Community Council and Eichmann's Central Office for Jewish Emigration. Relying on exhaustive archival research in Israel and Europe, Rabinovici contends that what happened in Vienna provided a "model" for both the expulsion of the Jews from Greater Germany and the establishment of *Judenräte* in occupied Poland.

Rabinovici's thesis is not altogether original, but he makes a compelling case. Where he differs from those who have written about Jewish Councils elsewhere—most notably Raul Hilberg and Hannah Arendt—is in his refutation of the claim that "if the Jewish people had really been unorganized and leaderless, there would have been chaos and plenty of misery but the total number of victims would hardly have been between four and a half million people."[9] In Austria, Rabinovici demonstrates, the opposite was the case. Cooperation with the SS and Gestapo made it possible for all but a third of the Jewish populace to escape the Holocaust. Even so, there was no other choice: Nazi policy between 1938 and 1941 was one of expropriation and expulsion, not extermination. At the time, collaboration made sense.

Unlike Freidenreich and Rosenkranz, Rabinovici focuses on a handful of historical actors. He covers familiar ground in order to analyze the high politics of the impotent. The central figures discussed are Josef Löwenherz, chief executive of the post-Anschluss *Kultusgemeinde*, his close associate Rabbi Benjamin Murmelstein, and a dozen or so other dignitaries permitted by the Nazis to retain relative freedom of action. Prominent among them were Alois Rothenberg, chief of the Palestine Office, Berthold Sofer, an international businessman in charge of "Overseas Transport," and Franzi Löw-Danneberg, a social worker who managed to survive the Holocaust and save the lives of scores of coreligionists. In addition, Rabinovici provides disturbing portraits of several "evacuators" and "catchers" recruited by the Gestapo to hunt down fellow Jews.

Immediately following the Anschluss, the Nazis dissolved the *Kultusgemeinde* and arrested its officers. On 2 May 1938, the thirty-two-year-old Adolf Eichmann reopened its offices and appointed Löwenherz chief executive. While the reconstituted Jewish Council was dominated by Zionists, Rabinovici reminds us that it was a Nazi creation possessing no autonomy and little leverage. Whether its members shared Hitler's goal of Jewish emigration is a moot point; the Jewish Council was literally powerless. Its officials did not shy away from cooperation, but the volcanic eruption of popular anti-Semitism left them no other alternative. Accustomed to the relative protection of the Dollfuss-Schuschnigg dictatorship, they concluded that the Central Office for Jewish Emigration might shelter them from the Viennese mob.

There was, however, little real cause for hope. Eichmann abused Löwenstern mercilessly, treating him with contempt and manipulating him to advance his own career. Hence, after a brief interlude violence resumed, and the Central Office for Jewish Emigration set up a "conveyor belt system" of expropriation and expulsion. Rabinovici devotes considerable attention to this scheme that robbed Austrian Jews of their assets but also enabled 104,000 of them to escape abroad before December 1939. His detailed account provides new information on the internal debates of the *Kultusgemeinde*, even if it does not significantly alter our knowledge of what happened. Rabinovici also offers a convincing defense of Benjamin Murmelstein, the driving force within the Jewish Council, who was later castigated for his collaborative, harsh, and seemingly arbitrary behavior. While conceding personality flaws, Rabinovici argues that Murmelstein's ruthless approach saved countless lives. The question of motivation remains, however, unresolved.

After Hitler's conquest of Poland, Eichmann and his superior, Franz Stahlecker, proposed "resettling" the remaining Austrian Jews in Nisko, near Lublin. By this time, the plight of Viennese Jewry had become so desperate that Löwenherz welcomed the idea and 830 Jews even volunteered to make the trip. Rabinovici recounts this first Nazi experiment at "resettlement" in horrific detail, reiterating his case for an Austrian model in the evolution of the Holocaust. While this assessment may be sound, one should not lose sight of Saul Friedländer's observation that "what happened in Austria after the Anschluss was simply the better organized part of a general policy adopted throughout the Reich."[10]

Between November 1939 and February 1941, there ensued a hiatus in the assaults on those Jews still living in the *Ostmark*, even though random evictions, beatings, and petty harassment persisted. Rabinovici makes the interesting suggestion that Löwenherz may have dissuaded Eichmann, now in charge of formulating an overall plan for evacuation, from further deportations by reminding him that a reversal of the emigration policy would sever the flow of much-needed foreign currency from the American Joint Distribution Committee. Even after Hitler ordered the expulsion of Vienna's remaining Jews on 3 December 1940, Löwenherz and his associates managed to help six thousand coreligionists find refuge abroad.

Rabinovici devotes two chapters to the waves of deportations that dispatched sixty-five thousand Austrian Jews to Riga, Theresienstadt, and the gas ovens in Poland. The first wave, precipitated by the housing crisis in Vienna, lasted from 15 February to 12 March 1941. It was followed by an interlude of renewed violence, rumors of the mass murder of Jews in German-occupied Russia, and the notorious Yellow Star Decree of 1 September 1941. Shortly thereafter, on Yom Kippur, a sobbing Löwenherz revealed to his congregation the resumption of transports to the East. By the end of 1942 only 7,989 Jews remained in Vienna, two-thirds of them living in mixed marriages.

Rabinovici's account of the fate of those Austrian Jews who perished in the Holocaust parallels the works of others, notably that of Rosenkranz. Written with sensitivity and eloquence, it analyzes the Holocaust from the perspective of the *Kultusgemeinde*. The central issue, as might be expected, is the role of the Jewish Council in the deportation process. Rabinovici concedes that Löwenherz and his associates gathered data, filled out forms, and assembled victims at collection centers. But he also shows that while Council members deemed Auschwitz a dreaded destination, they failed to realize that it was an extermination camp until long after the deaths of the deportees. In this respect, Rabinovici stresses, the Viennese *Kultusgemeinde* knew less about Hitler's extermination program than most of the "Jewish Elders" in Poland, the World Jewish Congress, and particularly the Western Allies.

Were other options available? Rabinovici tackles this question in two ways. First, he assesses the character of the major Jewish functionaries, nearly all of whom were reviled by postwar survivors as careerists or collaborators. He shows that, while officials such as Murmelstein may have appeared harsh and domineering, they had ample opportunity to flee the Third Reich before 1941, a possibility never open to the "Jewish Elders" in Poland. Whatever their flaws, the leaders of the Viennese Council comported themselves in a generally selfless way. Second, Rabinovici reveals that in a number of small ways Löwenherz and his associates did manage to subvert Nazi orders; they, for example, fabricated documents, funneled money to those in hiding, and even forestalled the departure of several transports. Once the Nazis modulated to a program of total genocide, however, nothing could be done to prevent it. "Every Jewish strategy, whether resistance or cooperation, came to naught," he concludes (p. 420). Isolated in a compact metropolis, the surviving Children of Israel were doomed.

Exactly how many Jews remained alive in Vienna at the end of the war is unclear; estimates range from roughly 2000 to 5,512. While most had survived in mixed marriages, 450 members of the *Kultusgemeinde* continued at their posts in April 1945. In addition to the hardships suffered by the general population, they faced the daunting task of caring for the sick and elderly, provisioning survivors from Eastern Europe, and coping with bureaucratic directives from both the Second Republic and the occupying Allied powers. While the American Joint Distribution Committee and the United Nations Relief and Rehabilitation Administration (UNRRA) provided some material relief, the prospect of resurrecting the Viennese Jewish community seemed bleak. "There is not one single child of full Jewish parentage alive in the city," lamented one American observer. "Practically none of the Jews left in Vienna want to remain there. All of them have lost their families, their homes, their property. Nothing binds them now but the memories of horror and destruction."[11]

The revival of Viennese Jewish life against insuperable odds is the subject of Evelyn Adunka's mammoth survey of the postwar *Kultusgemeinde*. She writes lucidly and well, but unlike Rabinovici presents the results of her exhaustive research in the form of short biographies, lengthy testimonials, and newspaper commentaries. The format is not without merit as it allows readers to judge contentious issues on the basis of carefully selected primary material, including documents from American, European, and Israeli archives. And while Adunka plays down contextual analysis, her assessments are usually fair and judicious. Still, what she has written is a celebratory work useful to historians primarily as a compendium of well-organized information.

By 1946, Adunka shows, most Viennese Jews were receiving food parcels from the American Joint Distribution Committee. Many were able to eat their fill, but only five hundred managed to find jobs and a mere one hundred called reclaim their homes. While Austrian politicians professed sympathy and promised restitution, they conspired, as we have seen, to limit compensation, providing only minimal assistance in the form of loans. Jewish leaders, Adunka writes, were not deceived by the mendacity of the government but preferred to keep their own counsel. Intensely aware of the anti-Semitic sentiment still prevailing in Austria, they embraced the Zionist cause and organized rallies to pressure the British to "open the gates" to Palestine.

And yet, the Jewish community slowly began to recover. By 1948, there were nine thousand members. The almost imperceptible growth led to the renovation of a hospital on Seegasse, the establishment of three newspapers, and the revival of athletic clubs and other associations liquidated by the Nazis. It also led to changes within the *Kultusgemeinde*, which, as in the interwar period, tended to parallel the political developments of the larger Austrian stage. Thus, after several failed attempts by the Communists to gain control of the *Kultusgemeinde* and considerable feuding behind closed doors, democratic elections were held in 1946 and 1948. The second contest gave a clear mandate to David Schapira, a moderate Zionist and survivor of Theresienstadt, who, once in office, played a key role in the selection of Akiba Eisenberg as Chief Rabbi. According to Adunka, it was the youthful Eisenberg who inspired a downcast congregation, reorganized religious instruction, and restored a semblance of stability to Jewish life.

In 1951, for example, an Israeli correspondent indicated that the *Kultusgemeinde* remained hopelessly divided into contentious factions, primarily along political lines. Seven years later, however, the executive board reported a "gratifying upswing" (p. 148) in Jewish communal life. Adunka's evidence suggests that, while disputations persisted throughout the 1950s, they became less acrimonious once the Slansky trials in Czechoslovakia discredited the arguments of influential local Communists. The establishment of both a Hebrew school and an active student organization at the University of Vienna certainly provided cause for satisfaction. And in 1959, nearly everyone rejoiced when Bruno Kreisky joined the

Austrian government as foreign minister. Overshadowing this less than harmonious consensus, however, was the memory of the Holocaust and the virtual disappearance of religious commitment.

Adunka devotes a long chapter to the fierce debates dividing various Zionist factions in the 1950s, but she neglects to explain the issues at stake. She shows that, although the warring camps presented numerous lectures on Jewish subjects, most of the Viennese community, including returnees and newcomers, preferred the older tradition of secular assimilation. One outside observer complained: "If there is a Jewish community anywhere where unity of action and purpose seems imperative, it is Vienna. But there is still a long way to go" (p. 181).

Adunka unwittingly replicates the confusion and disarray of the era in a cut-and-paste narrative that sometimes borders on incoherence. She presents, for example, a chapter on the thorny issue of restitution that partially complements the articles in Stiefel's collection but fails to contextualize the historical conditions following the signing of the State Treaty. This is all the more regrettable as she provides much intriguing information on the invidious activities of Benjamin Schreiber, head of the tiny Orthodox community, who subverted the ongoing efforts of both the Community Council and the World Jewish Council in reaching a settlement.

Adunka's account of the turbulent 1960s is also disappointing. She reprints a good many articles lauding the presidencies of Ernst Feldsberg (1963-70) and Anton Pick (1970-76), but only adumbrates their close attachment to the SPÖ, a relationship that included questionable links to the FPÖ. What Adunka's material does reveal is that executive partisanship opened new fault lines within the Community Council and provoked the implacable resistance of the Nazi hunter Simon Wiesenthal. Obsessed with bringing Austrian war criminals to justice, Wiesenthal demanded complete withdrawal from politics and greater emphasis on purely Jewish affairs. His vitriolic rhetoric ignited a bitter feud that would persist for decades.

At first, the SPÖ faction managed to fend off Wiesenthal's inflammatory charges and to retain control of the Community Council. Attitudes changed once Chancellor Bruno Kreisky joined the fray. Brushing aside the cause of Hitler's victims, this post-imperial *Kaiser* awarded portfolios to former Nazis, welcomed Arab leaders to Vienna, and condemned his fellow Jews as a "wretched people." He also branded Wiesenthal a "Jewish fascist." Adunka believes that Kreisky's intemperate behavior rekindled the fires of anti-Semitism, but she is remarkably judicious in explaining his grievances both as an Austrian patriot and a religious agnostic.

She also describes the process by which in 1976 a coalition of reformers and Zionists wrested control of the Community Council from the SPÖ. Their victory was not without irony. Had 5,380 Viennese Jews disregarded Zionist pleas to emigrate to Israel, especially after the Six Day War, the Socialist hammerlock might have been broken much earlier.

In the final pages of her compendium, Adunka provides snapshots of Viennese Orthodox life, the reorganization of Jewish social services, and the erection of the stunning Holocaust memorial in the Judenplatz. There is also a fascinating chapter on the Waldheim affair that both recaptures the emotional climate of that tawdry episode and provides chilling examples of abuse suffered by Jewish citizens. For all its merits, though, Adunka's account fails to place the national catharsis in historical context or to offer the sort of overview provided, for example, by Heidemarie Uhl.[12] In the end, Adunka's abrupt conclusion neither sums up her enormous work nor assesses Jewish life in contemporary Vienna. One can only hope that in the future she may produce a more structured, analytic study.

Overall, the volumes reviewed here enrich our understanding of Nazi Austria and the Holocaust, especially the fate of Austrian Jewry and the complexities of postwar restitution. They also succeed in raising important questions for future research. What they do not address directly, except in a single essay,[13] is the searing experience of the Second World War, a conflict in which 1.2 million Austrians served in the German armed forces and nearly 300,000 lost their lives. Until the impact of the conflagration on Austrian soldiers and civilians is more thoroughly explored and placed in proper context, the history of Hitler's *Ostmark* will remain incomplete.

Notes

1. "Joint Statement on Holocaust Restitution," retrieved 26 November 2001 from the World Wide Web: http://www.cnn.com/2000/WORLD/europe/10/24/austria.nazi; http://www.usembassy-vienna.at.

2. See, for example, "Österreichs unendliches Trauma," *Format* 23 (1 June 2001): 46-53.

3. Kurt Tweraser, "Die Linzer Wirtschaft im Nationalsozialismus: Anmerkungen zur strukturellen Transformation ('Modernisierung') und zum NS-Krisenmanagement," in *Nationalsozialismus in Linz*, vol. 1, ed. Fritz Mayrhofer and Walter Shuster (Linz: Archiv der Stadt Linz, 2001), 387-555.

4. Gordon J. Horwitz, *In the Shadow of Death: Living Outside the Gates of Mauthausen* (New York: Free Press, 1990).

5. Gerald D. Feldman, "Confiscation of Insurance Assets: Special Issues," in *Washington Conference on Holocaust Era Assets, November 30-December 3, 1998*, ed. J.D. Bindenagel (Washington, DC: U.S.G.P.O., 1999), 599.

6. Gerald D. Feldman, *Allianz and the German Insurance Business, 1933-1945* (Cambridge: Cambridge University Press, 2001); Harold James, *The Deutsche Bank and the Nazi Economic War Against the Jews* (Cambridge: Cambridge University Press, 2001).

7. Hella Pick, *Austria from the Holocaust to Hitler* (London: J.B. Tauris, 2000), 120.

8. Harriet Pass Freidenreich, *Jewish Politics in Vienna 1918-1938* (Bloomington: Indiana University Press, 1991); Herbert Rosenkranz, *Die Verfolgung und Selbstbehauptung: Die Juden in Österreich 1938-1945* (Vienna: Herold, 1978).

9. Hannah Arendt, *Eichmann in Jerusalem: A Report on the Banality of Evil* (New York: The Viking Press, 1967), 125.

10. Saul Friedländer, *Nazi Germany and the Jews: The Years of Persecution, 1933-1939* (New York: Harper Collins, 1997), 247.

11. Quoted in Adunka, *Die vierte Gemeinde*, 28.

12. Heidemarie Uhl, *Zwischen Versöhnung und Verstörung. Eine Kontroverse um Österreichs historische Identität fünfzig Jahre nach dem "Anschluß"* (Vienna: Böhlau, 1992).

13. Walter Manoschek and Hans Safrian, "Österreicher in der Wehrmacht," in Tálos et al., *NS-Herrschaft*, 123-158.

The Waldheim Matter: Old Issues and Perplexing Questions

Kurt Waldheim, *Die Antwort* (Vienna: Amalthea, 1996)

Harold H. Tittmann III, *The Waldheim Affair: Democracy Subverted* (Dunkirk, NY: Olin Frederick, Inc., 2000)

Robert E. Herzstein

As I comment on recent literature and documentation concerning Dr. Kurt Waldheim, readers deserve to know my perspective. To a minor extent, I am cited in all of them, and I was a participant in many of the events surrounding the Waldheim controversy. In 1986, the World Jewish Congress asked me to research the former U.N. secretary-general's wartime career. Later, I continued my inquiry on my own, and eventually published my book on the subject.[1] I concluded that Waldheim had neither ordered nor carried out atrocities. He had, however, transmitted illegal orders resulting in criminal deportations of prisoners; and, of course, he had deceived his contemporaries in regard to his wartime service.

As he rose in prominence, Waldheim ignored his service in the Balkans, and, later, the secretary-general made evasive and deceptive comments about it. He continues to torture language in misguided attempts at self-vindication. *Die Antwort* replies that Irangate showed that even American politicians have "memory lapses." This comment hardly inspires faith in Waldheim's veracity. But, Waldheim protests, the partisans whom he fought in Greece, later came into conflict with the United States. "How bad can I be?," the former federal president seems to ask.

Not surprisingly, Waldheim cites my book when it exposes the politically motivated fabrications of the Yugoslavs against him. Other passages, as, for example, those where I show how he transmitted illegal orders and provided information that could have endangered civilians, are not mentioned. It seems everything Waldheim does is selective, defensive, evasive. Waldheim loves to display friendly letters from world leaders, whom he uses as character witnesses. But what do these boring pro forma exercises have to do with Army Group E and the deportation to slave labor of Italian prisoners? Absolutely nothing. Always, Waldheim returns to the "real villains": the Jews, Mossad, the ultra-left, intellectuals, the World Jewish Congress, the SPÖ. Bragging about his visits as federal president to foreign countries, Waldheim misses the irony inherent in their names: Saudi Arabia and Syria and other Arab states as well, including Iraq. Did these invitations have to do with Waldheim's anti-Israeli or anti-Jewish bias? Why did they invite him? Does he really think that the Saudis or Syrians admired his "even-handed" Middle East policies?

When he addresses the subject of the *Historikerkommission*, Waldheim plays his usual games. He blasts the "*Scharfmacher*" around Professor Manfred Messerschmidt and praises General Collins and Colonel Vanwelkenhuyzen (the "doves," as he calls them)—only to admit that the latter were not comfortable with the German-language documentation (p. 191)! And in a rather pompous distortion, Waldheim claims that his being put on the "Watch List" was an insult to the entire Austrian nation ("*die Beleidigung einer ganzen Nation*," p. 151). In fact, one good thing to emerge from this affair was the growing interest displayed by younger Austrians in the compromised past of their country. About this, Waldheim says little or nothing.

Instead, the former federal president is both angry and dismissive. The "Watch List" decision continues to irritate Waldheim. And, like his political allies, he prefers to dwell upon the political origins of the affair that bears his name. It seems easier to attack the Socialist conspirators of 1985-86 than to present an honest portrait of his role in the events of 1942-1945. Ironically, both Waldheim and his most severe critics seem to share one trait: They eschew a calm, scholarly in-depth analysis of wartime documents bearing Waldheim's name. So, *Die Antwort* dwells at length on Socialist perfidy and campaign tactics, on the U.N. and world politics, and on the "Watch List" infamy, but says little new about the war. As before, Kurt Waldheim sees himself as a survivor, neither a hero, nor a resister, nor a collaborator. This view contains some truth but seems misleading when used to justify evasion and amnesia. Does Waldheim really think that he would have become secretary-general had his role (as a staff officer) in the deportation of Italians, Serbs, and perhaps Jews, been known? *Die Antwort* does not ask, much less answer, this crucial question. Perhaps it is too painful; perhaps even asking it would lead to the unmasking of the self-deception in which so many of Waldheim's countrymen participated.

Waldheim blames the Jews in the United States for his troubles. He alleges that his incomplete answer to a question from Congressman Stephen J. Solarz about his wartime service was taken out of context—by Jews upset about his "even-handed" policy towards the Middle East (p. 100). Waldheim does admit, though, that a more complete listing of his wartime units might have spared him anguish in the long run. Yet, his invocation of "the Jews were out to get me" theme does not inspire confidence in Waldheim's veracity.

With *The Waldheim Affair*, the attorney Harold H. Tittmann III has written a brief for this difficult client of his. He has little new to say and seems unfamiliar with much of the documentation concerning Kurt Waldheim. His one-sided little book rehashes stories about the uneven work of the *Historikerkommission* and reveals nothing new about the HBO Waldheim "trial" or the Ministry of Defense's review of Waldheim's putative contacts with British commandos. Indeed, Tittmann's text reminds me of the lessons I received long ago from two of Waldheim's aides, Dr. Ferdinand Trauttmansdorff and Dr. Ralph Scheide. Ever amiable but determined, they carefully explained that Waldheim saw himself as innocent and wronged and invariably hinted at their own agreement with his position. Mr. Tittmann seems to owe a lot to these apologists, whom he cites in his book. I can still recall their polite, long lectures that almost persuaded me— until I studied the records of Army Group E, and perused Waldheim's post-1972 comments.

According to Tittmann, it was a socialist conspiracy that hatched the Waldheim affair. Perhaps so, but that has nothing to do with the documents signed by Waldheim in Athens in 1943. Nor am I alone in claiming that the Germans and Croatians "massacred their opponents" at Kozara in 1942. Moreover, Tittmann ignores the mass deportation of Serbs from Kozara to slave labor and death far from home. Yet, Waldheim was a transport officer on the divisional staff in that campaign, and he later made confusing and amnesiac statements about his role—which remains unclear to this day. Tittmann glosses over the fact that "Waldheim had not discussed his Balkan service in his writings . . ." (p. 20). This omission is remarkable in the light of the ferocity of the Balkan theater of war.

Gerhard Waldheim once told me that when he was young he asked his father about some antique weapon acquired in the Balkans. Father Kurt burst out, "Mein Gott, das waren Jahre!," then changed the subject. Yes, those were incredible years, about which Waldheim chose to remain silent—or evasive. Though his family had been "black" and anti-Nazi, it turns out that Waldheim did not suffer reprisals at the *Konsularakademie* at all, as had been implied. Indeed, his career flourished after the Anschluss. And one marvels at the flexibility of a man who later married a Nazi, the daughter of an "illegal." But back to *The Waldheim Affair*.

Tittmann seems uncomfortable with historical research. Though he has read my fully documented book, he still insists that "the historians produced no evidence of Waldheim's involvement in, or even knowledge of, this matter" (p 49). Tittmann refers to the deportations of Italian soldiers from the Athens area in the autumn of 1943. In fact, on 22 September, at 9:30 pm, Lt. Waldheim telephoned operations at Army Group Headquarters in

Arsakli, reporting that the "deportation of the Italians from Attica and Boeotia has been concluded." These prisoners, who thought they were being repatriated to Italy, would wind up as forced laborers in Germany. Waldheim played an important role in this deception since, as a colleague later recalled, "He spoke very good Italian and he transmitted the ongoing discussions with the Italian army leadership."[2] This illegal deportation of disarmed soldiers, whose country was not even at war with Germany, was the kind of activity that Kurt Waldheim chose not to remember. So much for Tittmann's assertion that a staff officer "would not have been a recipient of unlawful orders . . ." (p. 52). He further muddies the waters by telling us that there is no evidence of Waldheim's involvement in the deportations. Then he claims that Waldheim lacked "authority to order the transfer of Italian prisoners to Germany" (p. 77). Of course not. He deceived the Italian officers he knew so well and persuaded them that they and their men were destined for repatriation to Italy. In so doing, Waldheim helped transmit illegal orders resulting in mass deportations to slave labor. That is involvement; to claim he lacked authority is to set up the proverbial straw man.

As I have stated on numerous occasions, Waldheim, so far as I know, never ordered or personally carried out illegal actions; instead, he transmitted illegal orders and facilitated their implementation. In the case of certain Greek Jews, I carefully spelled out Waldheim's role in receiving and transmitting (to Ia of the high command of Army Group E) information that can only have endangered this Jewish community.

My refusal to call Waldheim a war criminal angered some Jewish groups, as Tittmann relates, but I stand by my position: Kurt Waldheim was a functionary, not a perpetrator. He worked for and knowingly transmitted orders for a regime that was committing war crimes and crimes against humanity. This explains why Waldheim avoided all public or autobiographical comments on his career in the Balkans—until cornered by historical evidence in 1986. So Tittmann has a hard time trying to explain why Waldheim lied to a U.S. congressman who had asked him to list his wartime units between 1939-1945. He mentioned Russia but omitted the Balkans altogether. Tittmann lamely defends this deception, adding that the revelations publicized by the World Jewish Congress prove that Waldheim's records were "available in various archives . . ." (p. 89). Then why would he conceal his Balkan past? But, of course, Waldheim did so quite effectively until I and others uncovered those records after 1985. Forty years of concealment is not unimpressive. However, it seems strange—or maybe not—that a lawyer should defend such obfuscation. His placement on the "Watch List" continues to rankle Waldheim and his apologists, and Tittmann's book is a belated attempt to remove that stain from the old soldier's record. In this, it has failed. But other records are incomplete, too.

I have worked for several years on behalf of the legislation later entitled the "Nazi War Crimes Disclosure Act." My efforts began back in 1986, when I suggested that during the cold war American and other intelligence services might have assisted and used Kurt Waldheim. This legislation would require the release of documents concerning accused Nazi war criminals, with certain exceptions, and it became law in October 1998. Unfortunately, the "Waldheim file" released in 2001 contains little that is new or important.[3] Most of these papers concern an innocuous document generated by British intelligence in 1945. That report identifies Waldheim as a staff officer in the Balkans but says next to nothing about him. Other released files concern Waldheim's misleading responses to Congressman Stephen J. Solarz (whom I advised in this matter). Press clippings and sanitized internal correspondences were also part of the package released a year ago. It is no wonder that, having reviewed these files, Professor Richard Breitman claimed that they do not depict Waldheim as an asset for the CIA. Yet, he may be wrong.

Ironically, I obtained better documentation on Waldheim *before* "my" War Crimes Disclosure Act was passed. In the early 1990s, I gained access to Waldheim-related documents engendered by both the State Department and the Central Intelligence Agency. Contrary to the packet cited by Professor Breitman, these documents depict Waldheim as a man working closely with Americans, on behalf of U.S. interests. The documents cover a long period of time; they also show a peculiar American disinterest in Waldheim's incomplete and lacking military biography—which he had provided to the Americans in Vienna in the early 1950s. In due course, when I can provide further context and documentation, I will publish these intriguing cold war documents.

The books and documents reviewed here show that Waldheim's defenders, along with those who accuse him of having committed war crimes, have failed to substantiate their more extreme claims. But there is more work for the historian: These materials also show that Waldheim and his friends still refuse to confront his wartime past in any depth. They also indicate that the puzzling relationship between Waldheim and U.S. intelligence agencies needs to be investigated.

The Waldheim matter is not over. The final chapter has yet to be written.

Notes

1. Robert E. Herzstein, *Waldheim: The Missing Years* (New York: Morrow, 1988).
2. Ibid., 104-5.

3. CIA documents were released on 27 April 2001 under the Nazi War Crimes Disclosure Act, signed into law by President Clinton in 1998. See also the article by David Johnston in the *New York Times*, 28 April 2001 on the release of those CIA documents.

Studies in Nazi Business History in the *Ostmark* during World War II

Oliver Rathkolb, ed., *NS-Zwangsarbeit: Der Standort Linz der Reichswerke Hermann Göring AG, Berlin, 1938-1945*, 2 vols. (Vienna: Böhlau, 2001)

Dieter Stiefel, *Die österreichischen Lebensversicherungen und die NS-Zeit* (Vienna: Böhlau, 2001)

Herman Freudenberger

More than a half century after the end of a war that caused untold suffering, including the deaths of tens of millions of human beings, efforts are still being made to clean up the human obligations that are left over. Oliver Rathkolb, the editor of one of the works here discussed, referred to these obligations as "sleeping accounts" (*"schlafende Konten"*), which came to the forefront of international attention when Switzerland refused to account for liabilities that its banks and insurance firms still held on their books. Encouraged by the formation of a Swiss commission headed by the well-known economic historian Jean-François Bergier, the Austrian government, interestingly comprised of two conservative parties, established a similar commission in 1998. Its purpose is to investigate the human obligations emanating from the Nazi period that have not yet been fully accounted for and to provide restitution and indemnification for the ascertainable harm administered to people who may by good fortune still be alive. Headed by the president of the administrative court (*Verwaltungsgerichtshof*), Clemens Jabloner, this commission is to examine and presumably analyze the entire mass of data concerning the damages to the incomes of forced workers in Austria during the Nazi period and to propose methods of restitution and indemnification. The Rathkolb study was commissioned by the *Voest Alpine* steel firm, the successor to the *Hütte Linz*, a subsidiary of the *Hermann Göring Werke* (HGW). The latter itself was a huge conglomerate, estimated to have included over 400 separate enterprises in 1944.[1] The HGW was a creation of the Nazi government and oriented completely to the German war effort.

As Jabloner reemphasizes in the introduction to Stiefel's study, Austria has no legal obligation under international law to compensate the injured parties and so far has found it politically unpalatable to seriously undertake this "moral" obligation. This is a complicated question that can hardly be answered with the seriousness that it deserves in a short review. In a way—to paraphrase the 17th century English poet John Donne, who reminds us not to ask for whom the bell tolls, it tolls for thee—we all bear responsibility for that historical obscenity of all obscenities, the Hitler system, which caused such misery, of which many of us still bear personal witness. Yet, those who were closest to the scene of human depravity and all too often implicit in the propagation of this historic tragedy, the Germans and the Austrians, cannot escape being charged with greater complicity than other ethnic groups. They lacked the "civil courage" (*Zivilcourage*) to oppose the inhumanity and the legal irregularities, the "bizarre legalism" of the Nazi government, as Gerhard Mollin has called it.[2] And it was the Germans and Austrians who indeed would have needed such courage most since the foul stench of Nazism emanated most strongly from their precincts. The air was certainly not sweetened by the speed with which the Austrians restored the confiscated property of convicted Nazis after the war (Stiefel, p. 241).

The odor of death and decay inevitably accompanies a reading of the books here under review. One can only hope that at least some token may be offered to the few persons whose justified claims of payment for damages reach back as long as sixty years. It would, however, be an injustice to them and especially to the millions of people who have not survived to this day, if one would present to the few still living some alms and consider the historical account closed. However the accounting is being done, the few living witnesses of Nazism themselves are obliged to hold high the bloody banner of suffering of those who were persecuted and otherwise exposed to the brutality and the inhumanity of their fellow human beings—if that term can apply to the perpetrators of Nazi atrocities. At the same time, one must reject the idea of mass guilt since it is unjust to the righteous, who would thus be painted with the same brush. Moreover, such a broad indictment unfairly represents a historical accusation of a new generation of people who should be allowed to make their own record. At the same time, since history is a seamless web held together by the deeds and misdeeds of the predecessors, every generation, while it hopefully builds on those parts of its past that are sound and promising for a better future, must be prepared to pay for the crimes and errors committed by its forebears.

Here, we are dealing with Austria's "moral" obligation as the subject of inquiry. However, the purpose of the volumes under review goes well beyond a mere re-creation and understanding of the past. In the end, these studies are meant to provide a basis for restitution for and indemnification of injuries for which an exact accounting is often impossible to establish.[3] To realize a fair and compassionate solution one should go beyond legalistic quibbling. Besides compensating victims for ascertainable damages that they incurred for no reason of their own, an entire society should willingly take upon itself the responsibility to make some sort of redress, somewhat like supporting people in times of great emergency. As in the case of earthquakes and floods, it would take especially cold and insensitive persons who could reject a common approach to suffering, even if it has happened in the increasingly distant past. Such indemnification would be akin to the UNRRA and the Marshall Plan aid of which Austria, in particular, was a major beneficiary. This would indeed be even more apropos when compensation for harm done has been denied over these many decades and when a cynic could easily point to the low amount of liability payments that would have to be made to the tiny remainder of those harmed most directly by Nazi policies who are still alive in the 21st century. Yet, if one adopts a rigorous business-like approach, one should point out that the cost of indemnification goes up significantly with delay; using a modest rate of discount of, say, 6% per year in compound interest, the compensation for damages which a forced worker has incurred for wages below the going rate would be something in the area of 20-25 times the original income of which he was unfairly deprived. This includes only the most simple and easily ascertainable damage and excludes physical and psychological suffering, which may have negatively impacted the future income and well-being of the affected persons.

Aside from the simple accounting principle that requires the computation of lost income due to the underpayment of wages and the ascertainable physical harm done to workers who were subject to involuntary servitude, there are the stories of human suffering and the brutality that was inflicted on persons whose main guilt was that by reasons of birth they were treated as inferior categories of humanity. While Jews were graced with the Mogen David on a yellow field—which the Danish king adopted as a sign of honor for himself during the German occupation of his country—others were forced to wear alphabetic letters on their clothing that identified their land of origin, as if it were a point of disgrace. The chapter by Michael John in Rathkolb's first volume as well as the entire second volume, which incorporates Karl Fallend's interviews with persons formerly associated with the *Hermann Göring Werke* in the Linz area, give eloquent testimony to the horrors experienced by foreign forced laborers. Among other things, wage payments were calibrated to the standing of the workers' "racial" quality, with the French, Italians, and Czechs, for example, being more highly rewarded for their work than Poles, Ukrainians, Russians, and, of course, Jews, who were worth only 50% of the wage paid to members of the Reich. Somewhat curiously, the wage payments owed to Jews went into the treasury of the SS, which is curious because in the competitive climate of Nazi institutions, one might have expected that the SS would want to maximize its revenues by taking 100% of the Jews' wages. To be sure, the income from the "rental" (*Mietgebühr*, as Mark Spoerer calls it in a recently published book on Nazi forced labor) of laborers did not remain with the SS but was commingled with the general funds of the German state. It might, of course, be argued that the SS was being charitable to its competing institutions, not charging them the going rate. Or, possibly, the SS understood that the labor it was providing to the productive enterprises was so poor, due to the physical and psychological conditions of the workers, that 50% of a normal output of work was all that the Jewish and other concentration camp inmates were able to provide. If, however, the SS, as all other parts of the Nazi war machine, was to contribute the maximum possible to the war effort, this way of treating its labor resources was hardly optimal.

John's chapter of over 120 pages on the conditions under which the forced workers were required to operate is suggestive but rather incomplete. A considerable amount of space is dedicated to the choice of Linz as a location for a major steel mill. While not uninteresting, this question could have been more properly left to the two-volume history of National Socialism in Linz that was also published in 2001.[4] It is unquestionably important to specify how the foreign labor was recruited and how it was subsequently treated in the *Hermann Göring Werke*, especially in light of the object of this study, which is to ascertain the damages that these workers incurred. Beyond that, however, the organization of work in the plants deserves considerably more attention. These were after all industrial establishments which were meant to contribute critically to the German war effort. The supply of German and Austrian labor was being increasingly depleted by the need for more "warm bodies" in the military campaigns, especially the one in the Soviet Union. Reliance on forced labor thus became greater, and the chances for sabotage also increased. Nevertheless, numerous workers belonged to the "master race" in these plants. Consequently, it would have been desirable to have more details concerning the interaction between the various ethnic groups within the factories. We get glimpses of this problem; German and foreign laborers were often not allowed to speak with each other. Unquestionably, this policy had to be detrimental to the production process since communication was thus made extremely difficult. Even much of the German labor had to work under rather insecure conditions. If the experience of the steel works at Salzgitter near Braunschweig, the original firm belonging to the HGW conglomerate, is pertinent, then few workers came without some form of compulsion or coercion, even when higher wages than normal were being offered.[5] In short, a plant producing critically needed goods for the war effort, one would think, would have to operate at maximum efficiency. Himmler's dictum, *Vernichtung durch Arbeit*, i.e., extermination of undesirable people by working them to death, hardly fit into a program that required greater output of military goods.[6]

Even though one cannot push the moral questions aside when investigating the Nazi war economy, one should nevertheless concern oneself also with the more purely economic elements. If a large output of goods was required for the war effort, then the managers and officials, inside as well as outside of government, had to be aware that productivity and the well-being of workers were closely correlated. In fact, Germany was in the forefront in the research of the optimization of work. The *Kaiser Wilhelm Institut für Arbeitsphysiologie* had been actively pursuing this question since the 1920s and, during the war, was able to show that caloric input of food had a direct and positive impact on work. More food calories meant higher output.[7] Yet, working laborers to death was the preferred solution in Linz as well as in other places where concentration camp inmates and other "subhuman" workers were employed. To say the least, such policies were counterproductive and were certainly inappropriate for any rational approach. Josef Moser, in his article in the Rathkolb work, approaches this problem, but quickly drops it from further consideration. Yet, it seems to deserve a much more detailed and analytical treatment. From time to time, in this volume there are suggestions that Paul Pleiger, the head of the *Hermann Göring Werke* complex, was aware of this problem but felt himself incapable of dealing with it in the political climate within which he was forced to operate, even though his only objective was maximum production. He can certainly not be accused of having had soft, humane purposes in mind. In short, the conflict between winning the war and exterminating unwanted human beings was decided in favor of the latter. This makes the term "slave labor" inoperative since, as Mark Spoerer has recently and correctly pointed out, slaves, at least in the American context in the first half of the 19th century, represented valuable capital, whose welfare was associated with the owner's own income and wealth.[8] In this connection, Michael John's definition of forced labor in the Rathkolb volume seems unnecessarily restrictive. As Spoerer in the cited work and Gabriella Hauch in the Rathkolb volume point out, forced labor could take on a number of guises in which economic and non-economic motivations were intermingled. Was it forced labor when a young man in Poland signed a contract to work in Germany and, at the same time, was given to understand that his family would be punished if he did not sign? Or was it a voluntary agreement when the recruiter in France or Italy knowingly falsified the conditions under which the worker would exist without having recourse to complain or to return home?

To a very large extent the Rathkolb volumes deal with moral and human interest stories. It is certainly interesting that two Jewish girls in the Ukraine unsuccessfully tried to pass themselves off as Christians and audaciously volunteered for work in Germany. Hauch, in her chapter on female forced workers and their children, reported these and other anecdotes on the recruitment and coercion of foreign women workers but made little effort to integrate them into the narrative. Anecdotal evidence is indeed valuable, especially where the data are incomplete, but it would be helpful to the reader if the author went beyond the anecdotes and explained their significance. Probably Betrand Perz, in his chapter on the concentration camp inmates who were laborers in the HGW in Linz, did the best job in this respect. He emphasized the cruel inefficiency of using labor under the inhuman conditions that prevailed in the concentration camp Mauthausen and its branch camps. With the extreme scarcity of labor in the industries of the Greater German Reich, it seemed imbecilic to employ a labor force whose productivity was estimated to be half of that of non-inmate civilians. In short, pure self-interest would suggest that a somewhat better treatment of labor would redound to the benefit of the German war machine. Even as unfeeling and unscrupulous a Nazi operative as Fritz Saukel, the plenipotentiary for labor use (*Generalbevollmächtigter für den Arbeitseinsatz*), was forced to remind the *Gauleiter*, the regional leaders of the Nazi party, that starving and physically beaten Soviet workers could hardly be expected to produce much coal.[9] Moreover, it seems clear that competent skilled labor services could scarcely be expected from workers who were being starved to death and whose health was seriously impaired. Terror and corporal punishment as means to drive people to work, especially in plants where sophisticated equipment was widely used and where an output of precisely calibrated goods was required, seem at best counterproductive.

Questions that deal with labor economics deserve considerably more attention than they have received in the volumes under discussion. It may, of course, be true that the authors' main focus was the human factor; in this respect, the Rathkolb volumes did a commendable job. But a great opportunity was missed to analyze such an awkward and self-destructive organization of work. Numerous scholars have concerned themselves for decades, if not centuries, with this topic. What combination of incentives, punishment, and supervision facilitates the most effective organization of labor forces? Fear and terror only, which seemed to have been principally employed in the Linz factories, have rarely proven to be successful in the long run. Nevertheless, judging by the length of the war, they proved remarkably productive, much more than one could have predicted. There is little doubt, however, that in times of peace, a system of such crudity could not have succeeded even for a short period of time.

If a good opportunity was missed concerning the efficient organization of labor in industry, the industrial organization of the *Hermann Göring Werke* in Austria as well as in Germany and in captured territories also deserved to be examined more intensively. To be sure, the particular focus of the Rathkolb volumes was on forced labor with the objective of laying the factual groundwork for restitution and compensation for past injuries. Even with such strictures in mind, it becomes important to know how this immense conglomerate was being operated, to discover whether the labor policies were being administered uniformly or whether the HGW was, in fact, a loosely connected amalgamation of firms with a great deal of local autonomy.

This huge complex clearly produced massive internal organizational problems, let alone those that dealt with external competitors such as the SS and the Speer ministry. Historians like to deal with the machinations of personalities in leading positions whose battles over turf can be traced in documents and whose ego-driven comments make for good reading. For example, Paul Pleiger, who managed this complex that was largely owned by the German state, was especially interested in demonstrating success in opposition to private industry, as with his bet with Fritz Thyssen that in five years he would no longer be dependent on Swedish iron. Rathkolb's own chapter on the management of the Linz enterprises and their relationship with the larger complex is all too short to satisfy the questions that come to mind on this topic. For students of industrial organizations it is a very intriguing problem how such a huge complex could be held together to produce in a more or less acceptable way. Pleiger and Göring several times tried to reorganize the HGW on more rational lines.

The HGW emanated from the four-year plan that was established in 1936 with the purpose of preparing the industry for war. It evolved increasingly in opposition to the private sector, which was concerned with its position in international trade and apparently was not convinced that war was a good solution for Germany's problems.[10] Hermann Göring, who supposedly was largely illiterate in economic affairs, was placed in charge of the government program. We need not concern ourselves with the personalities that were involved but should emphasize that Göring served apparently as a convenient cover for Pleiger, a man who had some business experience in a mid-sized context, as did Hitler's economic advisor Keppler. There seems to have been considerable animosity between these outsiders and the captains of industry in the Ruhr area. The HGW got its start in 1937 with the founding of a large steel firm in Salzgitter, near Braunschweig, whose purpose it was to make use of poor quality iron ore that had previously been unusable for large-scale production. When Austria was annexed to the Reich in 1938, Linz was chosen as another site for a large iron works because Hitler wanted to elevate his old home town to world renown and because it was located near a good source of high grade iron ore in Styria. After a comparatively modest beginning, the HGW soon amassed numerous other firms, mostly in conquered territory, including the Vitkovice iron works in northern Moravia, the Skoda armament firm in western Bohemia, the de Wendel firm in France, and numerous others. In 1944, the HGW in Austria alone employed well over 54,000 workers. Needless to say, the organization that managed this huge complex of some 400 firms was unwieldy. Gigantism is a failing of our day and is not unique to Nazi Germany. One need only be reminded of the centralized, huge industrial establishments in the defunct Soviet Union to be convinced of the inefficiency of such arrangements. Studying the HGW may also prove to be a giant headache for anyone who wishes to disentangle the lines of authority. But the question remains whether any economies of scale can be drawn up for the HGW in general and the Linz properties in particular. Specialists in the field of industrial organization have long contended that the problems of communication up and down the hierarchy, especially after a concern hits a particularly large size, tend to become very costly, often erasing much of the potential benefits of a large-scale operation.

Beside the problems of internal organization within a huge industrial complex like the *Hermann Göring Werke*, the mere fact of creating large firms has been a subject of discussion among specialists in industrial organization. One leading hypothesis suggests that performing relevant activities on the market has become so costly that it can be done more cheaply within a firm where the fiat of the managers can be substituted for market procedures that are less predictable. It is, of course, true that even in the most market-oriented countries, like the United States, war production is largely removed from the market nexus by having firms manufacture goods on a cost-plus basis. The struggle between the Nazi potentates and the leaders of Germany's private industry demonstrates adequately that market orientation was largely abandoned quite early especially following the "anti-liberal" concepts of men like Pleiger (Rathkolb, p. 289). These are questions that beg a detailed examination. In his short chapter, Rathkolb makes a good start in that direction, and writers such as Helmut Fiereder in his work about the HGW in Linz and August Meyer in his book about the entire conglomerate have provided further evidence.[11]

One of the more baffling components of the first volume of Rathkolb's work is the tediously long recital of statistical data. Comprising 140 pages, this volume informs the reader, for example, of the year of birth and country of origin of workers segregated by gender. The reader thus learns, for instance, that one male worker born in 1881 and no female worker came from Denmark. It would have helped greatly if the author, Michaela Schober, had suggested how such data could be useful. A member of the historical archive of the *Voest-Alpine Montan A.G.*, Schober unquestionably did a fine job in ferreting out all sorts of data, but it would have been welcome if she had been joined in this endeavor by a statistician who could have provided the reader with some analysis. It may, of course, have been the case that this volume was composed in too much of a hurry to meet all the desiderata. After all, it took only two years to produce this rather formidable work. Actually, the few tables that are found at the end of Josef Moser's chapter (pp. 351-54) provide some very interesting statistical data and demonstrate the value of concise information in the study of a complex organization on a local level.

Certainly the most gripping part of the Rathkolb work is the second volume. In it the psychologist Karl Fallend presents a panorama of personal experiences of persons engaged in various occupations in the steel mill in Linz. Fallend carefully explains his method of examination, which depended heavily on personal interviews. Even though these interviews clearly do not represent a scientific sample of persons associated with the firm, they spell out a fairly chilling picture of the goings-on in the Linz industry. Over all, however, they raise many more questions than they answer. As in another work of this genre, Valentina Maria Stefanski's *Zwangsarbeit in*

Leverkusen (Osnabrück: Fibre, 2000), the interrogator had to be concerned that her/his questions might in fact arouse long dormant traumas. Nevertheless, Fallend's contribution to the Rathkolb work is indeed valuable and provides anyone dealing with social problems in the near or distant past with an outline of how such examinations can take place. It is naturally impossible to subject dead persons to direct psychological examination, and thus the experiences of the majority of those forced to work in the HGW complex will forever remain moot.

Many of the methodological problems that seem to have plagued the Rathkolb volumes are fortunately less apparent, if at all, in Dieter Stiefel's book on the implications of Nazi practices for the life insurance industry of Austria and on the devices used after the war to return the industry to its former state. It is likely that the treatment of the problems connected with insurance firms is less complex than the labor policies of industrial firms. Stiefel, an accomplished economic historian, combines all the required talents in his own person, thus obviating the problems that inevitably attend the merging of different approaches. Just as the Rathkolb volumes, Stiefel's book is forced to concern itself not only with Austrian firms but must consider the implications that flow from their incorporation into the greater German orbit. In this respect, Stiefel was undoubtedly aided greatly by being able to refer to the manuscript of Gerald Feldman's recently published book *Allianz and the German Insurance Business, 1933-1945* (Cambridge: Cambridge University, 2001). Despite the fact that Stiefel's volume was financed by the Austrian Association of Insurance Companies, it is clearly an objective study in which the investigator was able to exercise his judgment without any interference from interested parties.

A first-rate business history, Stiefel's examination of the life insurance industry reveals what should have been a considerably less problematic outcome in the way of compensating the injured parties for their damages. The Nazi government made itself the beneficiary of Jewish insurance policies and required insurance firms to pay the paid-up value to the Reich government. The remedy to the injured parties in this case seems straightforward: Such ill-concealed, blatant robbery of assets should be unambiguously paid back to its residual owners. Even if the title to life insurance policies that were in this way sequestered should be fairly easily ascertained, the problem of liability raises its ugly head since the Austrian firms were frequently merged with German firms. Incidentally, a further distinction between the Rathkolb work and Stiefel's should be alluded to in this connection: Stiefel devotes a considerably greater amount of space to the efforts that have been made since the end of the war to satisfy damage claims.

One of the great merits of Stiefel's book is that he recognizes the importance of tying the problems of the Austrian insurance industry in with that of Germany. Although this seems to be a clear and obvious requirement for such a study, it sets it off to some extent from the Rathkolb volumes. It is of course true that a huge and unwieldy industrial complex like the HGW poses many more problems than a considerably smaller industry like the life insurance companies. Rathkolb's authors do not completely ignore the all-German context of the subject of their investigation. Both the Stiefel and the Rathkolb studies indicate that Austria and Austrians did not fare especially well under German dominance. However, the Rathkolb authors may have been more restrictive in this respect and could thus have separated the Austrian context more diligently from that of Germany. The lack of this is regrettable since the economic integration within the German Reich was after all one of the most salient aspects of Austria's experience under Nazi domination.

Stiefel's treatment goes well beyond simply specifying the problems of the insurance industry. He also summarizes well the economic and political environment within which the insurance industry operated under the Nazi rule and the political milieu of the postwar period in Austria. Unquestionably a poor and rather battered country after the war, Austria did all it could to place itself into the category of victims of aggression and therefore proclaimed itself not responsible for the injuries that happened to other victims such as the Jews and the forced workers from abroad. Germany, an even poorer and more battered country after the end of the war than Austria, was, as Stiefel notes, the only country that faced up to its responsibilities. There were, of course, numerous difficulties associated with the German Republic's efforts to compensate all those persons and countries that had been harmed by the Nazi war machine.[12] In Austria, ambivalence ruled the day much more so than in Germany—excluding the Communist-ruled GDR—where Konrad Adenauer was able to push through a program of restitution quite early. Austria's position was in part articulated by its stand in 1945, when one memorandum of the foreign office asserted that all the persecutions were the fault of the German occupying troops. At the same time, the same government agency admitted that anti-Semitism in Vienna was actually more pronounced than in Germany. Coincidentally at about the same time the office of the Austrian chancellor found that world Jewry was so powerful that even without constituting a state it was the fifth greatest power and was responsible for the defeat of Hitlerite Germany. For this undeserved compliment, echoing Nazi propaganda, the Jews paid for with six million dead.

Notes

1. August Meyer, *Das Syndikat* (Braunschweig: Steinweg, 1986), 198.

2. Gerhard Mollin, *Montankonzerne und "Drittes Reich"* (Göttingen: Vandenhoek & Ruprecht, 1988), 125.

3. For the immense difficulties associated with this general problem see Hans Günter Hockerts, "Wiedergutmachung in Deutschland," *Vierteljahrshefte für Zeitgeschichte* 49 (2001): 167-214.

4. Fritz Mayrhofer and Walter Schuster, eds., *Nationalsozialsimus in Linz* (Linz: Archiv der Stadt Linz, 2001).

5. Gerd Wysocki, *Zwangsarbeit im Stahlkonzern* (Braunschweig: Magni, 1982), 44f.

6. Mark Spoerer, "Profitierten Unternehmer von KZ-Arbeit?," *Historische Zeitschrift* 268 (1999): 61-95, esp. 89.

7. H.A. Kraut and E.A. Muller, "Calorie Intake and Industrial Output," *Science* 104 (1946): 495-97.

8. Mark Spoerer, *Zwangsarbeit unter dem Hakenkreuz* (Stuttgart: Deutsche Verlagsanstalt, 2001).

9. Kurt Tweraser, "Die Linzer Wirtschaft im Nationalsozialismus," in *Nationalsozialismus in Linz*, ed. Fritz Mayrhofer and Walter Schuster (Linz: Archiv der Stadt Linz, 2001), 470.

10. For a good discussion on this topic see Mollin, *Montankonzerne*.

11. Helmut Fiereder, *Reichswerke "Hermann Göring" in Österreich* (Vienna: Geyer, 1983); Meyer, *Das Syndikat*.

12. See Hockerts, "Wiedergutmachung in Deutschland."

BOOK REVIEWS

Otto Klambauer, *Der Kalte Krieg in Österreich: Vom Dritten Mann zum Fall des Eisernen Vorhangs* (Vienna: Ueberreuter, 2000)

Matthias Pape, *Ungleiche Brüder: Österreich und Deutschland 1945-1965* (Cologne: Böhlau, 2000)

Wolfgang Krieger

Austria's place in the history of the cold war has been the subject of numerous excellent studies in recent years. Unfortunately, Otto Klambauer's book adds little to those debates. It is written in a superficial journalistic style. More importantly, it fails to address some of the key issues such as Austria's economic recovery, her rather controversial policies of denazification, the creation and purpose of her armed forces, and her economic, political, and psychological relationship with the German neighbor. Even the classical topic of Austria's neutrality as created by the State Treaty of 1955 is hardly mentioned. Thus, the reader gets little idea of the subtle interplay between the various factors which brought about Austria's almost miraculous recovery.

Much of the book's weakness is owed to the misplaced reliance upon interviews with former decision makers and other important Austrian figures, whom the author permits to tell their favorite little stories any which way they fancy. For obvious reasons, those witnesses have no inclination to discuss their own shortcomings, unresolved problems, and outright failures. It would have been up to the author to set them right, provide supplementary information, and put their statements into perspective.

Fortunately, there are a few worthwhile elements in the book as well, above all a short chapter on Cardinal Franz König, the former archbishop of Vienna. To appreciate his story, the reader must understand that König was and actually still is a veritable icon among liberal Catholics across Europe. It is with amazing frankness that the cardinal discusses some of his activities in cold war church diplomacy. He even criticizes some of the Vatican's policies vis-à-vis the communist world.

In 1960, König made an adventurous trip to Yugoslavia for the funeral of the bishop of Zagreb. That visit nearly caused his own premature funeral because König's car was hit by a truck, killing his driver and gravely injuring himself and his assistant. He survived surgery in a Yugoslav hospital and was eventually returned to Vienna. Could the KGB have been behind all this? Unlikely, König thinks even today. After the cardinal had made a full recovery, Pope John XXIII urged him to continue his activities behind the Iron Curtain and to pay a visit to Cardinal Mindszenty, who lived as a refugee in the U.S. embassy in Budapest: "It's not far [from Vienna]," the pope pleaded with König. "Just go to the station and buy yourself a ticket—it'll work out" (page 117). König did so in 1963. The two men first spoke Latin then English with each other. Years later König's diplomacy led to the release of the Hungarian cardinal. Eventually the battleground shifted to Poland. With the arrival of a Polish pope, Moscow feared that the church would fight openly against communism by putting human and political rights, such as the right to form labor unions, on its agenda.

In a way, König's initiative was typical of the role played by Austria in the cold war: from the formation of the Renner government in April 1945, to the Marshall Plan, and all the way to Vienna's special relationship with Budapest in the summer of 1989. Time and again, Austria was the site of experiments and initiatives which gradually helped to overcome the cold war division of Europe. In the end, Austria herself was released from her cold war shackles when, in September 1991, Soviet President Gorbachev pronounced his permission that Austria could join the European Union without violating Austria's 1955 pledge of neutrality.

Matthias Pape's *Ungleiche Brüder* is a completely different sort of book. It deals with an aspect of post-1945 Austrian history, which is perhaps more crucial than most Austrians would care to admit, namely Austrian-German relations between 1945 and 1965. Here we find all the painstaking research, all the detailed descriptions of practically each and every important (or perhaps not so important) diplomatic move made in Vienna and Bonn, which can possibly contribute to our understanding of this bilateral relationship. Most notably, Pape does not restrict his analysis to diplomacy in the narrow sense of the word, but includes public perceptions and debates which helped shape policies on both sides. While guiding the reader through a maze of diplomatic details, he keeps his eye firmly on a question which is very profound indeed: How did Austria's national identity emerge after the fall of the Third Reich?

To introduce his subject, Pape reaches far back into the19th century, when Prussia's victory in her brief war against Austria, in 1866, destroyed the German Federation. It had been created by the Congress of Vienna in an effort to restore the balance of powers in central Europe and to prevent both Prussia and Austria from gobbling up the several dozen medium-sized and smaller German states. This arrangement had been eroded first by Prussia's liberal trade policies of the 1830s, then by the popular forces of German nationalism and liberalism during the revolution of 1848, and finally by the clever political scheming of Prussia's Prime Minister Otto von Bismarck. A new German Empire emerged in 1870, which meant nothing less than a complete break of the political ties between the German-speaking Habsburg territories and the rest of the German nation, now looking to Prussia for leadership. The German-Austrian Alliance Treaty of 1879 was a poor substitute on several counts. It defined in rather vague terms the cooperation of the two empires in their foreign policies, particularly as far as Russia was concerned. For the Germans, it proved to be of little use in taming either Russian expansionism or France's strive for revanche. Eventually, Austria turned it into an instrument for chaining Berlin to Vienna's troubles in the Balkans, a strategy which tragically led to World War I and to the crushing of the Habsburg Empire.

The results are well known. While the non-German populations of the Austro-Hungarian Empire organized themselves into newly created sovereign states, the majority of the German-speaking populations wound up in the Austrian Republic, with several millions left to fight for themselves as minority groups scattered throughout central and eastern Europe. No wonder many people viewed this new republic to be both historically illogical and economically unviable. Austrian Socialists even went a step further and hoped to unite their new republic with the then Socialist-governed Republic of Germany. But the Allied powers, at their peace conference in Paris, strictly forebade such a union.

When the Allies finally changed their minds and agreed to the Anschluss of 1938, they did so under radically changed political and economic circumstances. Hitler's Germany had skillfully and brutally undermined the Austrian state, weakened as it was by the world economic crisis. In what seemed a "new Europe," an "appeased" Germany, indeed an economically strengthened and territorially enlarged Germany, seemed to promise stability and safety from the latent dangers of Soviet communism. As in 1919, Britain and France saw Austria as an annex to the German question. From the perspective of most Austrians, there was little reason to pass up this opportunity now that the Austrian political system was in such a bad state, mainly due to irreconcilable differences among its political parties and leaders. From an economic perspective, Hitler's apparent successes in overcoming mass unemployment in Germany was a ray of hope to many Austrians, too. Now seemed the time to overcome the legacy of 1866 and to form a single German nation, a feeling which Hitler as a native Austrian abused for his own purposes.

It is this ambivalence between an Austrian identity, mostly shaped by the newly discredited Habsburgs, and a difficult-to-define German-ness which underlay the policies of post-1945 Austria. Yet, in contrast to the ill-fated first Austrian Republic, the leadership of the Second Republic was determined to set out on a completely new political course, based on a new Austrian identity as far removed from a German identity as possible. Based on the Moscow Declaration of 1943 and eventually enshrined in the Austrian State Treaty of 1955, the Austrian Republic was restored and endowed with privileges which, in many ways, put Austria ahead of Germany in the international cold war pecking order. Apart from marginal border changes, Austria's territory was preserved in full while Germany lost her eastern provinces beyond the Oder-Neisse line. The occupying powers withdrew all their military forces from Austria by 1955 whereas up to 800,000 troops stayed in eastern and western Germany through 1994, of which some 70,000 are left in the united Germany even today. Austria had to pay considerable reparations to the Soviet Union but received—per head of population—about ten times as much in Marshall Plan aid as Germany and paid little compensation for Nazi crimes, whether to Jewish survivors or to Israel or to other European survivors of the Nazi camps.

How was this possible? Both the German public and the Bonn government rather angrily observed the strategy by which the new Austrian leadership managed to convince the world that Austria and her people had allegedly remained innocent of any Nazi crimes although the percentage of Nazi party members and SS volunteers was the same as in Germany, if not higher. By the same token, in proportion, the number of Jews and other minorities who were deported from Austria and killed was as bad or worse than in Germany. As a wisecrack once put it: "The greatest success of Austrian diplomacy was to make the world believe that Mozart and Beethoven were Austrians and Hitler was a German."

While most people know that Beethoven was a native of Bonn, fewer stop to think that Mozart's native city of Salzburg first became part of the Habsburg empire in 1805, or 14 years after the composer's death. Yet the year 1956, marking his 200th birthday, was shrewdly used by the Austrian leadership to present Mozart as part of the newly defined "Austrian heritage." This was somewhat curious since a number of prominent musicologists had to rewrite their earlier assessments, which had depicted Mozart as a typical product of "German culture"—some of their writings had been published only a few years earlier during the "Mozart year" of 1941, marking the composer's death 150 years earlier. The maestro himself would no doubt have been much amused by these transformations of his national identity. To him it was all about "German" musical drama competing against French and, most importantly, Italian opera. Beyond that, music was an international rather than a national business as his childhood concert tours had taught him.

But Austrian officials were far from amused by such cultural quarrels. In the fall of 1955, when the prestigious *Burgtheater* in Vienna was to be reopened, a noisy fight broke out over the first play to be performed there. Rather than *Egmont* by Goethe, born, alas, in Frankfurt, Austrian nationalists demanded that preference be given to a play by the Austrian dramatist Grillparzer. His *King Ottokar*, however, a play about a mediaeval family feud of the Habsburgs, was not entirely politically correct either. After all, King Rudolf von Habsburg claimed that "German blood" was flowing through his veins, and in the play's dramatic ending "the people" shouted "Hail Austria! Habsburg forever!" The drama, originally banned by censorship in 1823, was now performed in a "slightly altered" version.

The key to much of this confusion about Austrian identity lies in the way the Anschluss came to be viewed both legally and politically. If the Austrian government could claim, as it successfully did, that Hitler's move of March 1938 had been one of brute force, post-1945 Austria would herself claim to be a victim of Nazi Germany and would not have to pay compensation to other victims. It would even be entitled to compensation from Germany. On that basis, German property on Austrian territory could be confiscated for such compensation, and broadly speaking, this is what was actually done in the Austrian State Treaty of 1955.

It comes as no surprise that this famous treaty marks an all-time low in post-1945 relations between Austria and Germany. The issue of German property in Austria has a long and twisted history, which Pape unravels with great skill. There was of course the issue of Nazi investment and the penetration of German big business after 1938, which made the Austrian economy a part, indeed a most valuable part, of the German war economy. Quite understandably, the Allies wished to sever those ties in order to make Austrian independence viable. The Soviets went one step further and wished to make sure that Austria could not contribute to NATO's rearmament efforts, after West Germany had been admitted to NATO just a few months earlier. Therefore, German property was transferred wholesale to the Austrian government, and this was done without compensation. Even property from before 1938 was included in this package.

Not surprisingly, the Bonn government was furious and complained both to the Austrian government and to the Western powers, their new military allies. But nothing was achieved because, in this particular case, the Americans had no interest in protecting the Germans. Indeed, it was the American negotiators who had suggested this formula to their erstwhile war allies because, thus, German property questions were handled the same way as they had been with regard to German property in the United States. In other words, if this was a clause which contravened international law, as Bonn claimed, it was written by the Americans rather than the Austrian Socialists who Bonn suspected to be responsible for this. Indeed, this information was given to the Germans by the U.S. State Department.

If the Austrian State Treaty marked a low point in the relations between Bonn and Vienna, it was also an object of intense speculation, not just in Bonn but in many other places. If the Soviets were ready to withdraw their forces and to restore Austria to full sovereignty, what would it take to make them negotiate a similar treaty for Germany? Some observers wondered if Austria was merely a testing ground for an imminent settlement of the much larger German question. Had Moscow already made up its mind on that issue?

Among the number of questions which can be derived from this subject, the most interesting is still to some degree unanswerable. What were the Soviets' priorities with respect to Europe and how did they expect to achieve their goals? A comprehensive answer is still not possible and perhaps the Soviet leadership never had a clearly defined plan in the first place. Pape explores in considerable detail a narrower question which concerns the connection between the Austrian and the German questions. He takes a strong position against those scholars, like Rolf Steininger and Michael Gehler, who have argued or somehow implied that Austria had been able to negotiate with the Soviets autonomously, i.e., without the close support of the Western powers. Pape explicitly follows the argument, which was made privately by Austrian Chancellor Julius Raab, that Austrian neutrality and the withdrawal of all Western forces from Austrian territory was only acceptable, both to Austria and to the rest of Western Europe, because Western Allied forces were retained on West German territory. Therefore, the Austrian solution of 1955 was neither a model for Germany nor could it be used as an argument against the policies of West German Chancellor Konrad Adenauer, whose pro-NATO course was directed, among other things, against a quick compromise with the Soviets. For Julius Raab, Austrian neutrality was a means of "getting the Soviets out of the country." In case of war, "Austria would always side with the west," he said (page 308 and passim).

Much more could be said about this thoughtful and important work by Pape. Fellow researchers will note with interest that a major new body of sources on the subject was uncovered in the personal papers of Bonn's first representative in Vienna, Carl Hermann Mueller-Graaf, whose reporting was highly sensitive to the growing pains of the Second Austrian Republic. (Pape includes a few excerpts in the book's appendix.) A wealth of other papers were consulted, though the author admits that none could fully compensate for the failure to get access to the relevant security classified government files in Austria and Germany. One is really at a loss to explain what might still legitimately be hidden from researchers in those files. Today, very few papers could possibly qualify as state secrets or as truly private information.

Finally it is worth noting that Pape makes excellent use of press materials whereby he does not simply quote what he happens to come across. He tries to follow systematically what positions the major newspapers and their most prominent journalists took throughout the period and how they are relevant for the issues explored in this book. This deserves mentioning because contemporary history is all too often written in a manner which overemphasizes the value of government documents, without asking what might be missing in the available files and without having first fully explored what is available in the public domain. Of course, Pape also interviewed witnesses where he could find them. (And he found an amazing number of them!) But unlike Klambauer he took all the necessary precautions not to become their spokesperson. Together, those qualities mark Pape as one of the foremost younger experts on central European contemporary history.

Stephen E. Ambrose, *The Wild Blue. The Men and Boys Who Flew the B-24s over Germany* (New York: Simon & Schuster, 2001)

Siegfried Beer

Stephen Ambrose, the popular historian of American exploits in World War II, has done it again: He has written a readable, at times even gripping, account of the experiences of a fairly small segment of the American fighting forces, the Fifteenth Air Force of the Army Air Forces, which operated out of Italy. However, this time the celebrated author, sought-after television personality of elaborate documentaries as well as many talk shows, and movie consultant (as Steven Spielberg's military adviser), was caught and found wanting in his scholarly analysis. Not only did he not cover his subject adequately, but he has also opened himself up to the charge of plagiarism and scholarly misconduct, which has been widely discussed in the American print media as well as on campuses nationwide. Given his prolific output of market-oriented bestsellers on American heroics in the last world war, produced on market-demand over the last five years or so, none of this really comes as a surprise.

The Wild Blue is a narrative eulogy on the pilots and crews of the B-24 bomber, perhaps better known as the "Liberator." Like many of Ambrose's books, it focuses on representatives of what Ambrose (and Tom Brokaw) calls the "greatest generation" of young Americans, in particular the bomber crew of the "Dakota Queen," piloted by *the* later U.S. senator and presidential candidate, George S. McGovern. McGovern flew thirty-five combat missions against Hitler's Third Reich, several of them against Austrian targets, primary or secondary (Vienna, Moosbierbaum, Wiener Neustadt, Amstetten, Innsbruck, Steyr, Salzburg, Linz, Krieglach, and Graz). While Ambrose does describe how the U.S. Army Air Forces recruited, trained, and chose those who would fly and man the B-24s—pilots, bombardiers, navigators, and gunners—there is very little mention of the strategic thinking, planning, and operating of the Eighth and Fifteenth Air Forces in the European Theatre prior to the arrival of McGovern and his crew in November 1944. The author describes convincingly that dropping bombs on economic and military targets in at times vigorously defended enemy territory required not just great skill and stamina, but profound courage on the part of bomber crews. However, due to his usual patriotic focus on the history of these men and boys in their B-24s, he neglects many of the larger questions which other military historians have raised, as, for example, how effective the Allies' campaign of strategic bombing really was or whether military target bombing did not also involve a good deal of terror bombing of civilian populations. The perspectives, fears, and reactions of those at the receiving end are never mentioned.

When all of McGovern's requisite number of missions have been discussed, the book basically ends, followed only by a synopsis of what McGovern, whom Ambrose clearly reveres, did with the rest of his life. McGovern is portrayed as a skilled, courageous, and thoughtful pilot, who has well earned his Distinguished Flying Cross and who deserves the respect of his crew and colleagues. He is greatly concerned about the inadvertent bombing of an Austrian farmhouse on a troubled mission towards the end of the war. Ambrose even manages to solve this tricky and final plot detail: McGovern, a full forty years later, on a visit to Innsbruck, finds out that the attacked farmer was what McGovern considered one of the rare Austrian anti-Nazis, who even "thought at the time that if bombing our farm reduced the length of the war by one hour or one minute, it was well worth it" (p.263). Hollywood would (and, who knows, maybe will) savor this particular detail.

Needless to say, this book has little to do with a serious and scholarly treatment of the air war in World War II. Ambrose's approach is totally unilateral, patriotic, piecemeal, personal, and thus narrow in scope. It is based primarily on individual histories and oral interviews conducted many decades (presumably at least five) after the fact, and only scantily on the rich, expansive, and easily available international research, both literary and archival, about the Allied strategic and terror bombing in World War II. Though the author provides an almost three-page-long list of secondary literature and a fair amount of mostly skimpy endnotes, the alert and educated reader (not to mention the air war specialist) quickly senses the lack of grounding in solid research. Ambrose, for example, was not interested in consulting the Army Air Force planning and operational records at the Albert F. Simpson Historical Research Center at Maxwell Air Force Base, Alabama, or the various extensive record groups (RGs) at the National Archives in College Park, Maryland. There, he would have had access to RG 243: United States Strategic Bombing Survey and RG 331: Allied Operational and Occupation Headquarters—Mediterranean Allied Air Forces (MAAF), both of which should have been included in his research. Furthermore, he could have found useful documentation on the effect of these strategic bombardments on the ground, for example, in the German Federal Military Archives at Freiburg/Breisgau or at several regional archives, *again* for example in Austrian provincial capitals. Ambrose completely ignored German and Austrian research of the last decade on the Allied aerial bombardment of central Europe in World War II, which is generally based on a wide array of international archival and literary sources. Our bestseller historian would have discovered that, just to take the example of Austria, solid studies exist on the air war against western Austria, against the central Austrian province and city of Salzburg, and against the southern Austrian region routinely overflown by American and RAF-bombers since the late fall of 1943.[1] This merely refers to the more recent monographic publications on this topic.

As reflected in the substantiated accusations of Ambrose's plagiarism—drawing from another American study about World War II bomber pilots—this book has been put together and produced hastily and sloppily by author and publisher. A quick glance at the index corroborates this impression as it reveals several misspelled Austrian and German names of towns. Maps of southern and central Europe indicating the location of Allied bases and principal bombing targets would have been quite helpful, particularly to the American reader. Moreover, in serious works of historical research the dates of oral history interviews are generally offered as a reference for the close reader who wants to know about the distance between experience and memory of the author's main informants. Such references are, however, lacking here.

The Wild Blue is written in the same vein as Ambrose's earlier blockbuster books on World War II, only that it provides even less historical research and original analysis. It continues the "hero approach" for yet another segment of the American war experience. This time there are actually several types of protagonist-heroes: First, the strenuous yet rugged B-24 bomber plane represents one of America's forgotten workhorse weapons. Then, the twenty-two-year-old 2nd Lt. George McGovern, a typical U.S. Army Air Force pilot of the 741st Squadron, 455th Bomb Group of the Fifteenth Air Force, is the splendid representative of his war generation. Finally, there is his crew (and other Cerignola, Italy, crews) of young men, mostly in their late teens and early twenties who, as Ambrose assures us, "in doing good work . . . saved western civilization" (p. 251).

We now know that heroic, nostalgic, and patriotic history sells, certainly in America, but such work can and will not be deemed relevant by the international, academic community.

Notes

1. Thomas Albrich and Arno Gisinger, *Im Bombenkrieg. Tirol und Vorarlberg 1943-1945* (Innsbruck: Haymon, 1992); Erich Marx, ed., *Bomben auf Salzburg. Die "Gauhauptstadt" im "Totalen Krieg"* (Salzburg: Archiv der Stadt Salzburg, 1995); Siegfried Beer and Stefan Karner, *Der Krieg aus der Luft. Kärnten und Steiermark 1941-1945* (Graz: Weishaupt, 1992).

Peter Thaler, *The Ambivalence of Identity: The Austrian Experience of Nation-Building in a Modern Society*, Central European Studies, edited by Charles W. Ingrao (West Lafayette: Purdue University Press, 2001)

Peter Utgaard

Few historiographical questions in postwar Austria have been as provocative as those surrounding Austrian identity. The obvious, but often unspoken, reasons for controversy are that in the aftermath of the Great War many Austrians wanted to unite with Germany, and that in 1938 Austria became part of Nazi Germany. This meant that in postwar Austria the idea of the Austrian nation and a self-confident sense of Austrian identity could not be taken for granted. Of course, postwar Austria eventually became a great success as the country came to be defined by a stable government and prosperous citizens who, for the most part, saw themselves as Austrians and believed in the Austrian nation. But how this happened poses a fascinating and in some ways controversial question: To build an Austrian nation, it had to be assumed that there was always an Austria, specifically, an Austria that was *not* German. Peter Thaler examines these topics with an effective organization and a convincing theoretical framework.

Thaler begins by summarizing several theories of modern nationalism and concludes that national particularities make it difficult to apply any single theory with precision. Thaler points out that theories of nationalism are more complex with non-Western countries. However, here the author briefly loses focus: "But in China—and in Japan—one can observe the gradual development of collective identity based on cultural and territorial elements that also characterizes many European nations" (p. 14). Given that modern Chinese and Japanese national identity and nationalism developed rather differently from European countries, the author would have been better off eliminating this detour from his introduction. Ultimately, Thaler finds that the instrumentalist theory of nationalism, "... which ascribes the forming of national identities to the conscious efforts of nationalist elite" (p. 16), is the most appropriate for postwar Austria.

Thaler's adoption of the instrumentalist idea is developed in the subsequent three chapters, which collectively form the core of the work. In chapter 2, "Catalyst or Precondition: The Socioeconomic Environment of Austrian Nation-Building," Thaler argues that the social and economic success of the Second Republic was a key "precondition for the development of an Austrian national consciousness" (p. 43). Of particular interest in the chapter is how the Austrian economy was closely tied to the West German economy and to that of Western Europe in general (i.e., *not* to the successor states of the empire). In chapters 3 and 4, Thaler discusses the intellectual foundations and instruments of Austrian nation-building. In these chapters, the author provides a dispassionate and sophisticated analysis of oft-politicized themes in Austrian historiography. In particular, Thaler should be praised for his criticism of Austrianist historians who interpreted the past selectively and dismissed or ignored the German self-image of numerous Austrian constituencies throughout history. Thaler further debunks the *Mitteleuropa* idea popular in the 1980s—i.e., the notion that Austria's past and future lay with Central Europe (minus Germany), and the Danubian Basin—by pointing to empirical data which indicates that Austrians see themselves as much more similar to Germans than to Czechs, Hungarians, or Yugoslavs. Finally, Thaler also challenges the idea that a self-confident Austrian identity was born *during* the Second World War (rather than after). While he is convincing on this point, Thaler would have benefited from Evan Bukey's definitive work, *Hitler's Austria: Popular Sentiment in the Nazi Era, 1938-1945* (Chapel Hill: U of North Carolina P, 2000).

One thread uniting the two schools of thought, Austrianism and *Mitteleuropa*, is the stubborn insistence that Austria was both eternal and not German. While Thaler methodically deconstructs each of these notions, his purpose is not to imply that Austrian identity, as it came to be, was somehow false, but rather that it was produced out of postwar conditions and cultivated by Austrian political elites. Thaler's adoption of the instrumentalist theory is further born out in his discussions of judicial and educational instruments of nation-building. The transformation of Austrian identity is chronicled in the fifth chapter, "Measuring Identity," where Thaler (after appropriately discussing the limits of public opinion research) summarizes several important surveys about Austrian identity from the immediate postwar period through the 1990s. These surveys demonstrate the remarkable success of Austrian nation-building: For example, one study showed that in 1994 72% agreed that "The Austrians are a nation," as compared to 47% in 1964 (p.168).

Overall, Thaler's work, while mostly convincing and well argued, is not without flaw. The writing tends towards the passive construction and Thaler relegates too much important text to the notes. At times, this results in cumbersome reading and, more significantly, in a tendency to understate key points. Furthermore, Thaler does not clearly convey the gravity of Austria's position in the immediate postwar context and he understates the importance of the Four Powers. For example, in his discussion of economics Thaler barely mentions the Marshall Plan. A better conveyance of the significance of the occupation might have added nuance to the arguments and motivations of the postwar Austrianists. There is also a considerable literature on the idea of Austrian victimization as key to Austrian identity (admittedly my own area of interest) that Thaler does not take into account. In general, Thaler's reading of the relevant works, while extensive, is not comprehensive. Important works that should have been cited include Anton Pelinka, *Austria: Out of the Shadow of the Past* (Boulder: Westview Press, 1998), Ruth Wodak, et al., *The Discursive Construction of National Identity* (Edinburgh: Edinburgh University Press, 1999), and Günter Bischof, *Austria in the First Cold War, 1945-55: The Leverage of the Weak* (New York: St. Martin's Press, 1999). Also, he does not use enough primary sources, particularly in the chapter "Measuring Identity," which would have benefited from additional sources beyond the public opinion surveys. In the end, the reader understands that everyday Austrians came to see themselves as Austrians, but is not entirely sure how and why this happened.

These criticisms aside, Thaler's study makes a solid contribution to our understanding of postwar Austrian identity. He also successfully argues that Austria's postwar experience enhances our understanding of the conceptual foundations of nationhood. Depending of course on how one defines a nation, the Austrian case seems to demonstrate that deliberate nation-building can succeed. This is a sobering, and for Thaler, a seemingly troubling thought:

> [T]he malleability of consciousness suggested by the Austrian experience also raises questions about its formation and its interrelationship with objective social, political, cultural, and economic conditions. More than anything else, the Austrian experience of nation-building reveals a frequently underestimated aspect of this process: the potential ambivalence of identity (p.188).

This conclusion is not entirely satisfying. Based on the Austrian experience of five state structures in the twentieth century (Empire, First Republic, *Ständestaat*, Third Reich, and Second Republic), one is tempted to ask if Austrian identity is better characterized as ambivalent or as variegated, yet unequivocally Austrian.

Peter Berger, *Im Schatten der Diktatur. Die Finanzdiplomatie des Vertreters des Völkerbundes in Österreich, Meinoud Marinus Rost van Tonningen, 1931-1936* (Vienna: Böhlau, 2000)

Jens-Wilhelm Wessels

The League of Nations' financial reconstruction scheme and fiscal control in the 1920s and early 1930s strongly influenced the main events of Austrian economic diplomacy at the time, such as the Geneva Protocols of 1922, the collapse of the *Creditanstalt (CA)* and the Lausanne loan of 1932. However, the nature and course of the actual relationship of financial diplomacy between the League and Austria, between the League's representatives in Vienna, officials in Geneva and the big players of Western finance have never been traced in such great detail before the publication of Peter Berger's work. As most studies on the role of the League of Nations and its relationship to Austria have primarily focused on political aspects, this work also represents the first modern attempt to portray at length the financial politics of the League's effort to implement its orthodox reconstruction scheme.

By focusing on the political life of Rost van Tonningen, the main League representative in Austria after 1926, and his involvement in Austrian politics and financial policy-making, Berger not only reveals how Rost's life reflected the attempt of Western finance to exert its economic and political influence on Austria, but also why this attempt failed. The figure of Rost van Tonningen, a Dutch national who worked for the League's Financial Committee, is not an obvious target for a political biography of such length, since he was only a minor, not very influential, political player of his time. However, the astonishing fact that, in the course of his life, Rost changed from being an archetypical representative of Western orthodox finance and its principles to being a radical Nazi and SS member, vindicates such an extensive, non-structural historical analysis.

In addition, Rost's controversial involvements with some of the most important contemporary Austrian, German, and Dutch political and financial figures and events make this work a valuable research object and worthwhile reading. In his position as League representative of Western financial interests and fiscal adviser to the Austrian government, Rost interacted closely with such diversified groups as Western and Austrian central bankers, the members of the League's Financial Committee, the heads of the Austrian government (especially Dollfuß), the Austrian Social Democrats, *Heimwehr* representatives, the representatives of Nazi Germany (e.g. Himmler), and the main Dutch Nazis (e.g. Anton Mussert), to mention only the most important. By depicting Rost's involvement in major Austrian political and financial events, Berger circuitously describes the intriguing story of interwar financial diplomacy, the breakdown of parliamentary democracy, and the rise of fascism. The reader is taken through the gamut of not only Austrian, but also German and Dutch interwar financial and political history. The protagonist's connection to the implementation of the Geneva Protocols, the politics of the *CA* crisis, and the League loans are touched upon. Furthermore, the author tackles such different themes as the establishment of the *Ständestaat*, its struggle against German National Socialism, the impotence of the League, the history of the Dutch Nazi party (NSB), and the German occupation of the Netherlands. More events and historical figures could be mentioned to account for the length and thoroughness of Berger's biography of Rost van Tonningen.

Demonstrating how Rost's dramatic transformation from an agent of neo-liberal Western finance to an extreme Nazi was possible, Berger also makes clear that this transformation was not only due to the persuasive power of political extremism on the interwar European bourgeoisie. On a micro-political level, it also reveals the plain failure and essentially the inability of Western finance and the League to maintain the Versailles system. In addition, by describing how Rost turned his back on the League's attempt to sustain deflationary economic policy, the author indirectly also discloses the incapability of Western orthodox economic policies to cope with the enormous effects of the Depression on Austria. Rost, who represented the Committee of European International Finance, gradually changed from a staunch believer in economic and fiscal orthodoxy to someone who attempted to accommodate neo-liberalism with interventionist, reflationary Nazi economic policy. Moreover, Rost changed his attitude toward the League's financial stabilization scheme: While, at first, he saw it as an efficient and sincere effort of Central European reconstruction, he later came to regard it as an expression of humiliating Western financial imperialism aimed at the German peoples.

Through Rost's transformation, Berger also insinuates that the economic policies of conservative currency reconstruction and fiscal orthodoxy represented the central components of a failed European-wide reactionary movement that attempted to restore the favorable status quo of the prewar era. As these policies failed to tackle the Depression and aggravated the crisis not only in the small economically vulnerable Austria, they helped to facilitate the gradual turn to fascism. With this background, the seemingly incredible transformation of a weak, but easily swayed, ambitious, recognition-craving and power-hungry man becomes more intelligible.

At times, Berger's writing style is appropriately cynical and even amusing. The structure is strictly chronological. Because the work is a political biography, this approach seems useful, but causes the text to jump from one theme to another and back again. In addition, at the end of this long look, a summary or restatement of the main ideas is lacking. However, considering the size and complexity of this fascinating account supported by extensive use of archival material, these are minor points of criticism. All in all, this is a successful work, which is not only of interest to historians of financial diplomacy and the League of Nations, but also to the general reader fascinated by the changes and polarization of political life in interwar Europe.

ANNUAL REVIEW

Austria 2001

Reinhold Gärtner

Elections in Vienna
Temelin, Nuclear Energy, and the EU-Enlargement
Media Concentration
Anti-Semitism
Agreement on Compensation of NS Slave Labor
Haider and the Slovenes in Carinthia
Economic Data

Elections in Vienna

In March, the State Diet of Vienna was reelected. After the 2000 elections in Burgenland and Styria, Vienna's was the third regional election after the building of the ÖVP/FPÖ government in February 2000—and for the third time one striking feature was the losses incurred by the FPÖ in the votes cast.

	2001 percent	2001 seats	1996 percent	1996* seats
SPÖ	46.9	52	39.2	43
FPÖ	20.2	21	27.9	29
ÖVP	16.4	16	15.3	15
Grüne	12.5	11	7.9	7

* 6 seats for LiF – Liberales Forum

In 2001, the SPÖ and Vienna's Socialist mayor and governor, Michael Häupl, could regain the absolute majority which they had lost (for the first time since 1945) in the 1996 elections.

Temelin, Nuclear Energy, and the EU-Enlargement

Close to the Austrian border, the construction work on the nuclear plant of Temelin in the Czech Republic was finished. Since the referendum in 1978, Austria has abandoned nuclear energy, and, thus, parts of the population—especially in Upper Austria—were frightened about the prospect of having a new and possibly dangerous nuclear plant in the close vicinity.

All parties were eager to persuade the Czech Republic to improve security measures of Temelin, if not to actually close the plant down completely. The FPÖ, though, went one step further. If Temelin was not to be closed (or was to be opened), the FPÖ would veto the Czech Republic's application to become a member state of the European Union. The Temelin question became one of the topics which highlighted some serious tensions between the coalition partners ÖVP and FPÖ.

Media Concentration

One feature of Austria's print media has always been its enormous concentration. The most widely read paper, *Neue Kronen Zeitung*, reaches some 44% of newspaper readers every day, and it is combined with *Kurier*—the second largest daily—within the *Mediaprint* company. Two of the three big (political) weeklies, *News* and *Format*, belong to the Fellner group, which, in 2001, added the third Austrian weekly *Profil*. Thus, some 60% of dailies (*Neue Kronen Zeitung* and *Kurier*) and all three big (political) weekly magazines are members of one big news and media holding.

Anti-Semitism

Jörg Haider, former head of the FPÖ and now governor of Carinthia, cannot (or will not) deny his attitudes. During his speech on Ash Wednesday in Ried (Upper Austria), he fiercely attacked Ariel Muzicant, president of Austria's Jewish Community: "I don't understand how someone whose name is Ariel can have so much dirt sticking to him" (*"Ich versteh' nicht, wie einer, der Ariel heisst, soviel Dreck am Stecken hat"*), Haider said, punning on the washing powder brand-name. On other occasions, Haider repeatedly made more anti-Semitic remarks. Muzicant, so Haider's argument, an immigrant himself who was given shelter in Austria, would speak ill of Austria and declared war on Austria's democratically elected government. Muzicant, whose parents were forced out of Austria by the Nazis, responded by launching legal action against Haider, alleging anti-Semitism. Muzicant also claims that attacks on Jews have quadrupled since Haider's FPÖ joined the coalition government in 2000. According to *The Daily Telegraph* (23 March 2001), the Austrian EU-commissioner Franz Fischler pointed out that he, Fischler, deplored a certain brutalization in Austria and that "the people don't have a clear picture anymore of what anti-Semitism is. The thing is getting glazed over again."

In the court proceedings against the political scientist Anton Pelinka (University of Innsbruck), Jörg Haider lost. Haider had brought a slander suit against Pelinka, who had said—in an interview to the Italian *RAI*—that Haider, describing concentration camps as punishment centers, had played down the crimes of the Third Reich. In its final decision, the court pointed out that Haider had tried to minimize the intensity of NS crimes and that he had an ambivalent attitude towards NS language (*Diktion*). The court further claimed that one had to reproach Haider for a certain closeness to and coquetry with Nazism, and that he operated in the gray area in which the crimes of the NS regime are not accepted in their full dimension (OLG Wien – 24 BS 244/00).

Agreement on Compensation of NS Slave Labor

In January, the United States and Austria have taken last steps towards the "Reconciliation, Peace, and Cooperation Fund," which should provide a measure of justice to over one hundred thousand victims of the Nazi era. The Austrian government and Austrian companies have agreed to contribute ATS 6 billion (¬ 436 million) to establish this fund. In return, they seek legal closure with respect to claims against Austria and/or Austrian companies involving or relating to the use of slave or forced labor during the NS era. An agreement to compensate Austrian Jews and Eastern European victims forced to work as slave laborers during World War II had already been signed in October 2000.

Haider and the Slowenes in Carinthia

In December, the Supreme Court (*Verfassungsgerichtshof*) decided that in villages with a Slowene population of more than 10% topographical signs should be bilingual. In a fierce attack, Jörg Haider and the FPÖ vowed not to accept the court's decision, and Haider went even further by accusing the president of the *Verfassungsgerichtshof* of dishonorable behavior. Jörg Haider still insists that the bilingual place name signs will not be erected as long as he is governor of Carinthia.

Economic Data

In 2001, on average 3,148,000 people were employed, 203,900 unemployed (+ 4.9% compared to 2000); the rate of unemployment was 3.8% (ILO-criteria; + 0.1%) and 6.1% respectively (+ 0.3%).

The GDP was at ¬ 201.9 billion; inflation at 2.7%. According to Maastricht criteria, the public surplus was at 0.1% of the GDP (¬ 128 million) and public debt at ¬ 130 billion (61.7% of the GDP).

List of Authors

Bailer-Galanda Brigitte, vice-chair, Historical Commission of the Republic of Austria, Vienna

Beer Siegfried, professor of modern history, University of Graz

Berger Peter, professor of social and economic history, University of Economics and Business Administration, Vienna, and 2002/3 Marshall Plan Chair in Austrian Studies, University of New Orleans

Bischof Günter, professor of history and director, Center for Austrian Culture and Commerce, University of New Orleans

Blimlinger Eva, coordinator of research, Historical Commission of the Republic of Austria, Vienna

Bukey Evan Burr, professor of history, University of Arkansas at Fayetteville

Eichtinger Martin, Director, International Relations, Federation of Austrian Industry, Vienna

Freudenberger Herman, professor of economics emeritus, Tulane University

Gärtner Reinhold, associate professor of political science, University of Innsbruck, and secretary *Gesellschaft für Politische Aufklärung*

Greene Megan, research assistant, Liechtenstein Institute on Self-Determination, Woodrow Wilson School, Princeton University

Herzstein Robert Edwin, Carolina Distinguished Professor of History, University of South Carolina

Kirk Tim, lecturer in history, Newcastle University, United Kingdom

Klausinger Hansjörg, professor of economics, University of Economics and Business Administration, Vienna, and 2001-2 Schumpeter Fellow, Harvard University

Krieger Wolfgang, professor of modern history and dean of history and cultural studies, Marburg University, Germany

Lassner Alexander, assistant professor of history, International Security and Military Studies Department, U.S. Air Force Air Command and Staff College, Maxwell Air Force Base, Alabama

Miller James William, professor of history, University of Arkansas at Little Rock

Rathkolb Oliver, professor of contemporary history, University of Vienna, and research director of the Kreisky Foundation, Vienna

Reiter Margit, lecturer, Institute of Contemporary History, University of Vienna

Senft Gerhard, professor of social and economic history, University of Economics and Business Administration, Vienna

Stiefel Dieter, professor of social and economic history, University of Vienna

Utgaard Peter, chair of history & social sciences, Cuyamaca College, El Cajon, California

Wessels Jens-Wilhelm, research fellow in the department of history, Keele University, United Kingdom

Wohnout Helmut, historian, Chief of Staff of the State Secretary for the Arts and Media in the Federal Chancellery, and Executive Director of the Karl von Vogelsang-Institute, Vienna

For Product Safety Concerns and Information please contact our EU representative GPSR@taylorandfrancis.com
Taylor & Francis Verlag GmbH, Kaufingerstraße 24, 80331 München, Germany

www.ingramcontent.com/pod-product-compliance
Ingram Content Group UK Ltd.
Pitfield, Milton Keynes, MK11 3LW, UK
UKHW040855180926
475701UK00001B/13
9780765809704